I don't actually
have a pet dog.
—Tsugumi Ohba

Maybe it's because I've
pulled off too many all-
nighters but I've learnt to
sleep with my eyes open.
—Takeshi Obata

D0150056

Tsugumi Ohba

Born in Tokyo, Tsugumi Ohba is the author of the hit series *Death Note*.
His latest series *Bakuman。* was serialized in *Weekly Shonen Jump*.

Takeshi Obata

Takeshi Obata was born in 1969 in Niigata, Japan, and is the artist of
the wildly popular SHONEN JUMP title *Hikaru no Go*, which won the
2003 Tezuka Osamu Cultural Prize: Shinsei "New Hope" award and
the 2000 Shogakukan Manga award. Obata is also the artist of *Arabian
Majin Bokentan Lamp Lamp*, *Ayatsuri Sakon*, *Cyborg Jichan G.*, and
the smash hit manga *Death Note*. His latest series *Bakuman。* was
serialized in *Weekly Shonen Jump*.

Volume 18

SHONEN JUMP Manga Edition

Story by **TSUGUMI OHBA**
Art by **TAKESHI OBATA**

Translation | **Tetsuichiro Miyaki**
English Adaptation | **Julie Lutz**
Touch-up Art & Lettering | **James Gaubatz**
Design | **Fawn Lau**
Editor | **Alexis Kirsch**

BAKUMAN₀ © 2008 by Tsugumi Ohba, Takeshi Obata
All rights reserved.
First published in Japan in 2008 by SHUEISHA Inc., Tokyo.
English translation rights arranged by SHUEISHA Inc.

Printed in the U.S.A.

Published by VIZ Media, LLC
P.O. Box 77010
San Francisco, CA 94107

10 9 8 7 6 5 4 3 2 1
First printing, March 2013

18

LEEWAY and HELL

STORY BY TSUGUMI OHBA

ART BY TAKESHI OBATA

SHONEN JUMP MANGA

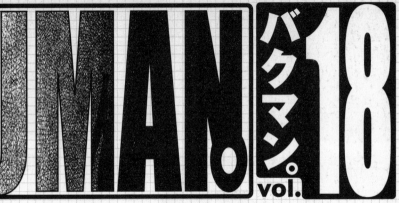

MAN。 バクマン。 vol. 18

A
B
C
D

EIJI
Nizuma

A manga prodigy and Tezuka Award winner at the age of 15. His goal is to create the world's best manga.

Age: 24

KAYA
Takagi

Miho's friend and Akito's wife. A nice girl who actively works as the interceder between Moritaka and Azuki.

Age: 23

AKITO
Takagi

Manga writer. An extremely smart guy who gets the best grades in his class. A cool guy who becomes very passionate when it comes to manga.

Age: 23

MIHO
Azuki

A girl who dreams of becoming a voice actress. She promised to marry Moritaka under the condition that they not see each other until their dreams come true.

Age: 23

MORITAKA
Mashiro

Manga artist. An extreme romantic who believes that he will marry Miho Azuki once their dreams come true.

Age: 23

*These ages are from February 2017.

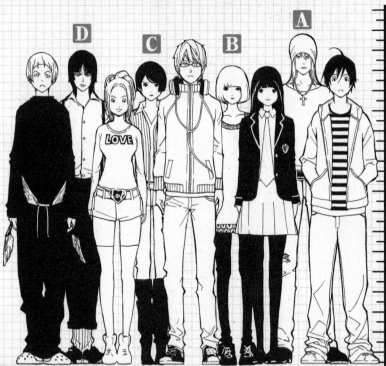

STORY In order to attain the glory that only a handful of people can, two young men decide to walk the rough "path of manga" and become professional manga creators. This is the story of a great artist, Moritaka Mashiro, a talented writer, Akito Takagi, and their quest to become manga legends!

6
1
4
5
2
I
L
N
J
E
M
G
8
H
K
9
7
3
F

WEEKLY SHONEN JUMP Editorial Department

1. Ex-Editor in Chief Sasaki
2. Editor in Chief Heishi
3. Deputy Editor in Chief Aida
4. Yujiro Hattori
5. Akira Hattori
6. Koji Yoshida
7. Goro Miura
8. Masakazu Yamahisa
9. Kosugi

The MANGA ARTISTS and ASSISTANTS

- A SHINTA FUKUDA
- B KO AOKI
- C AIKO IWASE
- D KAZUYA HIRAMARU
- E RYU SHIZUKA
- F NATSUMI KATO
- G YASUOKA
- H SHOYO TAKAHAMA
- I TAKURO NAKAI
- J SHUICHI MORIYA
- K SHUN SHIRATORI
- L ICHIRIKI ORIHARA
- M TOHRU NANAMINE
- N MIKIHIKO AZUMA

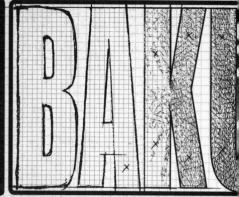

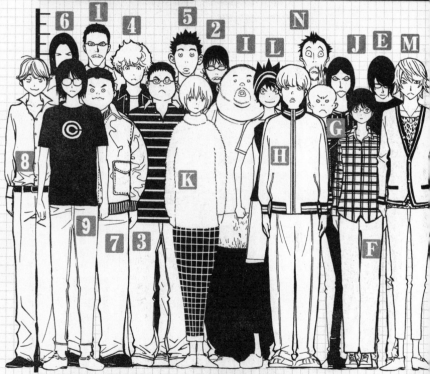

BAKUMAN。 vol.18

CONTENTS

(LEEWAY (AND HELL))

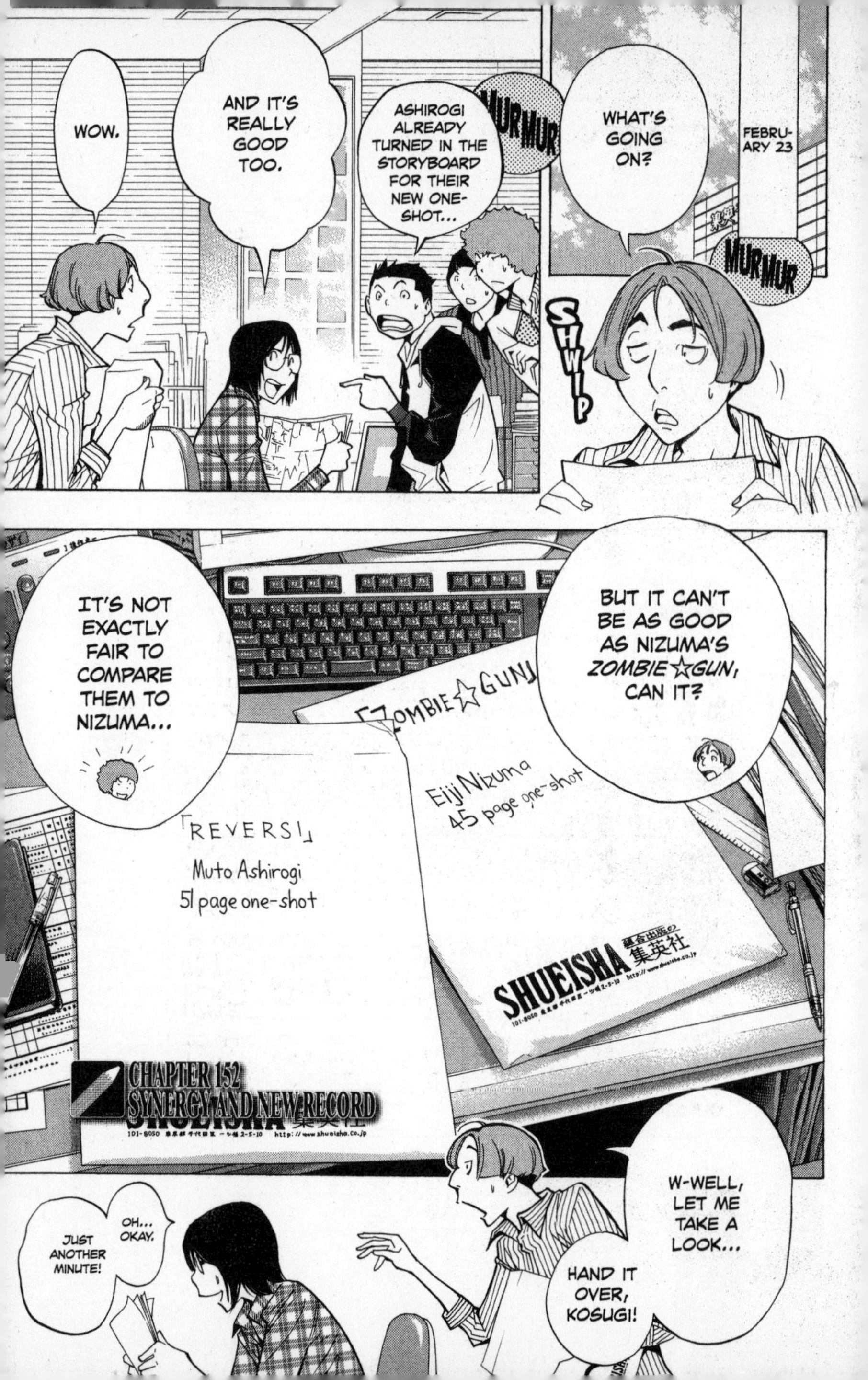
FEBRUARY 23
WHAT'S GOING ON?
MURMUR
SHWIP
MURMUR
ASHIROGI ALREADY TURNED IN THE STORYBOARD FOR THEIR NEW ONE-SHOT...
AND IT'S REALLY GOOD TOO.
WOW.
BUT IT CAN'T BE AS GOOD AS NIZUMA'S ZOMBIE☆GUN, CAN IT?
IT'S NOT EXACTLY FAIR TO COMPARE THEM TO NIZUMA...
「ZOMBIE☆GUN」
Eiji Nizuma
45 page one-shot
SHUEISHA 集英社
「REVERSI」
Muto Ashirogi
51 page one-shot
CHAPTER 152
SYNERGY AND NEW RECORD
W-WELL, LET ME TAKE A LOOK...
HAND IT OVER, KOSUGI!
OH... OKAY.
JUST ANOTHER MINUTE!

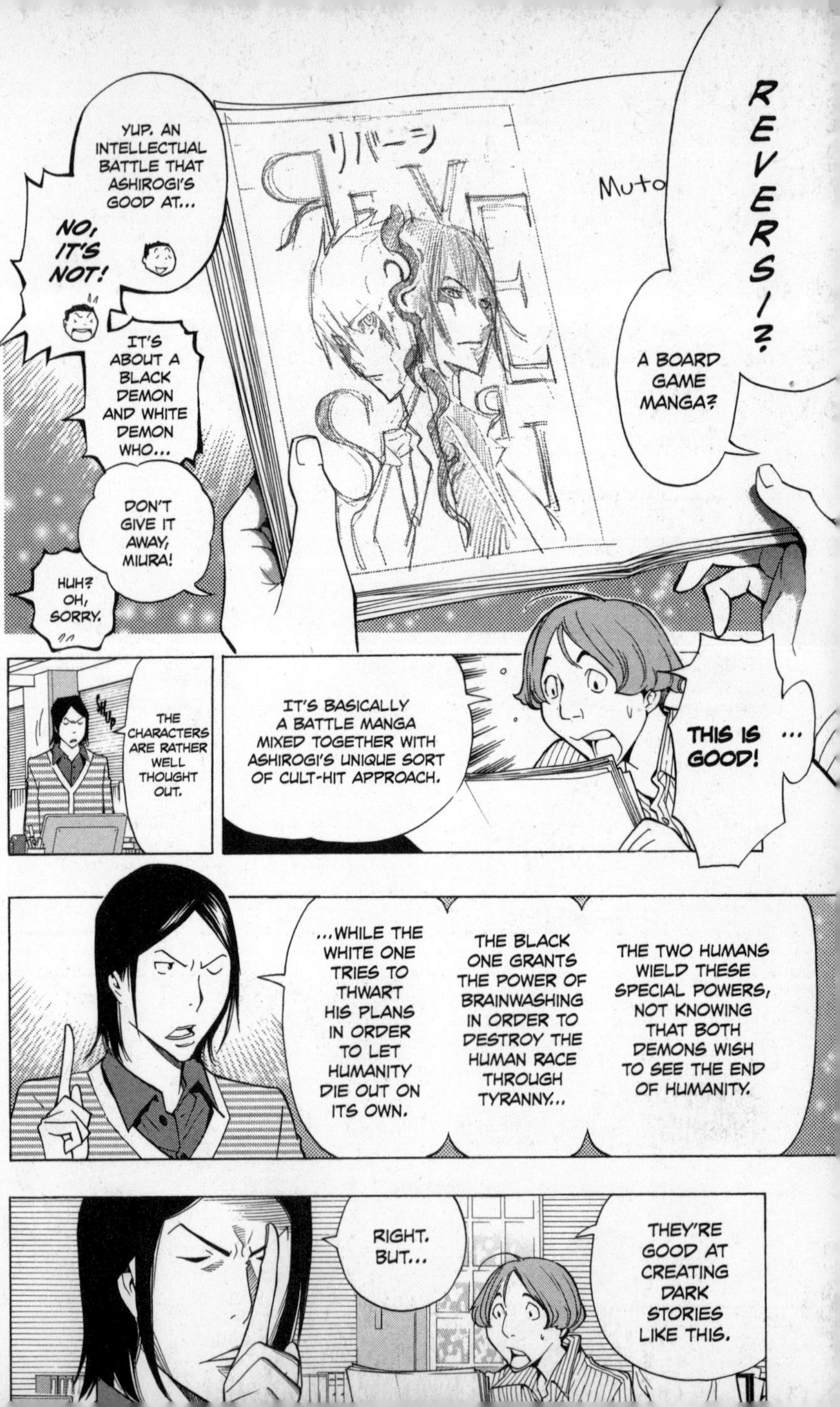
REVERSI!?
A BOARD GAME MANGA?
リバーシ
Muto
YUP. AN INTELLECTUAL BATTLE THAT ASHIROGI'S GOOD AT...
NO, IT'S NOT!
IT'S ABOUT A BLACK DEMON AND WHITE DEMON WHO...
DON'T GIVE IT AWAY, MIURA!
HUH? OH, SORRY.
THIS IS GOOD! ...
IT'S BASICALLY A BATTLE MANGA MIXED TOGETHER WITH ASHIROGI'S UNIQUE SORT OF CULT-HIT APPROACH.
SHUP
THE CHARACTERS ARE RATHER WELL THOUGHT OUT.
THE TWO HUMANS WIELD THESE SPECIAL POWERS, NOT KNOWING THAT BOTH DEMONS WISH TO SEE THE END OF HUMANITY.
THE BLACK ONE GRANTS THE POWER OF BRAINWASHING IN ORDER TO DESTROY THE HUMAN RACE THROUGH TYRANNY...
...WHILE THE WHITE ONE TRIES TO THWART HIS PLANS IN ORDER TO LET HUMANITY DIE OUT ON ITS OWN.
THEY'RE GOOD AT CREATING DARK STORIES LIKE THIS.
RIGHT. BUT...

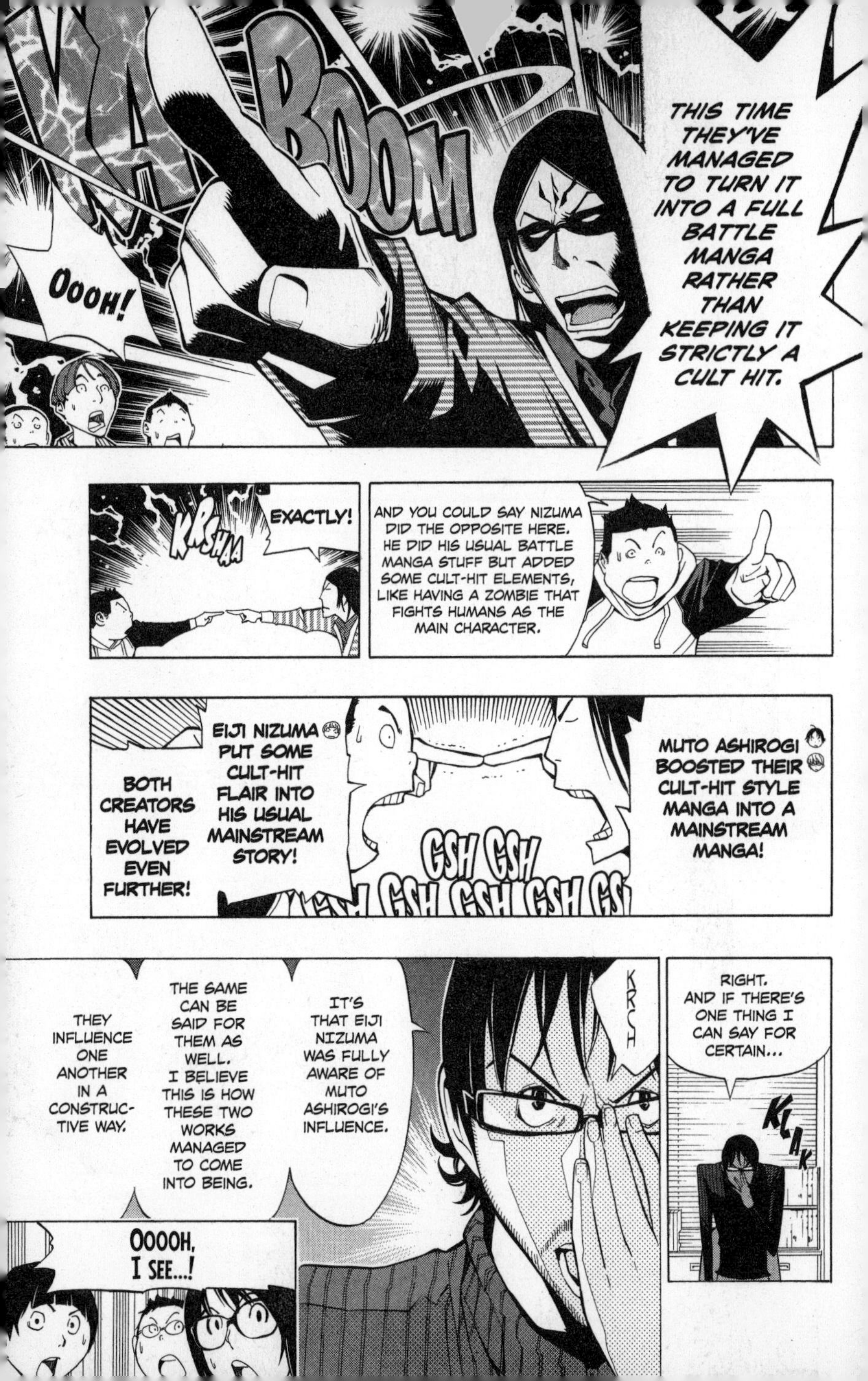
BOOM
THIS TIME THEY'VE MANAGED TO TURN IT INTO A FULL BATTLE MANGA RATHER THAN KEEPING IT STRICTLY A CULT HIT.
OOOH!
AND YOU COULD SAY NIZUMA DID THE OPPOSITE HERE. HE DID HIS USUAL BATTLE MANGA STUFF BUT ADDED SOME CULT-HIT ELEMENTS, LIKE HAVING A ZOMBIE THAT FIGHTS HUMANS AS THE MAIN CHARACTER.
EXACTLY!
KRSHAA
MUTO ASHIROGI BOOSTED THEIR CULT-HIT STYLE MANGA INTO A MAINSTREAM MANGA!
EIJI NIZUMA PUT SOME CULT-HIT FLAIR INTO HIS USUAL MAINSTREAM STORY!
BOTH CREATORS HAVE EVOLVED EVEN FURTHER!
GSH GSH GSH GSH GSH GSH
RIGHT. AND IF THERE'S ONE THING I CAN SAY FOR CERTAIN...
KLAK
KRSH
IT'S THAT EIJI NIZUMA WAS FULLY AWARE OF MUTO ASHIROGI'S INFLUENCE.
THE SAME CAN BE SAID FOR THEM AS WELL. I BELIEVE THIS IS HOW THESE TWO WORKS MANAGED TO COME INTO BEING.
THEY INFLUENCE ONE ANOTHER IN A CONSTRUCTIVE WAY.
OOOOH, I SEE...!

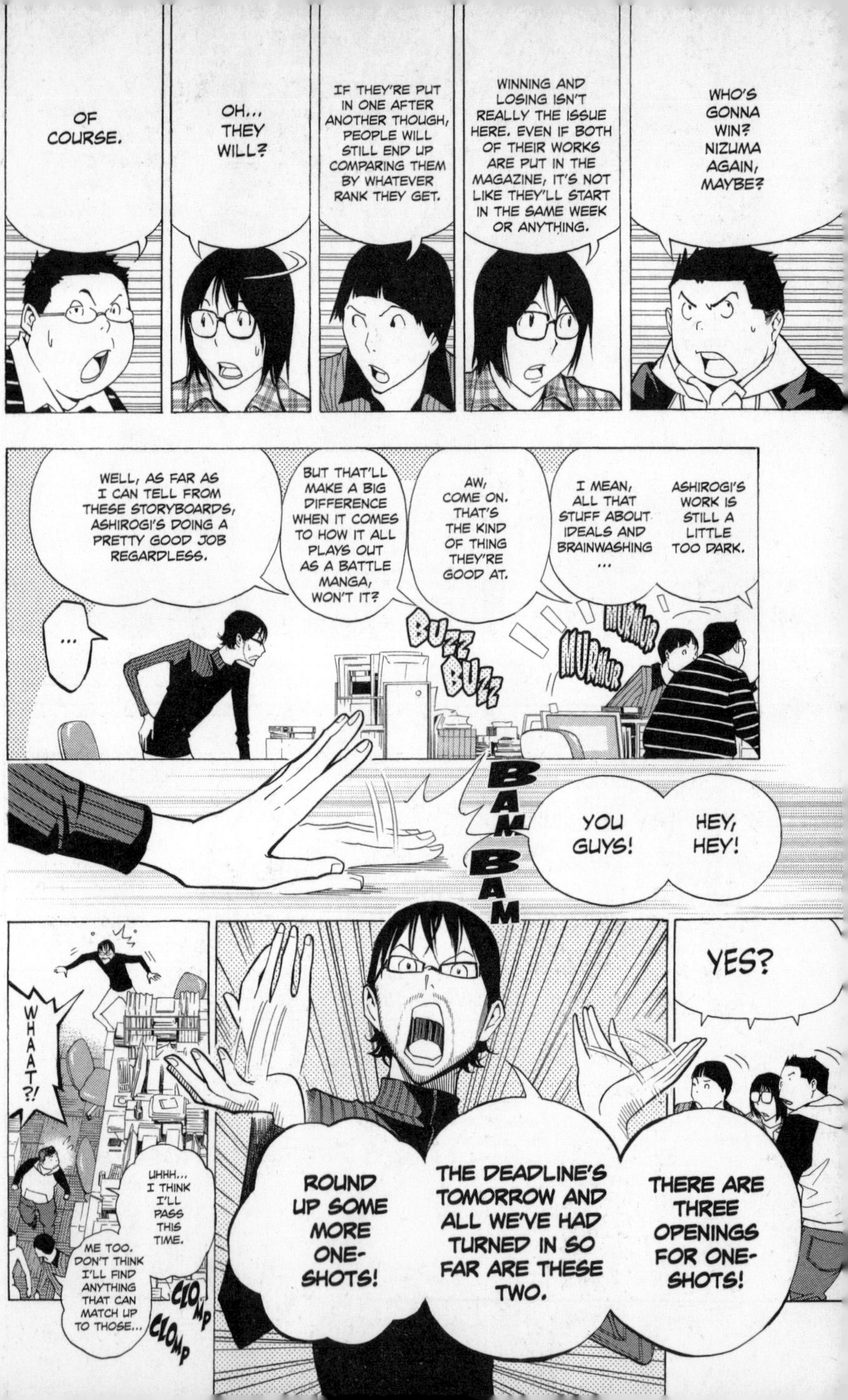
WHO'S GONNA WIN? NIZUMA AGAIN, MAYBE?
WINNING AND LOSING ISN'T REALLY THE ISSUE HERE. EVEN IF BOTH OF THEIR WORKS ARE PUT IN THE MAGAZINE, IT'S NOT LIKE THEY'LL START IN THE SAME WEEK OR ANYTHING.
IF THEY'RE PUT IN ONE AFTER ANOTHER THOUGH, PEOPLE WILL STILL END UP COMPARING THEM BY WHATEVER RANK THEY GET.
OH... THEY WILL?
OF COURSE.
ASHIROGI'S WORK IS STILL A LITTLE TOO DARK.
I MEAN, ALL THAT STUFF ABOUT IDEALS AND BRAINWASHING ...
AW, COME ON. THAT'S THE KIND OF THING THEY'RE GOOD AT.
BUT THAT'LL MAKE A BIG DIFFERENCE WHEN IT COMES TO HOW IT ALL PLAYS OUT AS A BATTLE MANGA, WON'T IT?
WELL, AS FAR AS I CAN TELL FROM THESE STORYBOARDS, ASHIROGI'S DOING A PRETTY GOOD JOB REGARDLESS.
MURMUR
MURMUR
BUZZ
BUZZ
...
BAM
BAM
HEY, HEY!
YOU GUYS!
YES?
THERE ARE THREE OPENINGS FOR ONE-SHOTS!
THE DEADLINE'S TOMORROW AND ALL WE'VE HAD TURNED IN SO FAR ARE THESE TWO.
ROUND UP SOME MORE ONE-SHOTS!
WHAAAT?!
UHHH... I THINK I'LL PASS THIS TIME.
ME TOO. DON'T THINK I'LL FIND ANYTHING THAT CAN MATCH UP TO THOSE...
CLOMP
CLOMP

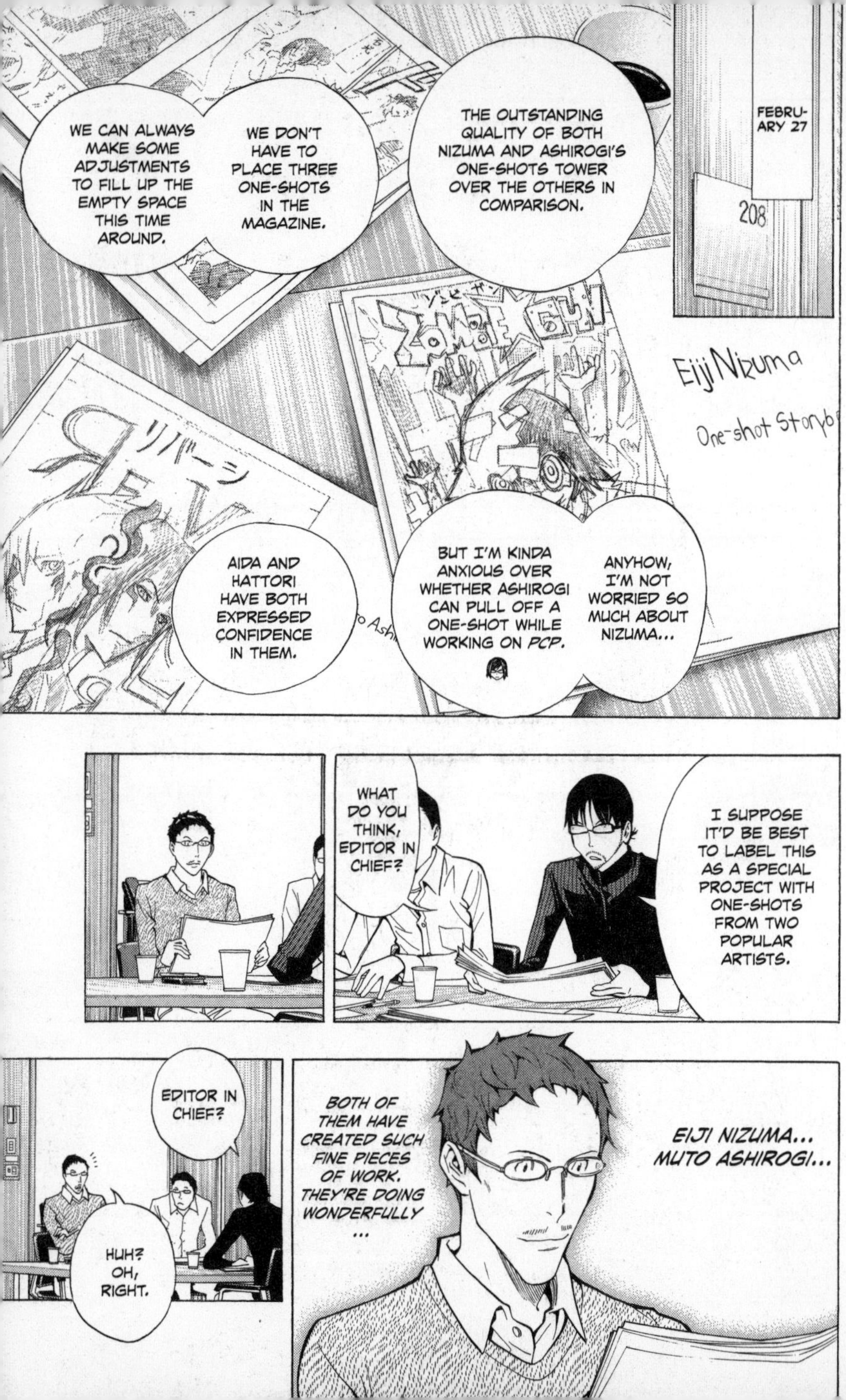
FEBRUARY 27
208
THE OUTSTANDING QUALITY OF BOTH NIZUMA AND ASHIROGI'S ONE-SHOTS TOWER OVER THE OTHERS IN COMPARISON.
WE DON'T HAVE TO PLACE THREE ONE-SHOTS IN THE MAGAZINE.
WE CAN ALWAYS MAKE SOME ADJUSTMENTS TO FILL UP THE EMPTY SPACE THIS TIME AROUND.
Eiji Nizuma
One-shot Storyb
ANYHOW, I'M NOT WORRIED SO MUCH ABOUT NIZUMA...
BUT I'M KINDA ANXIOUS OVER WHETHER ASHIROGI CAN PULL OFF A ONE-SHOT WHILE WORKING ON *PCP*.
AIDA AND HATTORI HAVE BOTH EXPRESSED CONFIDENCE IN THEM.
I SUPPOSE IT'D BE BEST TO LABEL THIS AS A SPECIAL PROJECT WITH ONE-SHOTS FROM TWO POPULAR ARTISTS.
WHAT DO YOU THINK, EDITOR IN CHIEF?
EIJI NIZUMA... MUTO ASHIROGI...
BOTH OF THEM HAVE CREATED SUCH FINE PIECES OF WORK. THEY'RE DOING WONDERFULLY...
EDITOR IN CHIEF?
HUH? OH, RIGHT.

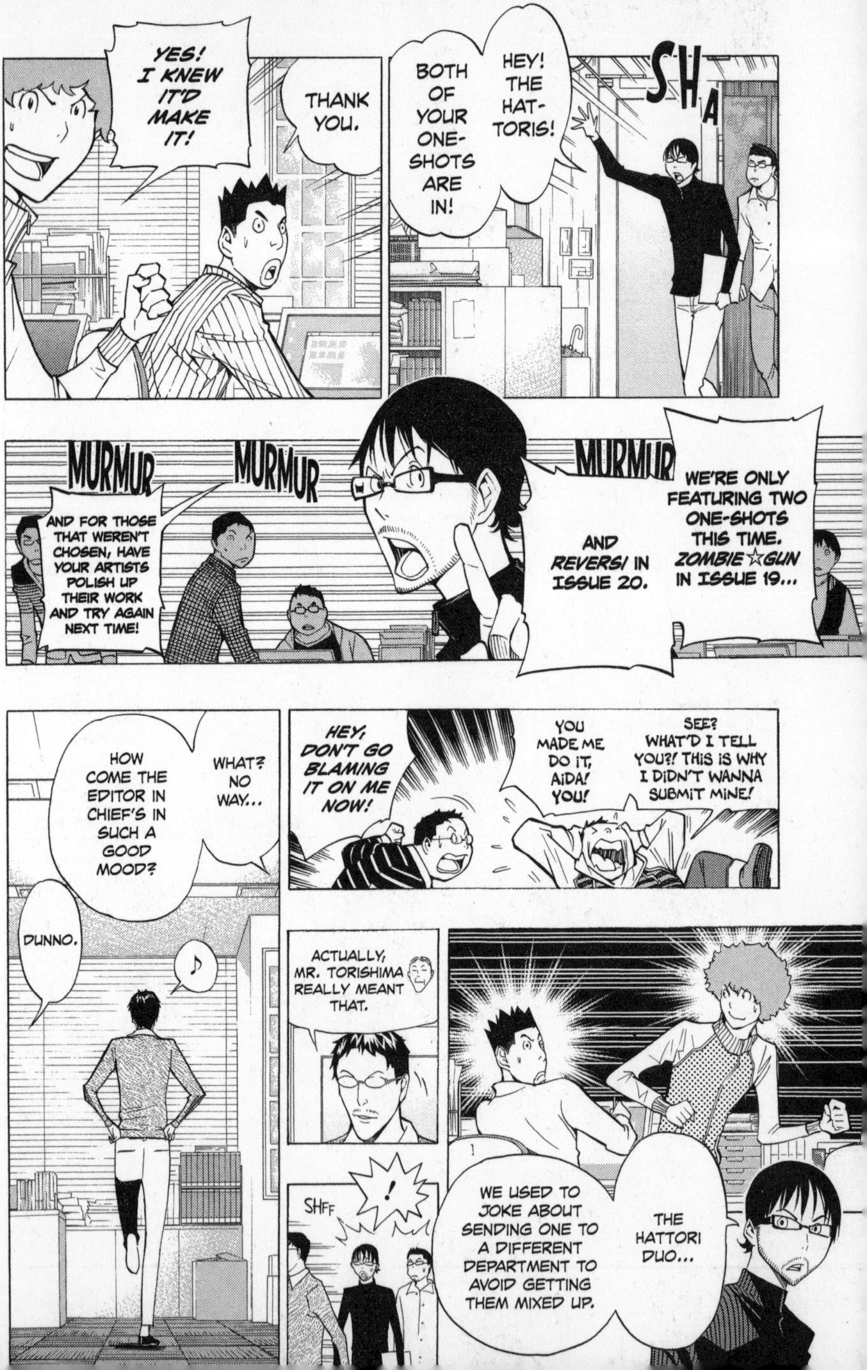
SHA
HEY! THE HAT-TORIS!
BOTH OF YOUR ONE-SHOTS ARE IN!
THANK YOU.
YES! I KNEW IT'D MAKE IT!
MURMUR
WE'RE ONLY FEATURING TWO ONE-SHOTS THIS TIME. ZOMBIE☆GUN IN ISSUE 19...
AND REVERSI IN ISSUE 20.
MURMUR
MURMUR
AND FOR THOSE THAT WEREN'T CHOSEN, HAVE YOUR ARTISTS POLISH UP THEIR WORK AND TRY AGAIN NEXT TIME!
SEE? WHAT'D I TELL YOU?! THIS IS WHY I DIDN'T WANNA SUBMIT MINE!
YOU MADE ME DO IT, AIDA! YOU!
HEY, DON'T GO BLAMING IT ON ME NOW!
ACTUALLY, MR. TORISHIMA REALLY MEANT THAT.
THE HATTORI DUO...
WE USED TO JOKE ABOUT SENDING ONE TO A DIFFERENT DEPARTMENT TO AVOID GETTING THEM MIXED UP.
!
SHFF
WHAT? NO WAY...
HOW COME THE EDITOR IN CHIEF'S IN SUCH A GOOD MOOD?
DUNNO.
♪

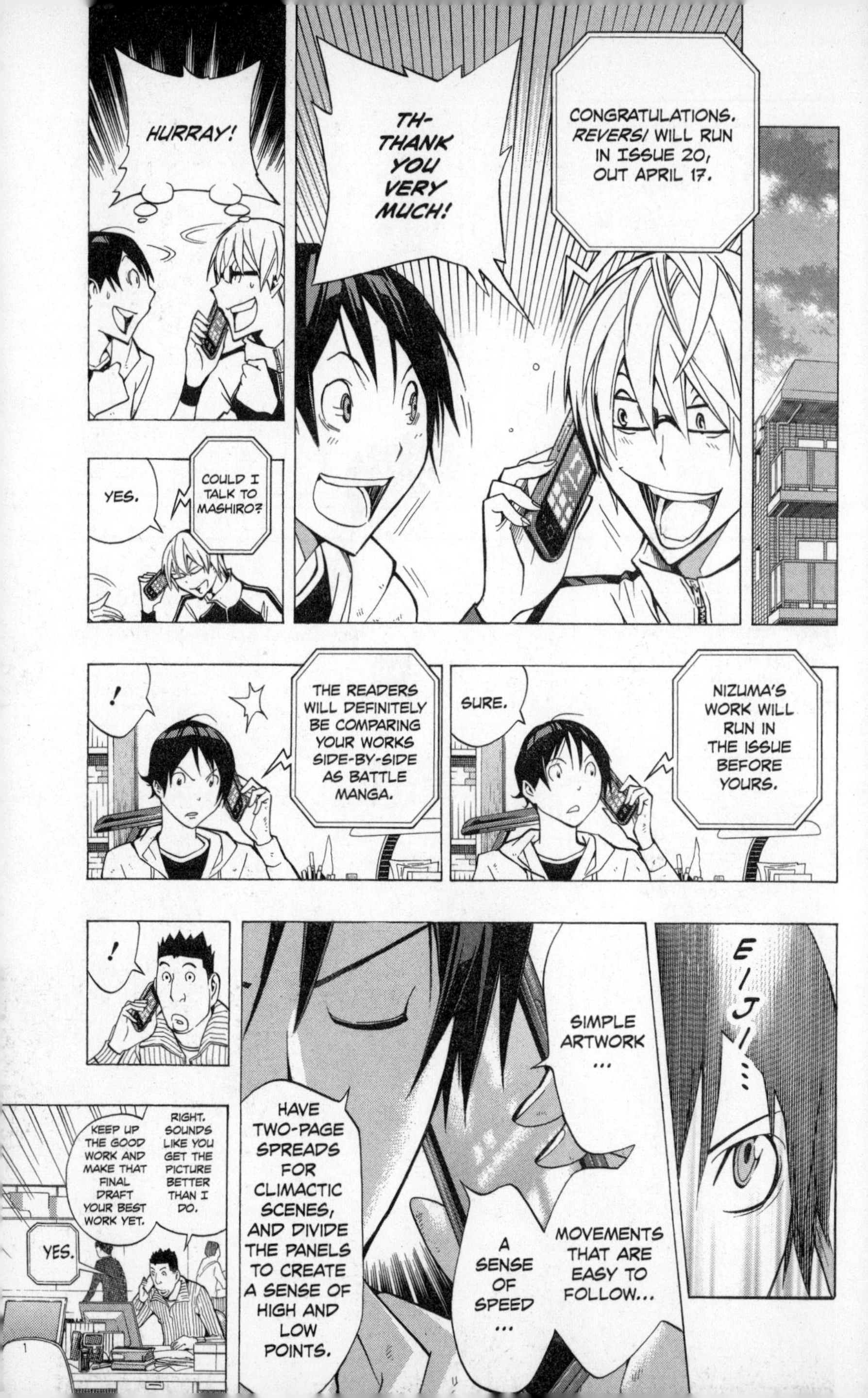
CONGRATULATIONS. *REVERSI* WILL RUN IN ISSUE 20, OUT APRIL 17.
TH-THANK YOU VERY MUCH!
HURRAY!
COULD I TALK TO MASHIRO?
YES.
NIZUMA'S WORK WILL RUN IN THE ISSUE BEFORE YOURS.
SURE.
THE READERS WILL DEFINITELY BE COMPARING YOUR WORKS SIDE-BY-SIDE AS BATTLE MANGA.
!
EIJI...
SIMPLE ARTWORK...
MOVEMENTS THAT ARE EASY TO FOLLOW...
A SENSE OF SPEED...
HAVE TWO-PAGE SPREADS FOR CLIMACTIC SCENES, AND DIVIDE THE PANELS TO CREATE A SENSE OF HIGH AND LOW POINTS.
!
RIGHT. SOUNDS LIKE YOU GET THE PICTURE BETTER THAN I DO.
KEEP UP THE GOOD WORK AND MAKE THAT FINAL DRAFT YOUR BEST WORK YET.
YES.

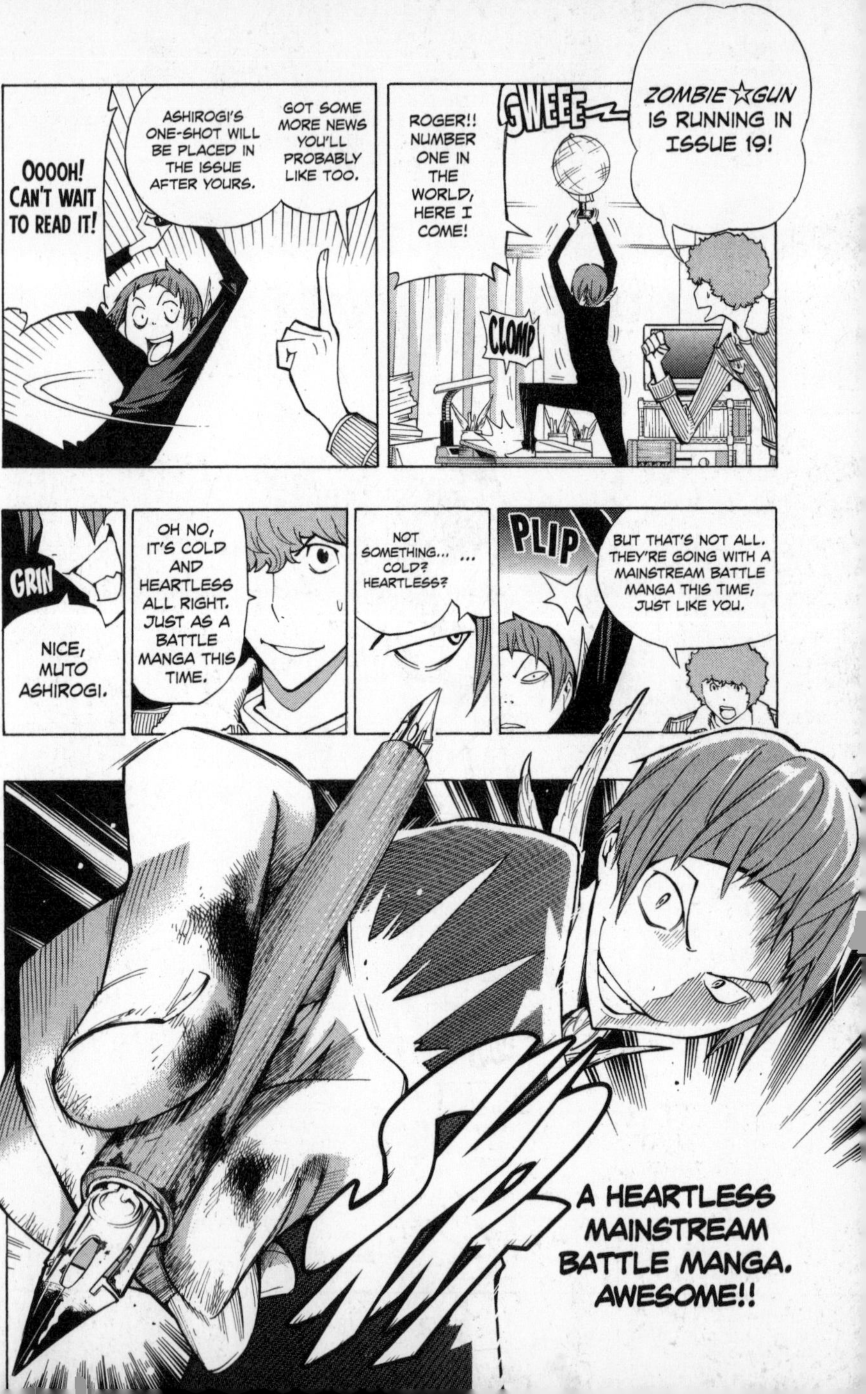
ZOMBIE☆GUN IS RUNNING IN ISSUE 19!
GWEEE
ROGER!! NUMBER ONE IN THE WORLD, HERE I COME!
CLOMP
GOT SOME MORE NEWS YOU'LL PROBABLY LIKE TOO.
ASHIROGI'S ONE-SHOT WILL BE PLACED IN THE ISSUE AFTER YOURS.
OOOOH! CAN'T WAIT TO READ IT!
PLIP
BUT THAT'S NOT ALL. THEY'RE GOING WITH A MAINSTREAM BATTLE MANGA THIS TIME, JUST LIKE YOU.
...
NOT SOMETHING... COLD? HEARTLESS?
OH NO, IT'S COLD AND HEARTLESS ALL RIGHT. JUST AS A BATTLE MANGA THIS TIME.
GRIN
NICE, MUTO ASHIROGI.
A HEARTLESS MAINSTREAM BATTLE MANGA. AWESOME!!

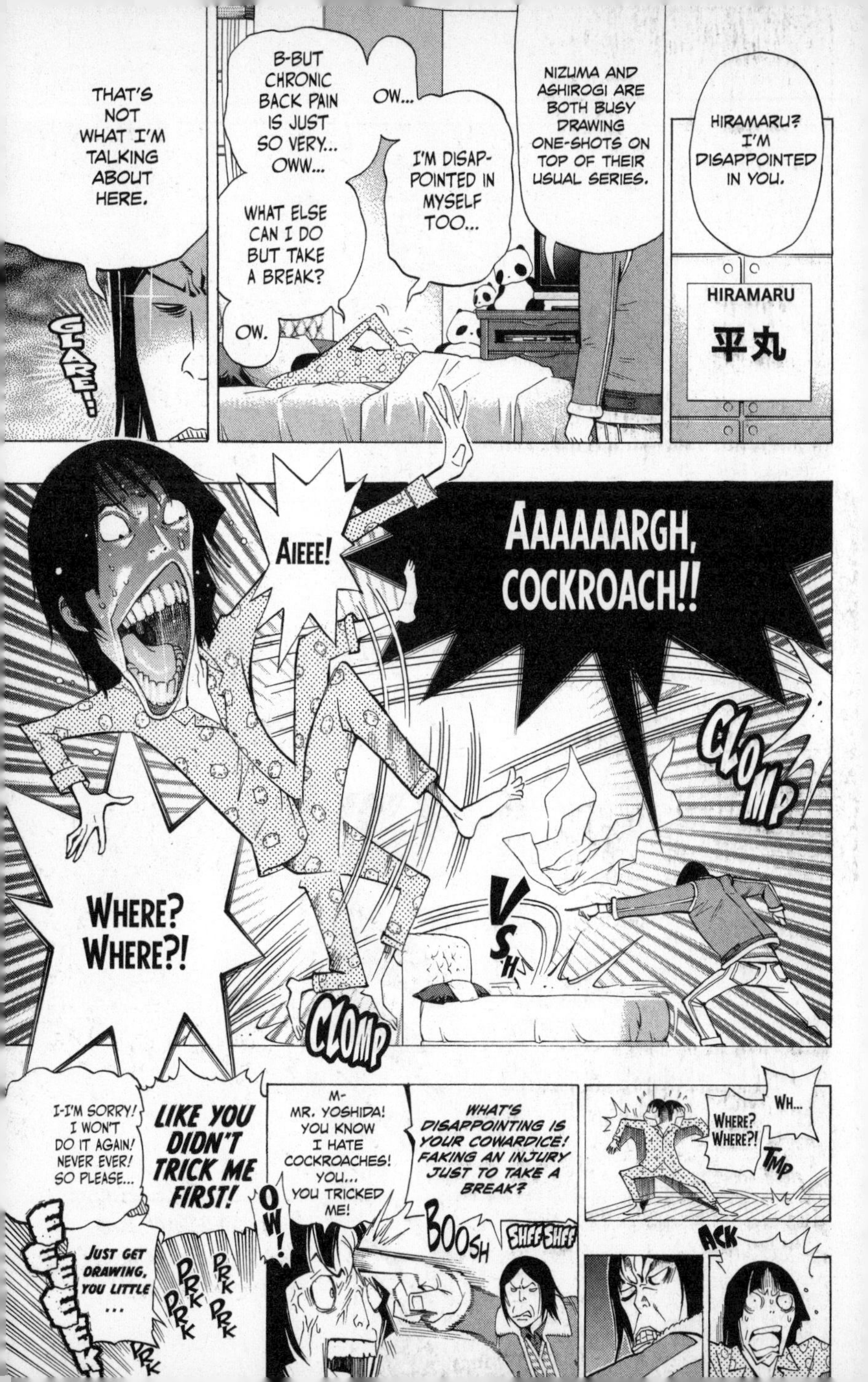
HIRAMARU? I'M DISAPPOINTED IN YOU.
HIRAMARU
平丸
NIZUMA AND ASHIROGI ARE BOTH BUSY DRAWING ONE-SHOTS ON TOP OF THEIR USUAL SERIES.
I'M DISAPPOINTED IN MYSELF TOO...
OW...
B-BUT CHRONIC BACK PAIN IS JUST SO VERY... OWW...
WHAT ELSE CAN I DO BUT TAKE A BREAK?
OW.
THAT'S NOT WHAT I'M TALKING ABOUT HERE.
GLARE!!
AAAAAARGH, COCKROACH!!
AIEEE!
CLOMP
VSH
WHERE? WHERE?!
CLOMP
WH...
WHERE? WHERE?!
TMP
ACK
WHAT'S DISAPPOINTING IS YOUR COWARDICE! FAKING AN INJURY JUST TO TAKE A BREAK?
M-MR. YOSHIDA! YOU KNOW I HATE COCKROACHES! YOU... YOU TRICKED ME!
BOOSH
SHFF SHFF
OW!
LIKE YOU DIDN'T TRICK ME FIRST!
I-I'M SORRY! I WON'T DO IT AGAIN! NEVER EVER! SO PLEASE...
JUST GET DRAWING, YOU LITTLE ...
DRK DRK DRK DRK DRK DRK
EEEEEK

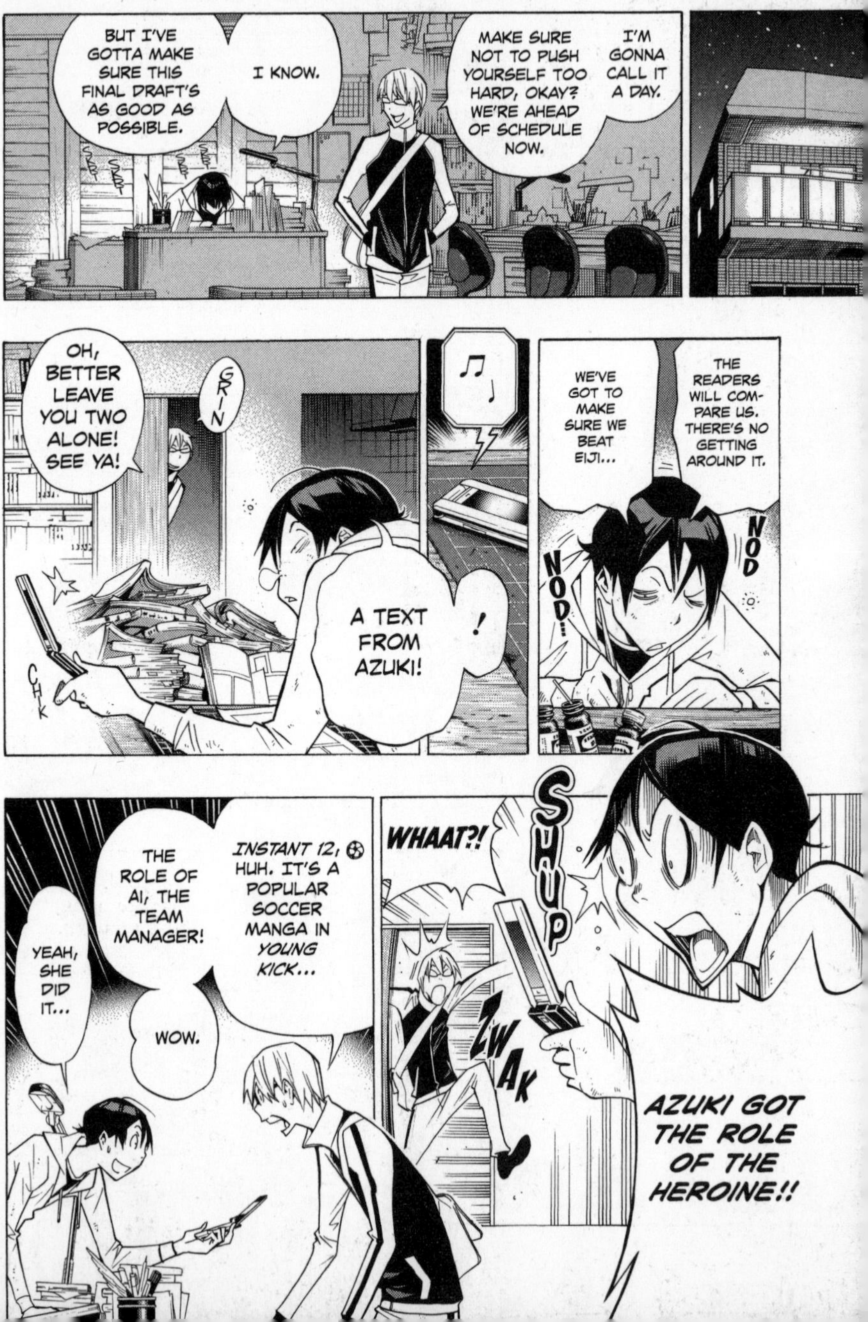
I'M GONNA CALL IT A DAY.
MAKE SURE NOT TO PUSH YOURSELF TOO HARD, OKAY? WE'RE AHEAD OF SCHEDULE NOW.
I KNOW.
BUT I'VE GOTTA MAKE SURE THIS FINAL DRAFT'S AS GOOD AS POSSIBLE.
THE READERS WILL COMPARE US. THERE'S NO GETTING AROUND IT.
WE'VE GOT TO MAKE SURE WE BEAT EIJI...
NOD
NOD
♫ ♩
GRIN
OH, BETTER LEAVE YOU TWO ALONE! SEE YA!
!
A TEXT FROM AZUKI!
CHK
SHUP
WHAAT?!
ZWAK
AZUKI GOT THE ROLE OF THE HEROINE!!
INSTANT 12, HUH. IT'S A POPULAR SOCCER MANGA IN YOUNG KICK...
THE ROLE OF AI, THE TEAM MANAGER!
WOW.
YEAH, SHE DID IT...

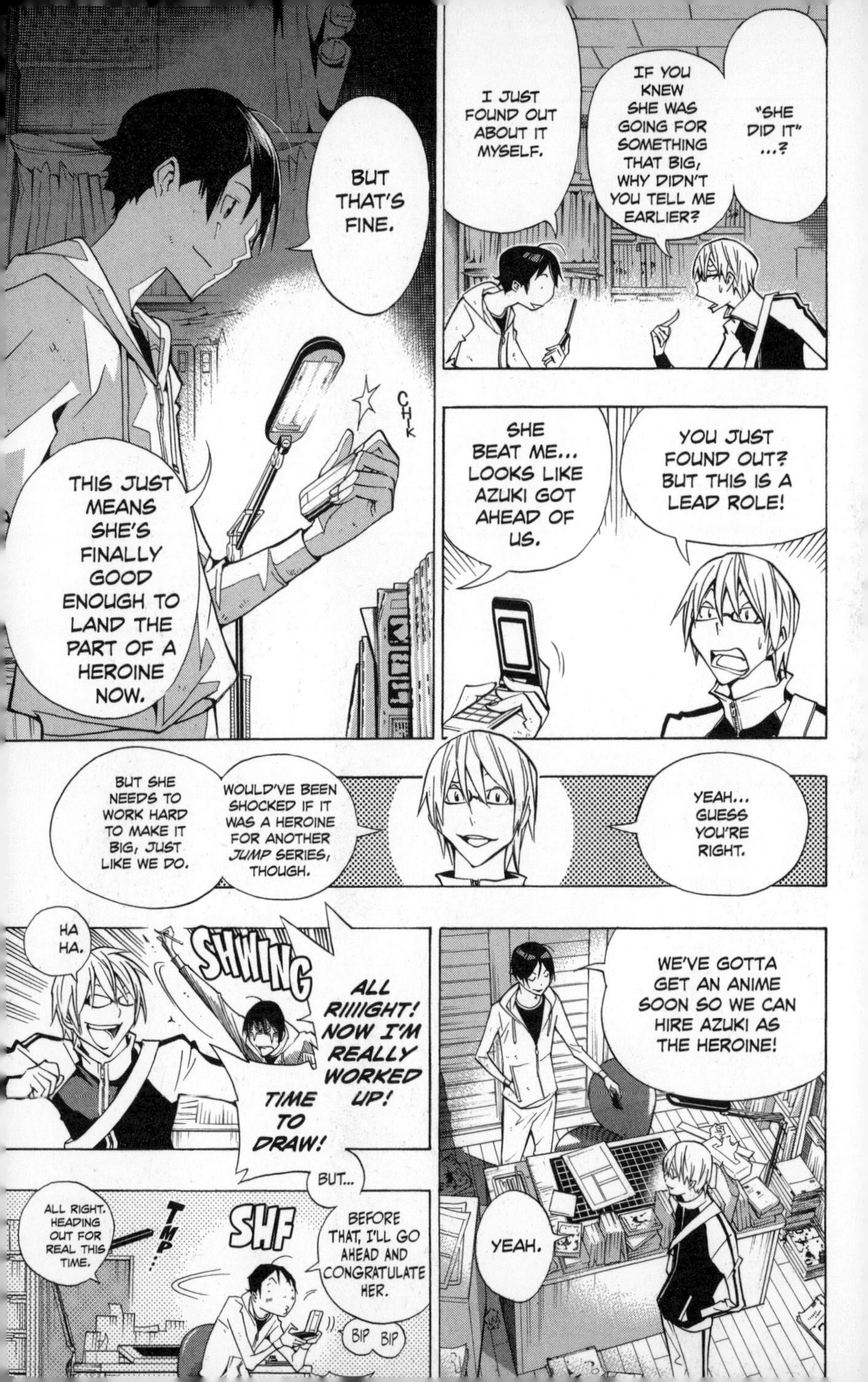
"SHE DID IT" ...?
IF YOU KNEW SHE WAS GOING FOR SOMETHING THAT BIG, WHY DIDN'T YOU TELL ME EARLIER?
I JUST FOUND OUT ABOUT IT MYSELF.
YOU JUST FOUND OUT? BUT THIS IS A LEAD ROLE!
SHE BEAT ME... LOOKS LIKE AZUKI GOT AHEAD OF US.
BUT THAT'S FINE.
CHIK
THIS JUST MEANS SHE'S FINALLY GOOD ENOUGH TO LAND THE PART OF A HEROINE NOW.
YEAH... GUESS YOU'RE RIGHT.
WOULD'VE BEEN SHOCKED IF IT WAS A HEROINE FOR ANOTHER *JUMP* SERIES, THOUGH.
BUT SHE NEEDS TO WORK HARD TO MAKE IT BIG, JUST LIKE WE DO.
WE'VE GOTTA GET AN ANIME SOON SO WE CAN HIRE AZUKI AS THE HEROINE!
YEAH.
HA HA.
SHWING
ALL RIIIIGHT! NOW I'M REALLY WORKED UP!
TIME TO DRAW!
BUT...
BEFORE THAT, I'LL GO AHEAD AND CONGRATULATE HER.
SHF
BIP BIP
TMP...
ALL RIGHT. HEADING OUT FOR REAL THIS TIME.

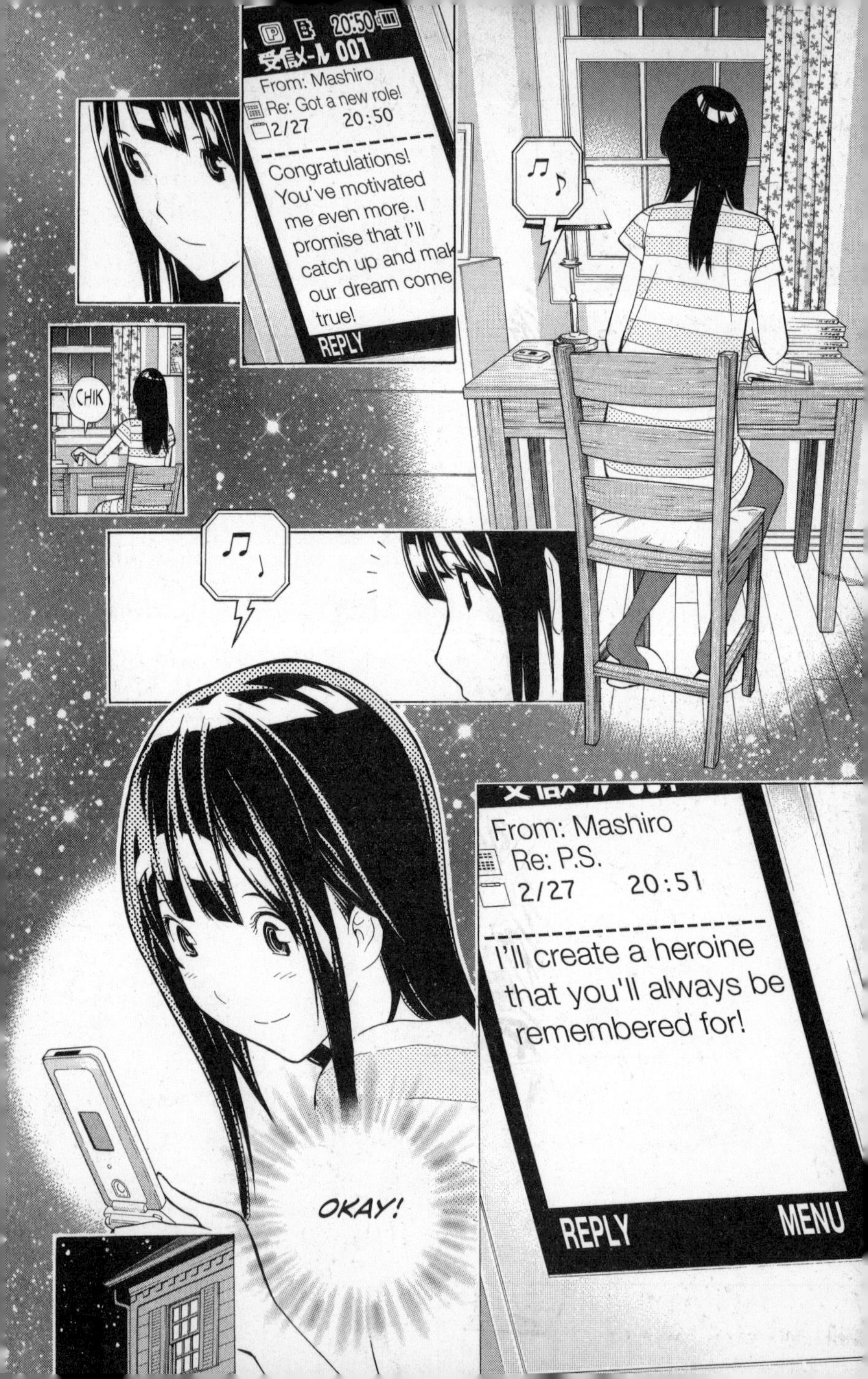

20:50
受信メール 001
From: Mashiro
Re: Got a new role!
2/27 20:50
Congratulations! You've motivated me even more. I promise that I'll catch up and mak our dream come true!
REPLY
CHIK
From: Mashiro
Re: P.S.
2/27 20:51
I'll create a heroine that you'll always be remembered for!
REPLY
MENU
OKAY!

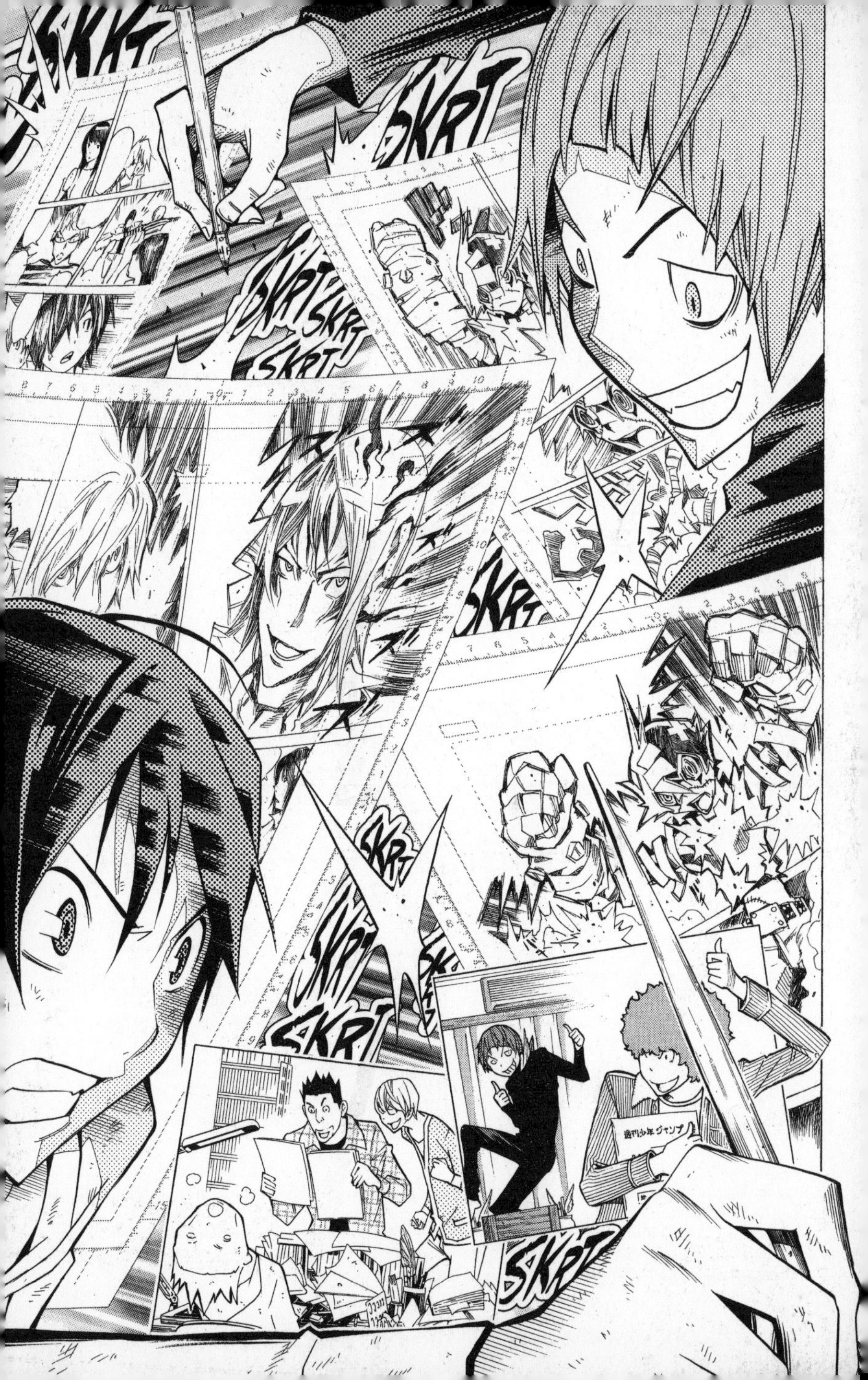

SKRT
SKRT
SKRT SKRT SKRT
SKRT
SKRT
SKRT
SKRT
週刊少年ジャンプ
SKRT

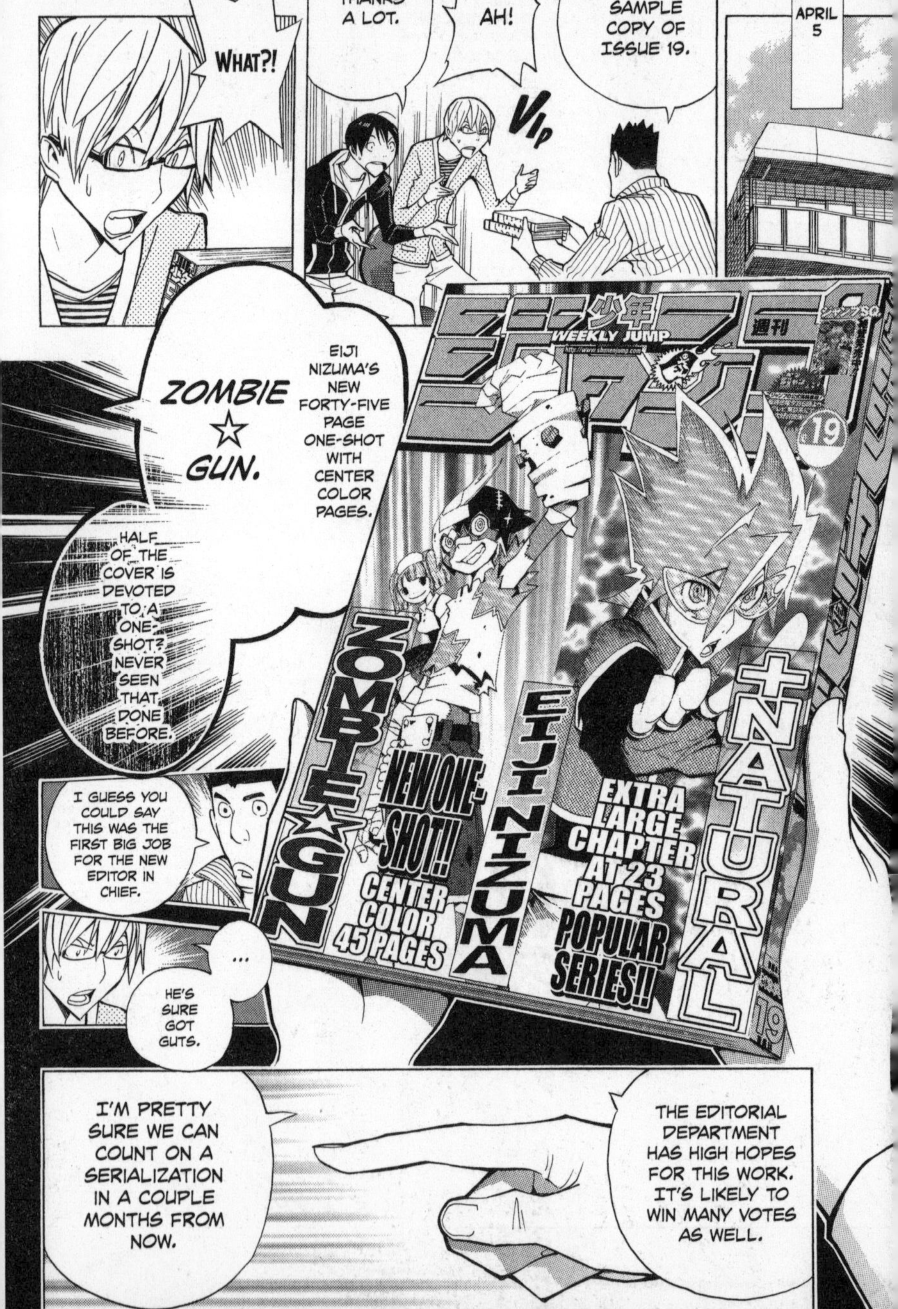

APRIL 5
HERE'S THE SAMPLE COPY OF ISSUE 19.
AH!
VIP
THANKS A LOT.
WHAT?!
EIJI NIZUMA'S NEW FORTY-FIVE PAGE ONE-SHOT WITH CENTER COLOR PAGES.
ZOMBIE ☆ GUN.
WEEKLY JUMP
19
+NATURAL
EXTRA LARGE CHAPTER AT 23 PAGES POPULAR SERIES!!
EIJI NIZUMA
NEW ONE-SHOT!! CENTER COLOR 45 PAGES
ZOMBIE☆GUN
HALF OF THE COVER IS DEVOTED TO A ONE-SHOT? NEVER SEEN THAT DONE BEFORE.
I GUESS YOU COULD SAY THIS WAS THE FIRST BIG JOB FOR THE NEW EDITOR IN CHIEF.
...
HE'S SURE GOT GUTS.
THE EDITORIAL DEPARTMENT HAS HIGH HOPES FOR THIS WORK. IT'S LIKELY TO WIN MANY VOTES AS WELL.
I'M PRETTY SURE WE CAN COUNT ON A SERIALIZATION IN A COUPLE MONTHS FROM NOW.

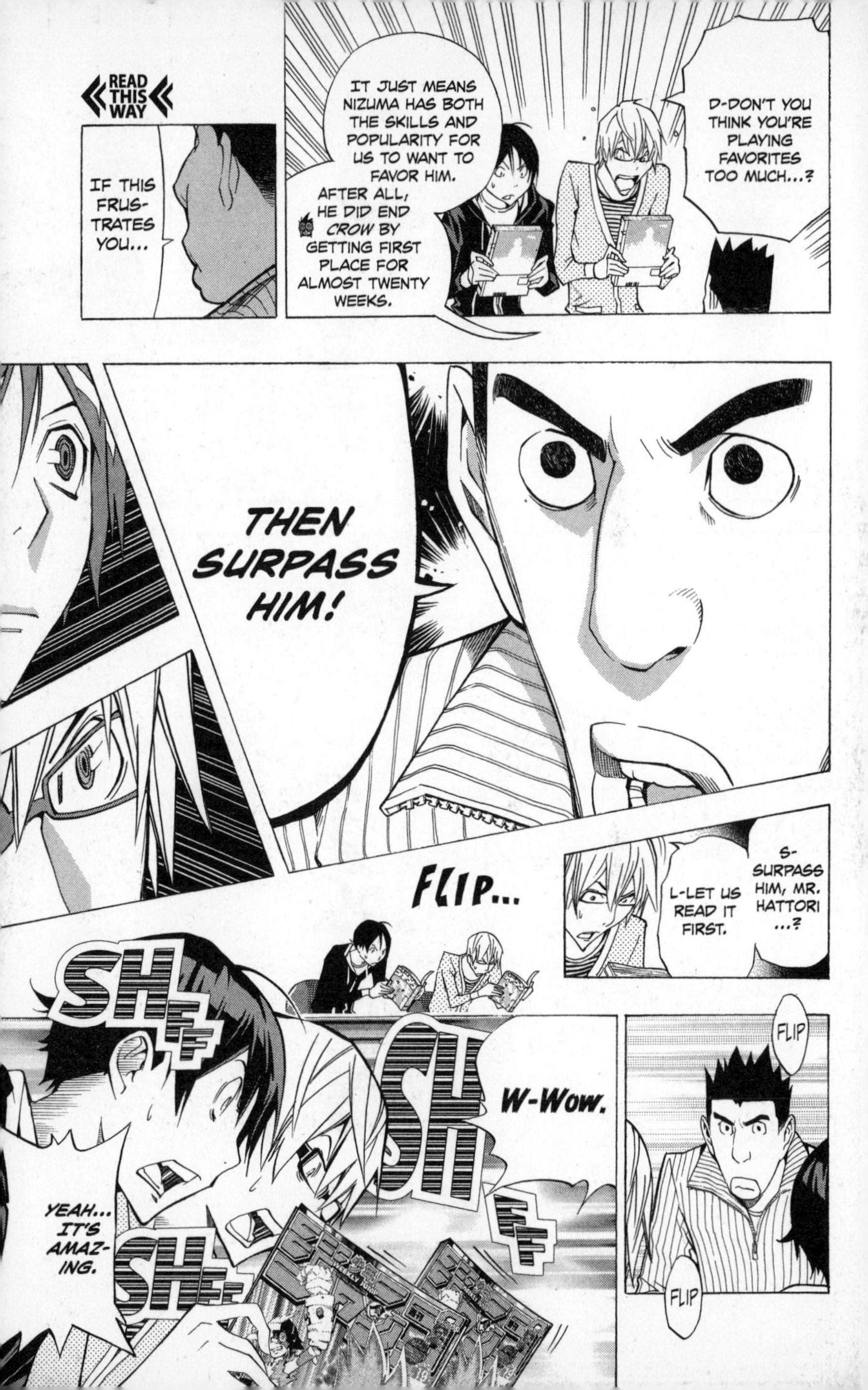
READ THIS WAY
D-DON'T YOU THINK YOU'RE PLAYING FAVORITES TOO MUCH...?
IT JUST MEANS NIZUMA HAS BOTH THE SKILLS AND POPULARITY FOR US TO WANT TO FAVOR HIM.
AFTER ALL, HE DID END *CROW* BY GETTING FIRST PLACE FOR ALMOST TWENTY WEEKS.
IF THIS FRUS-TRATES YOU...
THEN SURPASS HIM!
S-SURPASS HIM, MR. HATTORI ...?
L-LET US READ IT FIRST.
FLIP...
FLIP
FLIP
W-WOW.
YEAH... IT'S AMAZ-ING.

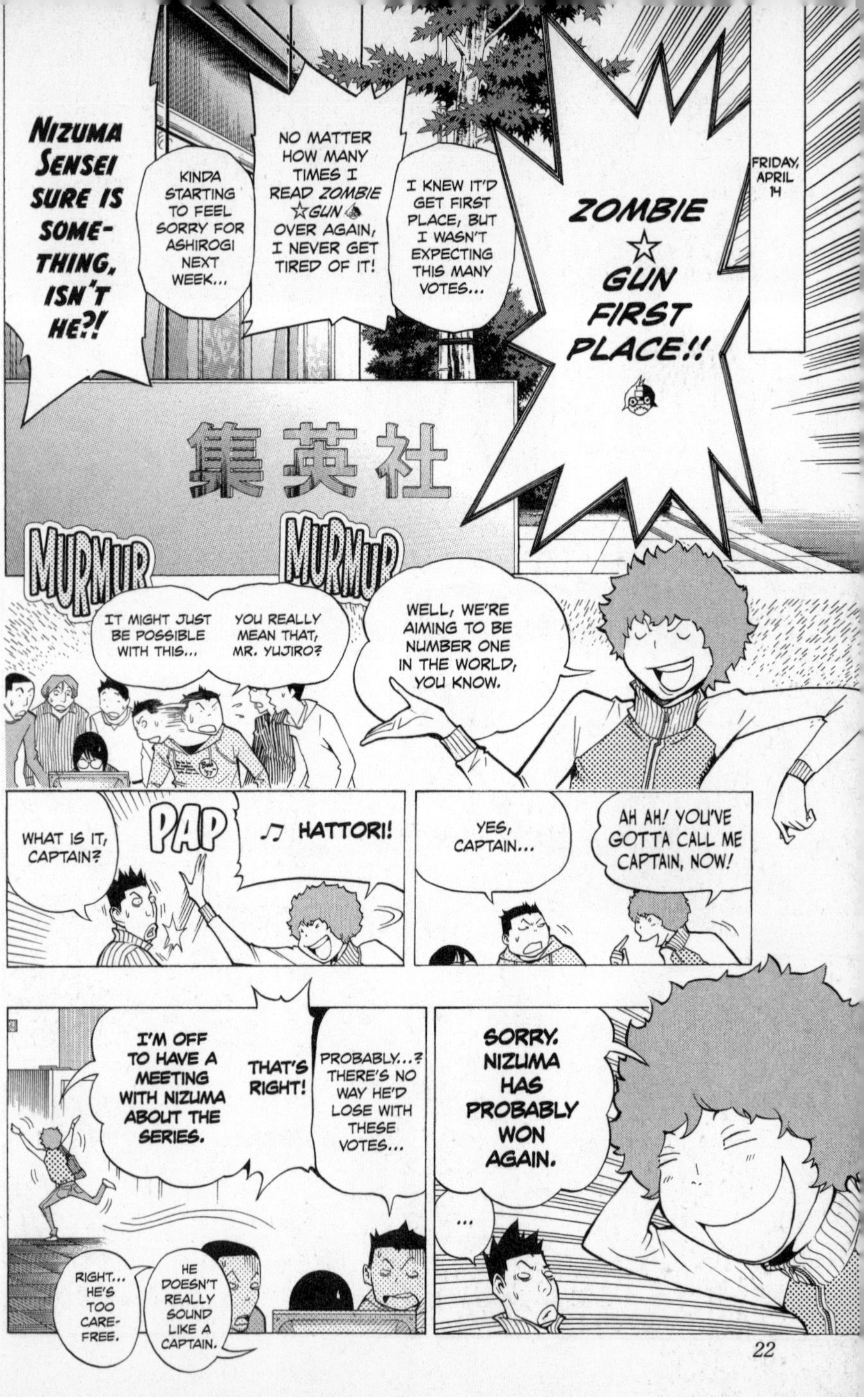
FRIDAY, APRIL 14
ZOMBIE ☆ GUN FIRST PLACE!!
I KNEW IT'D GET FIRST PLACE, BUT I WASN'T EXPECTING THIS MANY VOTES...
NO MATTER HOW MANY TIMES I READ *ZOMBIE ☆ GUN* OVER AGAIN, I NEVER GET TIRED OF IT!
KINDA STARTING TO FEEL SORRY FOR ASHIROGI NEXT WEEK...
NIZUMA SENSEI SURE IS SOME-THING, ISN'T HE?!
集英社
MURMUR
MURMUR
WELL, WE'RE AIMING TO BE NUMBER ONE IN THE WORLD, YOU KNOW.
YOU REALLY MEAN THAT, MR. YUJIRO?
IT MIGHT JUST BE POSSIBLE WITH THIS...
AH AH! YOU'VE GOTTA CALL ME CAPTAIN, NOW!
YES, CAPTAIN...
♫ HATTORI!
PAP
WHAT IS IT, CAPTAIN?
SORRY. NIZUMA HAS PROBABLY WON AGAIN.
...
PROBABLY...? THERE'S NO WAY HE'D LOSE WITH THESE VOTES...
THAT'S RIGHT!
I'M OFF TO HAVE A MEETING WITH NIZUMA ABOUT THE SERIES.
HE DOESN'T REALLY SOUND LIKE A CAPTAIN.
RIGHT... HE'S TOO CARE-FREE.

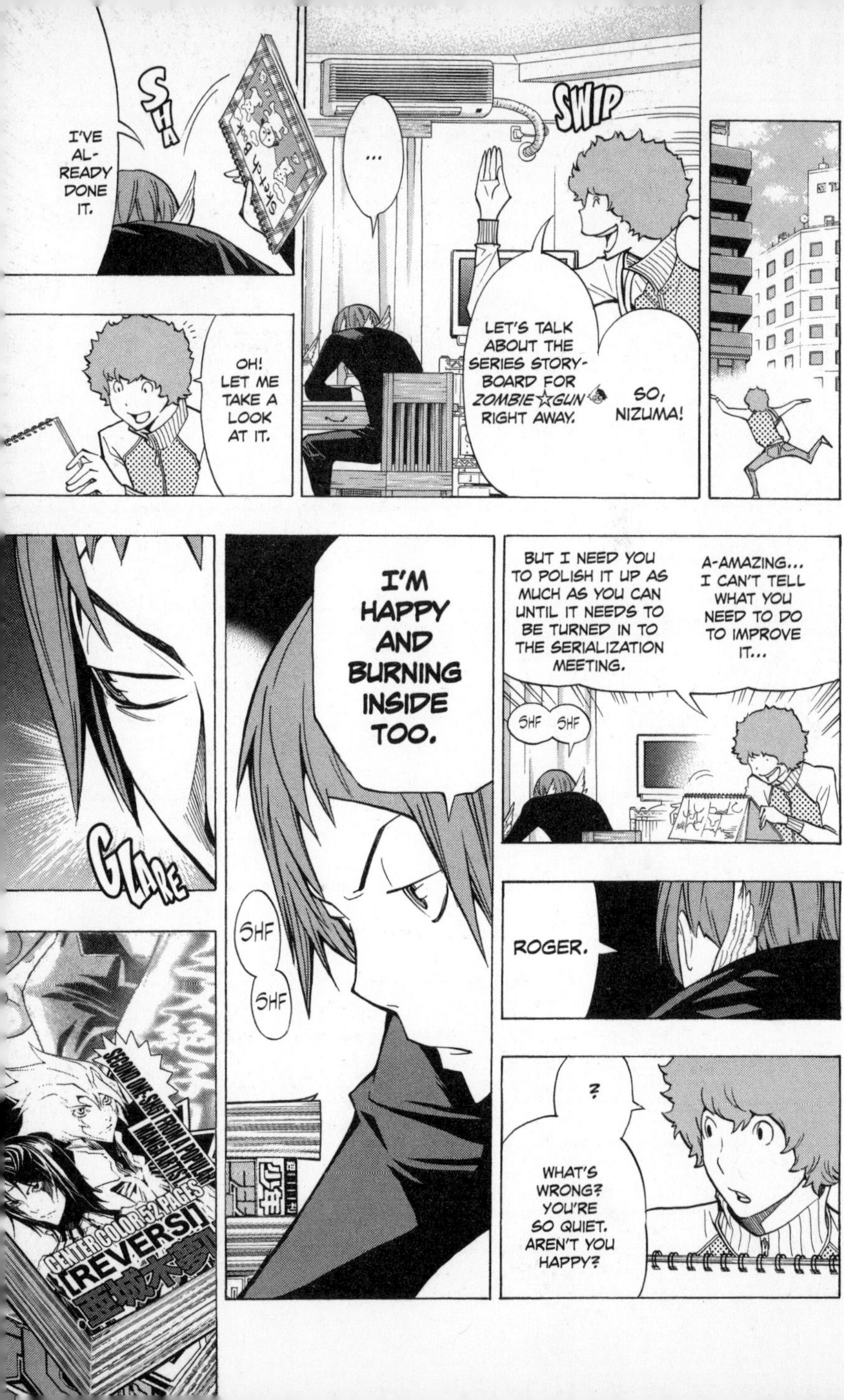
SWIP
SO, NIZUMA!
LET'S TALK ABOUT THE SERIES STORY-BOARD FOR ZOMBIE☆GUN RIGHT AWAY.
...
SHA
I'VE AL-READY DONE IT.
OH! LET ME TAKE A LOOK AT IT.
A-AMAZING... I CAN'T TELL WHAT YOU NEED TO DO TO IMPROVE IT...
BUT I NEED YOU TO POLISH IT UP AS MUCH AS YOU CAN UNTIL IT NEEDS TO BE TURNED IN TO THE SERIALIZATION MEETING.
SHF
SHF
ROGER.
?
WHAT'S WRONG? YOU'RE SO QUIET. AREN'T YOU HAPPY?
I'M HAPPY AND BURNING INSIDE TOO.
SHF
SHF
GLARE
SECOND ONE-SHOT FROM A POPULAR MANGA ARTIST!
CENTER COLOR 52 PAGES
[REVERSI]
少年

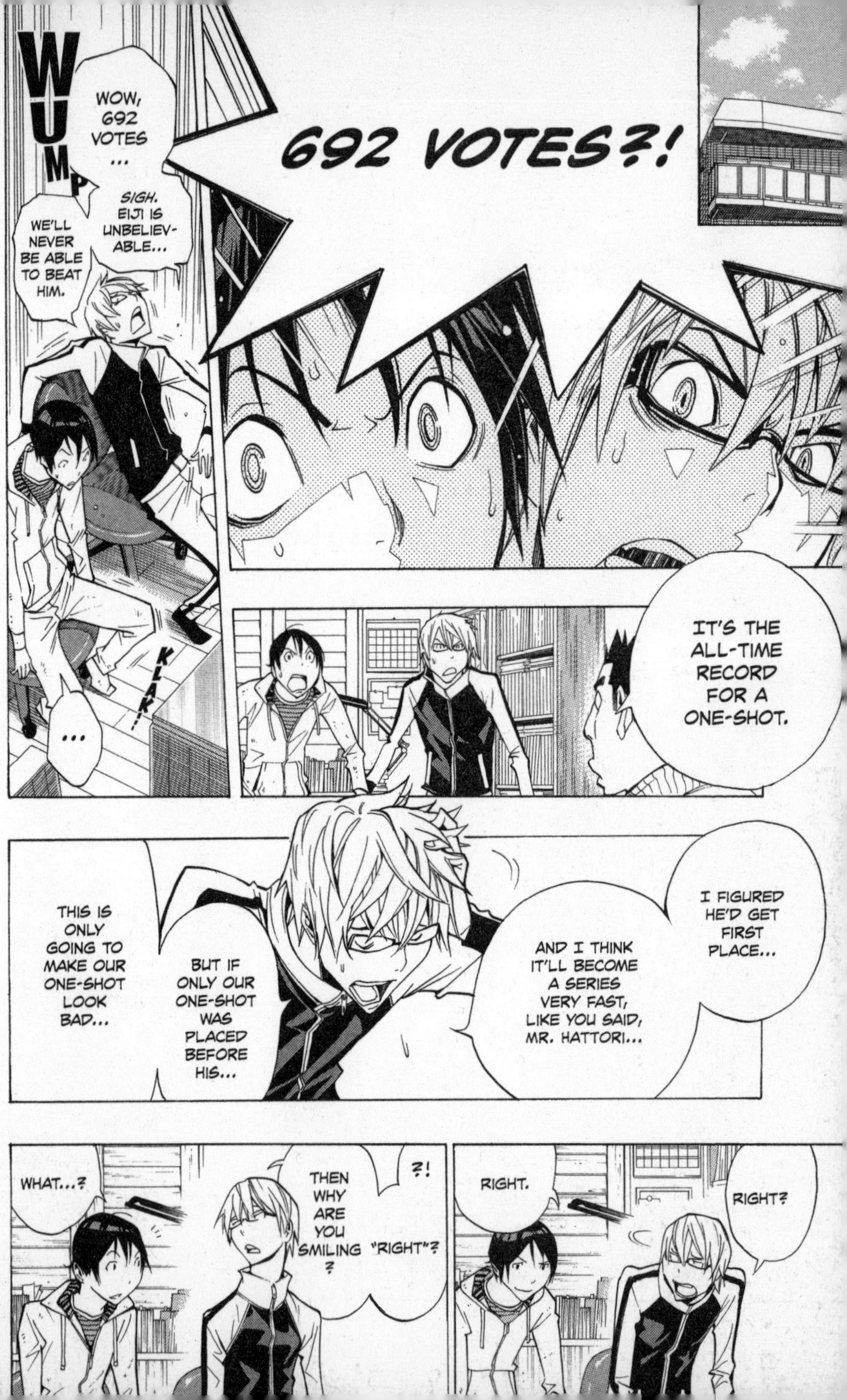
692 VOTES?!
IT'S THE ALL-TIME RECORD FOR A ONE-SHOT.
WOW, 692 VOTES ...
SIGH. EIJI IS UNBELIEV-ABLE...
WE'LL NEVER BE ABLE TO BEAT HIM.
WUMP
KLAK!!
...
I FIGURED HE'D GET FIRST PLACE...
AND I THINK IT'LL BECOME A SERIES VERY FAST, LIKE YOU SAID, MR. HATTORI...
BUT IF ONLY OUR ONE-SHOT WAS PLACED BEFORE HIS...
THIS IS ONLY GOING TO MAKE OUR ONE-SHOT LOOK BAD...
RIGHT?
RIGHT.
?!
THEN WHY ARE YOU SMILING "RIGHT"?
WHAT...?

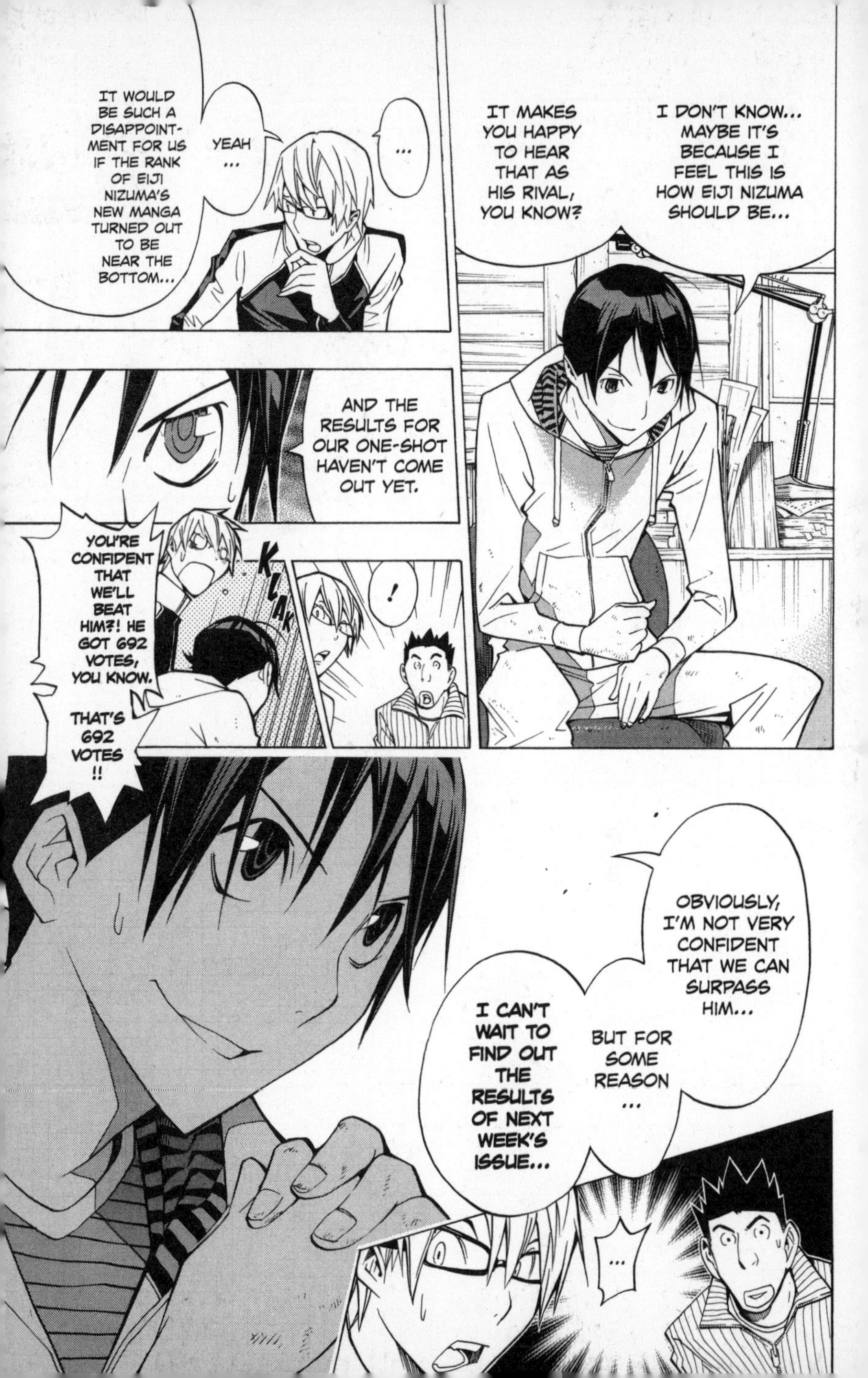
IT WOULD BE SUCH A DISAPPOINTMENT FOR US IF THE RANK OF EIJI NIZUMA'S NEW MANGA TURNED OUT TO BE NEAR THE BOTTOM...
YEAH ...
...
IT MAKES YOU HAPPY TO HEAR THAT AS HIS RIVAL, YOU KNOW?
I DON'T KNOW... MAYBE IT'S BECAUSE I FEEL THIS IS HOW EIJI NIZUMA SHOULD BE...
AND THE RESULTS FOR OUR ONE-SHOT HAVEN'T COME OUT YET.
!
KLAK
YOU'RE CONFIDENT THAT WE'LL BEAT HIM?! HE GOT 692 VOTES, YOU KNOW.
THAT'S 692 VOTES !!
OBVIOUSLY, I'M NOT VERY CONFIDENT THAT WE CAN SURPASS HIM...
BUT FOR SOME REASON ...
I CAN'T WAIT TO FIND OUT THE RESULTS OF NEXT WEEK'S ISSUE...
...

OHBA'S STORYBOARD

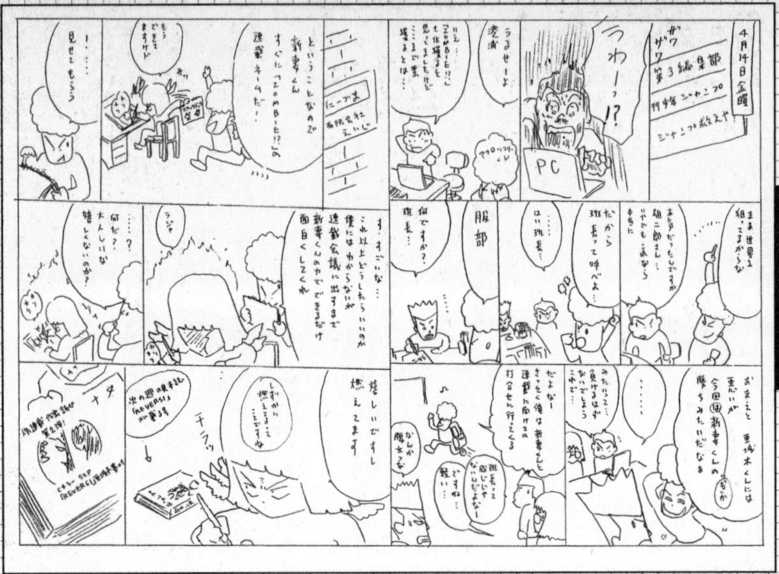

4月14日金曜
第3編集部
週刊少年ジャンプ
ジャンプ救えや!
ザワ ザワ
うわーっ!?
うるせーよ 港浦
いえ…「ZOMBIE!!」は作獲るを思ってましたけど ここまで票獲るとは…
まま世界1狙ってるからな
………
本気だったんですか 雄二郎さん… いやでも三本なら本当に
だから班長って呼べよ…
……はい班長…
服部
何ですか? 班長…
おまえと亜城木くんには悪いが 今回は新妻くんの勝ちみたいだなぁ
むか
……
みたいって… 負けるはずないでしょう これで…
だよなー さっそく俺は新妻くんと連載に向けての打合せ行ってくる
班長って感じじゃないんだよなー
軽い…ですね…
なんか腹立つな
にーづま
有限会社えいじ
ということなので 新妻くん すぐに「ZOMBIE!!」の連載ネームだ!
もうできてますケド
ガッ
……! 見せてもらう
す・すごいな… これ以上どうしたらいいのか僕にはわからないが 連載会議に出すまで 新妻くんの力でできるだけ面白くしてくれ
ラジャ
……? 何だ? 大人しいな 嬉しくないのか?
嬉しいですし 燃えてます
しずかに燃えてることですね
チラッ
次の週の原本誌「REVERSI」が載る号
ナヌ

OBATA'S STORYBOARD

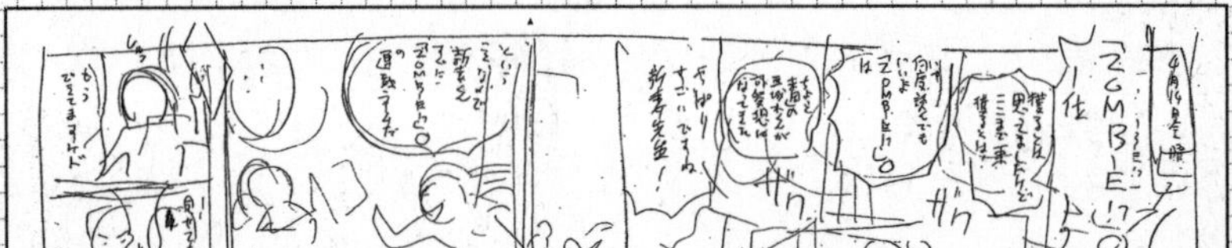

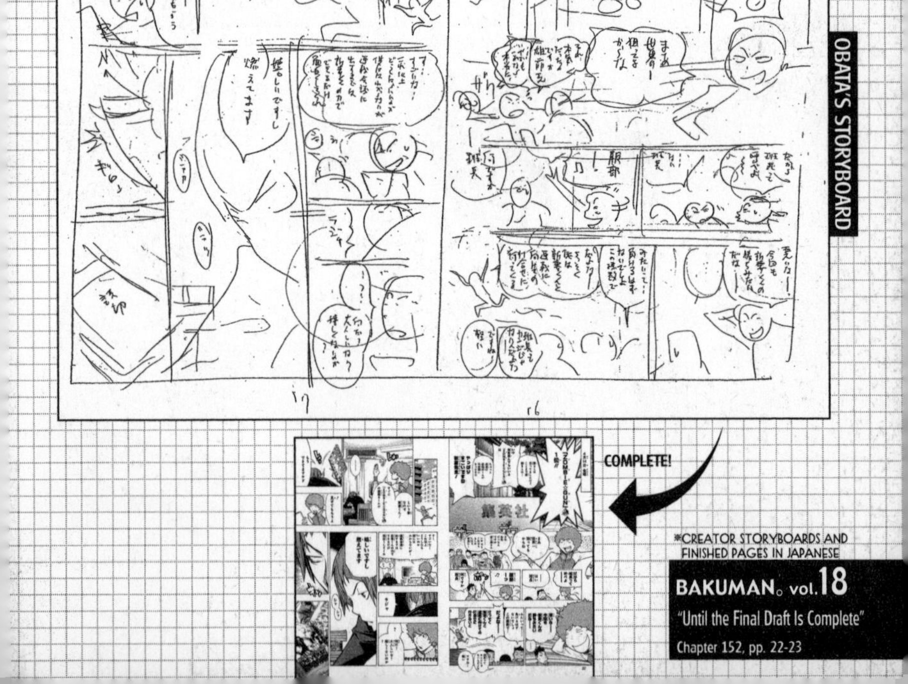

COMPLETE!

*CREATOR STORYBOARDS AND FINISHED PAGES IN JAPANESE

BAKUMAN。 vol.18

"Until the Final Draft Is Complete"

Chapter 152, pp. 22-23

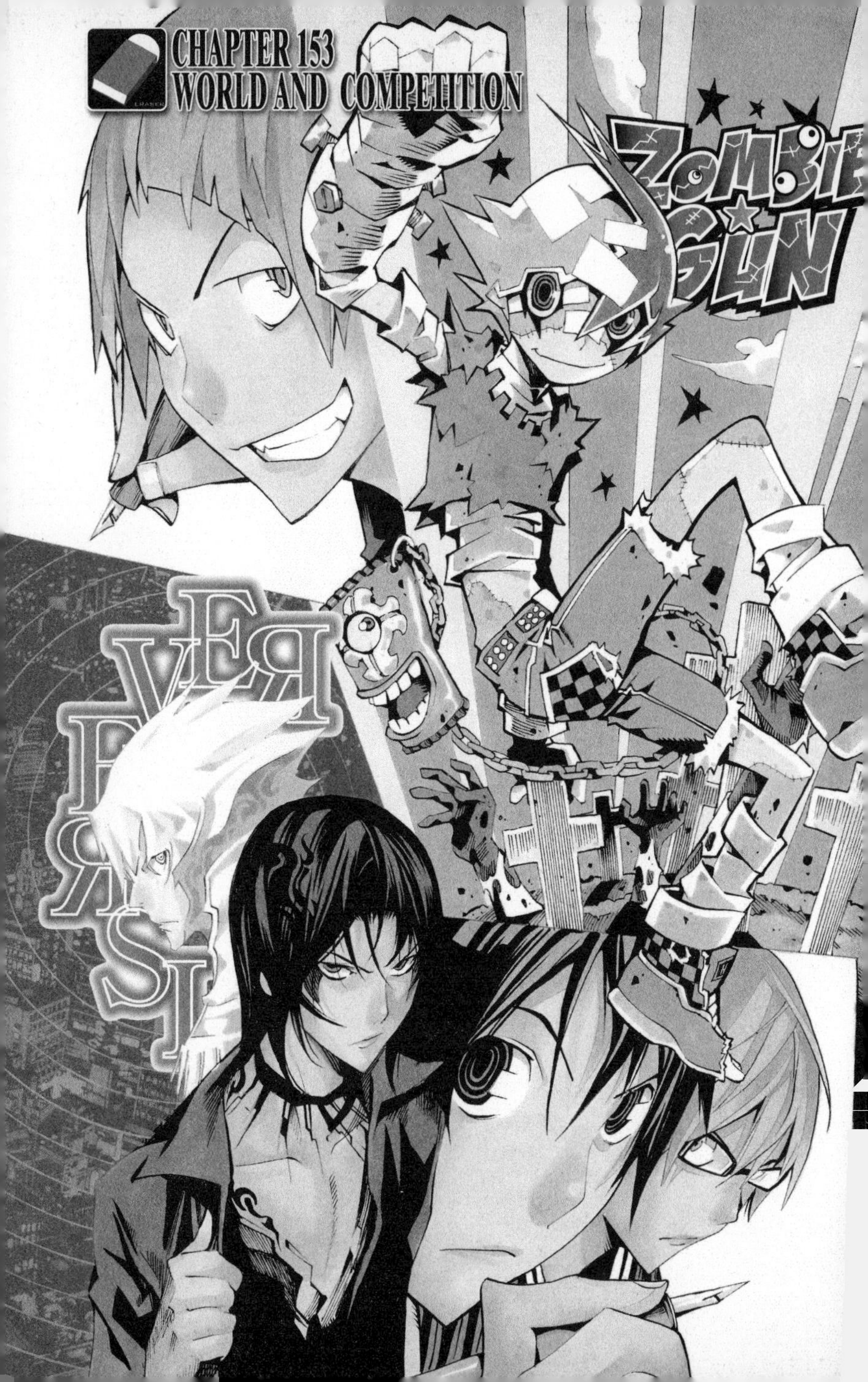
CHAPTER 153
WORLD AND COMPETITION
ZOMBIE GUN

BAKUMAN。

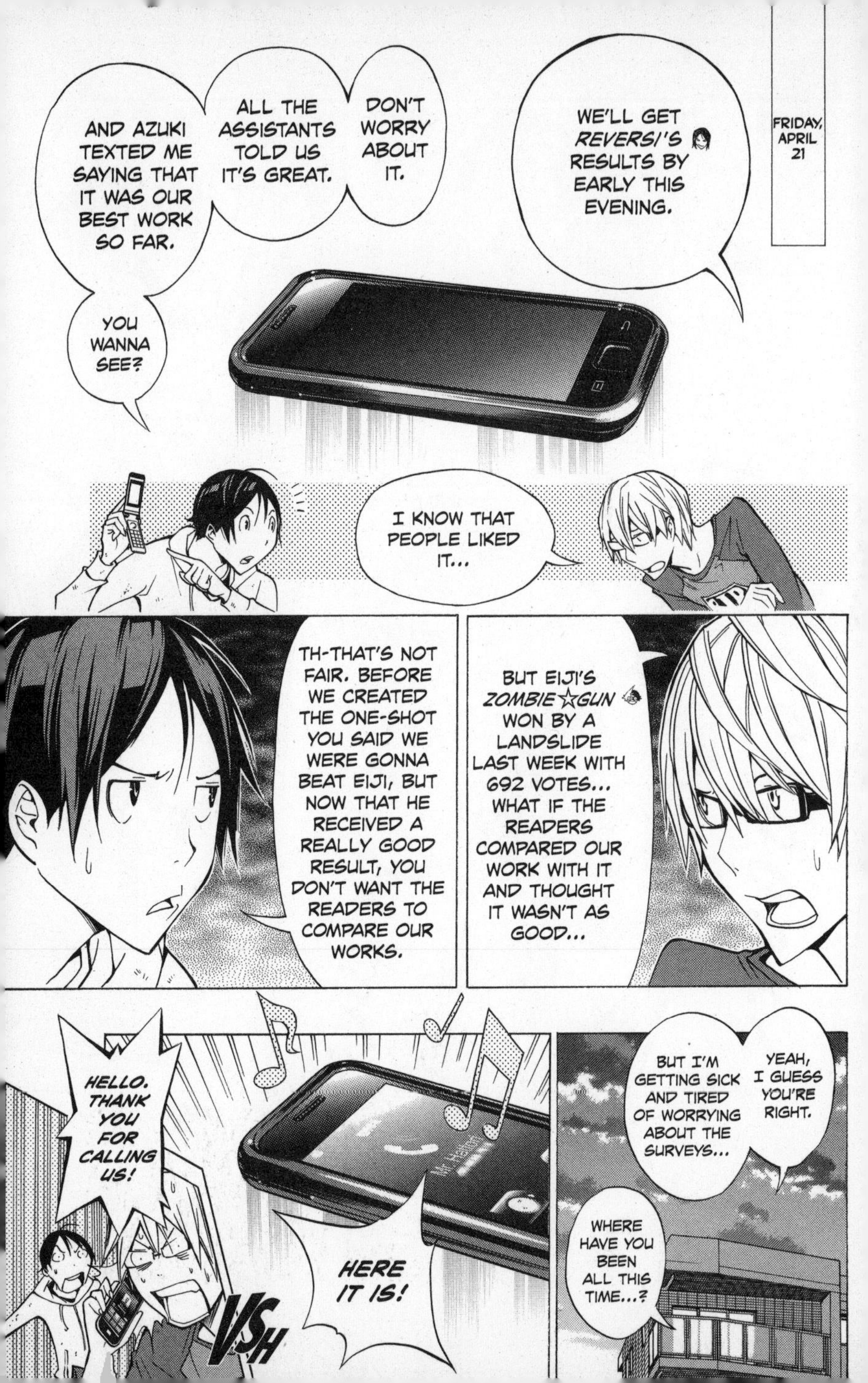
FRIDAY, APRIL 21
WE'LL GET *REVERSI*'S RESULTS BY EARLY THIS EVENING.
DON'T WORRY ABOUT IT.
ALL THE ASSISTANTS TOLD US IT'S GREAT.
AND AZUKI TEXTED ME SAYING THAT IT WAS OUR BEST WORK SO FAR.
YOU WANNA SEE?
I KNOW THAT PEOPLE LIKED IT...
BUT EIJI'S *ZOMBIE☆GUN* WON BY A LANDSLIDE LAST WEEK WITH 692 VOTES... WHAT IF THE READERS COMPARED OUR WORK WITH IT AND THOUGHT IT WASN'T AS GOOD...
TH-THAT'S NOT FAIR. BEFORE WE CREATED THE ONE-SHOT YOU SAID WE WERE GONNA BEAT EIJI, BUT NOW THAT HE RECEIVED A REALLY GOOD RESULT, YOU DON'T WANT THE READERS TO COMPARE OUR WORKS.
YEAH, I GUESS YOU'RE RIGHT.
BUT I'M GETTING SICK AND TIRED OF WORRYING ABOUT THE SURVEYS...
WHERE HAVE YOU BEEN ALL THIS TIME...?
HERE IT IS!
HELLO. THANK YOU FOR CALLING US!
VSH

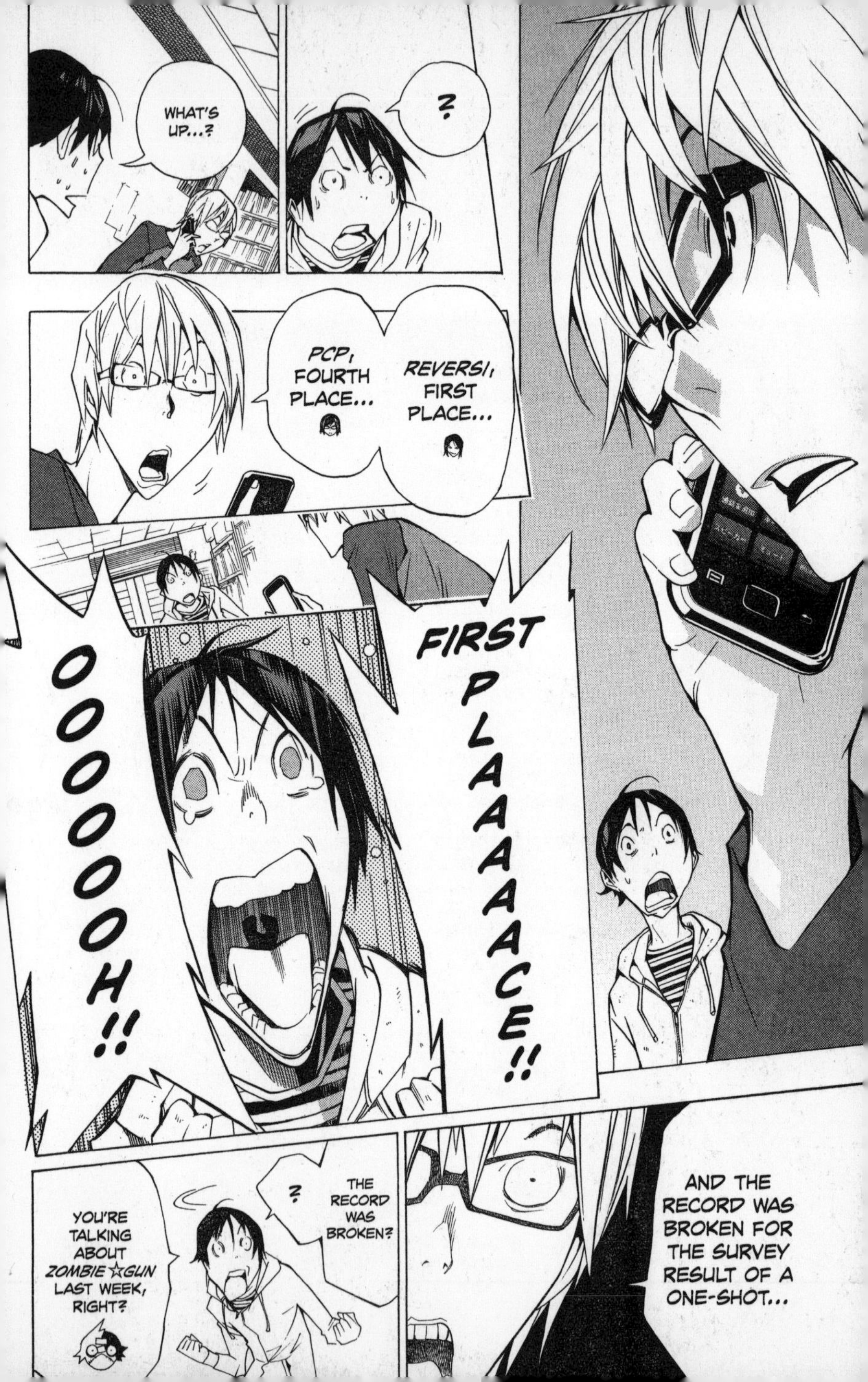
?
WHAT'S UP...?
REVERSI, FIRST PLACE...
PCP, FOURTH PLACE...
FIRST PLAAAAACE!!
OOOOOOH!!
AND THE RECORD WAS BROKEN FOR THE SURVEY RESULT OF A ONE-SHOT...
?
THE RECORD WAS BROKEN?
YOU'RE TALKING ABOUT ZOMBIE☆GUN LAST WEEK, RIGHT?

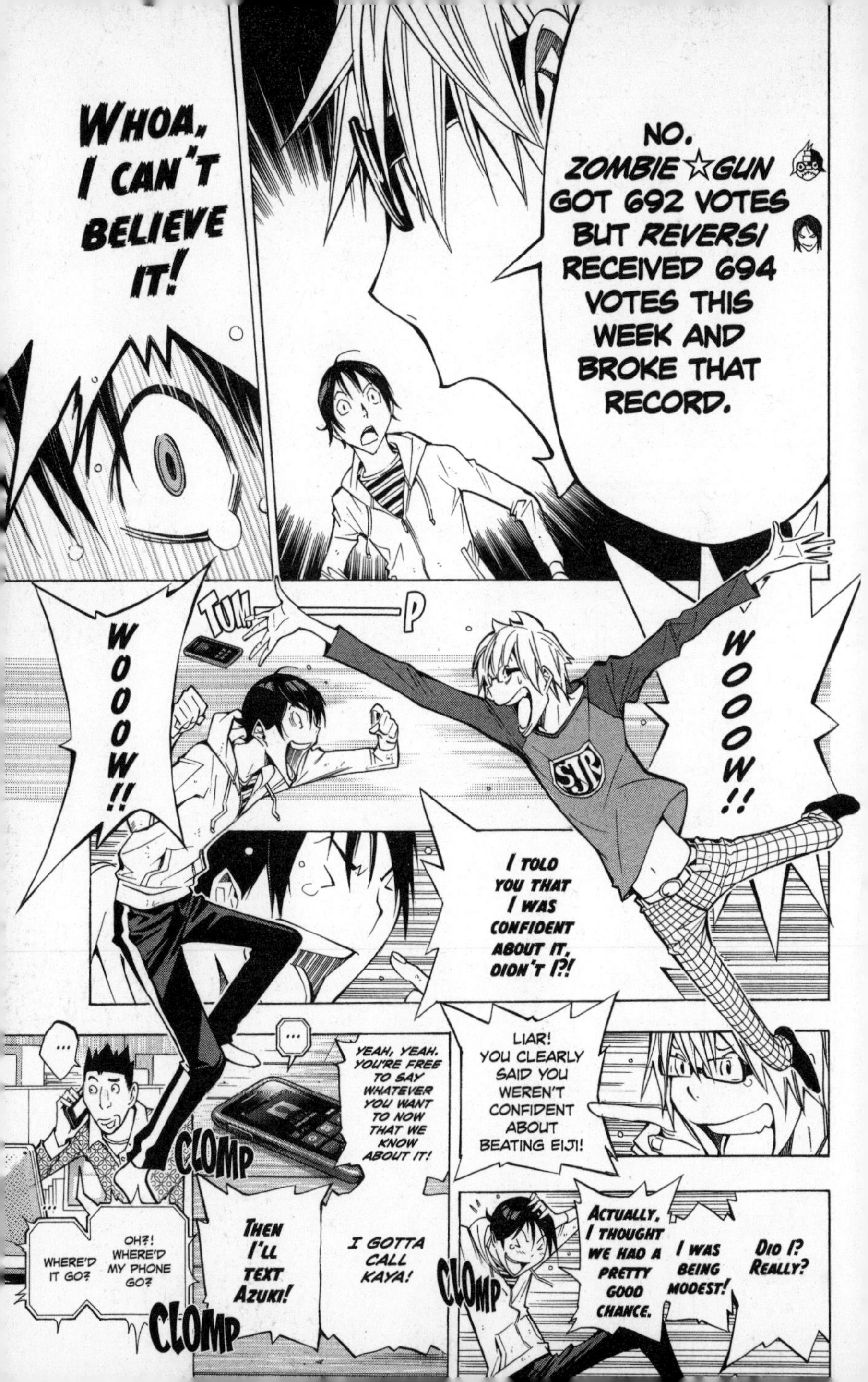
NO. ZOMBIE☆GUN GOT 692 VOTES BUT REVERSI RECEIVED 694 VOTES THIS WEEK AND BROKE THAT RECORD.
WHOA, I CAN'T BELIEVE IT!
WOOOOW!!
TUM—P
WOOOOW!!
I TOLD YOU THAT I WAS CONFIDENT ABOUT IT, DIDN'T I?!
LIAR! YOU CLEARLY SAID YOU WEREN'T CONFIDENT ABOUT BEATING EIJI!
YEAH, YEAH. YOU'RE FREE TO SAY WHATEVER YOU WANT TO NOW THAT WE KNOW ABOUT IT!
...
...
DID I? REALLY?
I WAS BEING MODEST!
ACTUALLY, I THOUGHT WE HAD A PRETTY GOOD CHANCE.
CLOMP
I GOTTA CALL KAYA!
THEN I'LL TEXT AZUKI!
CLOMP
OH?! WHERE'D MY PHONE GO?
WHERE'D IT GO?
CLOMP

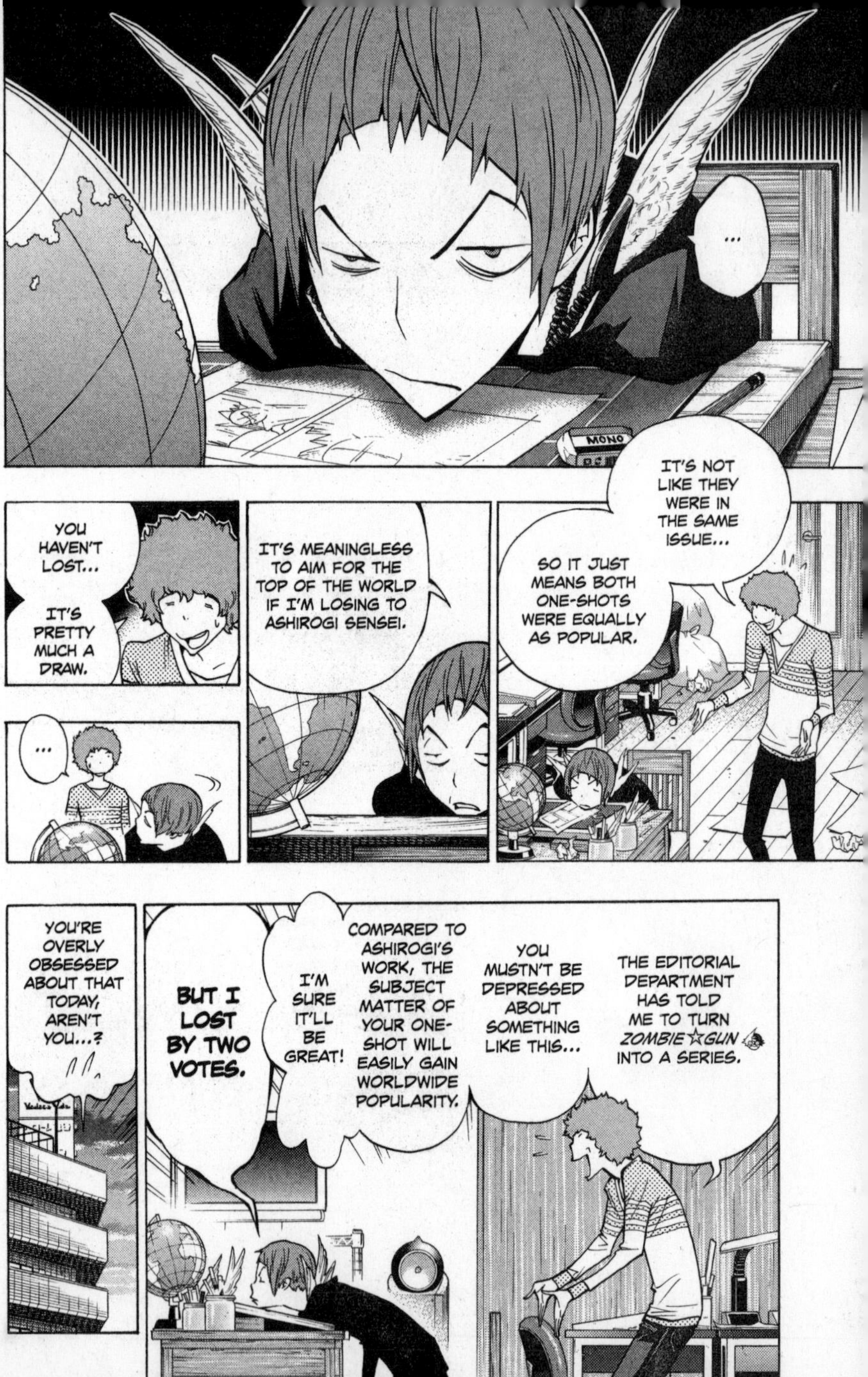
...
IT'S NOT LIKE THEY WERE IN THE SAME ISSUE...
SO IT JUST MEANS BOTH ONE-SHOTS WERE EQUALLY AS POPULAR.
IT'S MEANINGLESS TO AIM FOR THE TOP OF THE WORLD IF I'M LOSING TO ASHIROGI SENSEI.
YOU HAVEN'T LOST...
IT'S PRETTY MUCH A DRAW.
...
THE EDITORIAL DEPARTMENT HAS TOLD ME TO TURN ZOMBIE☆GUN INTO A SERIES.
YOU MUSTN'T BE DEPRESSED ABOUT SOMETHING LIKE THIS...
COMPARED TO ASHIROGI'S WORK, THE SUBJECT MATTER OF YOUR ONE-SHOT WILL EASILY GAIN WORLDWIDE POPULARITY.
I'M SURE IT'LL BE GREAT!
BUT I LOST BY TWO VOTES.
YOU'RE OVERLY OBSESSED ABOUT THAT TODAY, AREN'T YOU...?

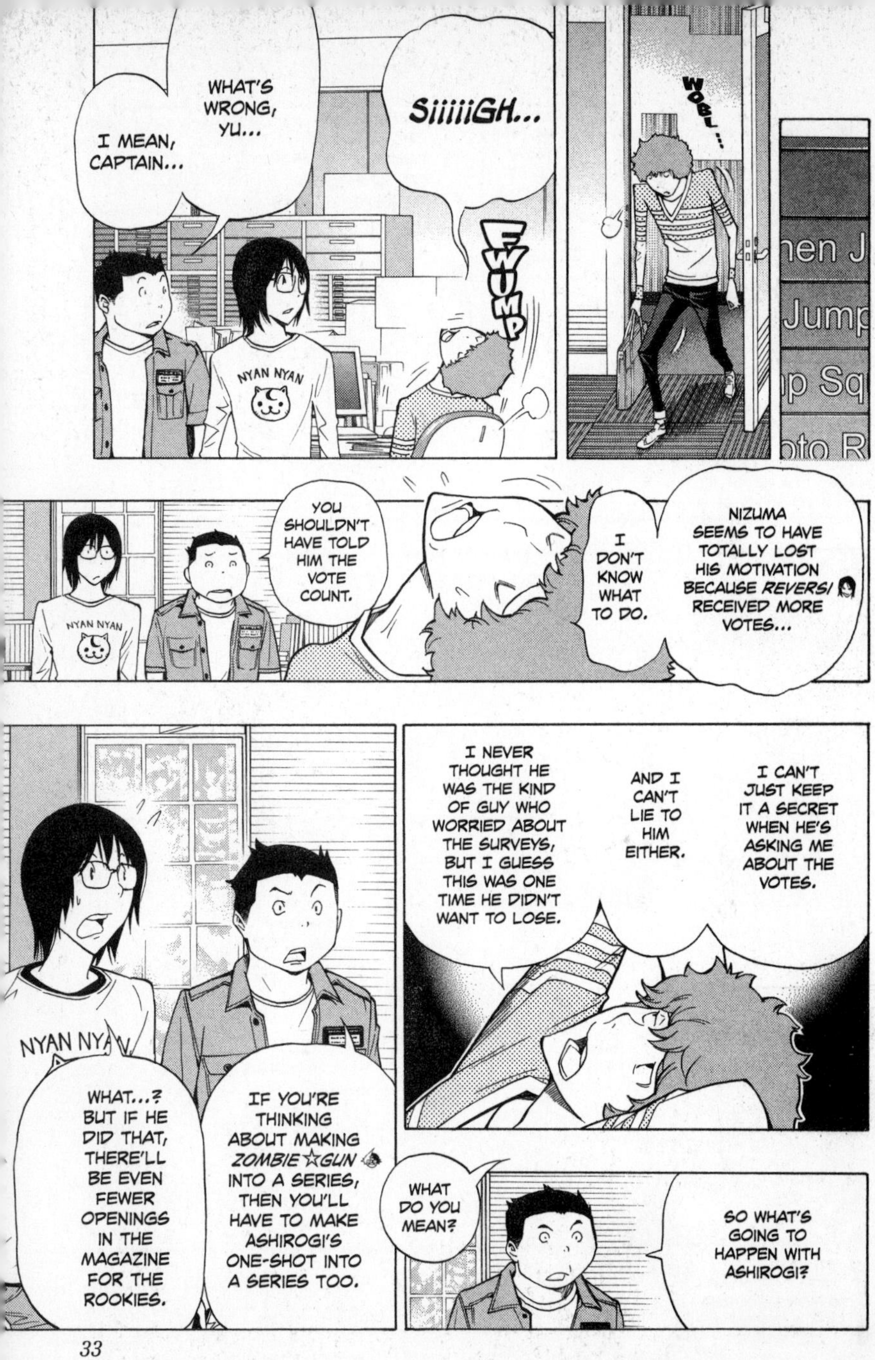
WOBL...
SIIIIGH...
FWUMP
WHAT'S WRONG, YU...
I MEAN, CAPTAIN...
NYAN NYAN
NIZUMA SEEMS TO HAVE TOTALLY LOST HIS MOTIVATION BECAUSE *REVERSI* RECEIVED MORE VOTES...
I DON'T KNOW WHAT TO DO.
YOU SHOULDN'T HAVE TOLD HIM THE VOTE COUNT.
NYAN NYAN
I CAN'T JUST KEEP IT A SECRET WHEN HE'S ASKING ME ABOUT THE VOTES.
AND I CAN'T LIE TO HIM EITHER.
I NEVER THOUGHT HE WAS THE KIND OF GUY WHO WORRIED ABOUT THE SURVEYS, BUT I GUESS THIS WAS ONE TIME HE DIDN'T WANT TO LOSE.
SO WHAT'S GOING TO HAPPEN WITH ASHIROGI?
WHAT DO YOU MEAN?
IF YOU'RE THINKING ABOUT MAKING *ZOMBIE☆GUN* INTO A SERIES, THEN YOU'LL HAVE TO MAKE ASHIROGI'S ONE-SHOT INTO A SERIES TOO.
WHAT...? BUT IF HE DID THAT, THERE'LL BE EVEN FEWER OPENINGS IN THE MAGAZINE FOR THE ROOKIES.

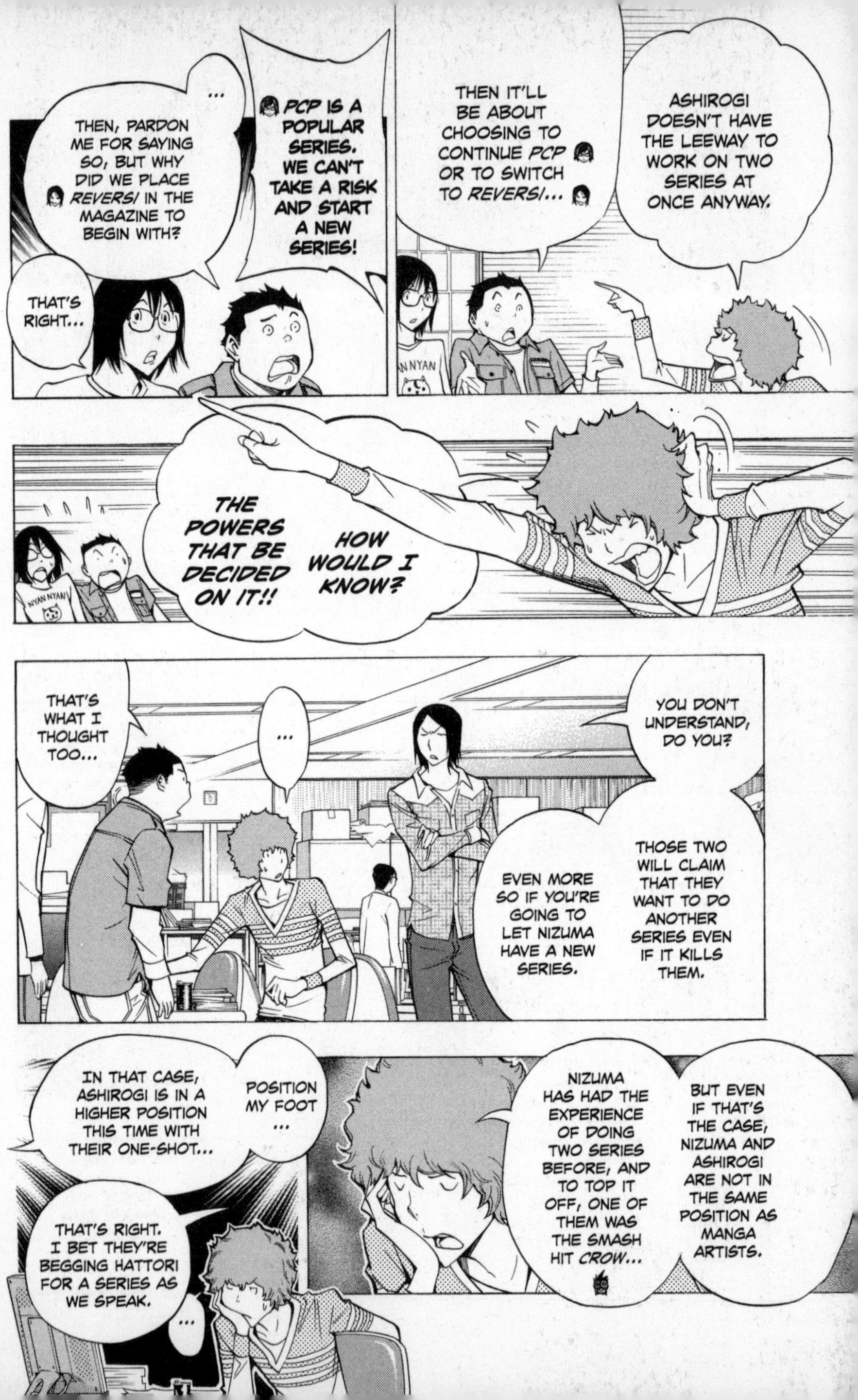
ASHIROGI DOESN'T HAVE THE LEEWAY TO WORK ON TWO SERIES AT ONCE ANYWAY.
THEN IT'LL BE ABOUT CHOOSING TO CONTINUE *PCP* OR TO SWITCH TO *REVERSI*...
PCP IS A POPULAR SERIES. WE CAN'T TAKE A RISK AND START A NEW SERIES!
...
THEN, PARDON ME FOR SAYING SO, BUT WHY DID WE PLACE *REVERSI* IN THE MAGAZINE TO BEGIN WITH?
THAT'S RIGHT...
HOW WOULD I KNOW?
THE POWERS THAT BE DECIDED ON IT!!
YOU DON'T UNDERSTAND, DO YOU?
...
THAT'S WHAT I THOUGHT TOO...
THOSE TWO WILL CLAIM THAT THEY WANT TO DO ANOTHER SERIES EVEN IF IT KILLS THEM.
EVEN MORE SO IF YOU'RE GOING TO LET NIZUMA HAVE A NEW SERIES.
BUT EVEN IF THAT'S THE CASE, NIZUMA AND ASHIROGI ARE NOT IN THE SAME POSITION AS MANGA ARTISTS.
NIZUMA HAS HAD THE EXPERIENCE OF DOING TWO SERIES BEFORE, AND TO TOP IT OFF, ONE OF THEM WAS THE SMASH HIT *CROW*...
POSITION MY FOOT...
IN THAT CASE, ASHIROGI IS IN A HIGHER POSITION THIS TIME WITH THEIR ONE-SHOT...
THAT'S RIGHT. I BET THEY'RE BEGGING HATTORI FOR A SERIES AS WE SPEAK.
...

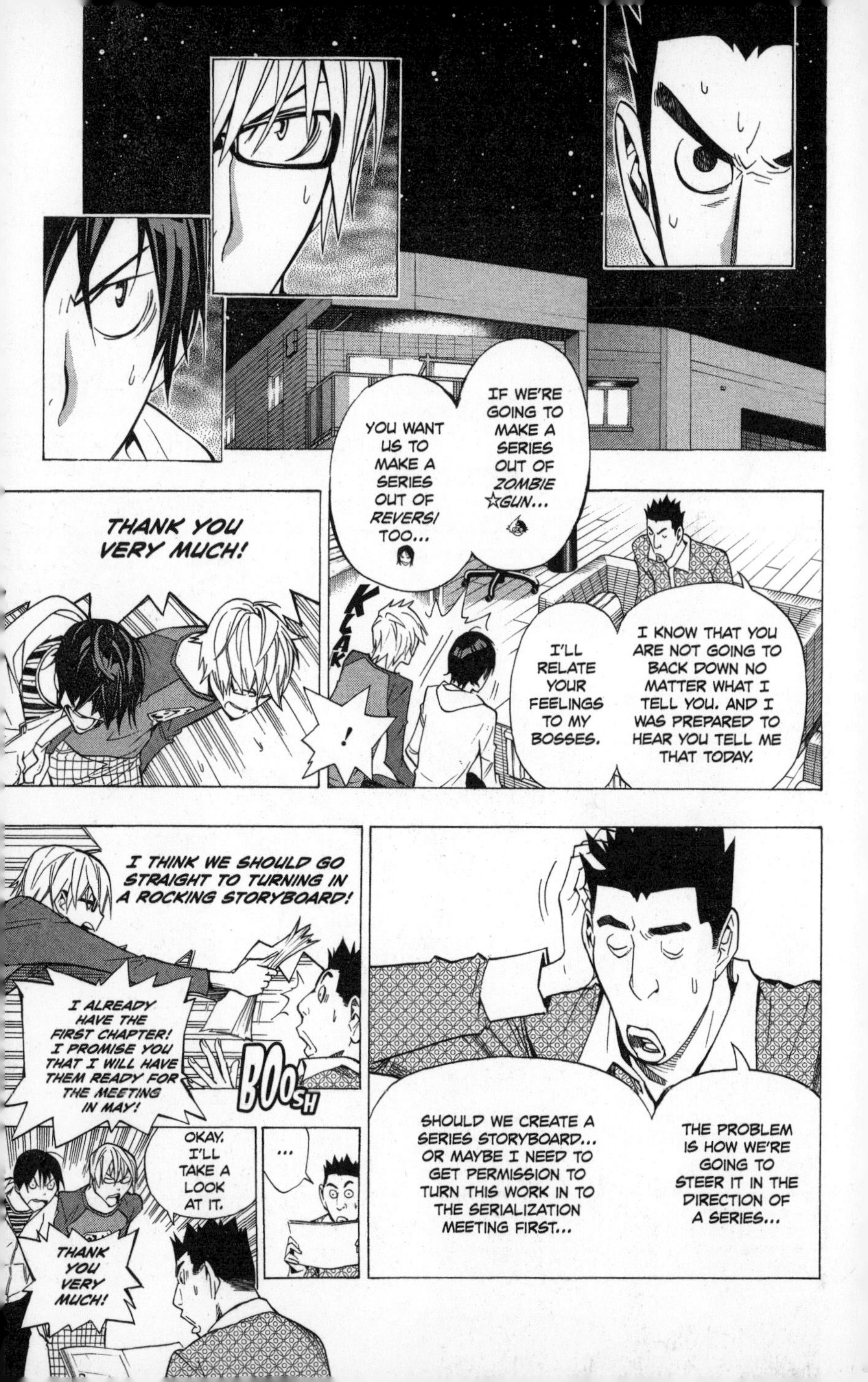
I KNOW THAT YOU ARE NOT GOING TO BACK DOWN NO MATTER WHAT I TELL YOU. AND I WAS PREPARED TO HEAR YOU TELL ME THAT TODAY.
I'LL RELATE YOUR FEELINGS TO MY BOSSES.
IF WE'RE GOING TO MAKE A SERIES OUT OF ZOMBIE☆GUN...
YOU WANT US TO MAKE A SERIES OUT OF REVERSI TOO...
KLAK
!
THANK YOU VERY MUCH!
THE PROBLEM IS HOW WE'RE GOING TO STEER IT IN THE DIRECTION OF A SERIES...
SHOULD WE CREATE A SERIES STORYBOARD... OR MAYBE I NEED TO GET PERMISSION TO TURN THIS WORK IN TO THE SERIALIZATION MEETING FIRST...
I THINK WE SHOULD GO STRAIGHT TO TURNING IN A ROCKING STORYBOARD!
I ALREADY HAVE THE FIRST CHAPTER! I PROMISE YOU THAT I WILL HAVE THEM READY FOR THE MEETING IN MAY!
BOOSH
...
OKAY. I'LL TAKE A LOOK AT IT.
THANK YOU VERY MUCH!

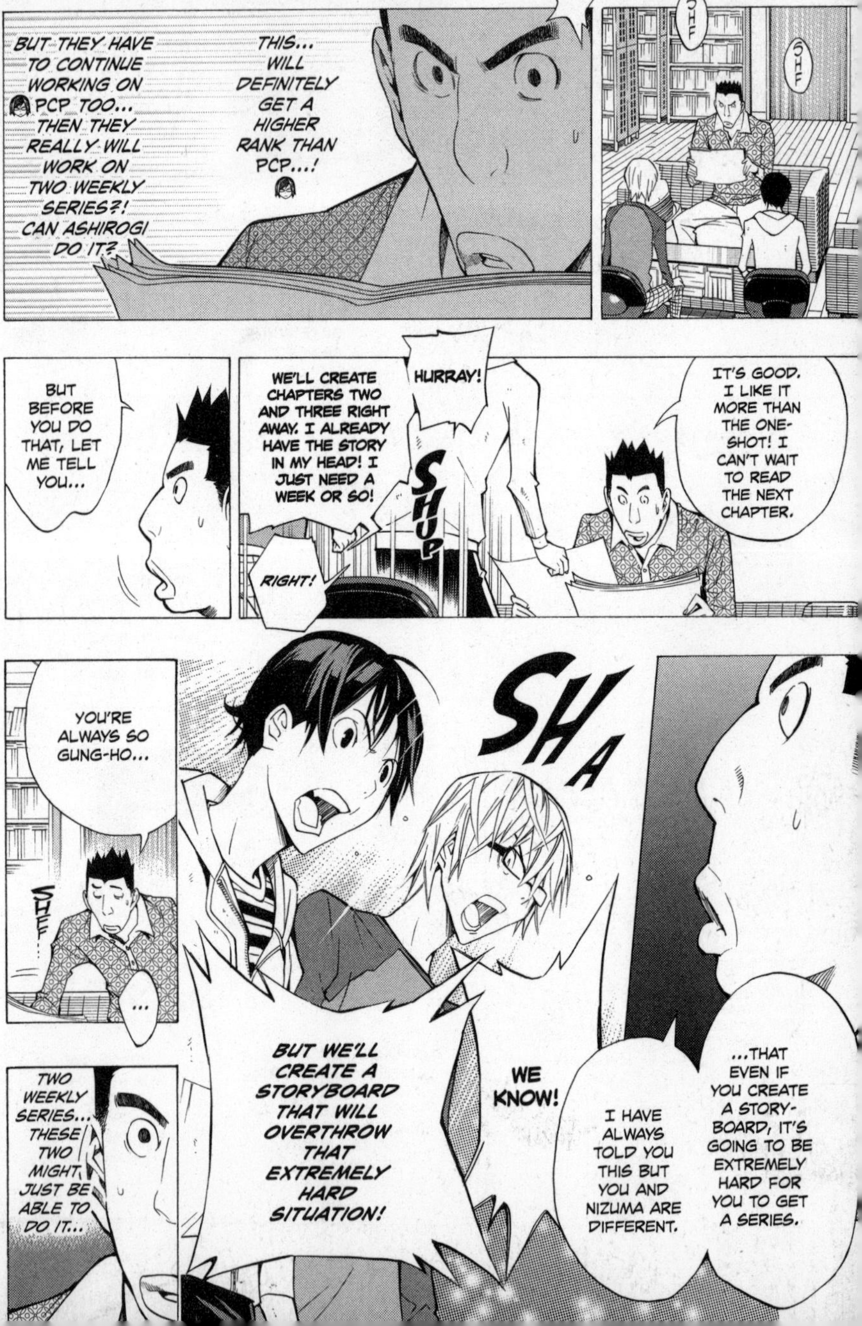
SHF
SHF
THIS... WILL DEFINITELY GET A HIGHER RANK THAN PCP...!
BUT THEY HAVE TO CONTINUE WORKING ON PCP TOO... THEN THEY REALLY WILL WORK ON TWO WEEKLY SERIES?! CAN ASHIROGI DO IT?
IT'S GOOD. I LIKE IT MORE THAN THE ONE-SHOT! I CAN'T WAIT TO READ THE NEXT CHAPTER.
HURRAY!
WE'LL CREATE CHAPTERS TWO AND THREE RIGHT AWAY. I ALREADY HAVE THE STORY IN MY HEAD! I JUST NEED A WEEK OR SO!
SHUP
RIGHT!
BUT BEFORE YOU DO THAT, LET ME TELL YOU...
...THAT EVEN IF YOU CREATE A STORY-BOARD, IT'S GOING TO BE EXTREMELY HARD FOR YOU TO GET A SERIES.
I HAVE ALWAYS TOLD YOU THIS BUT YOU AND NIZUMA ARE DIFFERENT.
SHA
WE KNOW!
BUT WE'LL CREATE A STORYBOARD THAT WILL OVERTHROW THAT EXTREMELY HARD SITUATION!
YOU'RE ALWAYS SO GUNG-HO...
SHEF...
...
TWO WEEKLY SERIES... THESE TWO MIGHT JUST BE ABLE TO DO IT...

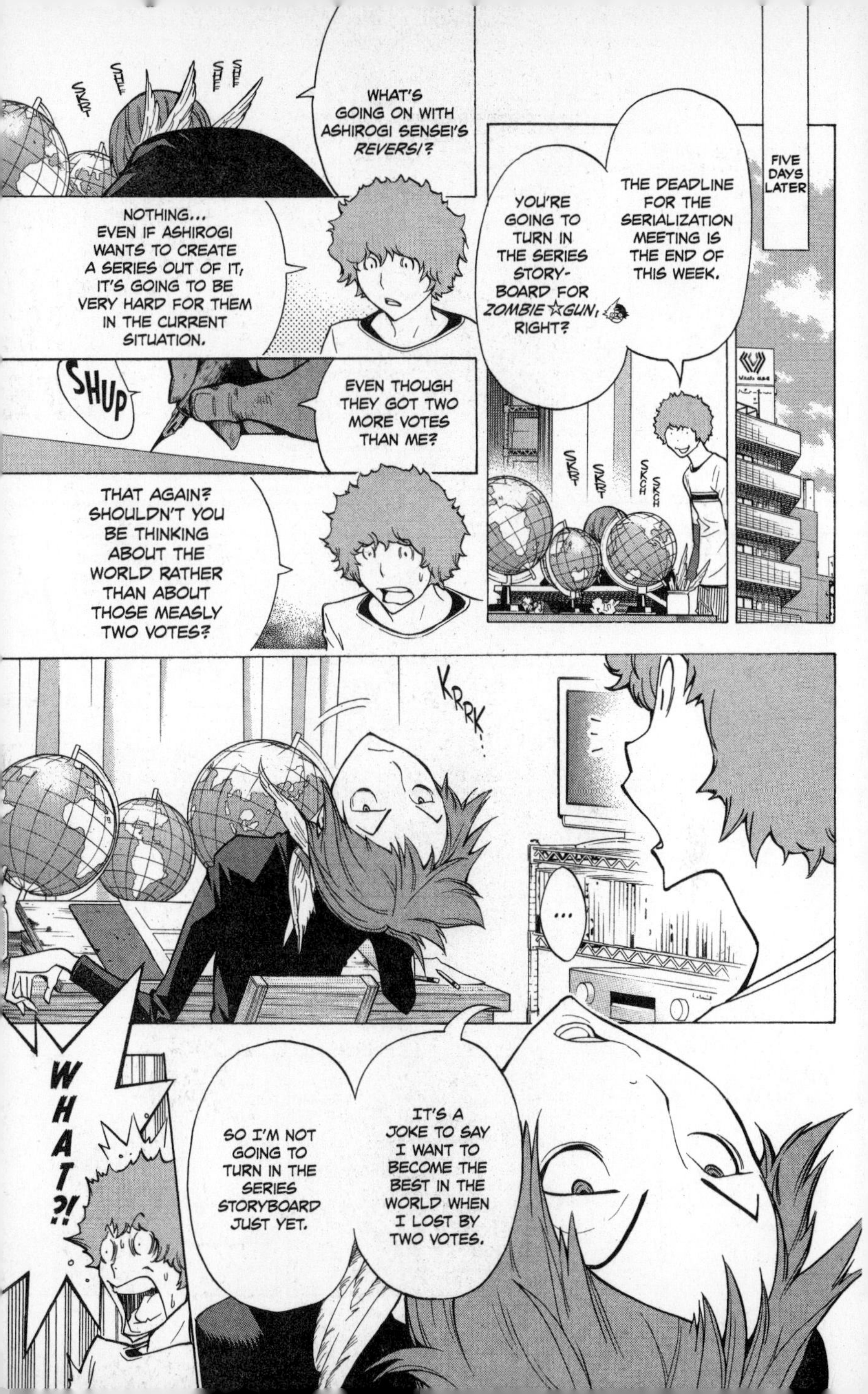

FIVE DAYS LATER
THE DEADLINE FOR THE SERIALIZATION MEETING IS THE END OF THIS WEEK.
YOU'RE GOING TO TURN IN THE SERIES STORY-BOARD FOR *ZOMBIE☆GUN*, RIGHT?
SKRT
SKRT
SKCH
SKCH
SHF
SHF
SHF
SKRT
WHAT'S GOING ON WITH ASHIROGI SENSEI'S *REVERSI*?
NOTHING... EVEN IF ASHIROGI WANTS TO CREATE A SERIES OUT OF IT, IT'S GOING TO BE VERY HARD FOR THEM IN THE CURRENT SITUATION.
EVEN THOUGH THEY GOT TWO MORE VOTES THAN ME?
SHUP
THAT AGAIN? SHOULDN'T YOU BE THINKING ABOUT THE WORLD RATHER THAN ABOUT THOSE MEASLY TWO VOTES?
KRRK
...
IT'S A JOKE TO SAY I WANT TO BECOME THE BEST IN THE WORLD WHEN I LOST BY TWO VOTES.
SO I'M NOT GOING TO TURN IN THE SERIES STORYBOARD JUST YET.
WHAT?!

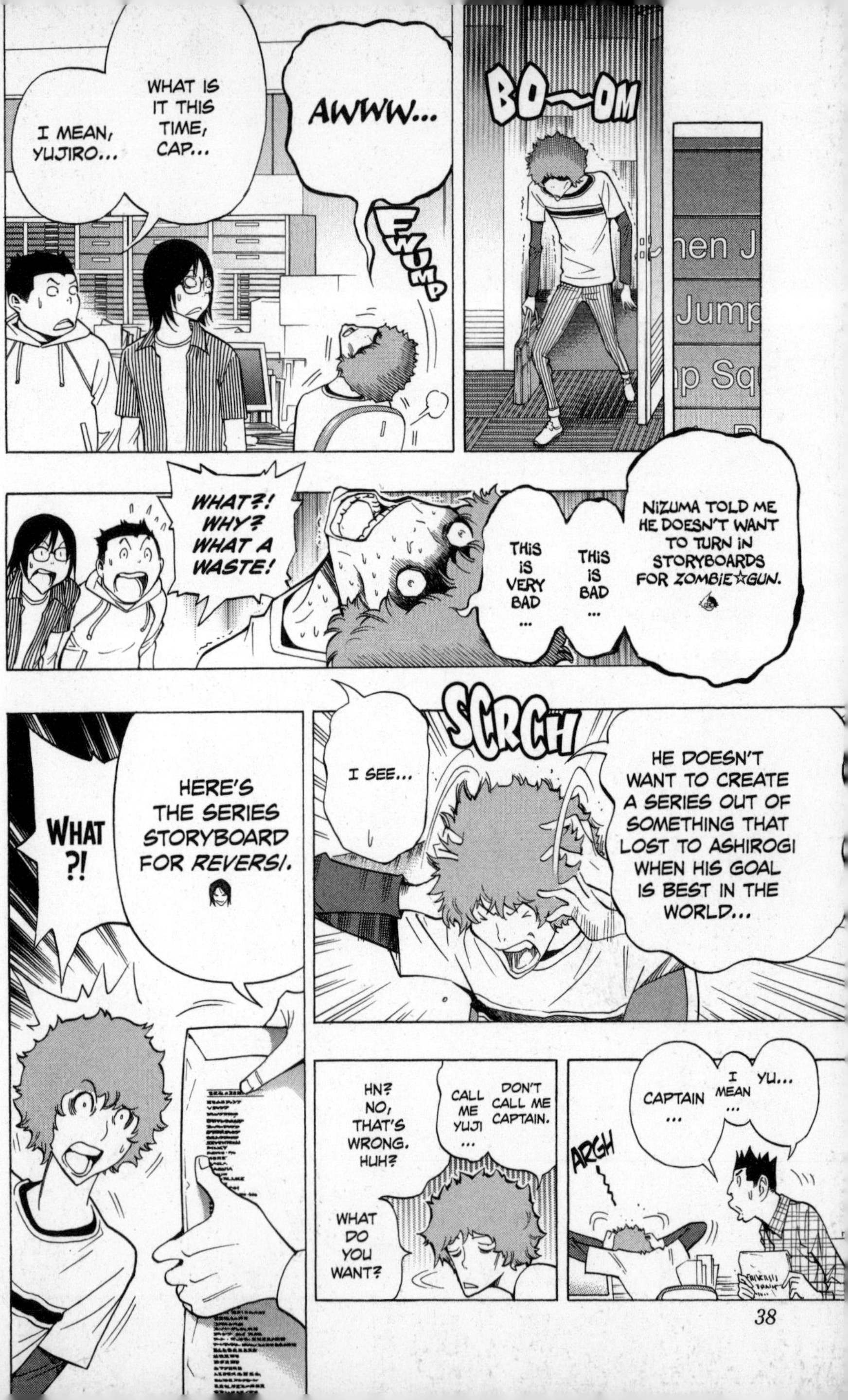
BO~OM
AWWW...
FWUMP
WHAT IS IT THIS TIME, CAP...
I MEAN, YUJIRO...
NIZUMA TOLD ME HE DOESN'T WANT TO TURN IN STORYBOARDS FOR ZOMBIE☆GUN.
THIS IS BAD ...
THIS IS VERY BAD ...
WHAT?! WHY? WHAT A WASTE!
SCRCH
HE DOESN'T WANT TO CREATE A SERIES OUT OF SOMETHING THAT LOST TO ASHIROGI WHEN HIS GOAL IS BEST IN THE WORLD...
I SEE...
YU...
I MEAN ...
CAPTAIN ...
ARGH
DON'T CALL ME CAPTAIN.
CALL ME YUJI ...
HN? NO, THAT'S WRONG. HUH?
WHAT DO YOU WANT?
HERE'S THE SERIES STORYBOARD FOR REVERSI.
WHAT ?!

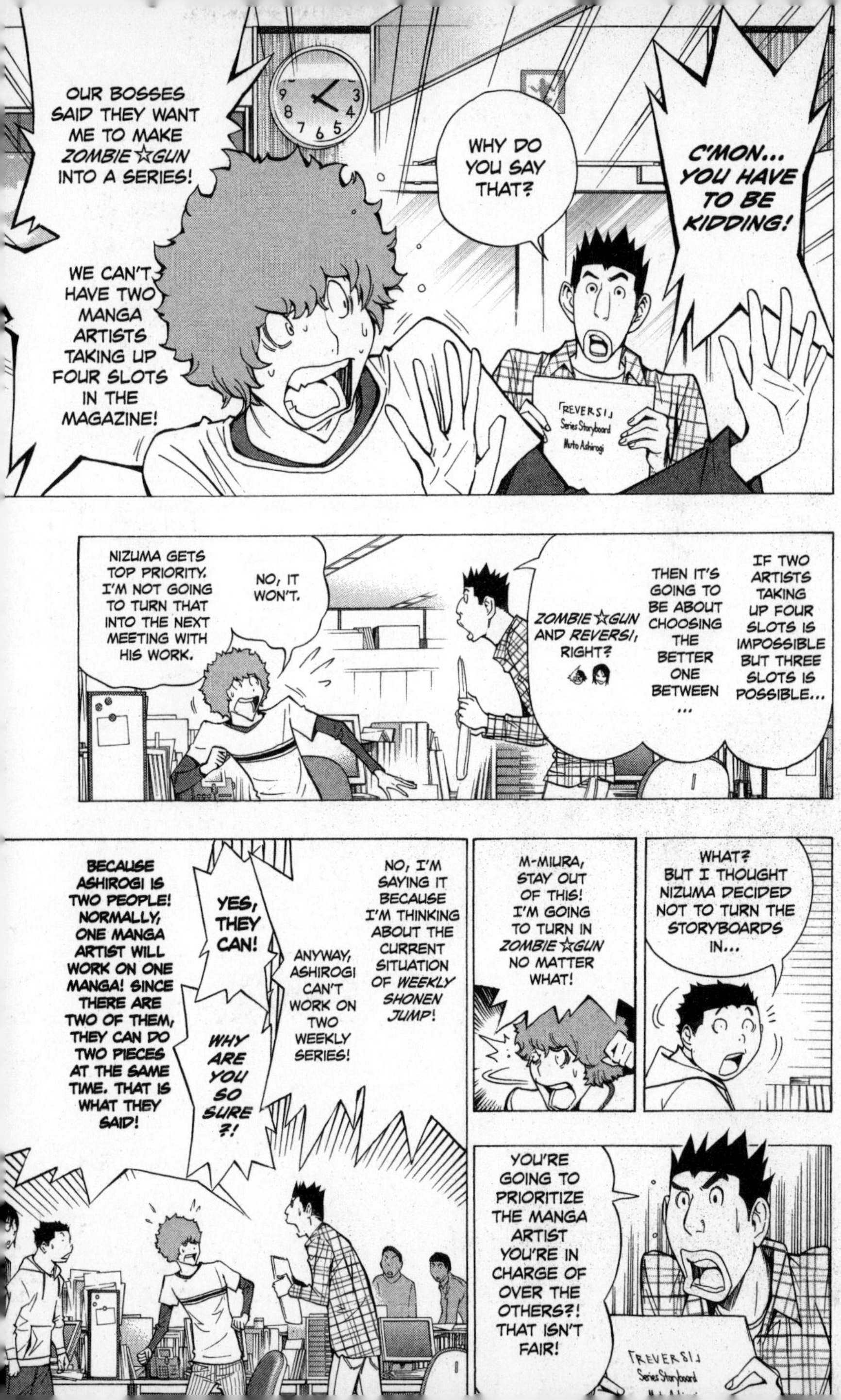
C'MON... YOU HAVE TO BE KIDDING!
WHY DO YOU SAY THAT?
OUR BOSSES SAID THEY WANT ME TO MAKE ZOMBIE☆GUN INTO A SERIES!
WE CAN'T HAVE TWO MANGA ARTISTS TAKING UP FOUR SLOTS IN THE MAGAZINE!
「REVERSI」 Series Storyboard Muto Ashirogi
IF TWO ARTISTS TAKING UP FOUR SLOTS IS IMPOSSIBLE BUT THREE SLOTS IS POSSIBLE...
THEN IT'S GOING TO BE ABOUT CHOOSING THE BETTER ONE BETWEEN...
ZOMBIE☆GUN AND REVERSI, RIGHT?
NO, IT WON'T.
NIZUMA GETS TOP PRIORITY. I'M NOT GOING TO TURN THAT INTO THE NEXT MEETING WITH HIS WORK.
WHAT? BUT I THOUGHT NIZUMA DECIDED NOT TO TURN THE STORYBOARDS IN...
M-MIURA, STAY OUT OF THIS! I'M GOING TO TURN IN ZOMBIE☆GUN NO MATTER WHAT!
YOU'RE GOING TO PRIORITIZE THE MANGA ARTIST YOU'RE IN CHARGE OF OVER THE OTHERS?! THAT ISN'T FAIR!
「REVERSI」 Series Storyboard
NO, I'M SAYING IT BECAUSE I'M THINKING ABOUT THE CURRENT SITUATION OF WEEKLY SHONEN JUMP!
ANYWAY, ASHIROGI CAN'T WORK ON TWO WEEKLY SERIES!
YES, THEY CAN!
WHY ARE YOU SO SURE?!
BECAUSE ASHIROGI IS TWO PEOPLE! NORMALLY, ONE MANGA ARTIST WILL WORK ON ONE MANGA! SINCE THERE ARE TWO OF THEM, THEY CAN DO TWO PIECES AT THE SAME TIME. THAT IS WHAT THEY SAID!

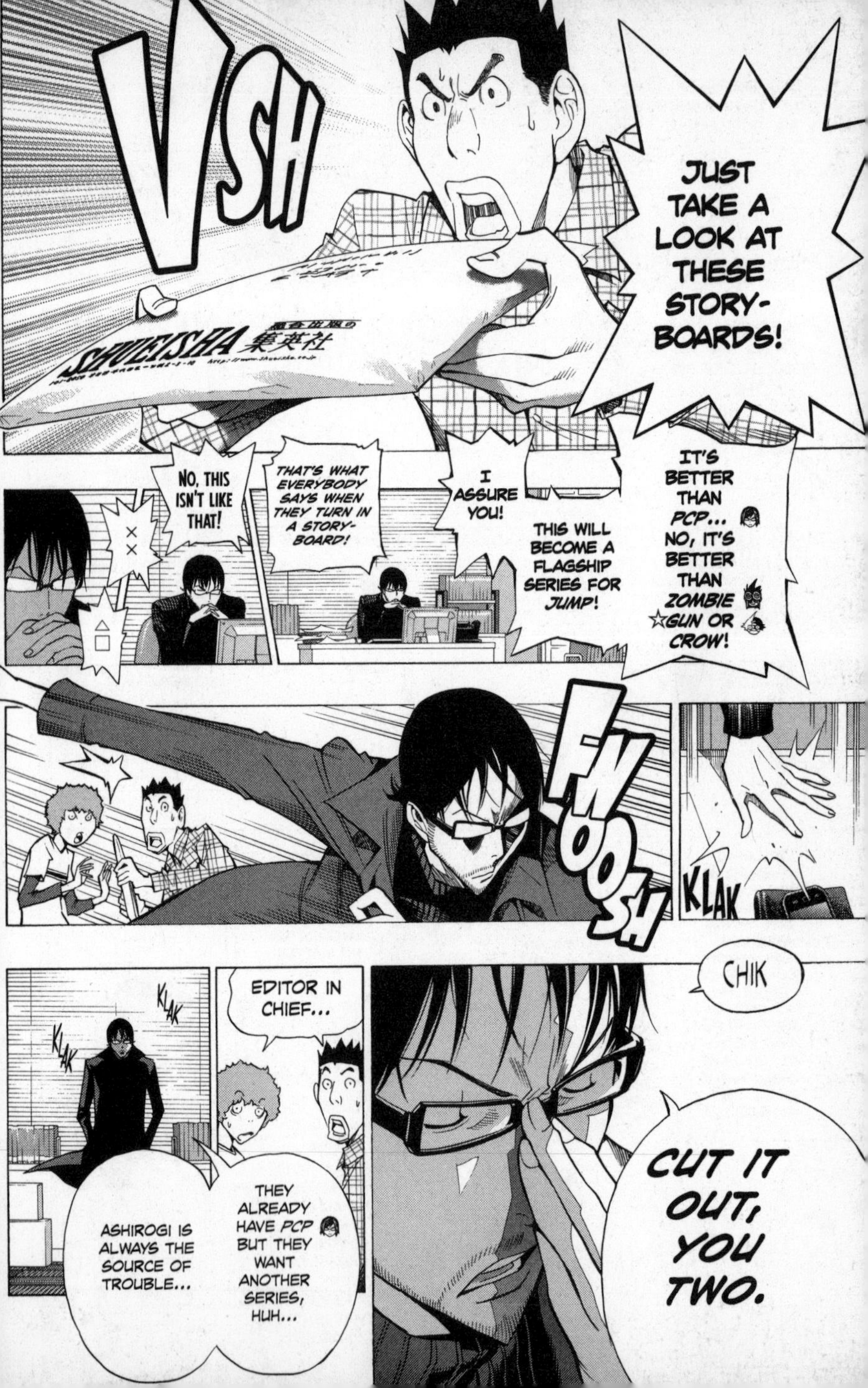
JUST TAKE A LOOK AT THESE STORY-BOARDS!
VSH
SHUEISHA 集英社
IT'S BETTER THAN PCP... NO, IT'S BETTER THAN ZOMBIE☆GUN OR CROW!
THIS WILL BECOME A FLAGSHIP SERIES FOR JUMP!
I ASSURE YOU!
THAT'S WHAT EVERYBODY SAYS WHEN THEY TURN IN A STORY-BOARD!
NO, THIS ISN'T LIKE THAT!
KLAK
FWOOSH
CHIK
CUT IT OUT, YOU TWO.
EDITOR IN CHIEF...
KLAK
KLAK
THEY ALREADY HAVE PCP BUT THEY WANT ANOTHER SERIES, HUH...
ASHIROGI IS ALWAYS THE SOURCE OF TROUBLE...

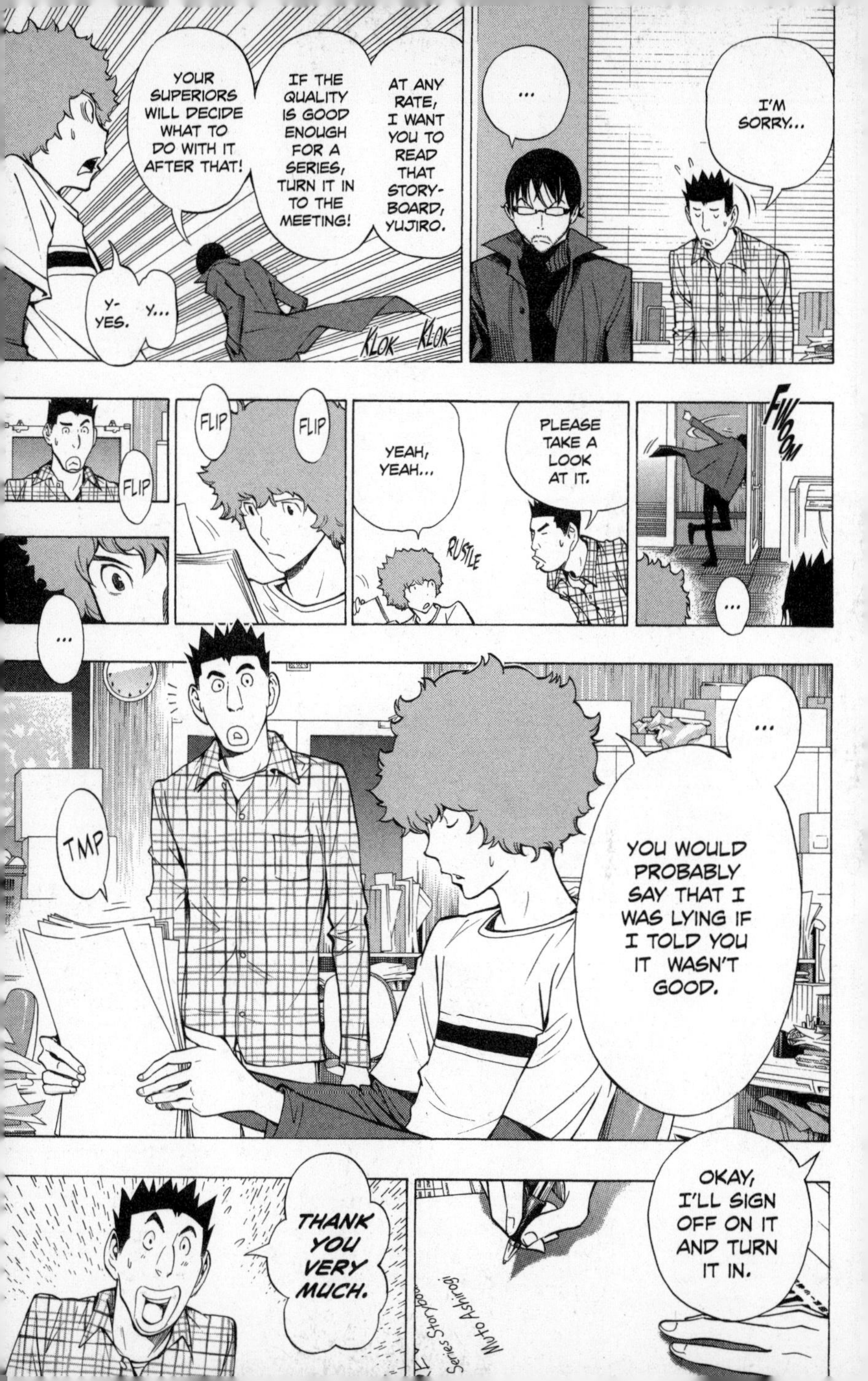
I'M SORRY...
...
AT ANY RATE, I WANT YOU TO READ THAT STORYBOARD, YUJIRO.
IF THE QUALITY IS GOOD ENOUGH FOR A SERIES, TURN IT IN TO THE MEETING!
YOUR SUPERIORS WILL DECIDE WHAT TO DO WITH IT AFTER THAT!
Y... Y-YES.
KLOK KLOK
FWOOM
...
PLEASE TAKE A LOOK AT IT.
YEAH, YEAH...
RUSTLE
FLIP
FLIP
FLIP
...
...
YOU WOULD PROBABLY SAY THAT I WAS LYING IF I TOLD YOU IT WASN'T GOOD.
TMP
OKAY, I'LL SIGN OFF ON IT AND TURN IT IN.
Muto Ashirogi
Series Storyboa
THANK YOU VERY MUCH.

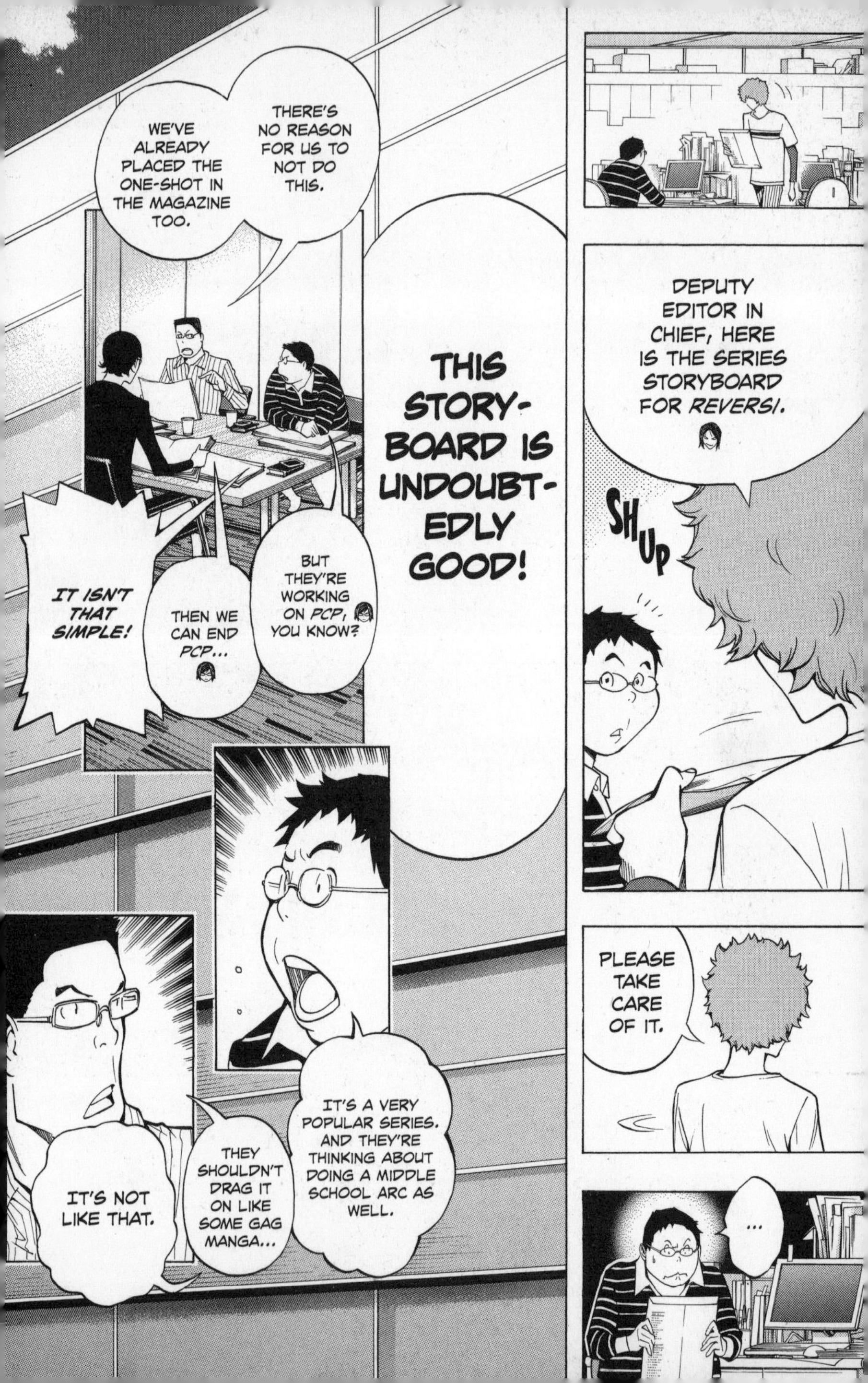
DEPUTY EDITOR IN CHIEF, HERE IS THE SERIES STORYBOARD FOR *REVERSI*.
SHUP
PLEASE TAKE CARE OF IT.
...
THERE'S NO REASON FOR US TO NOT DO THIS.
WE'VE ALREADY PLACED THE ONE-SHOT IN THE MAGAZINE TOO.
THIS STORY-BOARD IS UNDOUBT-EDLY GOOD!
BUT THEY'RE WORKING ON *PCP*, YOU KNOW?
THEN WE CAN END *PCP*...
IT ISN'T THAT SIMPLE!
IT'S A VERY POPULAR SERIES. AND THEY'RE THINKING ABOUT DOING A MIDDLE SCHOOL ARC AS WELL.
THEY SHOULDN'T DRAG IT ON LIKE SOME GAG MANGA...
IT'S NOT LIKE THAT.

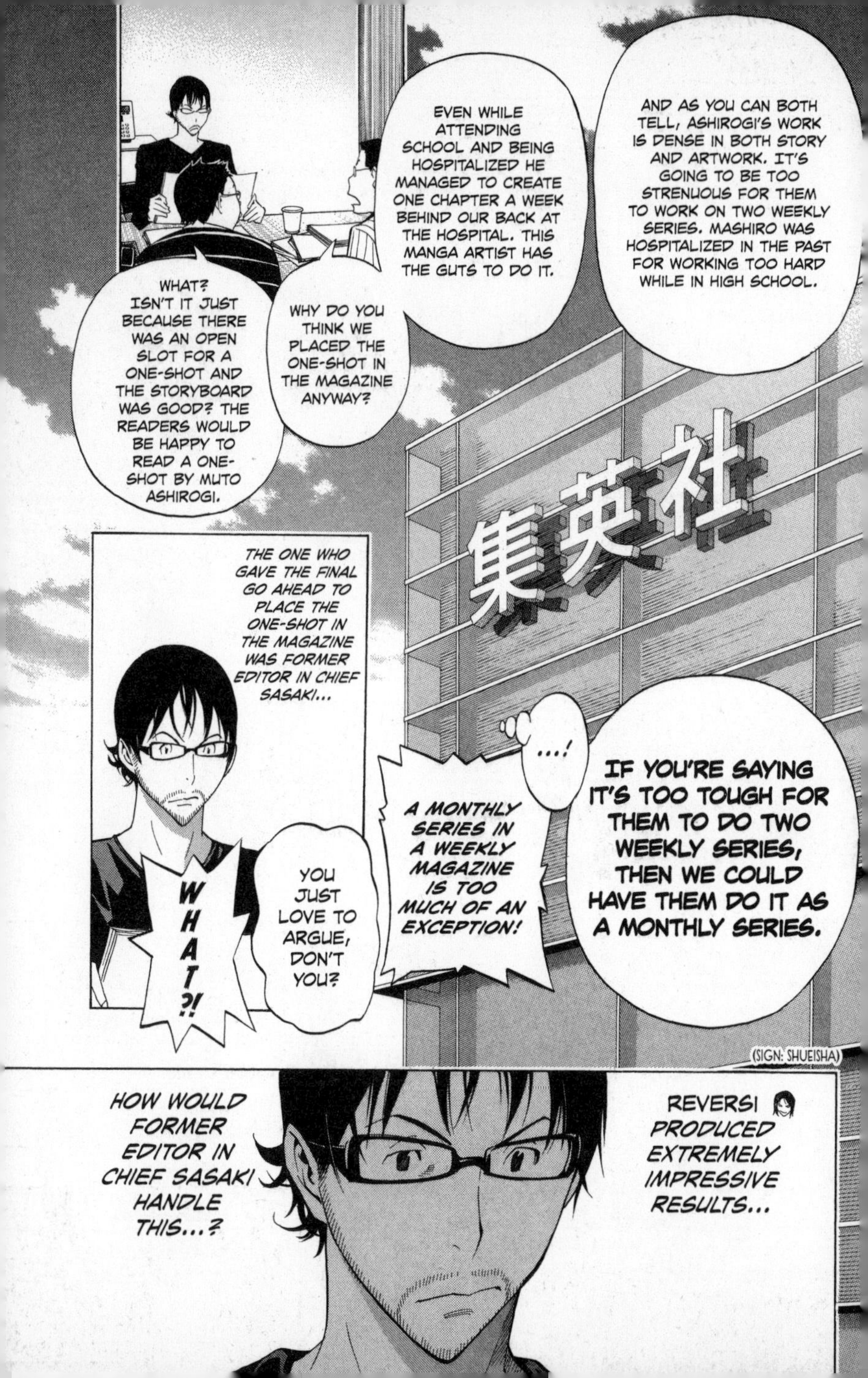
AND AS YOU CAN BOTH TELL, ASHIROGI'S WORK IS DENSE IN BOTH STORY AND ARTWORK. IT'S GOING TO BE TOO STRENUOUS FOR THEM TO WORK ON TWO WEEKLY SERIES. MASHIRO WAS HOSPITALIZED IN THE PAST FOR WORKING TOO HARD WHILE IN HIGH SCHOOL.
EVEN WHILE ATTENDING SCHOOL AND BEING HOSPITALIZED HE MANAGED TO CREATE ONE CHAPTER A WEEK BEHIND OUR BACK AT THE HOSPITAL. THIS MANGA ARTIST HAS THE GUTS TO DO IT.
WHY DO YOU THINK WE PLACED THE ONE-SHOT IN THE MAGAZINE ANYWAY?
WHAT? ISN'T IT JUST BECAUSE THERE WAS AN OPEN SLOT FOR A ONE-SHOT AND THE STORYBOARD WAS GOOD? THE READERS WOULD BE HAPPY TO READ A ONE-SHOT BY MUTO ASHIROGI.
集英社
IF YOU'RE SAYING IT'S TOO TOUGH FOR THEM TO DO TWO WEEKLY SERIES, THEN WE COULD HAVE THEM DO IT AS A MONTHLY SERIES.
...!
A MONTHLY SERIES IN A WEEKLY MAGAZINE IS TOO MUCH OF AN EXCEPTION!
THE ONE WHO GAVE THE FINAL GO AHEAD TO PLACE THE ONE-SHOT IN THE MAGAZINE WAS FORMER EDITOR IN CHIEF SASAKI...
YOU JUST LOVE TO ARGUE, DON'T YOU?
WHAT?!
(SIGN: SHUEISHA)
REVERSI PRODUCED EXTREMELY IMPRESSIVE RESULTS...
HOW WOULD FORMER EDITOR IN CHIEF SASAKI HANDLE THIS...?

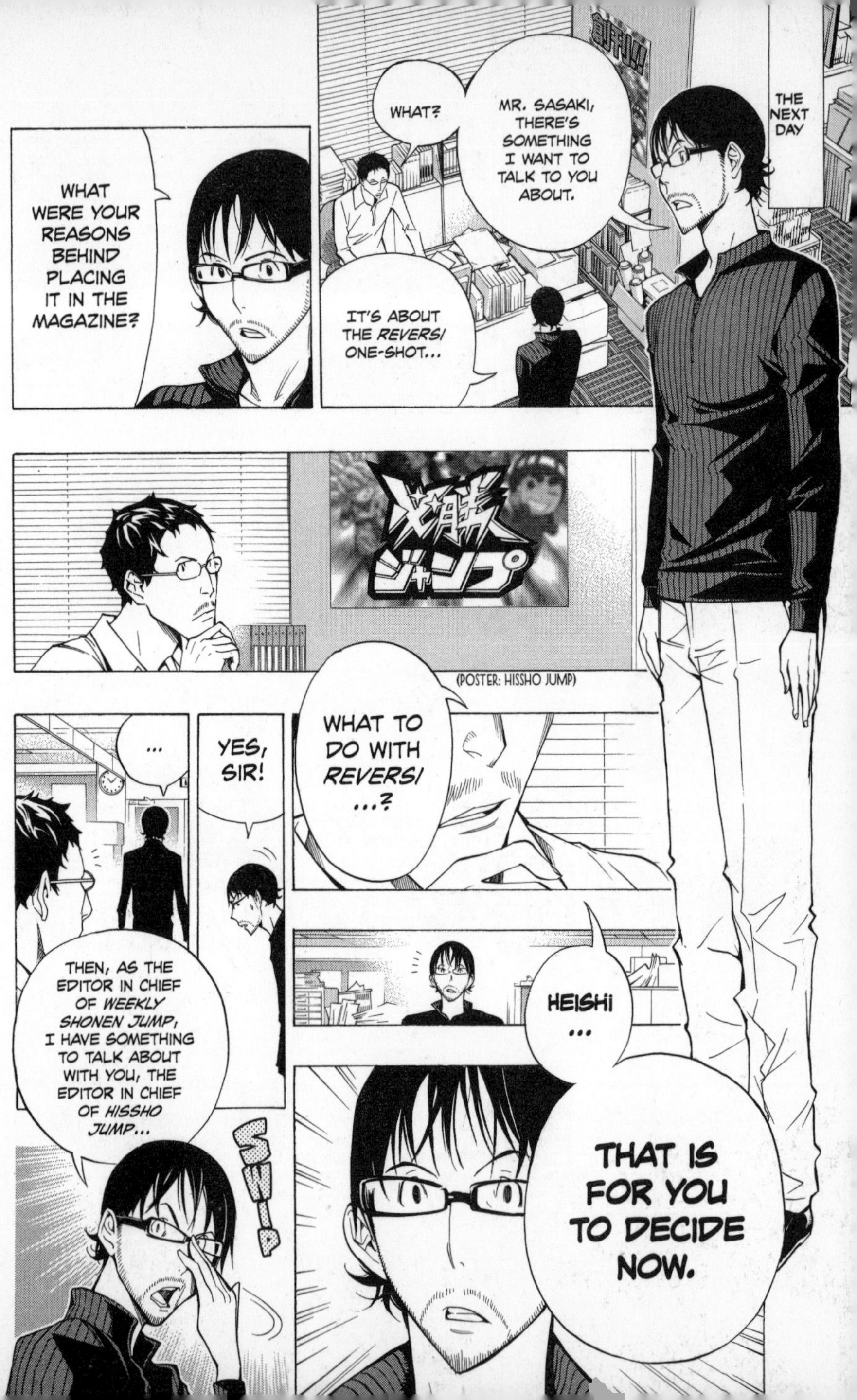
THE NEXT DAY
MR. SASAKI, THERE'S SOMETHING I WANT TO TALK TO YOU ABOUT.
WHAT?
IT'S ABOUT THE *REVERSI* ONE-SHOT...
WHAT WERE YOUR REASONS BEHIND PLACING IT IN THE MAGAZINE?
(POSTER: HISSHO JUMP)
WHAT TO DO WITH *REVERSI* ...?
YES, SIR!
...
HEISHI ...
THEN, AS THE EDITOR IN CHIEF OF *WEEKLY SHONEN JUMP*, I HAVE SOMETHING TO TALK ABOUT WITH YOU, THE EDITOR IN CHIEF OF *HISSHO JUMP*...
SWIP
THAT IS FOR YOU TO DECIDE NOW.

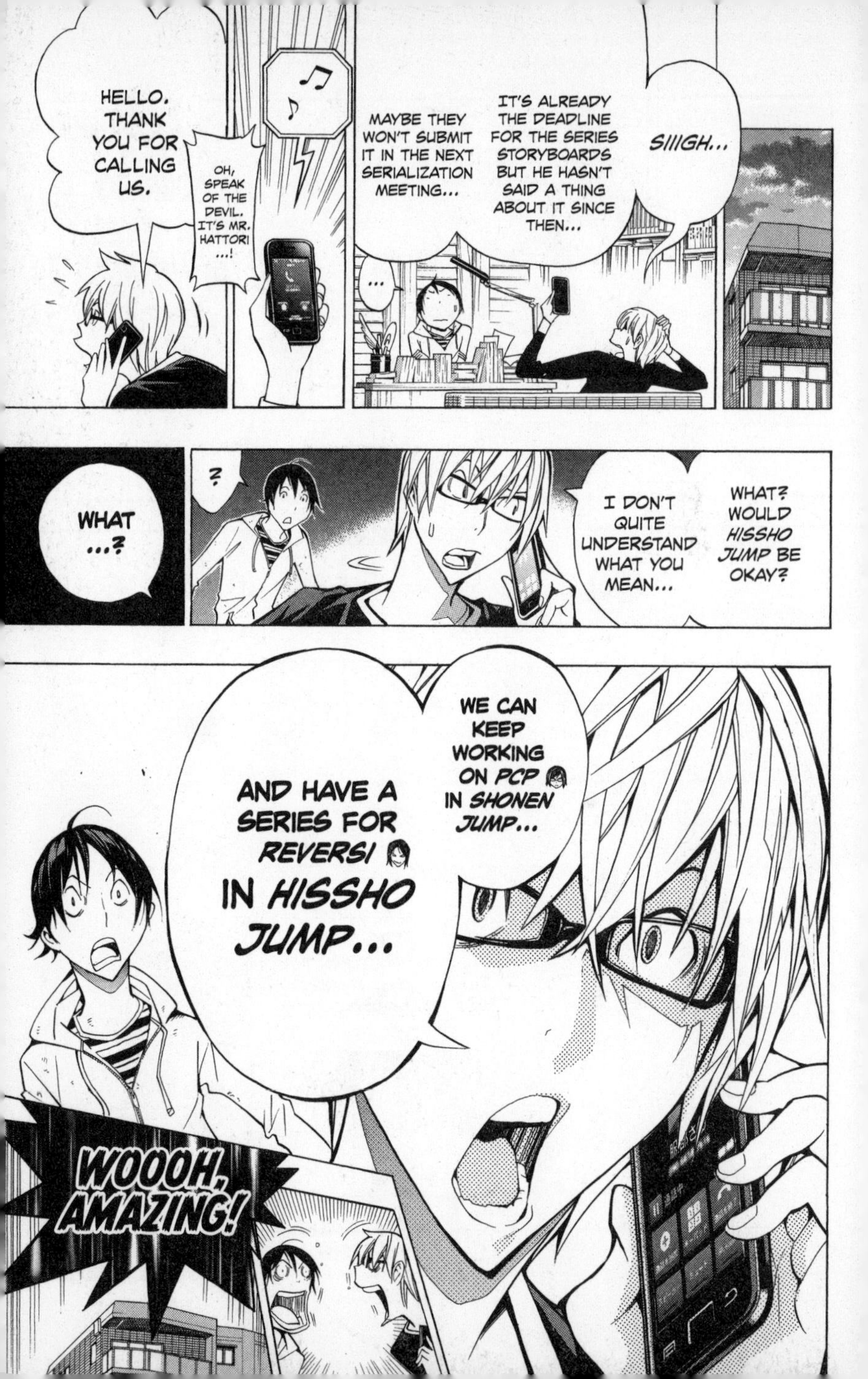
SIIIGH...
IT'S ALREADY THE DEADLINE FOR THE SERIES STORYBOARDS BUT HE HASN'T SAID A THING ABOUT IT SINCE THEN...
MAYBE THEY WON'T SUBMIT IT IN THE NEXT SERIALIZATION MEETING...
...
OH, SPEAK OF THE DEVIL. IT'S MR. HATTORI ...!
HELLO. THANK YOU FOR CALLING US.
WHAT? WOULD HISSHO JUMP BE OKAY?
I DON'T QUITE UNDERSTAND WHAT YOU MEAN...
?
WHAT ...?
WE CAN KEEP WORKING ON PCP IN SHONEN JUMP...
AND HAVE A SERIES FOR REVERSI IN HISSHO JUMP...
WOOOH, AMAZING!

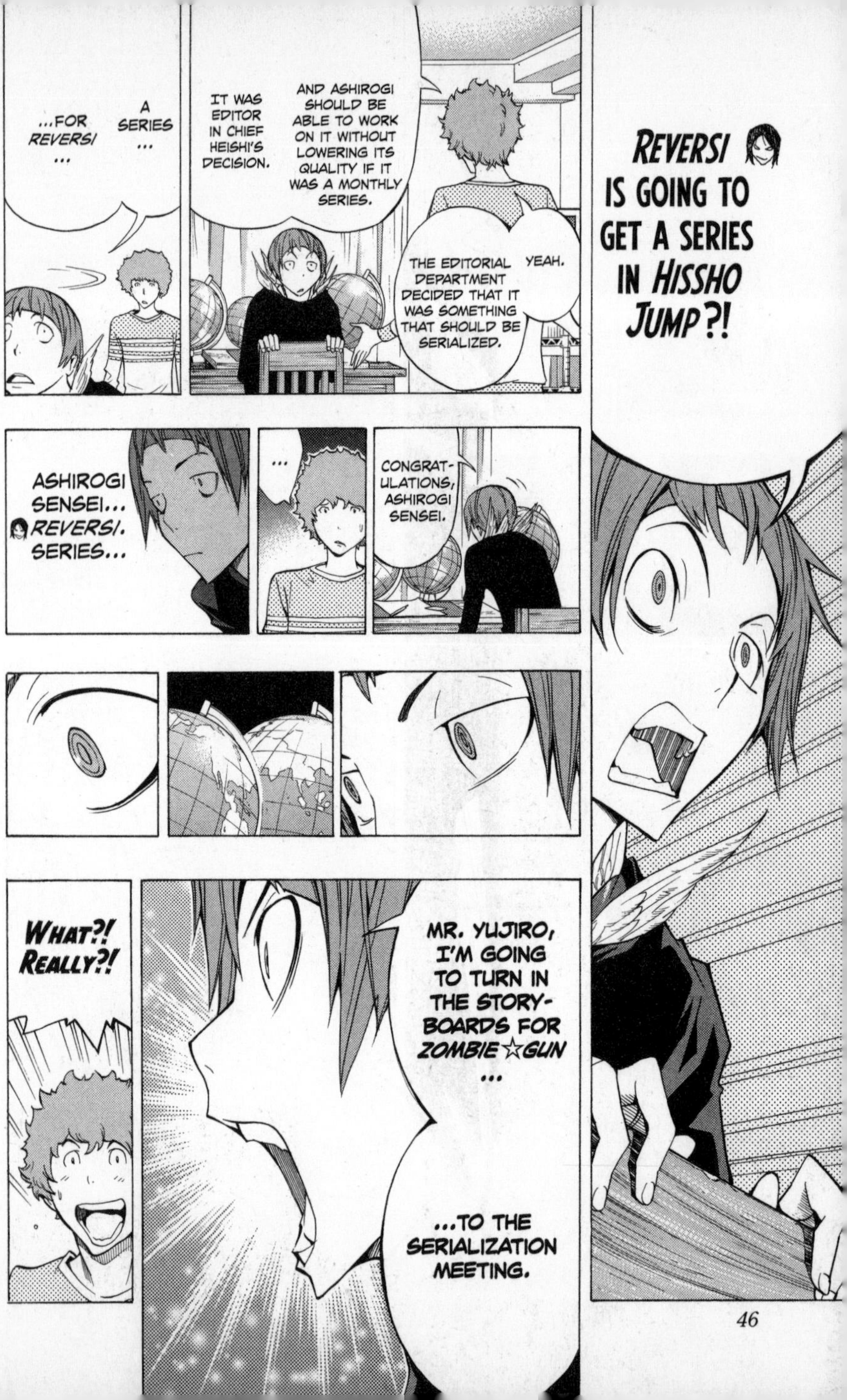
REVERSI IS GOING TO GET A SERIES IN HISSHO JUMP?!
YEAH.
THE EDITORIAL DEPARTMENT DECIDED THAT IT WAS SOMETHING THAT SHOULD BE SERIALIZED.
IT WAS EDITOR IN CHIEF HEISHI'S DECISION.
AND ASHIROGI SHOULD BE ABLE TO WORK ON IT WITHOUT LOWERING ITS QUALITY IF IT WAS A MONTHLY SERIES.
A SERIES...
...FOR REVERSI...
CONGRATULATIONS, ASHIROGI SENSEI.
...
ASHIROGI SENSEI... REVERSI. SERIES...
MR. YUJIRO, I'M GOING TO TURN IN THE STORYBOARDS FOR ZOMBIE☆GUN...
...TO THE SERIALIZATION MEETING.
WHAT?! REALLY?!

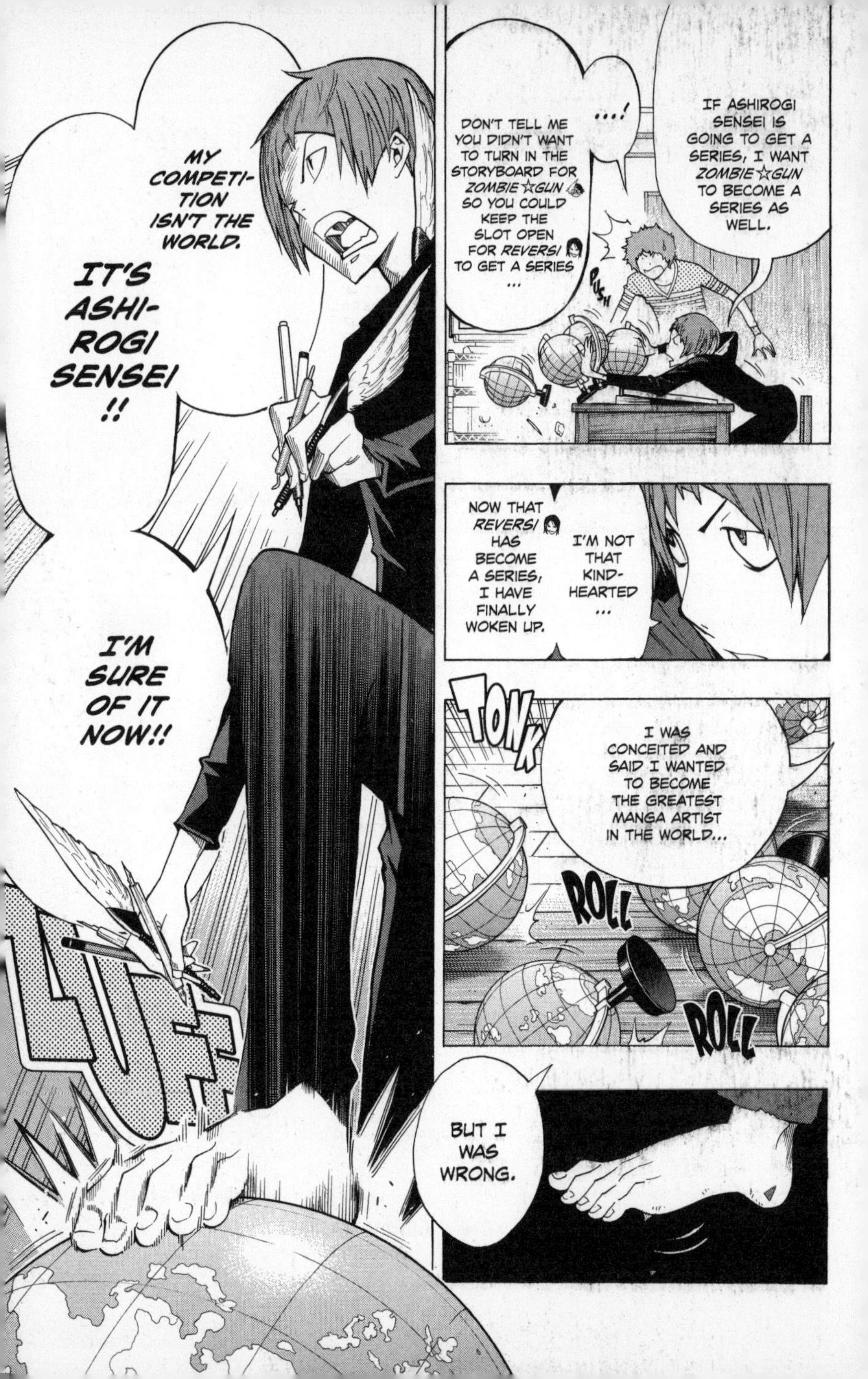
IF ASHIROGI SENSEI IS GOING TO GET A SERIES, I WANT ZOMBIE☆GUN TO BECOME A SERIES AS WELL.
...!
DON'T TELL ME YOU DIDN'T WANT TO TURN IN THE STORYBOARD FOR ZOMBIE☆GUN SO YOU COULD KEEP THE SLOT OPEN FOR REVERSI TO GET A SERIES ...
PUSH
I'M NOT THAT KIND-HEARTED ...
NOW THAT REVERSI HAS BECOME A SERIES, I HAVE FINALLY WOKEN UP.
TONK
I WAS CONCEITED AND SAID I WANTED TO BECOME THE GREATEST MANGA ARTIST IN THE WORLD...
ROLL
ROLL
BUT I WAS WRONG.
MY COMPETITION ISN'T THE WORLD.
IT'S ASHIROGI SENSEI!!
I'M SURE OF IT NOW!!

OHBA'S STORYBOARD

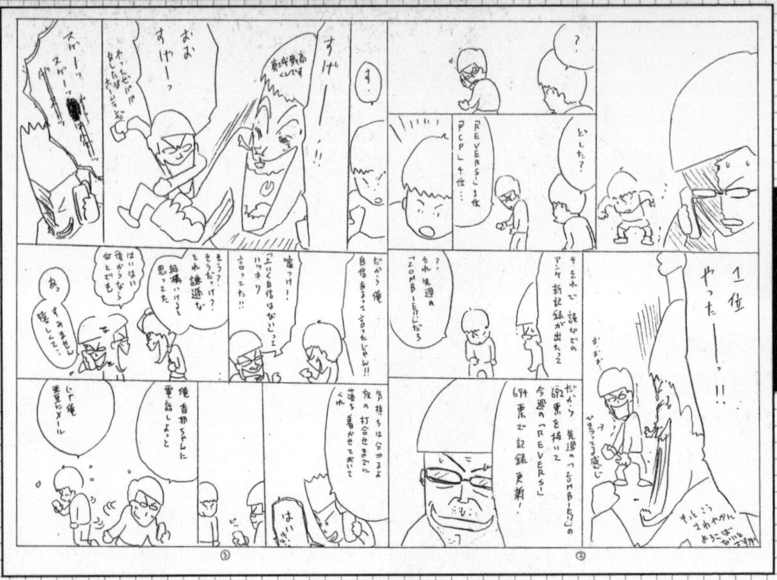
?
どした？
「REVERSI」1位
「PCP」4位…
1位
やった――っ!!
それ先週の「ZOMBIE☆GUN」だろ
だから先週の「ZOMBIE☆GUN」の692票を抜いて今週の「REVERSI」694票で記録更新!
す…
すげ――っ!!
おお すげ――っ
だから俺自信あるって言ったじゃん!!
嘘つけ!
はいはい
あっ すみません
気持ちは分かるよ 夜の打合せまでに落ち着かせておいてくれ
はい
俺 香耶ちゃんに電話しようと

OBATA'S STORYBOARD

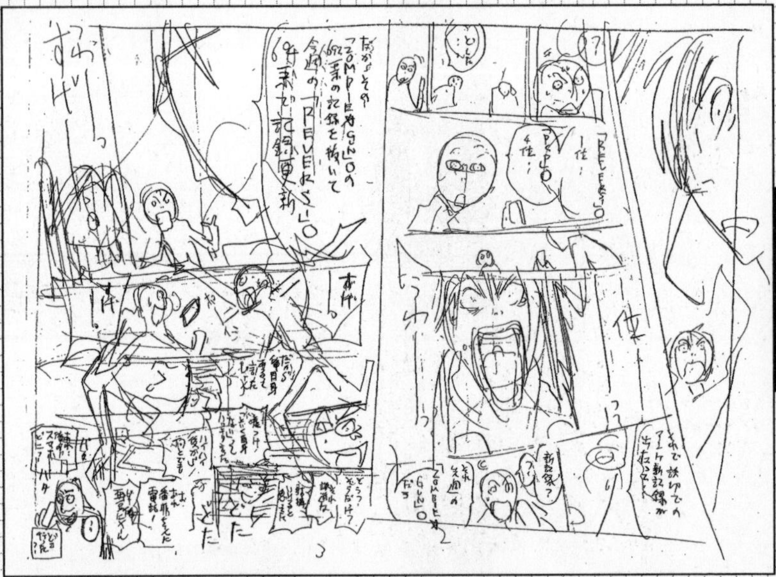

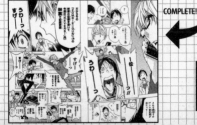

COMPLETE!

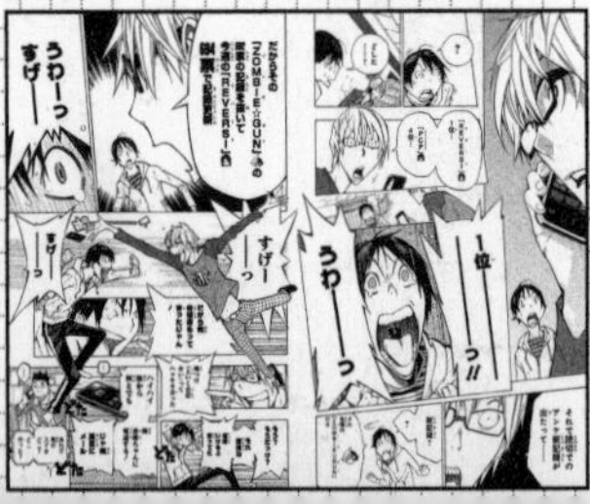

*CREATOR STORYBOARDS AND FINISHED PAGES IN JAPANESE

BAKUMAN。 vol.18

"Until the Final Draft Is Complete"

Chapter 153, pp. 30-31

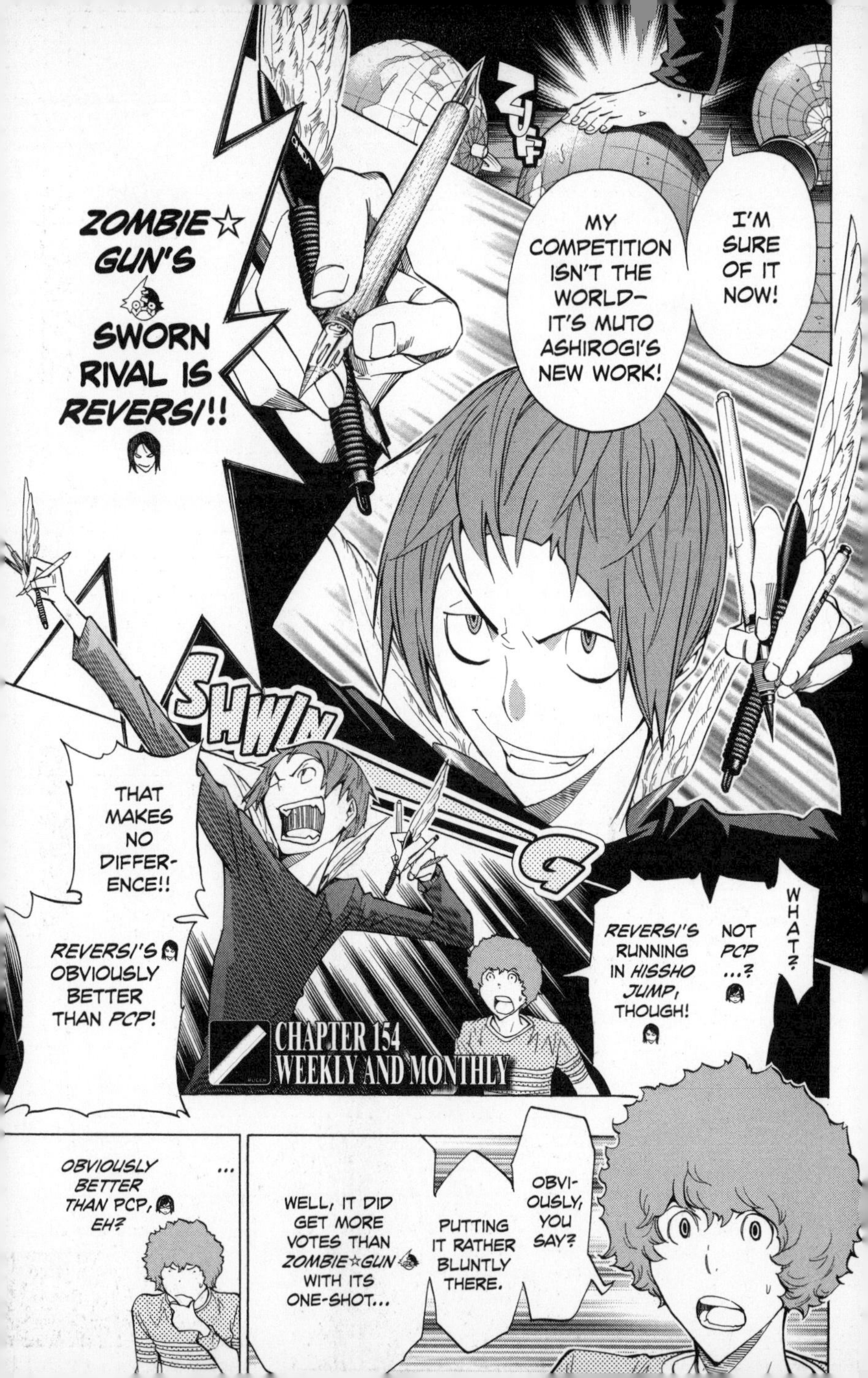
I'M SURE OF IT NOW!
MY COMPETITION ISN'T THE WORLD— IT'S MUTO ASHIROGI'S NEW WORK!
ZOMBIE☆GUN'S SWORN RIVAL IS REVERSI!!
SHWIN
G
WHAT?
NOT PCP ...?
REVERSI'S RUNNING IN HISSHO JUMP, THOUGH!
THAT MAKES NO DIFFERENCE!!
REVERSI'S OBVIOUSLY BETTER THAN PCP!
CHAPTER 154
WEEKLY AND MONTHLY
OBVIOUSLY, YOU SAY?
PUTTING IT RATHER BLUNTLY THERE.
WELL, IT DID GET MORE VOTES THAN ZOMBIE☆GUN WITH ITS ONE-SHOT...
...
OBVIOUSLY BETTER THAN PCP, EH?

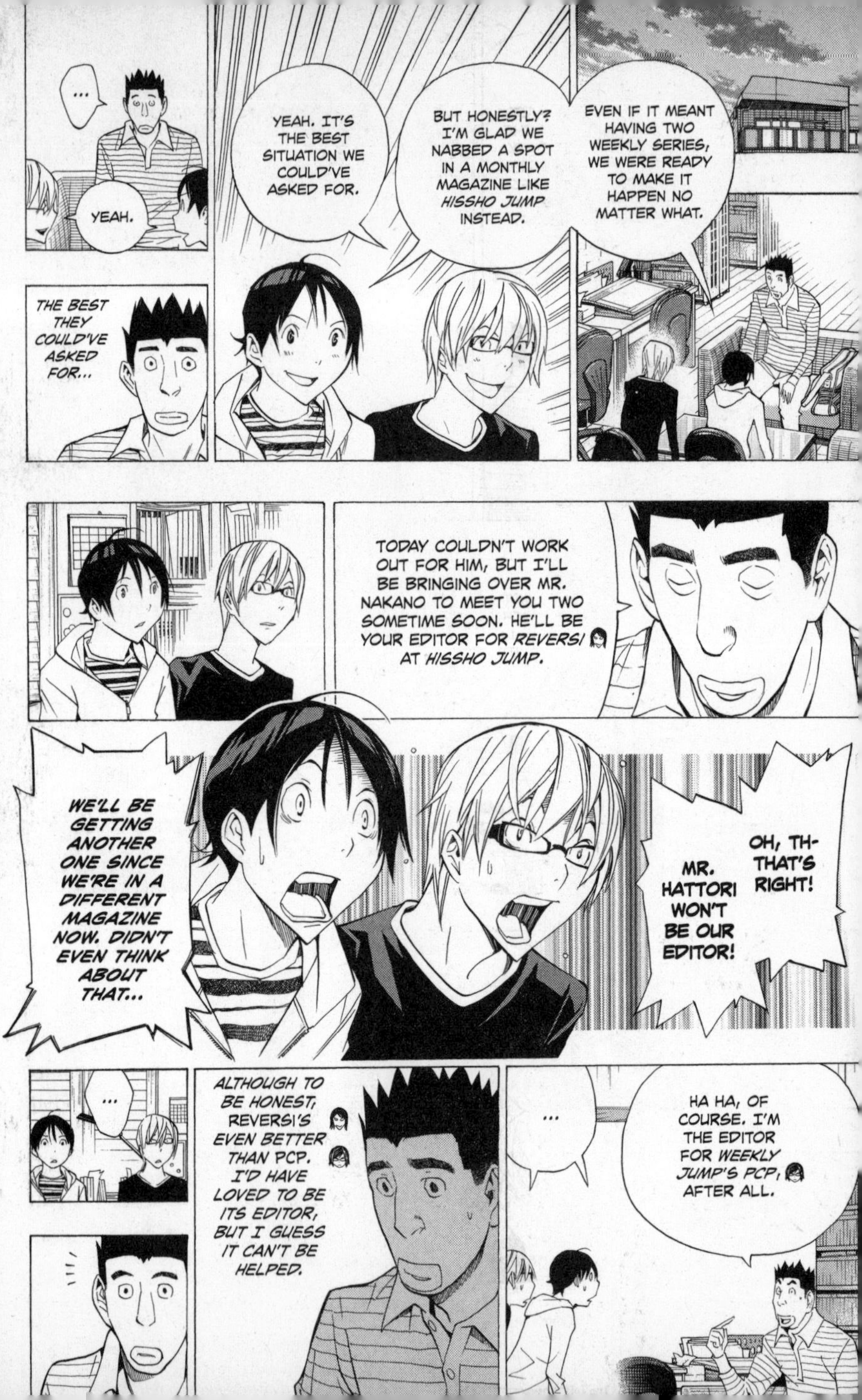
EVEN IF IT MEANT HAVING TWO WEEKLY SERIES, WE WERE READY TO MAKE IT HAPPEN NO MATTER WHAT.
BUT HONESTLY? I'M GLAD WE NABBED A SPOT IN A MONTHLY MAGAZINE LIKE *HISSHO JUMP* INSTEAD.
YEAH. IT'S THE BEST SITUATION WE COULD'VE ASKED FOR.
...
YEAH.
THE BEST THEY COULD'VE ASKED FOR...
TODAY COULDN'T WORK OUT FOR HIM, BUT I'LL BE BRINGING OVER MR. NAKANO TO MEET YOU TWO SOMETIME SOON. HE'LL BE YOUR EDITOR FOR *REVERSI* AT *HISSHO JUMP*.
OH, TH-THAT'S RIGHT!
MR. HATTORI WON'T BE OUR EDITOR!
WE'LL BE GETTING ANOTHER ONE SINCE WE'RE IN A DIFFERENT MAGAZINE NOW. DIDN'T EVEN THINK ABOUT THAT...
HA HA, OF COURSE. I'M THE EDITOR FOR *WEEKLY JUMP'S PCP*, AFTER ALL.
...
ALTHOUGH TO BE HONEST, REVERSI'S EVEN BETTER THAN PCP. I'D HAVE LOVED TO BE ITS EDITOR, BUT I GUESS IT CAN'T BE HELPED.
...

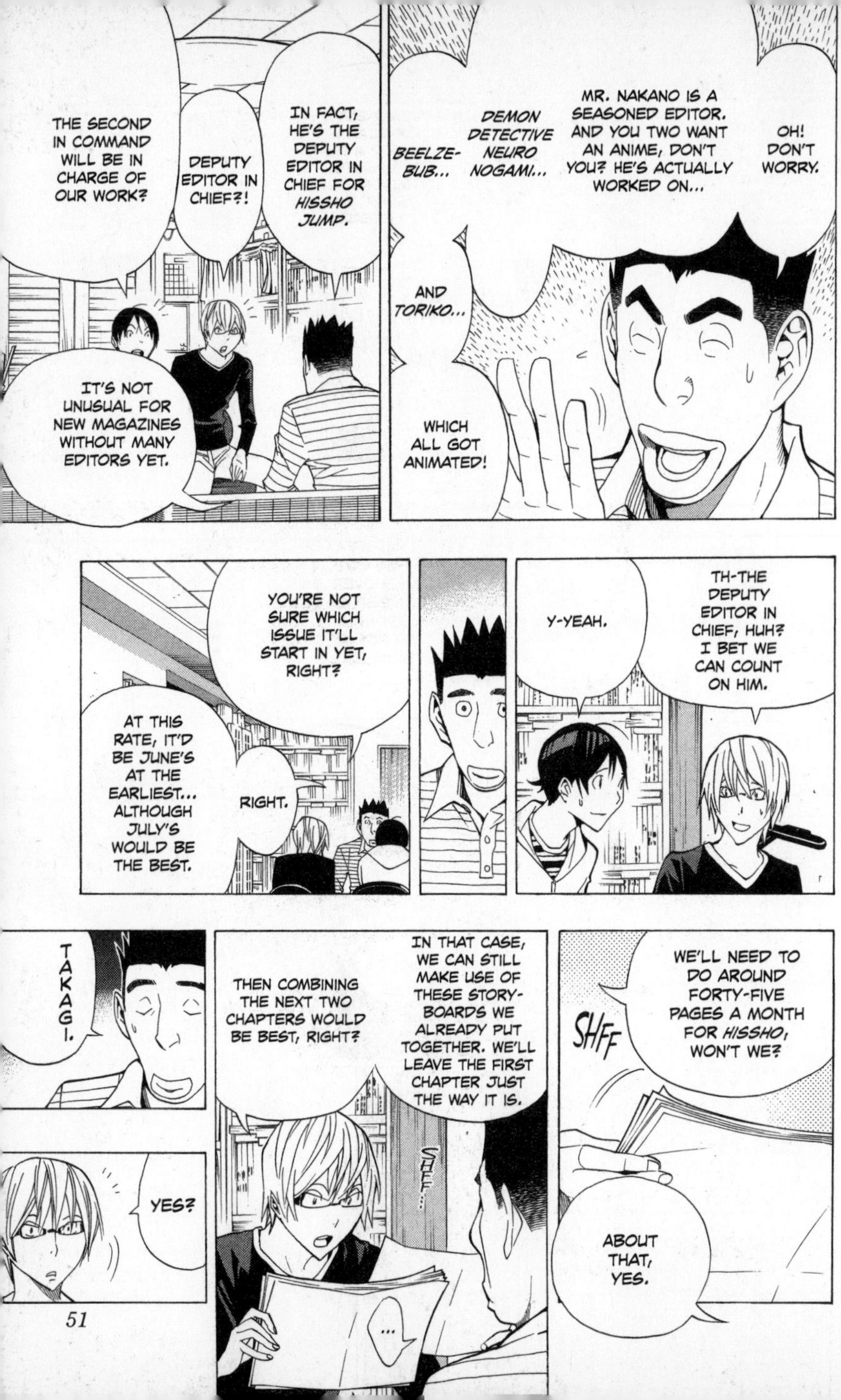
OH! DON'T WORRY.
MR. NAKANO IS A SEASONED EDITOR. AND YOU TWO WANT AN ANIME, DON'T YOU? HE'S ACTUALLY WORKED ON...
DEMON DETECTIVE NEURO NOGAMI...
BEELZEBUB...
AND *TORIKO*...
WHICH ALL GOT ANIMATED!
IN FACT, HE'S THE DEPUTY EDITOR IN CHIEF FOR *HISSHO JUMP*.
DEPUTY EDITOR IN CHIEF?!
THE SECOND IN COMMAND WILL BE IN CHARGE OF OUR WORK?
IT'S NOT UNUSUAL FOR NEW MAGAZINES WITHOUT MANY EDITORS YET.
TH-THE DEPUTY EDITOR IN CHIEF, HUH? I BET WE CAN COUNT ON HIM.
Y-YEAH.
YOU'RE NOT SURE WHICH ISSUE IT'LL START IN YET, RIGHT?
RIGHT.
AT THIS RATE, IT'D BE JUNE'S AT THE EARLIEST... ALTHOUGH JULY'S WOULD BE THE BEST.
WE'LL NEED TO DO AROUND FORTY-FIVE PAGES A MONTH FOR *HISSHO*, WON'T WE?
SHFF
ABOUT THAT, YES.
IN THAT CASE, WE CAN STILL MAKE USE OF THESE STORYBOARDS WE ALREADY PUT TOGETHER. WE'LL LEAVE THE FIRST CHAPTER JUST THE WAY IT IS.
THEN COMBINING THE NEXT TWO CHAPTERS WOULD BE BEST, RIGHT?
SHFF...
...
TAKAGI.
YES?

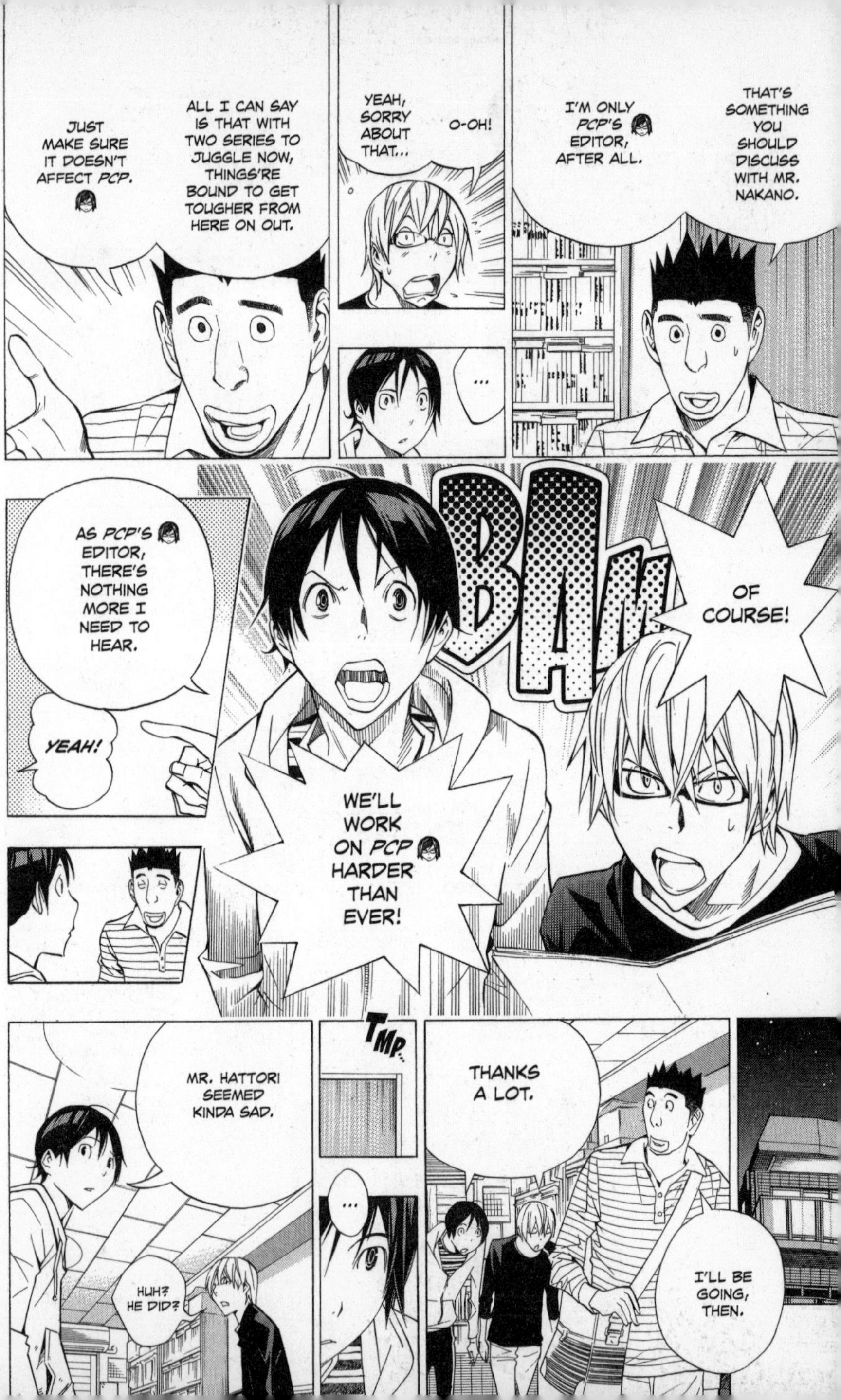
THAT'S SOMETHING YOU SHOULD DISCUSS WITH MR. NAKANO.
I'M ONLY *PCP*'S EDITOR, AFTER ALL.
O-OH!
YEAH, SORRY ABOUT THAT...
...
ALL I CAN SAY IS THAT WITH TWO SERIES TO JUGGLE NOW, THINGS'RE BOUND TO GET TOUGHER FROM HERE ON OUT.
JUST MAKE SURE IT DOESN'T AFFECT *PCP*.
BAM
OF COURSE!
WE'LL WORK ON *PCP* HARDER THAN EVER!
AS *PCP*'S EDITOR, THERE'S NOTHING MORE I NEED TO HEAR.
YEAH!
I'LL BE GOING, THEN.
THANKS A LOT.
TMP
...
MR. HATTORI SEEMED KINDA SAD.
HUH? HE DID?

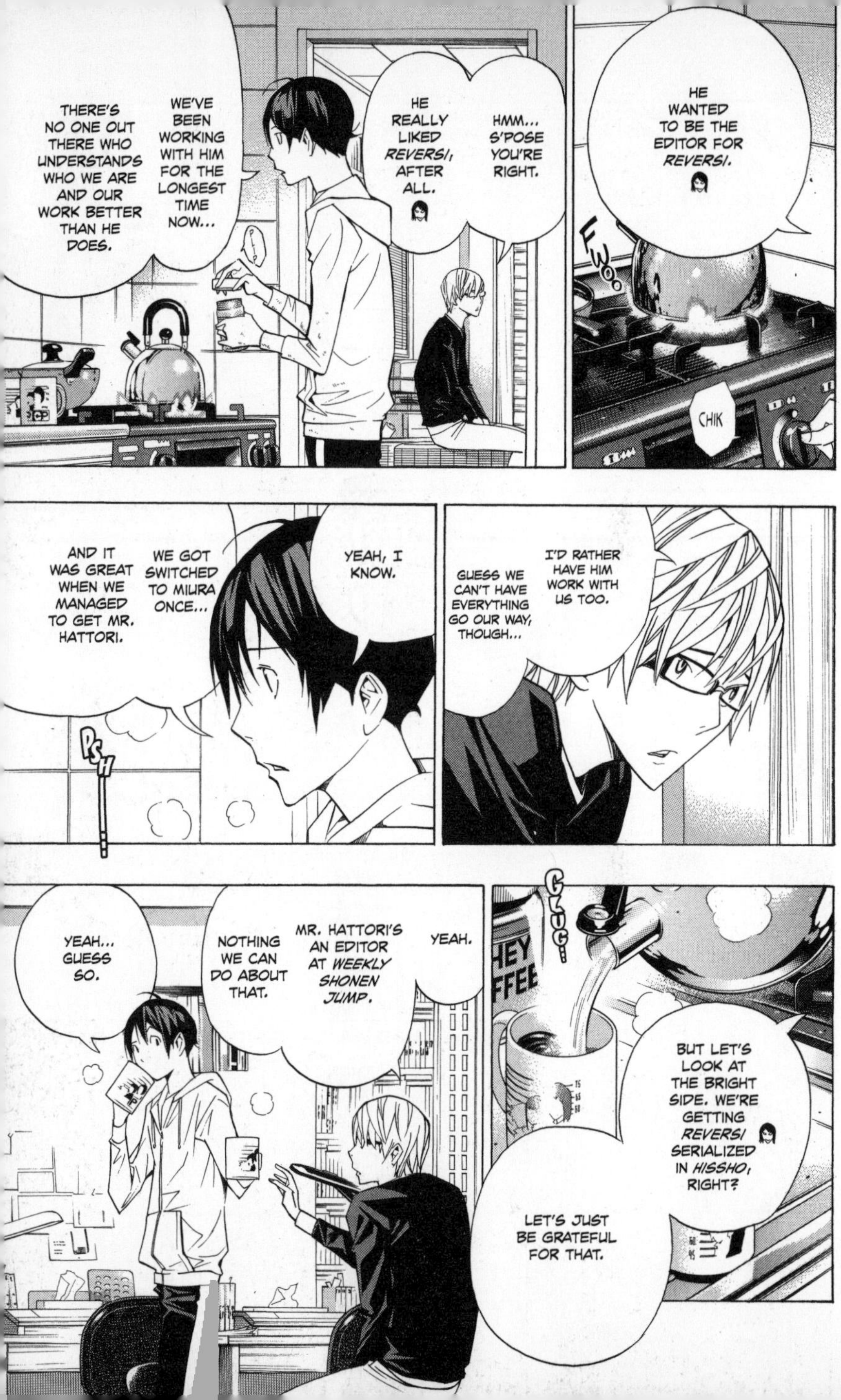
HE WANTED TO BE THE EDITOR FOR *REVERSI*.
FWOO
CHIK
HMM... S'POSE YOU'RE RIGHT.
HE REALLY LIKED *REVERSI*, AFTER ALL.
WE'VE BEEN WORKING WITH HIM FOR THE LONGEST TIME NOW...
THERE'S NO ONE OUT THERE WHO UNDERSTANDS WHO WE ARE AND OUR WORK BETTER THAN HE DOES.
PLIP
I'D RATHER HAVE HIM WORK WITH US TOO.
GUESS WE CAN'T HAVE EVERYTHING GO OUR WAY, THOUGH...
YEAH, I KNOW.
WE GOT SWITCHED TO MIURA ONCE...
AND IT WAS GREAT WHEN WE MANAGED TO GET MR. HATTORI.
PSH
GLUG
BUT LET'S LOOK AT THE BRIGHT SIDE. WE'RE GETTING *REVERSI* SERIALIZED IN *HISSHO*, RIGHT?
LET'S JUST BE GRATEFUL FOR THAT.
YEAH.
MR. HATTORI'S AN EDITOR AT *WEEKLY SHONEN JUMP*.
NOTHING WE CAN DO ABOUT THAT.
YEAH... GUESS SO.

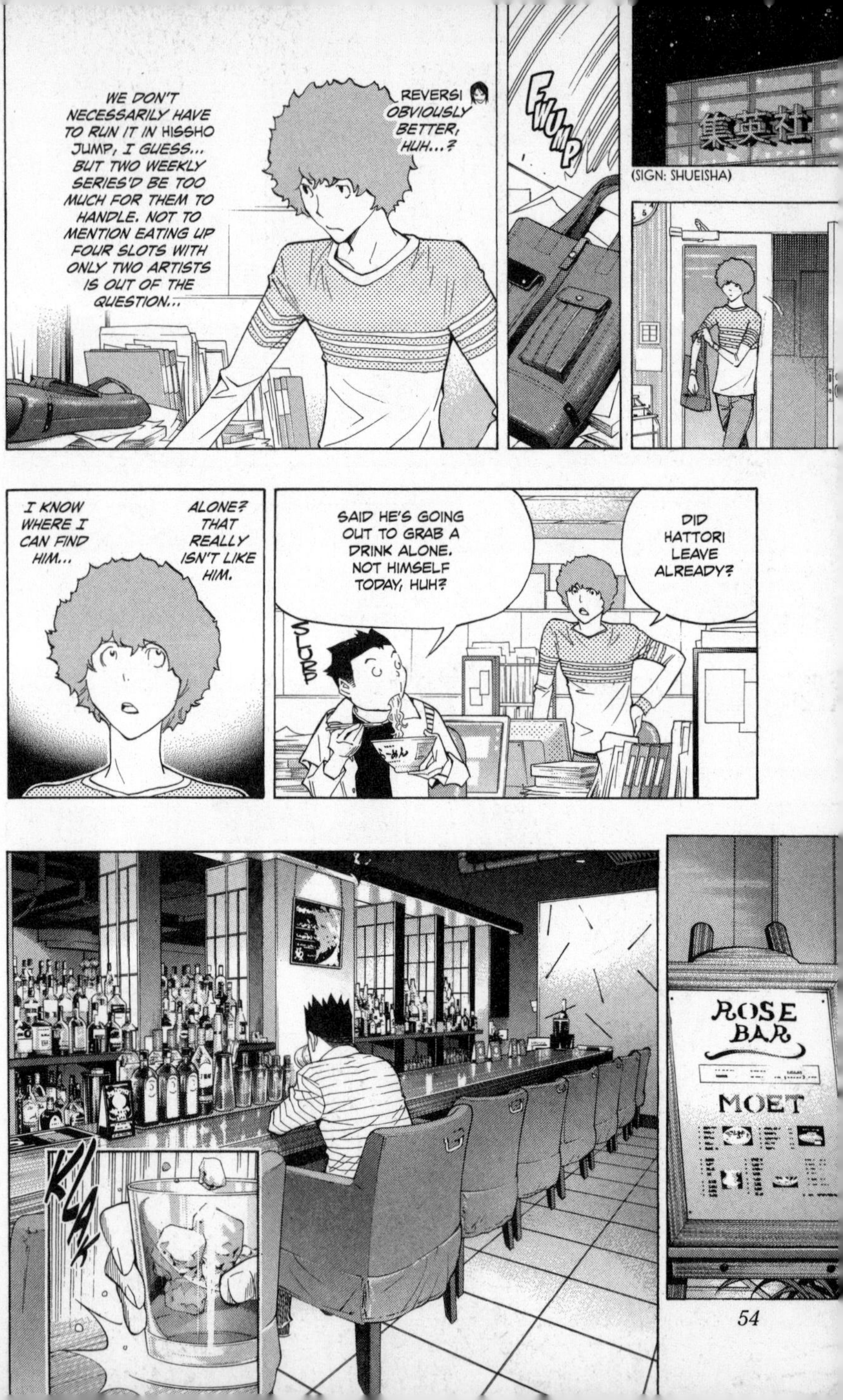
集英社
(SIGN: SHUEISHA)
FWUMP
REVERSI OBVIOUSLY BETTER, HUH...?
WE DON'T NECESSARILY HAVE TO RUN IT IN HISSHO JUMP, I GUESS... BUT TWO WEEKLY SERIES'D BE TOO MUCH FOR THEM TO HANDLE. NOT TO MENTION EATING UP FOUR SLOTS WITH ONLY TWO ARTISTS IS OUT OF THE QUESTION...
DID HATTORI LEAVE ALREADY?
SAID HE'S GOING OUT TO GRAB A DRINK ALONE. NOT HIMSELF TODAY, HUH?
SLURP
ALONE? THAT REALLY ISN'T LIKE HIM.
I KNOW WHERE I CAN FIND HIM...
ROSE BAR
MOET
KLAK

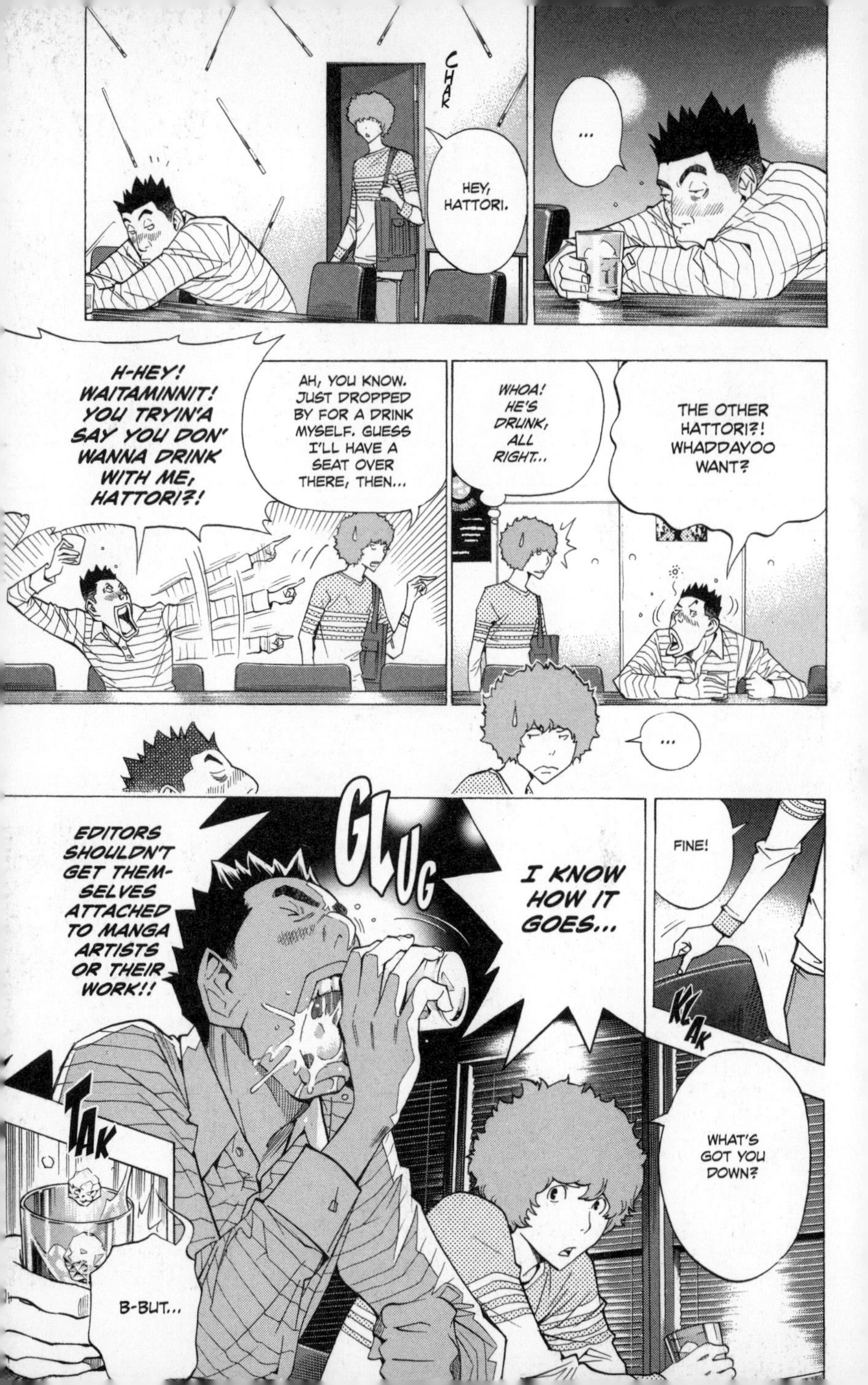
...
CHAK
HEY, HATTORI.
THE OTHER HATTORI?! WHADDAYOO WANT?
WHOA! HE'S DRUNK, ALL RIGHT...
AH, YOU KNOW. JUST DROPPED BY FOR A DRINK MYSELF. GUESS I'LL HAVE A SEAT OVER THERE, THEN...
H-HEY! WAITAMINNIT! YOU TRYIN'A SAY YOU DON' WANNA DRINK WITH ME, HATTORI?!
...
FINE!
KLAK
I KNOW HOW IT GOES...
GLUG
EDITORS SHOULDN'T GET THEMSELVES ATTACHED TO MANGA ARTISTS OR THEIR WORK!!
WHAT'S GOT YOU DOWN?
TAK
B-BUT...

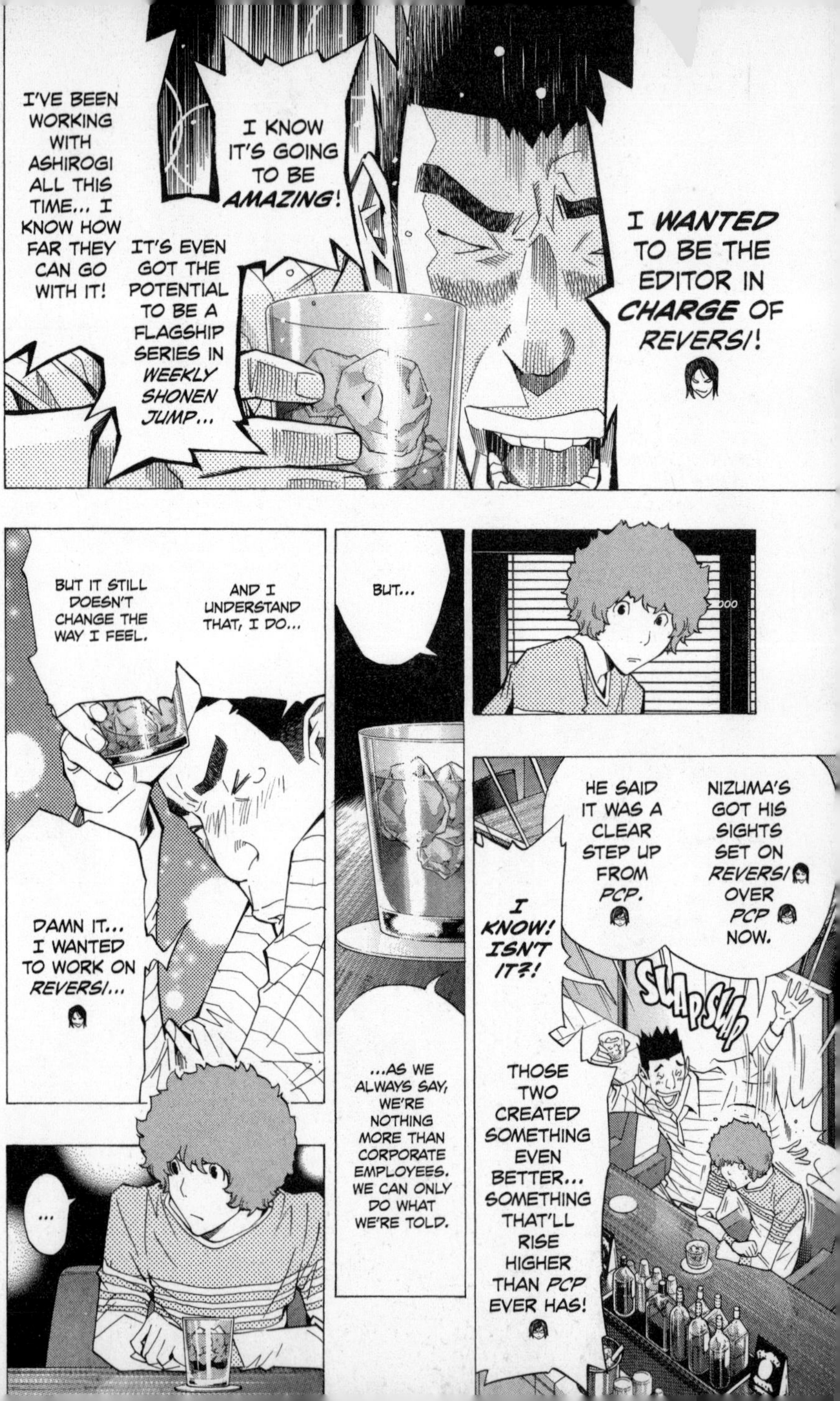
I *WANTED* TO BE THE EDITOR IN *CHARGE* OF *REVERSI*!
I KNOW IT'S GOING TO BE *AMAZING*!
I'VE BEEN WORKING WITH ASHIROGI ALL THIS TIME... I KNOW HOW FAR THEY CAN GO WITH IT!
IT'S EVEN GOT THE POTENTIAL TO BE A FLAGSHIP SERIES IN *WEEKLY SHONEN JUMP*...
NIZUMA'S GOT HIS SIGHTS SET ON *REVERSI* OVER *PCP* NOW.
HE SAID IT WAS A CLEAR STEP UP FROM *PCP*.
I KNOW! ISN'T IT?!
SLAP SLAP
THOSE TWO CREATED SOMETHING EVEN BETTER... SOMETHING THAT'LL RISE HIGHER THAN *PCP* EVER HAS!
BUT...
...AS WE ALWAYS SAY, WE'RE NOTHING MORE THAN CORPORATE EMPLOYEES. WE CAN ONLY DO WHAT WE'RE TOLD.
AND I UNDERSTAND THAT, I DO...
BUT IT STILL DOESN'T CHANGE THE WAY I FEEL.
DAMN IT... I WANTED TO WORK ON *REVERSI*...
...

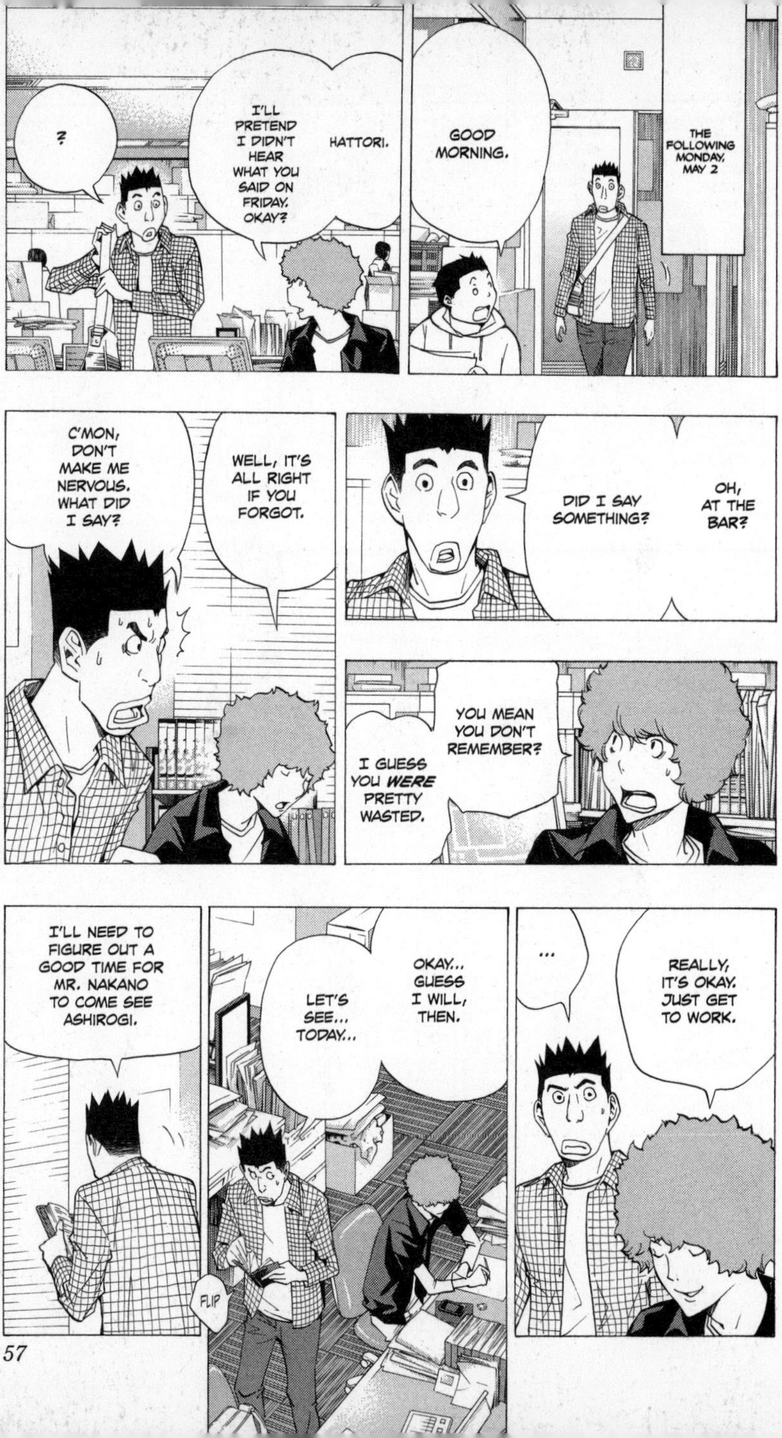
THE FOLLOWING MONDAY, MAY 2
GOOD MORNING.
HATTORI.
I'LL PRETEND I DIDN'T HEAR WHAT YOU SAID ON FRIDAY. OKAY?
?
OH, AT THE BAR?
DID I SAY SOMETHING?
YOU MEAN YOU DON'T REMEMBER?
I GUESS YOU *WERE* PRETTY WASTED.
WELL, IT'S ALL RIGHT IF YOU FORGOT.
C'MON, DON'T MAKE ME NERVOUS. WHAT DID I SAY?
REALLY, IT'S OKAY. JUST GET TO WORK.
...
OKAY... GUESS I WILL, THEN.
LET'S SEE... TODAY...
FLIP
I'LL NEED TO FIGURE OUT A GOOD TIME FOR MR. NAKANO TO COME SEE ASHIROGI.

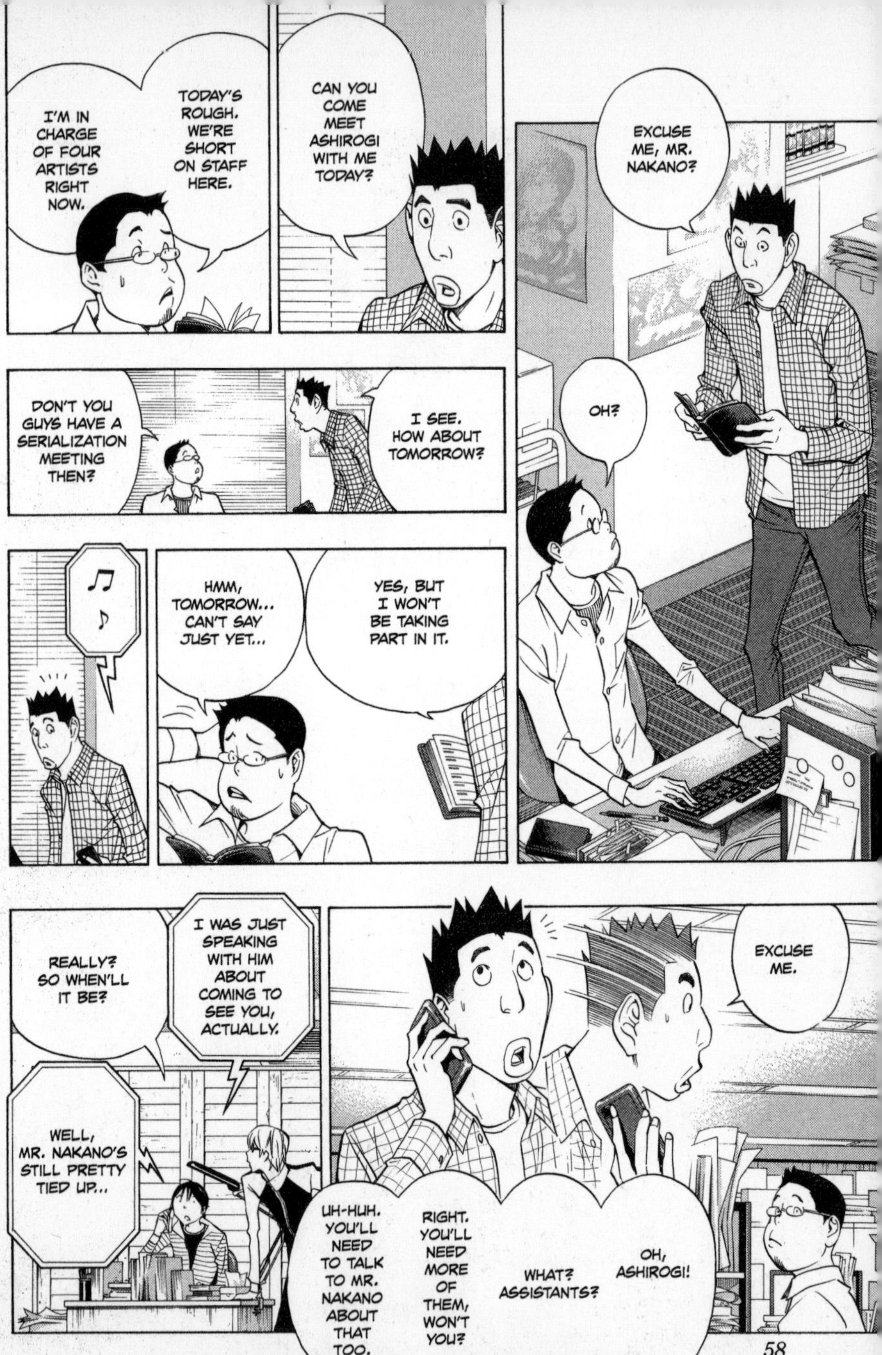
EXCUSE ME, MR. NAKANO?
OH?
CAN YOU COME MEET ASHIROGI WITH ME TODAY?
TODAY'S ROUGH. WE'RE SHORT ON STAFF HERE.
I'M IN CHARGE OF FOUR ARTISTS RIGHT NOW.
I SEE. HOW ABOUT TOMORROW?
DON'T YOU GUYS HAVE A SERIALIZATION MEETING THEN?
YES, BUT I WON'T BE TAKING PART IN IT.
HMM, TOMORROW... CAN'T SAY JUST YET...
♫ ♪
EXCUSE ME.
OH, ASHIROGI!
WHAT? ASSISTANTS?
RIGHT. YOU'LL NEED MORE OF THEM, WON'T YOU?
UH-HUH. YOU'LL NEED TO TALK TO MR. NAKANO ABOUT THAT TOO.
I WAS JUST SPEAKING WITH HIM ABOUT COMING TO SEE YOU, ACTUALLY.
REALLY? SO WHEN'LL IT BE?
WELL, MR. NAKANO'S STILL PRETTY TIED UP...

READ THIS WAY

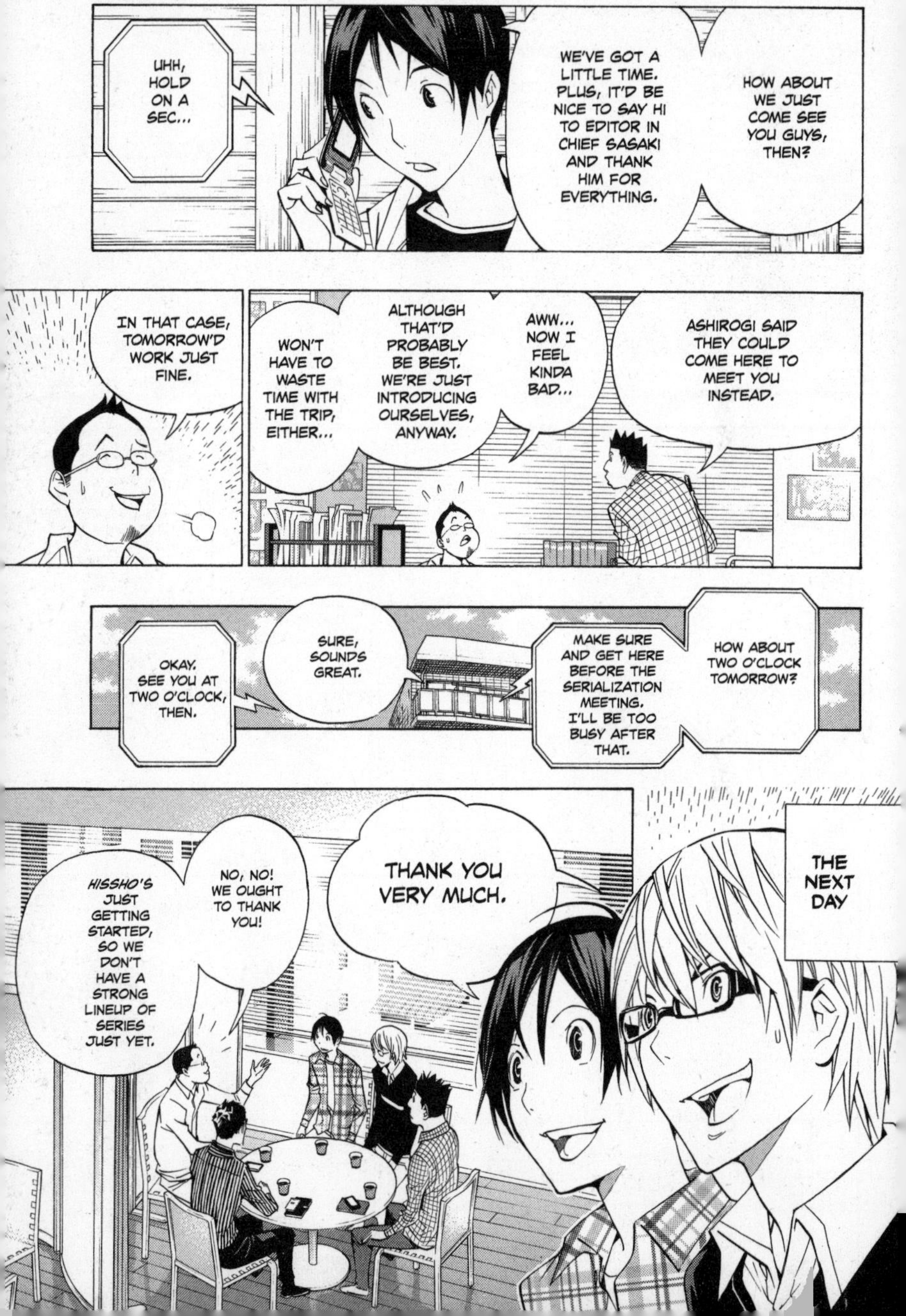
HOW ABOUT WE JUST COME SEE YOU GUYS, THEN?
WE'VE GOT A LITTLE TIME. PLUS, IT'D BE NICE TO SAY HI TO EDITOR IN CHIEF SASAKI AND THANK HIM FOR EVERYTHING.
UHH, HOLD ON A SEC...
ASHIROGI SAID THEY COULD COME HERE TO MEET YOU INSTEAD.
AWW... NOW I FEEL KINDA BAD...
ALTHOUGH THAT'D PROBABLY BE BEST. WE'RE JUST INTRODUCING OURSELVES, ANYWAY.
WON'T HAVE TO WASTE TIME WITH THE TRIP, EITHER...
IN THAT CASE, TOMORROW'D WORK JUST FINE.
HOW ABOUT TWO O'CLOCK TOMORROW?
MAKE SURE AND GET HERE BEFORE THE SERIALIZATION MEETING. I'LL BE TOO BUSY AFTER THAT.
SURE, SOUNDS GREAT.
OKAY. SEE YOU AT TWO O'CLOCK, THEN.
THE NEXT DAY
THANK YOU VERY MUCH.
NO, NO! WE OUGHT TO THANK YOU!
HISSHO'S JUST GETTING STARTED, SO WE DON'T HAVE A STRONG LINEUP OF SERIES JUST YET.

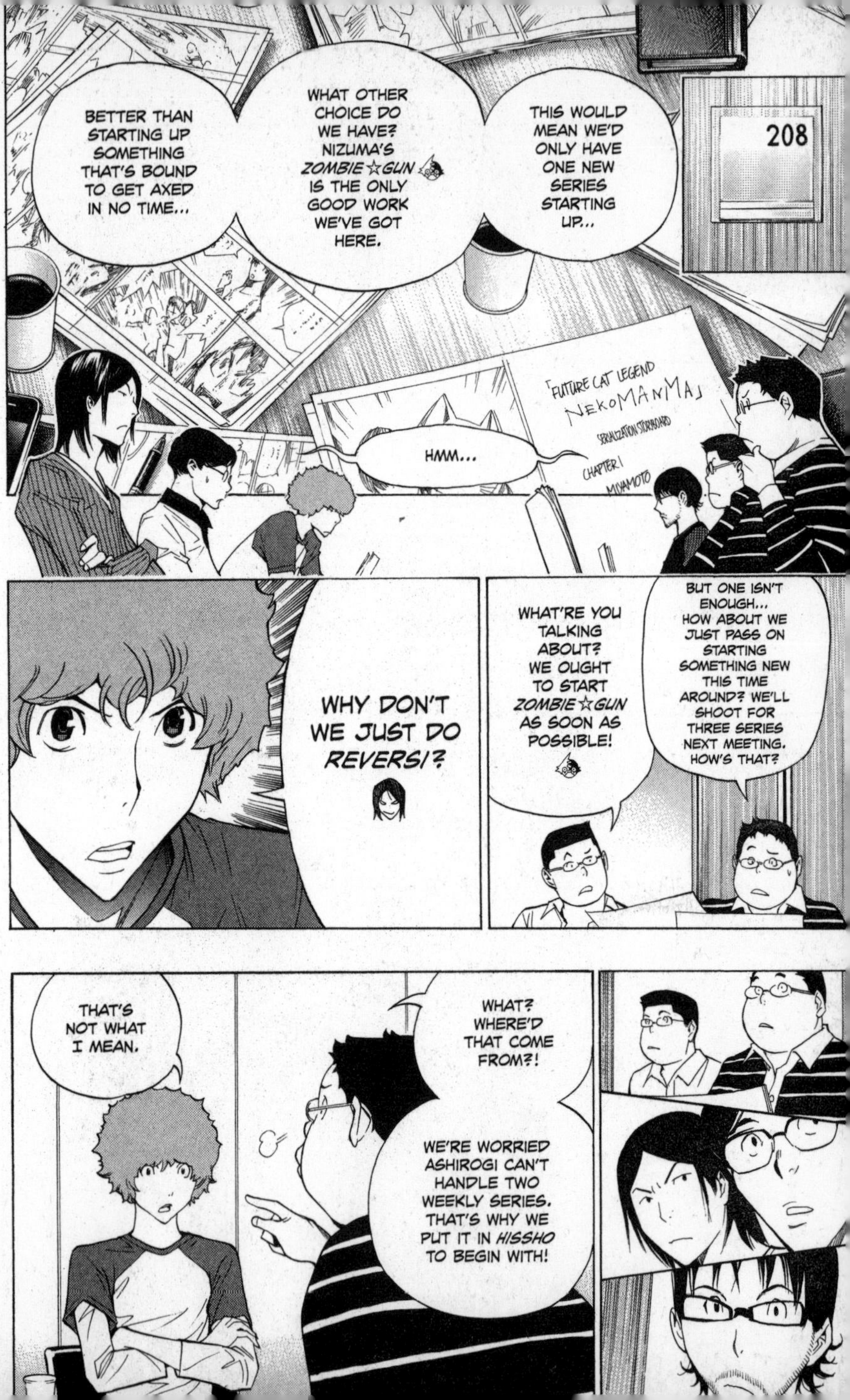
208
THIS WOULD MEAN WE'D ONLY HAVE ONE NEW SERIES STARTING UP...
WHAT OTHER CHOICE DO WE HAVE? NIZUMA'S *ZOMBIE☆GUN* IS THE ONLY GOOD WORK WE'VE GOT HERE.
BETTER THAN STARTING UP SOMETHING THAT'S BOUND TO GET AXED IN NO TIME...
"FUTURE CAT LEGEND NEKOMANMA"
SERIALIZATION STORYBOARD
CHAPTER 1
MIYAMOTO
HMM...
BUT ONE ISN'T ENOUGH... HOW ABOUT WE JUST PASS ON STARTING SOMETHING NEW THIS TIME AROUND? WE'LL SHOOT FOR THREE SERIES NEXT MEETING. HOW'S THAT?
WHAT'RE YOU TALKING ABOUT? WE OUGHT TO START *ZOMBIE☆GUN* AS SOON AS POSSIBLE!
WHY DON'T WE JUST DO *REVERSI*?
WHAT? WHERE'D THAT COME FROM?!
WE'RE WORRIED ASHIROGI CAN'T HANDLE TWO WEEKLY SERIES. THAT'S WHY WE PUT IT IN *HISSHO* TO BEGIN WITH!
THAT'S NOT WHAT I MEAN.

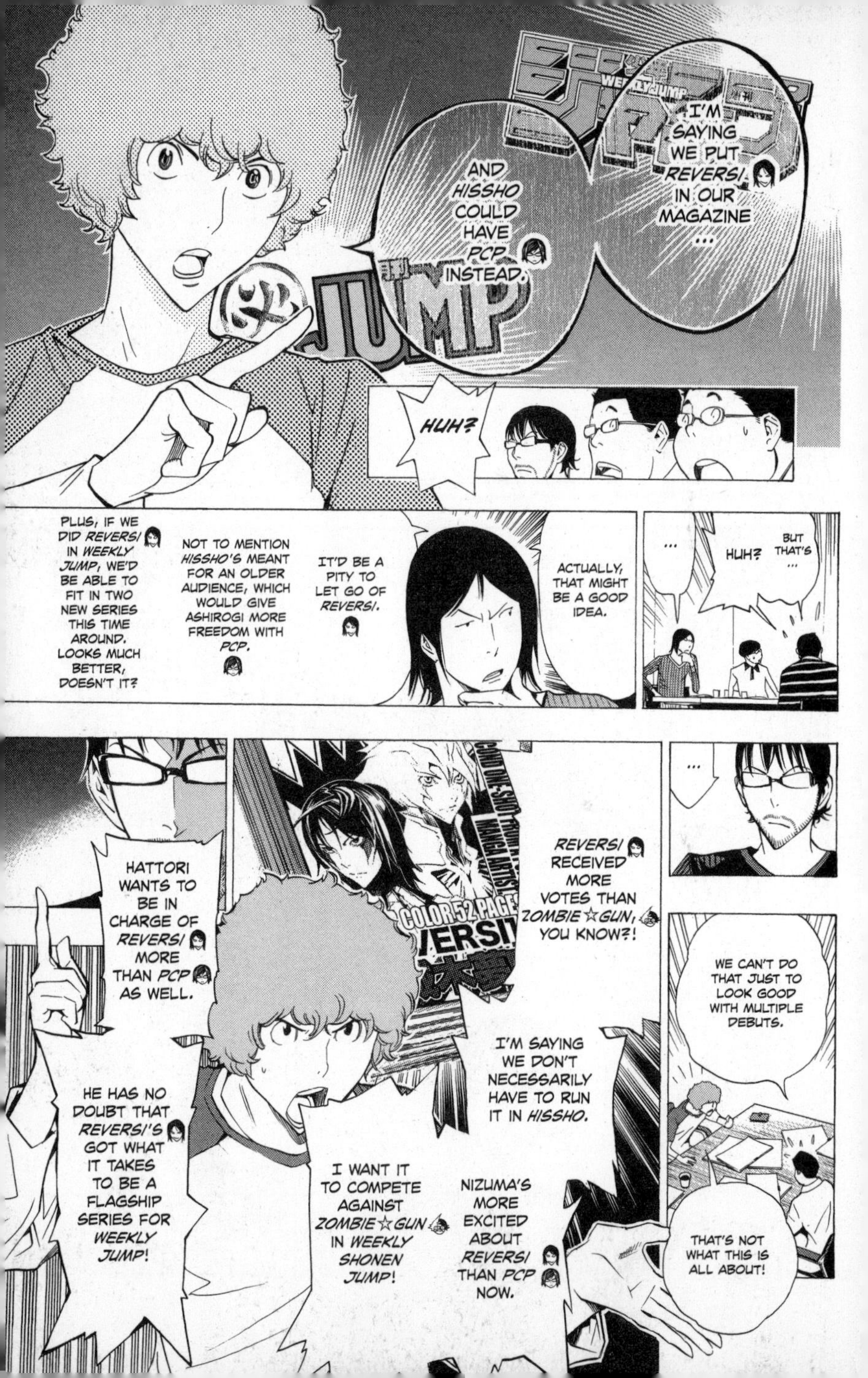
I'M SAYING WE PUT REVERSI IN OUR MAGAZINE ...
AND HISSHO COULD HAVE PCP INSTEAD.
HUH?
HUH? BUT THAT'S ...
...
ACTUALLY, THAT MIGHT BE A GOOD IDEA.
IT'D BE A PITY TO LET GO OF REVERSI.
NOT TO MENTION HISSHO'S MEANT FOR AN OLDER AUDIENCE, WHICH WOULD GIVE ASHIROGI MORE FREEDOM WITH PCP.
PLUS, IF WE DID REVERSI IN WEEKLY JUMP, WE'D BE ABLE TO FIT IN TWO NEW SERIES THIS TIME AROUND. LOOKS MUCH BETTER, DOESN'T IT?
...
WE CAN'T DO THAT JUST TO LOOK GOOD WITH MULTIPLE DEBUTS.
THAT'S NOT WHAT THIS IS ALL ABOUT!
REVERSI RECEIVED MORE VOTES THAN ZOMBIE☆GUN, YOU KNOW?!
I'M SAYING WE DON'T NECESSARILY HAVE TO RUN IT IN HISSHO.
NIZUMA'S MORE EXCITED ABOUT REVERSI THAN PCP NOW.
I WANT IT TO COMPETE AGAINST ZOMBIE☆GUN IN WEEKLY SHONEN JUMP!
HATTORI WANTS TO BE IN CHARGE OF REVERSI MORE THAN PCP AS WELL.
HE HAS NO DOUBT THAT REVERSI'S GOT WHAT IT TAKES TO BE A FLAGSHIP SERIES FOR WEEKLY JUMP!

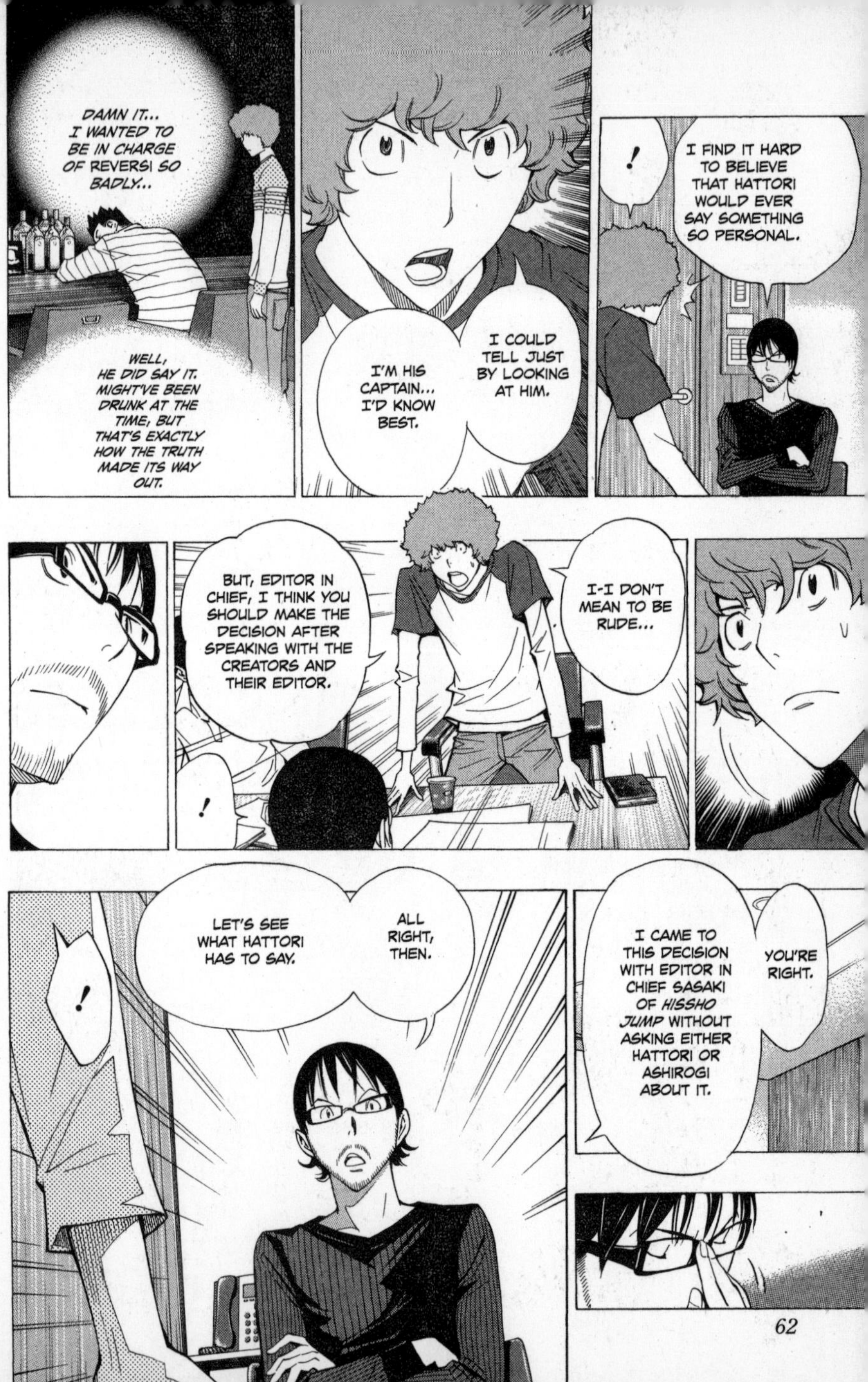
!
I FIND IT HARD TO BELIEVE THAT HATTORI WOULD EVER SAY SOMETHING SO PERSONAL.
I COULD TELL JUST BY LOOKING AT HIM.
I'M HIS CAPTAIN... I'D KNOW BEST.
DAMN IT... I WANTED TO BE IN CHARGE OF REVERSI SO BADLY...
WELL, HE DID SAY IT. MIGHT'VE BEEN DRUNK AT THE TIME, BUT THAT'S EXACTLY HOW THE TRUTH MADE ITS WAY OUT.
I-I DON'T MEAN TO BE RUDE...
BUT, EDITOR IN CHIEF, I THINK YOU SHOULD MAKE THE DECISION AFTER SPEAKING WITH THE CREATORS AND THEIR EDITOR.
!
YOU'RE RIGHT.
I CAME TO THIS DECISION WITH EDITOR IN CHIEF SASAKI OF *HISSHO JUMP* WITHOUT ASKING EITHER HATTORI OR ASHIROGI ABOUT IT.
ALL RIGHT, THEN.
LET'S SEE WHAT HATTORI HAS TO SAY.
!

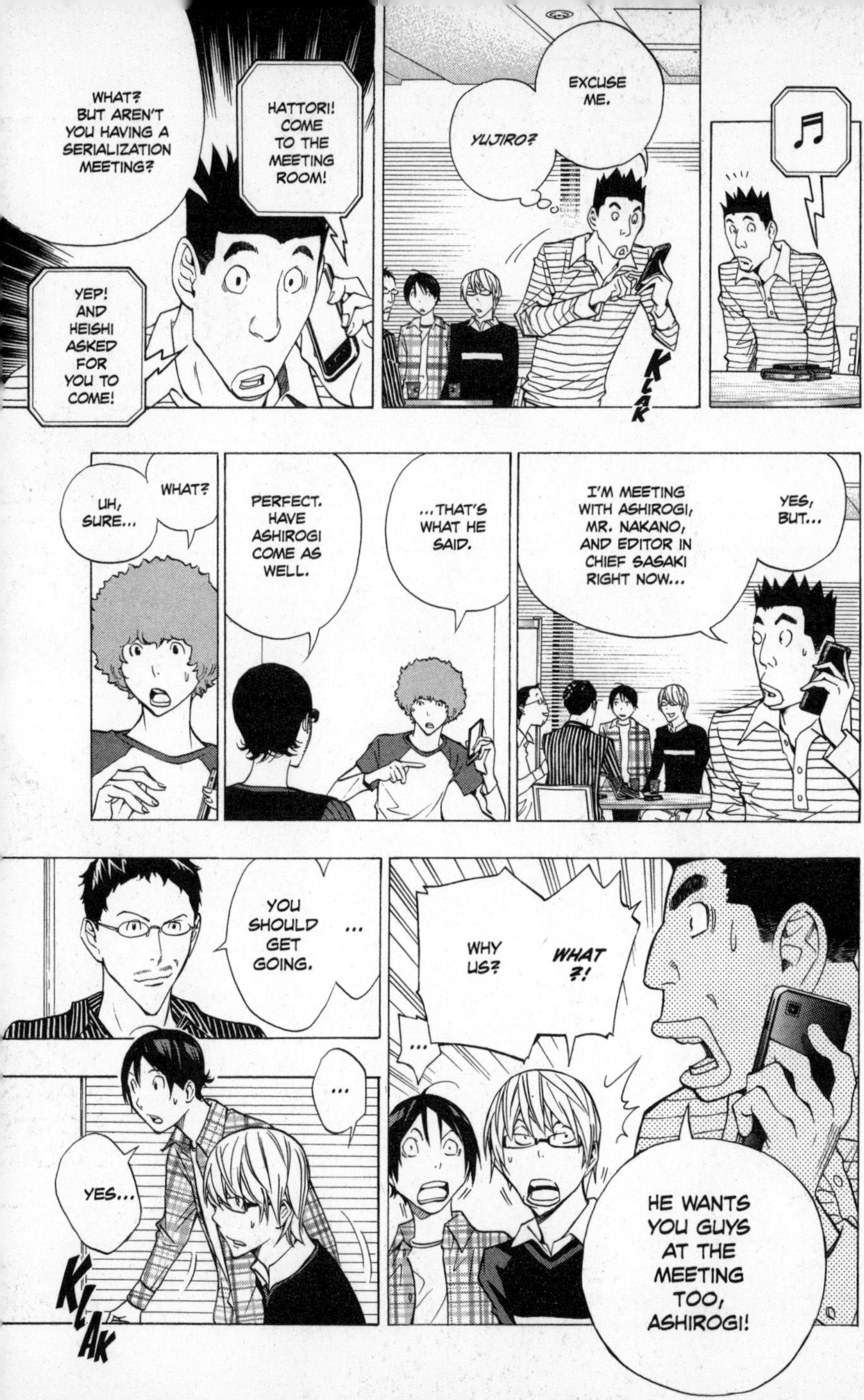
♪
EXCUSE ME.
YUJIRO?
KLAK
HATTORI! COME TO THE MEETING ROOM!
WHAT? BUT AREN'T YOU HAVING A SERIALIZATION MEETING?
YEP! AND HEISHI ASKED FOR YOU TO COME!
YES, BUT...
I'M MEETING WITH ASHIROGI, MR. NAKANO, AND EDITOR IN CHIEF SASAKI RIGHT NOW...
...THAT'S WHAT HE SAID.
PERFECT. HAVE ASHIROGI COME AS WELL.
WHAT?
UH, SURE...
WHAT?!
WHY US?
...
HE WANTS YOU GUYS AT THE MEETING TOO, ASHIROGI!
...
YOU SHOULD GET GOING.
...
YES...
KLAK

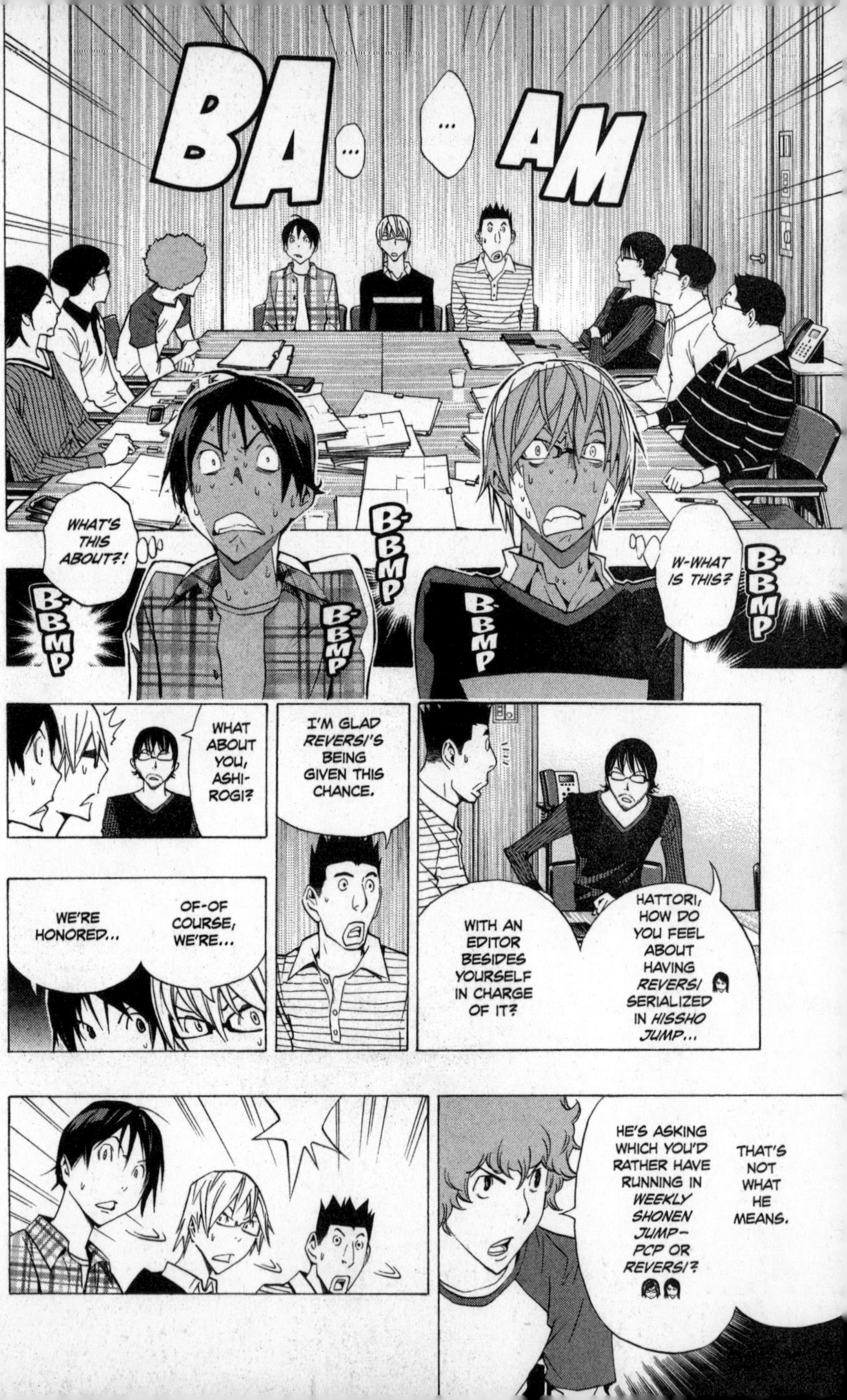
BA
...
...
AM
B-BMP
W-WHAT IS THIS?
B-BMP
B-BMP
WHAT'S THIS ABOUT?!
B-BMP
B-BMP
HATTORI, HOW DO YOU FEEL ABOUT HAVING REVERSI SERIALIZED IN HISSHO JUMP...
WITH AN EDITOR BESIDES YOURSELF IN CHARGE OF IT?
I'M GLAD REVERSI'S BEING GIVEN THIS CHANCE.
WHAT ABOUT YOU, ASHIROGI?
OF-OF COURSE, WE'RE...
WE'RE HONORED...
THAT'S NOT WHAT HE MEANS.
HE'S ASKING WHICH YOU'D RATHER HAVE RUNNING IN WEEKLY SHONEN JUMP—PCP OR REVERSI?

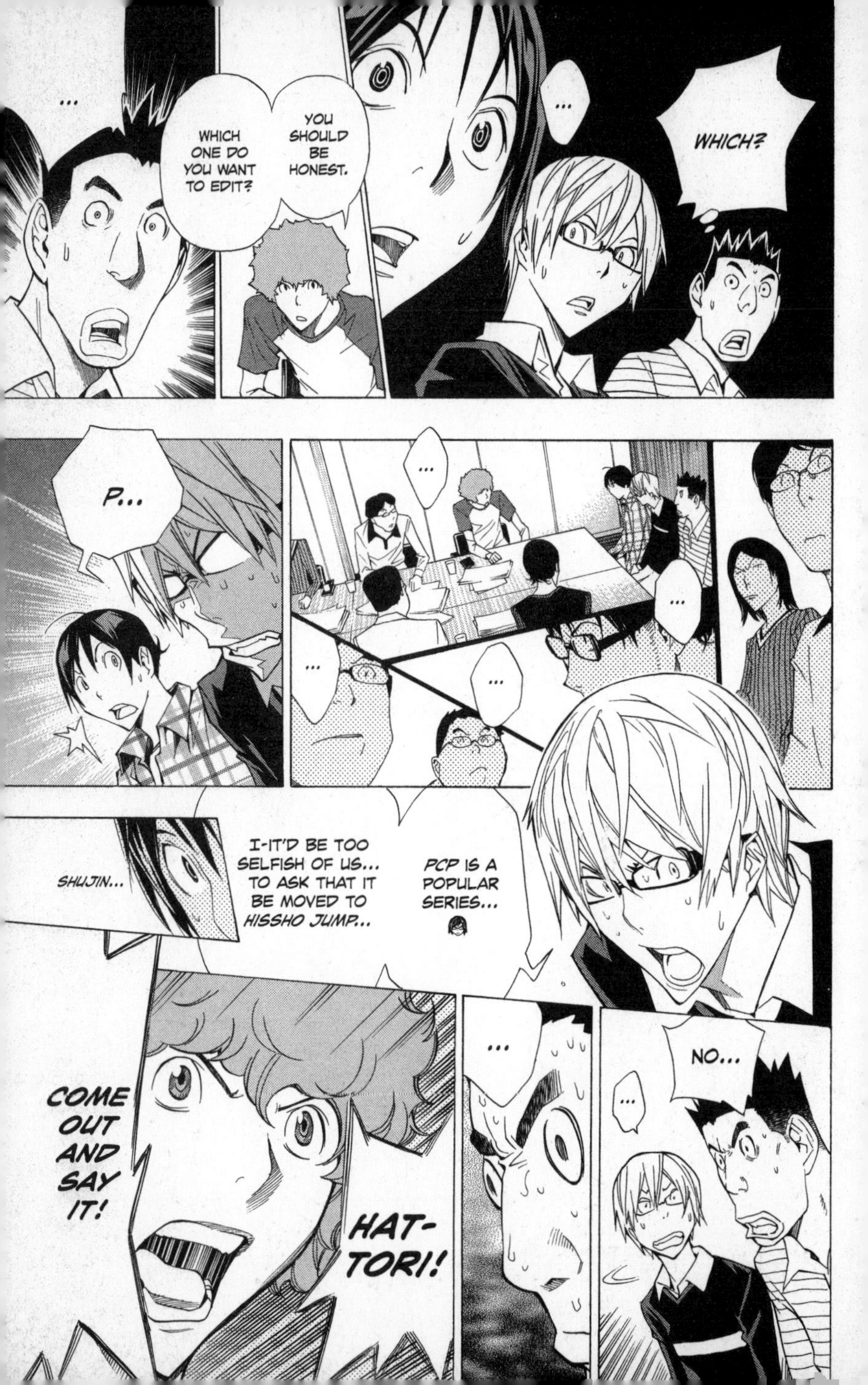
WHICH?
...
YOU SHOULD BE HONEST.
WHICH ONE DO YOU WANT TO EDIT?
...
...
...
...
...
P...
PCP IS A POPULAR SERIES...
I-IT'D BE TOO SELFISH OF US... TO ASK THAT IT BE MOVED TO HISSHO JUMP...
SHUJIN...
NO...
...
...
HAT-TORI!
COME OUT AND SAY IT!

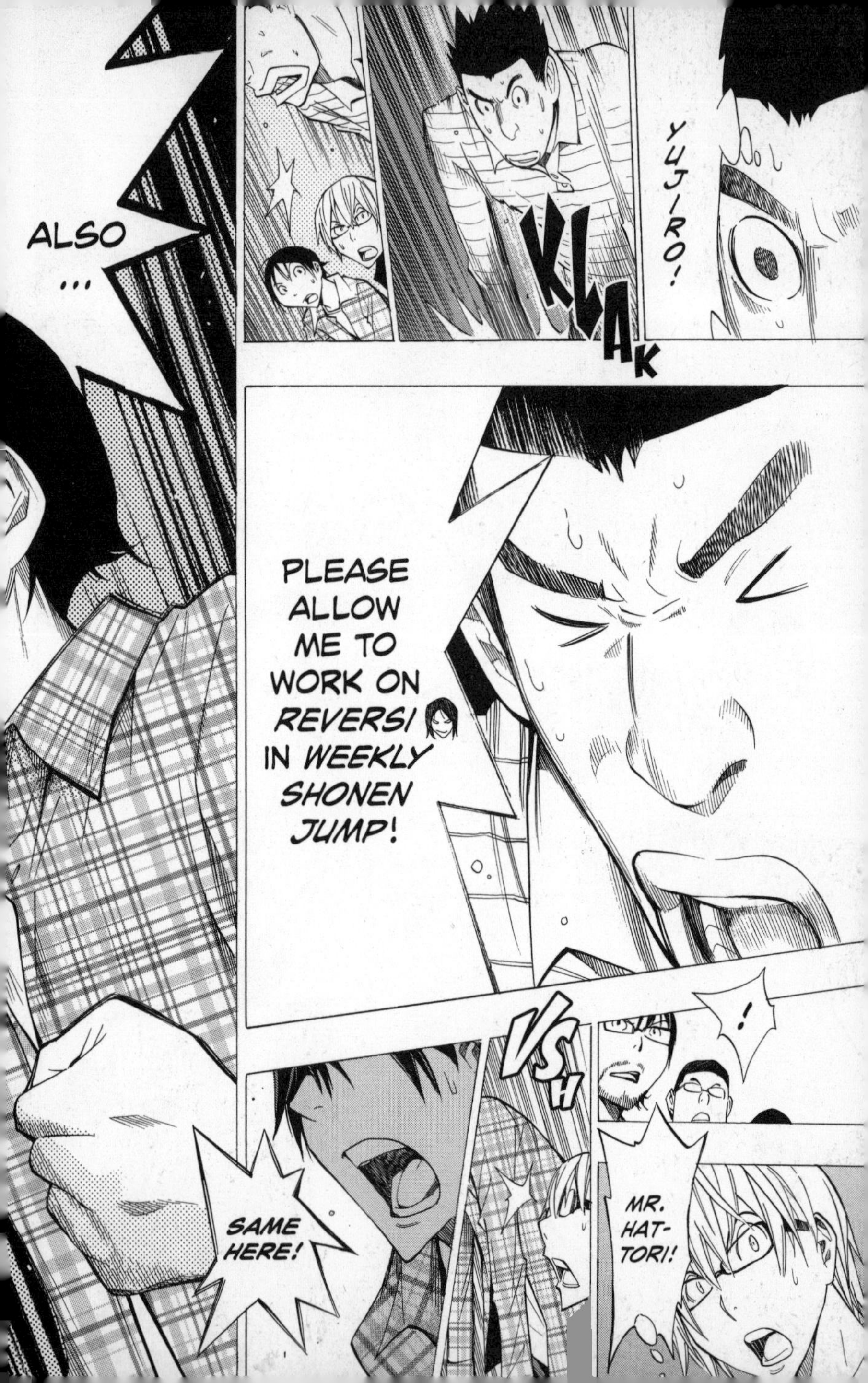
YUJIRO!
KLAK
PLEASE ALLOW ME TO WORK ON REVERSI IN WEEKLY SHONEN JUMP!
MR. HATTORI!
!
VSH
SAME HERE!
ALSO ...

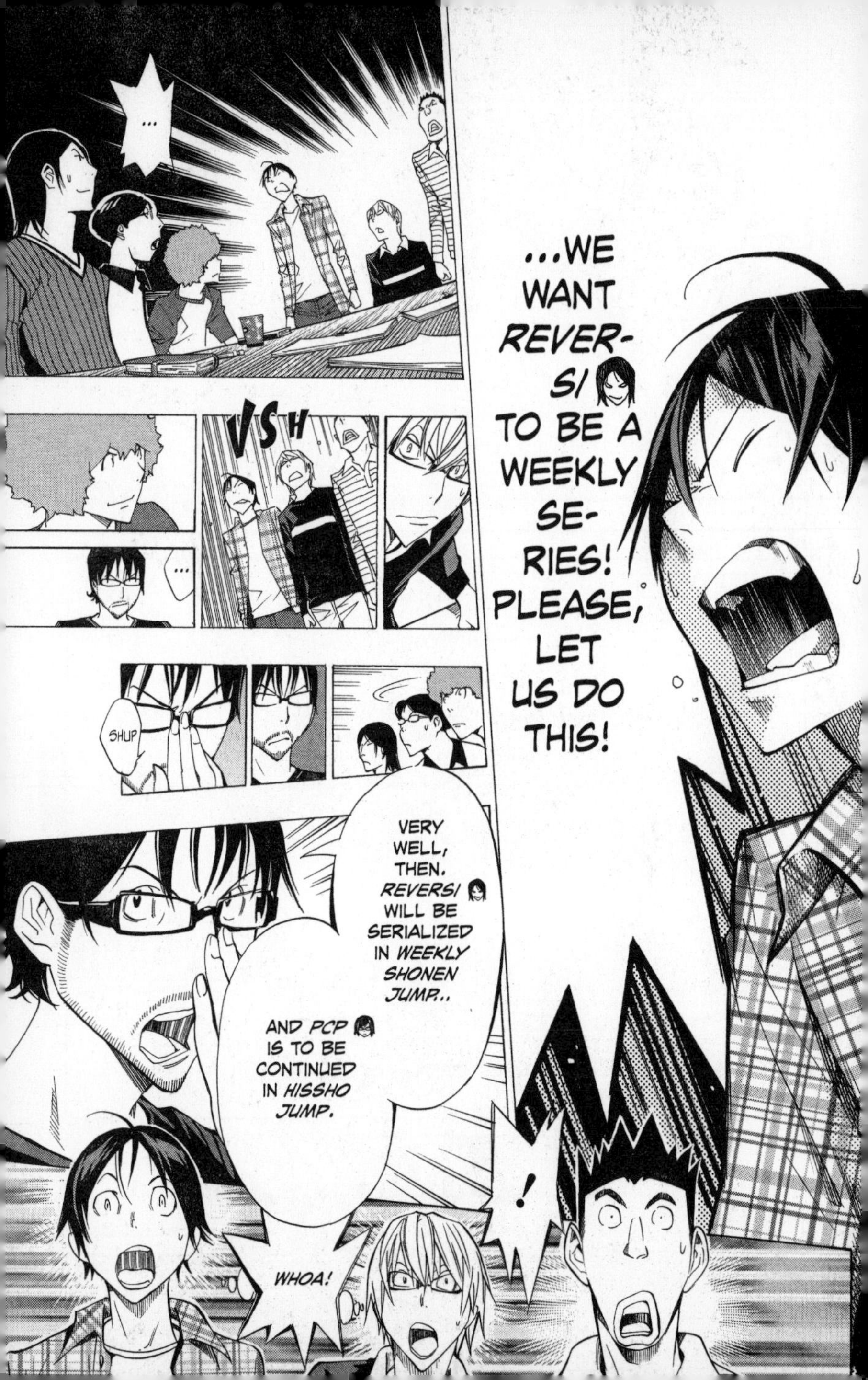
...WE WANT REVERSI TO BE A WEEKLY SERIES! PLEASE, LET US DO THIS!
...
VSH
...
SHUP
VERY WELL, THEN. REVERSI WILL BE SERIALIZED IN WEEKLY SHONEN JUMP...
AND PCP IS TO BE CONTINUED IN HISSHO JUMP.
!
WHOA!

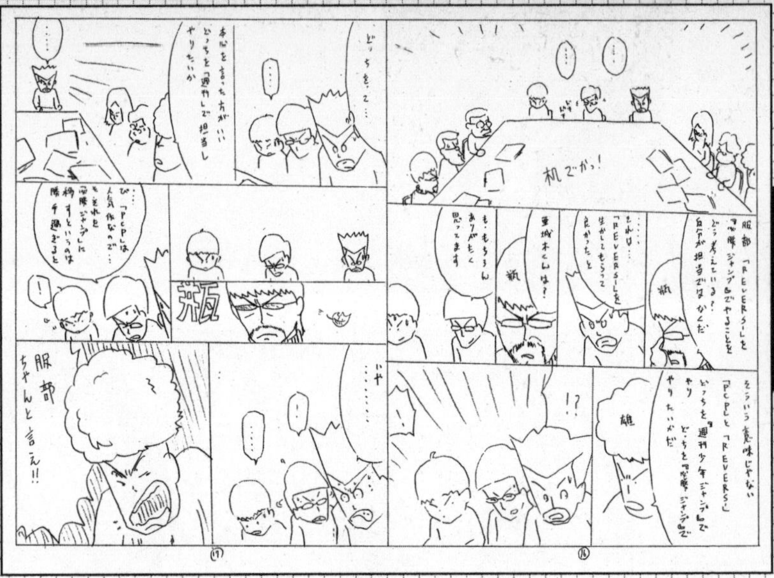
……
……
ドギ
机でかっ!
服部「REVERSI」を『必勝ジャンプ』でやることをどう考えている? 自分が担当ではなかくだ
瓶
……それは…「REVERSI」を生かしてもらって良かったと
亜城木くんは?
瓶
も・もちろんありがたく思ってます
そういう意味じゃない 「PCP」と「REVERSI」どっちを『週刊少年ジャンプ』でやりどっちを『必勝ジャンプ』でやりたいかだ
雄
!?
!
いや……
!
……
どっちを、て…
……
本心を言った方がいいどっちを「週刊」で担当しやりたいか
……
……「PCP」は人気作なので…それを『必勝ジャンプ』に移すというのは勝手過ぎると
!
瓶
服部ちゃんと言え!!
⑰
⑯

OHBA'S STORYBOARD

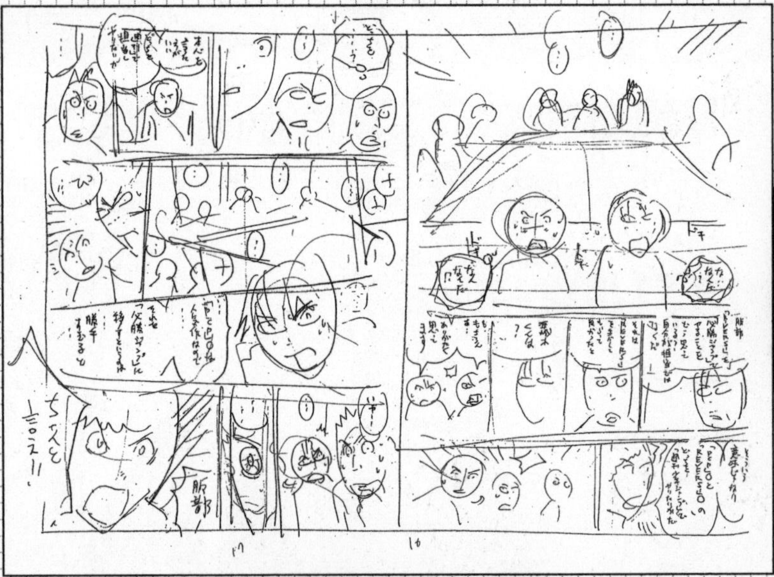

OBATA'S STORYBOARD

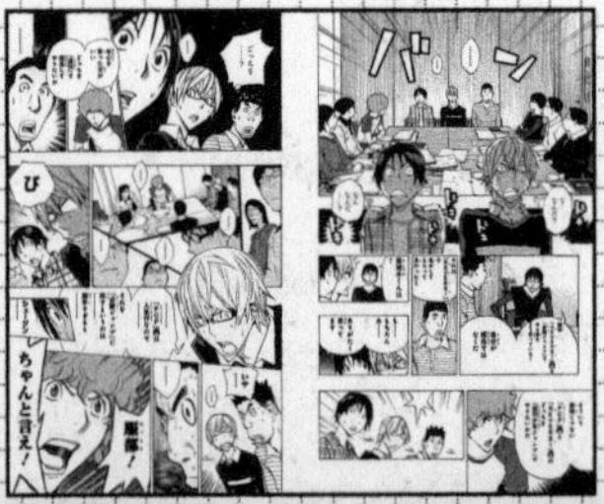

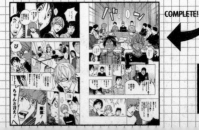

COMPLETE!

※CREATOR STORYBOARDS AND FINISHED PAGES IN JAPANESE

BAKUMAN。 vol.18

"Until the Final Draft Is Complete"

Chapter 154, pp. 64-65

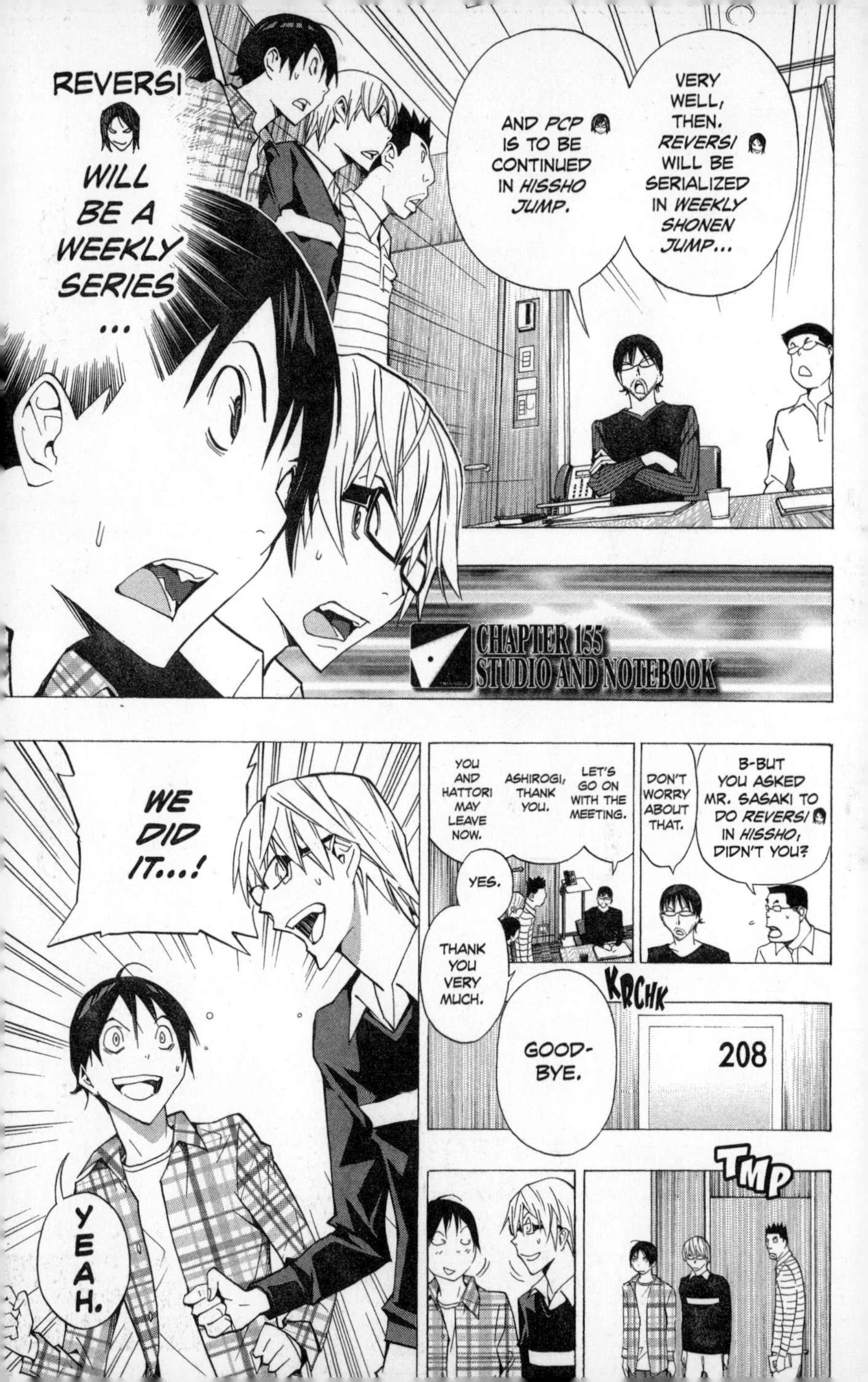
VERY WELL, THEN. REVERSI WILL BE SERIALIZED IN WEEKLY SHONEN JUMP...
AND PCP IS TO BE CONTINUED IN HISSHO JUMP.
REVERSI WILL BE A WEEKLY SERIES ...
CHAPTER 155
STUDIO AND NOTEBOOK
B-BUT YOU ASKED MR. SASAKI TO DO REVERSI IN HISSHO, DIDN'T YOU?
DON'T WORRY ABOUT THAT.
LET'S GO ON WITH THE MEETING.
ASHIROGI, THANK YOU.
YOU AND HATTORI MAY LEAVE NOW.
YES.
THANK YOU VERY MUCH.
KRCHK
208
GOOD-BYE.
TMP
WE DID IT...!
YEAH.

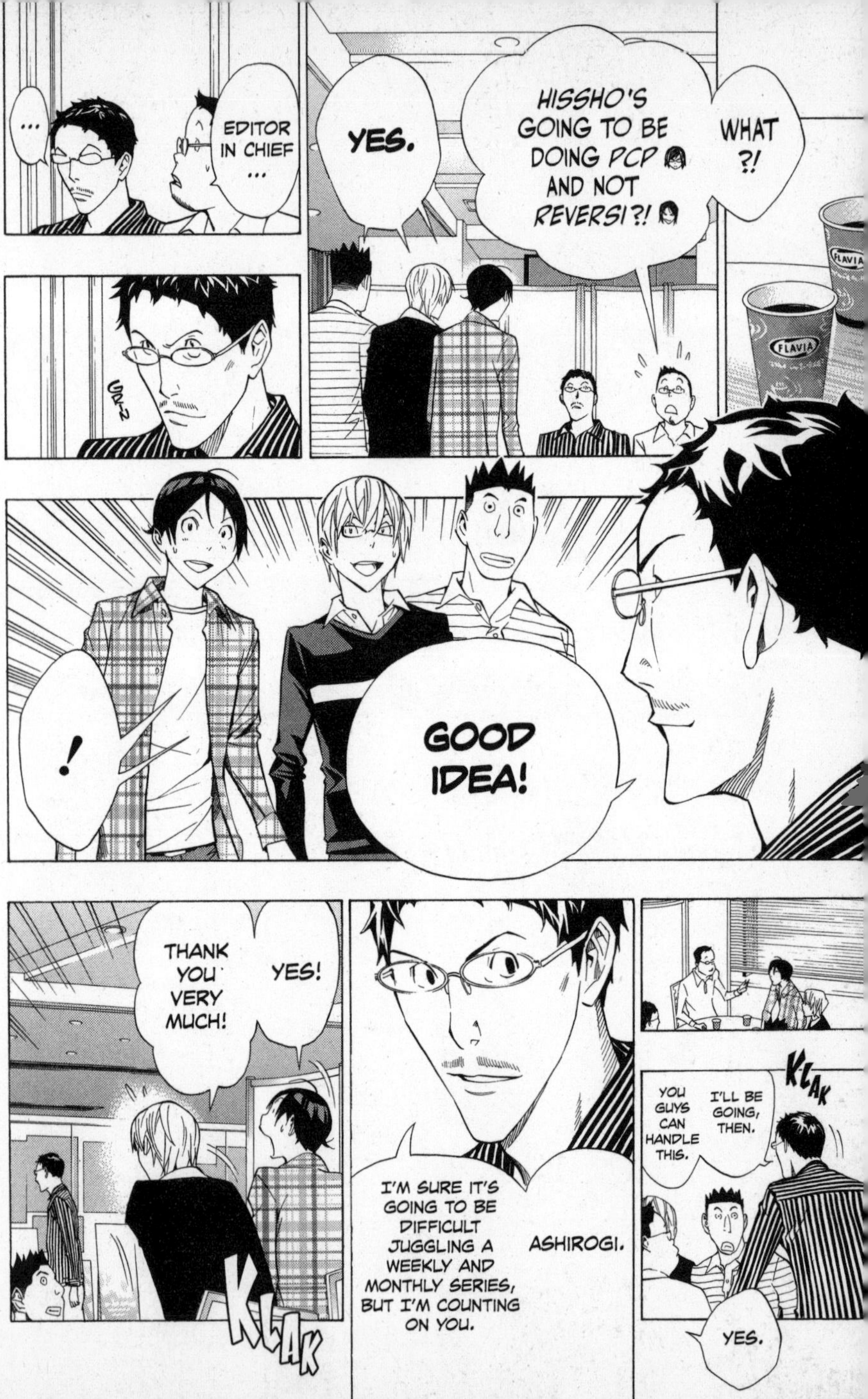
WHAT ?!
HISSHO'S GOING TO BE DOING PCP AND NOT REVERSI?!
YES.
EDITOR IN CHIEF ...
...
GRIN
GOOD IDEA!
!
KLAK
I'LL BE GOING, THEN.
YOU GUYS CAN HANDLE THIS.
YES.
ASHIROGI.
I'M SURE IT'S GOING TO BE DIFFICULT JUGGLING A WEEKLY AND MONTHLY SERIES, BUT I'M COUNTING ON YOU.
YES!
THANK YOU VERY MUCH!
KLAK

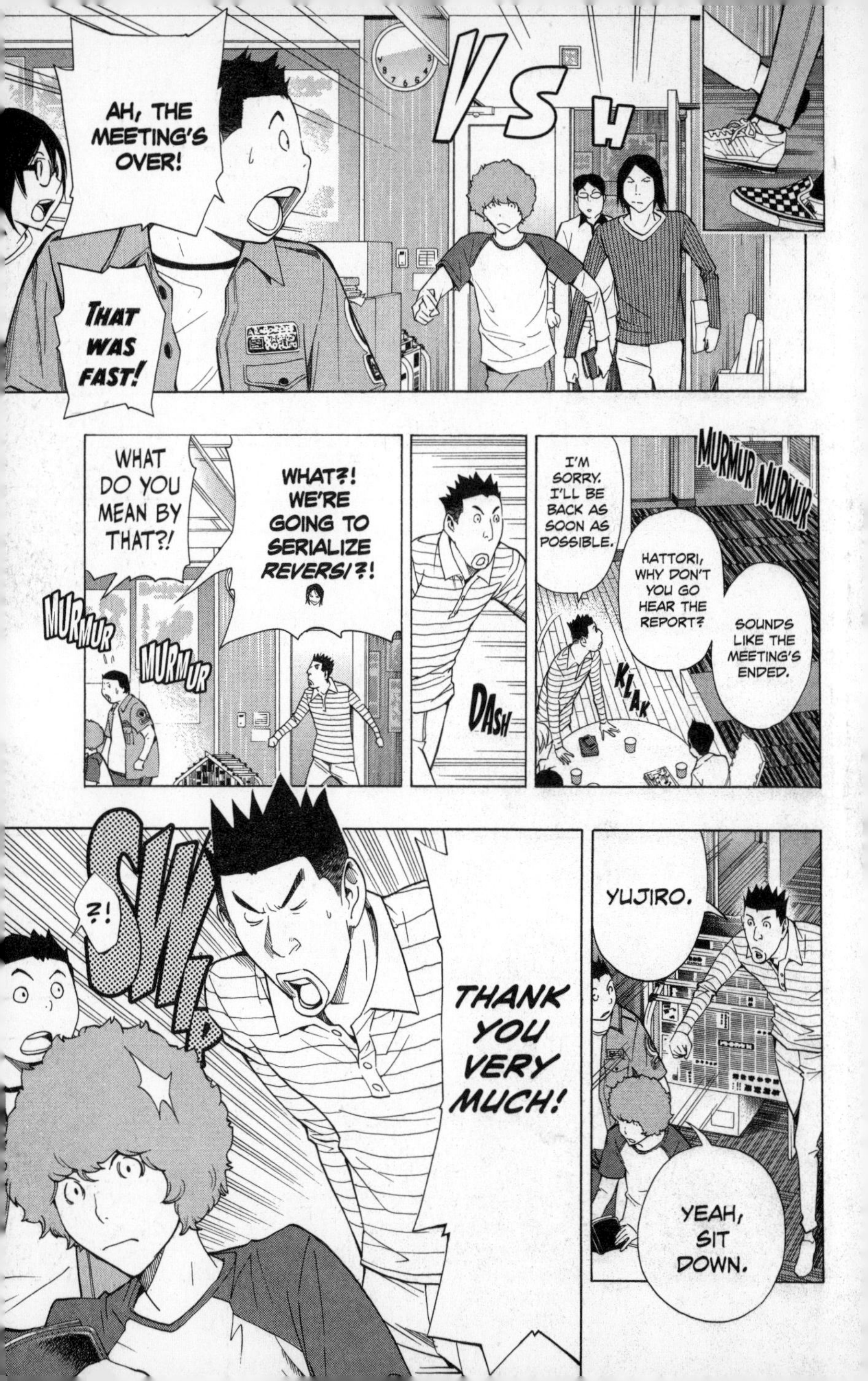
VSH
AH, THE MEETING'S OVER!
THAT WAS FAST!
MURMUR MURMUR
SOUNDS LIKE THE MEETING'S ENDED.
HATTORI, WHY DON'T YOU GO HEAR THE REPORT?
I'M SORRY. I'LL BE BACK AS SOON AS POSSIBLE.
KLAK
DASH
WHAT?! WE'RE GOING TO SERIALIZE *REVERSI*?!
WHAT DO YOU MEAN BY THAT?!
MURMUR
MURMUR
YUJIRO.
YEAH, SIT DOWN.
THANK YOU VERY MUCH!
SWIP
?!

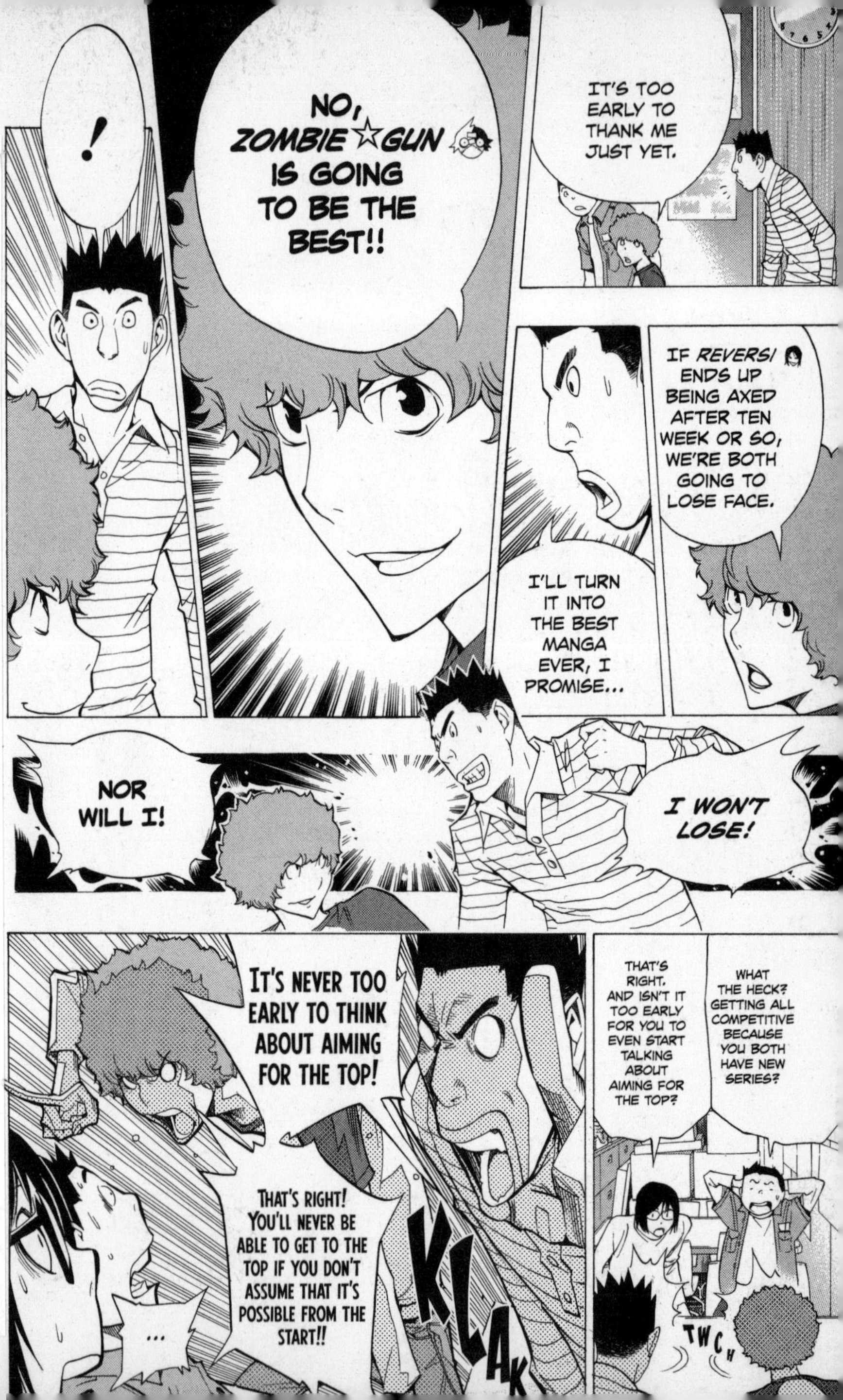
IT'S TOO EARLY TO THANK ME JUST YET.
IF REVERSI ENDS UP BEING AXED AFTER TEN WEEK OR SO, WE'RE BOTH GOING TO LOSE FACE.
I'LL TURN IT INTO THE BEST MANGA EVER, I PROMISE...
NO, ZOMBIE☆GUN IS GOING TO BE THE BEST!!
!
I WON'T LOSE!
NOR WILL I!
WHAT THE HECK? GETTING ALL COMPETITIVE BECAUSE YOU BOTH HAVE NEW SERIES?
THAT'S RIGHT. AND ISN'T IT TOO EARLY FOR YOU TO EVEN START TALKING ABOUT AIMING FOR THE TOP?
TWCH
IT'S NEVER TOO EARLY TO THINK ABOUT AIMING FOR THE TOP!
THAT'S RIGHT! YOU'LL NEVER BE ABLE TO GET TO THE TOP IF YOU DON'T ASSUME THAT IT'S POSSIBLE FROM THE START!!
KLAK
...

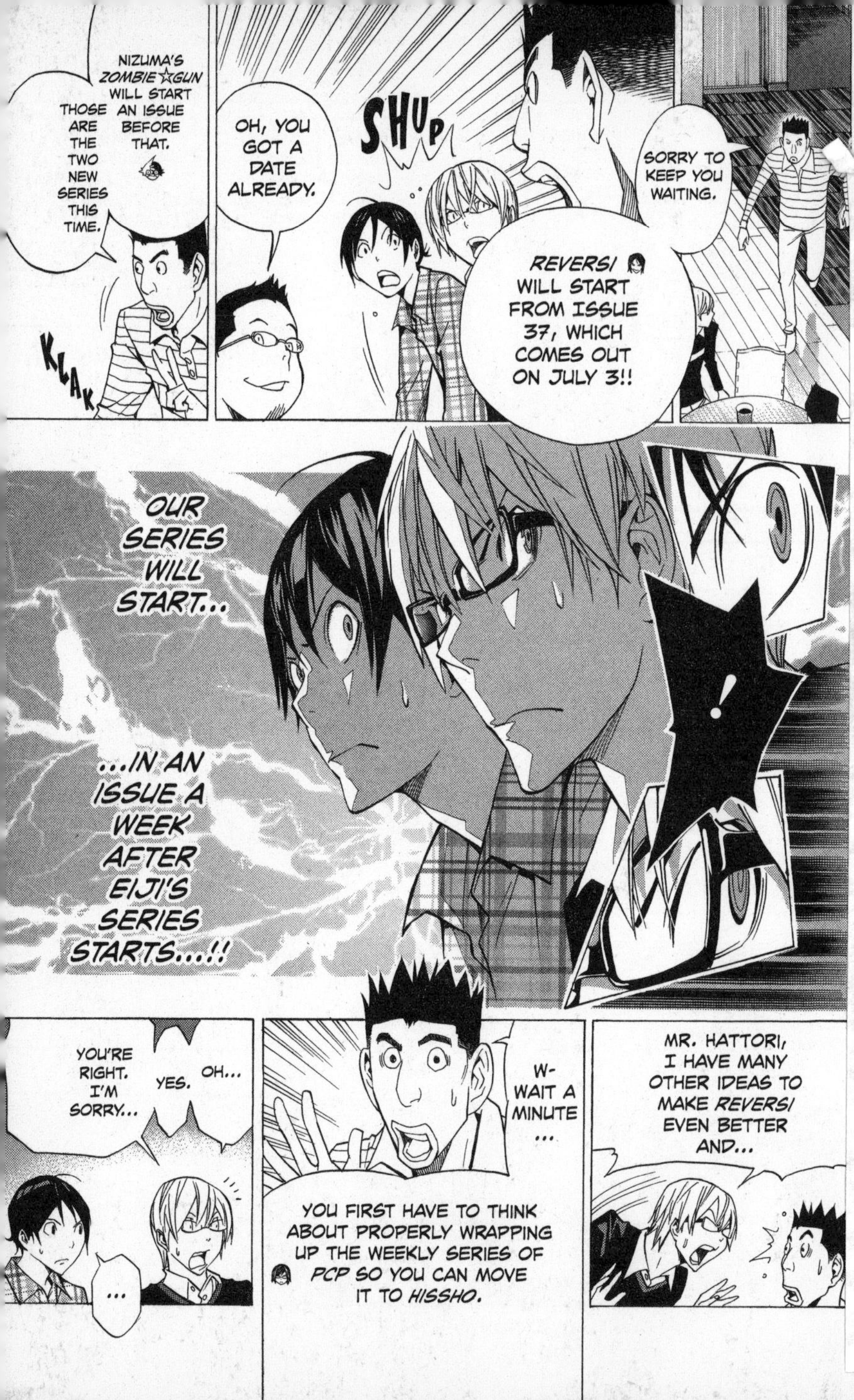
SORRY TO KEEP YOU WAITING.
REVERSI WILL START FROM ISSUE 37, WHICH COMES OUT ON JULY 3!!
SHUP
OH, YOU GOT A DATE ALREADY.
NIZUMA'S ZOMBIE☆GUN WILL START AN ISSUE BEFORE THAT.
THOSE ARE THE TWO NEW SERIES THIS TIME.
KLAK
OUR SERIES WILL START...
...IN AN ISSUE A WEEK AFTER EIJI'S SERIES STARTS...!!
!
MR. HATTORI, I HAVE MANY OTHER IDEAS TO MAKE REVERSI EVEN BETTER AND...
W-WAIT A MINUTE...
YOU FIRST HAVE TO THINK ABOUT PROPERLY WRAPPING UP THE WEEKLY SERIES OF PCP SO YOU CAN MOVE IT TO HISSHO.
OH...
YES.
YOU'RE RIGHT. I'M SORRY...
...

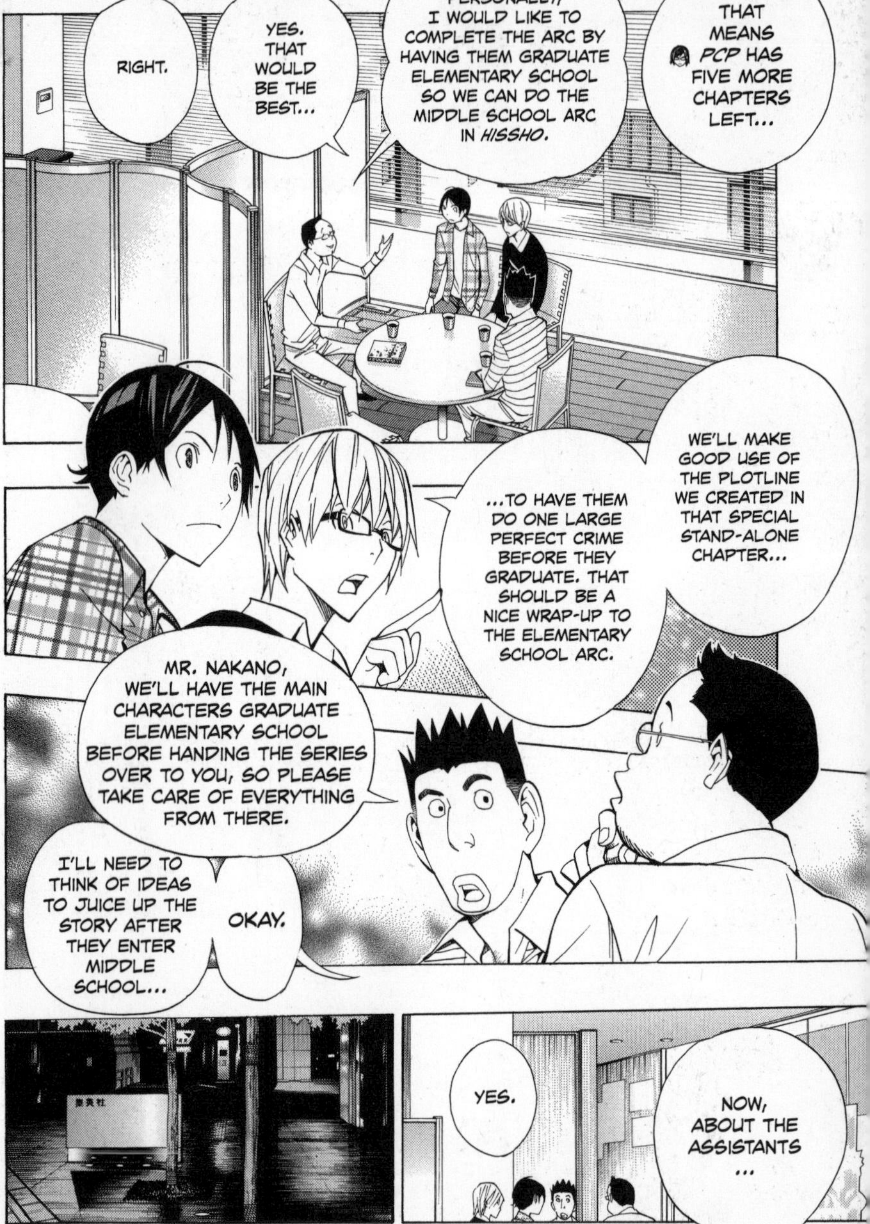
THAT MEANS PCP HAS FIVE MORE CHAPTERS LEFT...
PERSONALLY, I WOULD LIKE TO COMPLETE THE ARC BY HAVING THEM GRADUATE ELEMENTARY SCHOOL SO WE CAN DO THE MIDDLE SCHOOL ARC IN *HISSHO*.
YES. THAT WOULD BE THE BEST...
RIGHT.
WE'LL MAKE GOOD USE OF THE PLOTLINE WE CREATED IN THAT SPECIAL STAND-ALONE CHAPTER...
...TO HAVE THEM DO ONE LARGE PERFECT CRIME BEFORE THEY GRADUATE. THAT SHOULD BE A NICE WRAP-UP TO THE ELEMENTARY SCHOOL ARC.
MR. NAKANO, WE'LL HAVE THE MAIN CHARACTERS GRADUATE ELEMENTARY SCHOOL BEFORE HANDING THE SERIES OVER TO YOU, SO PLEASE TAKE CARE OF EVERYTHING FROM THERE.
OKAY.
I'LL NEED TO THINK OF IDEAS TO JUICE UP THE STORY AFTER THEY ENTER MIDDLE SCHOOL...
NOW, ABOUT THE ASSISTANTS ...
YES.

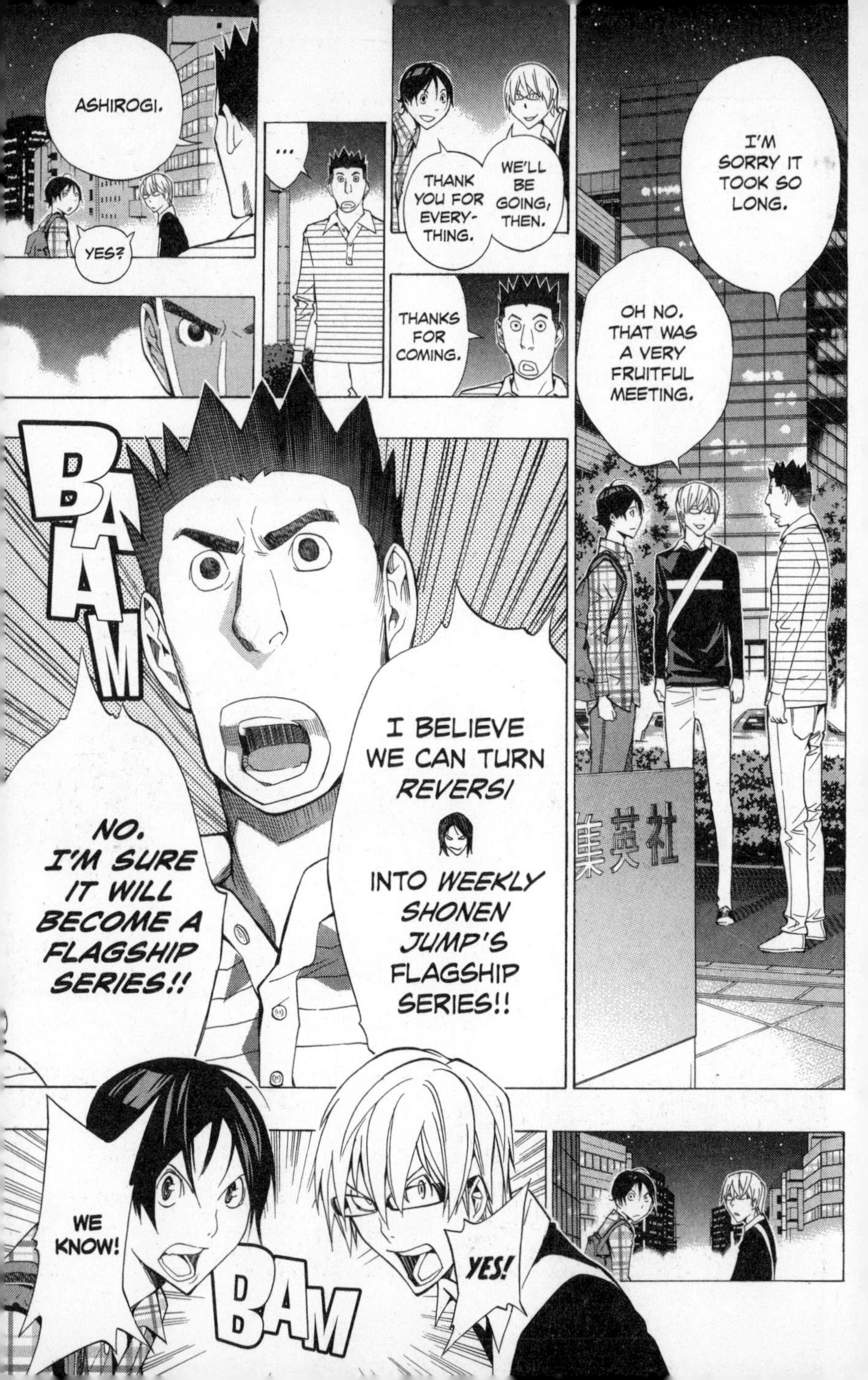

I'M SORRY IT TOOK SO LONG.
OH NO. THAT WAS A VERY FRUITFUL MEETING.
集英社
WE'LL BE GOING, THEN.
THANK YOU FOR EVERYTHING.
THANKS FOR COMING.
...
ASHIROGI.
YES?
BAM
I BELIEVE WE CAN TURN *REVERSI* INTO *WEEKLY SHONEN JUMP'S* FLAGSHIP SERIES!!
NO. I'M SURE IT WILL BECOME A FLAGSHIP SERIES!!
YES!
BAM
WE KNOW!

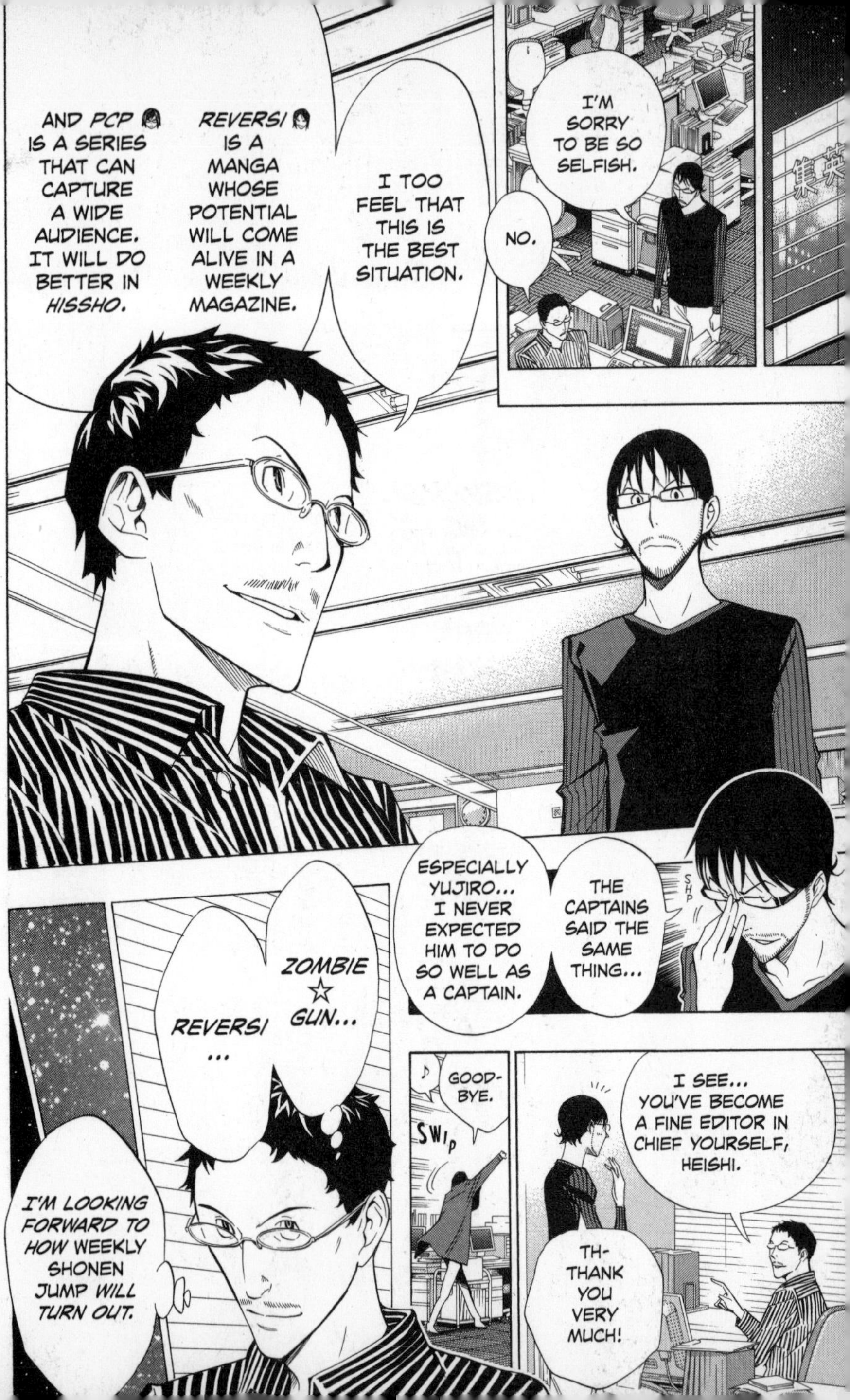
I'M SORRY TO BE SO SELFISH.
NO.
I TOO FEEL THAT THIS IS THE BEST SITUATION.
REVERSI IS A MANGA WHOSE POTENTIAL WILL COME ALIVE IN A WEEKLY MAGAZINE.
AND *PCP* IS A SERIES THAT CAN CAPTURE A WIDE AUDIENCE. IT WILL DO BETTER IN *HISSHO*.
SHP
THE CAPTAINS SAID THE SAME THING...
ESPECIALLY YUJIRO... I NEVER EXPECTED HIM TO DO SO WELL AS A CAPTAIN.
I SEE... YOU'VE BECOME A FINE EDITOR IN CHIEF YOURSELF, HEISHI.
TH-THANK YOU VERY MUCH!
GOOD-BYE.
SWIP
ZOMBIE☆GUN...
REVERSI...
I'M LOOKING FORWARD TO HOW WEEKLY SHONEN JUMP WILL TURN OUT.

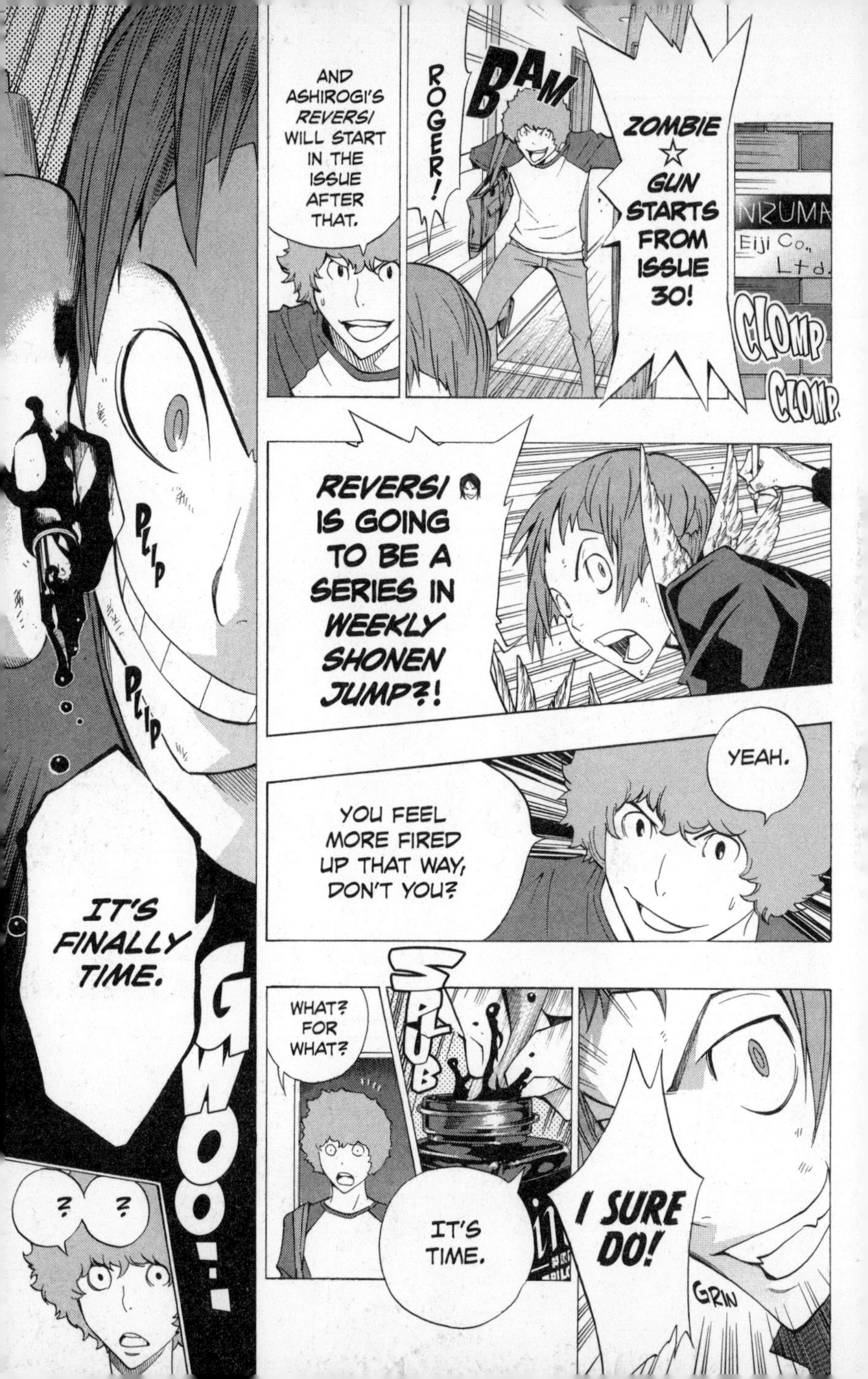
NIZUMA Eiji Co., Ltd.
CLOMP CLOMP
ZOMBIE☆GUN STARTS FROM ISSUE 30!
BAM
ROGER!
AND ASHIROGI'S REVERSI WILL START IN THE ISSUE AFTER THAT.
REVERSI IS GOING TO BE A SERIES IN WEEKLY SHONEN JUMP?!
YEAH.
YOU FEEL MORE FIRED UP THAT WAY, DON'T YOU?
I SURE DO!
GRIN
SPLUB
IT'S TIME.
WHAT? FOR WHAT?
PLIP
PLIP
IT'S FINALLY TIME.
GWOO...
? ?

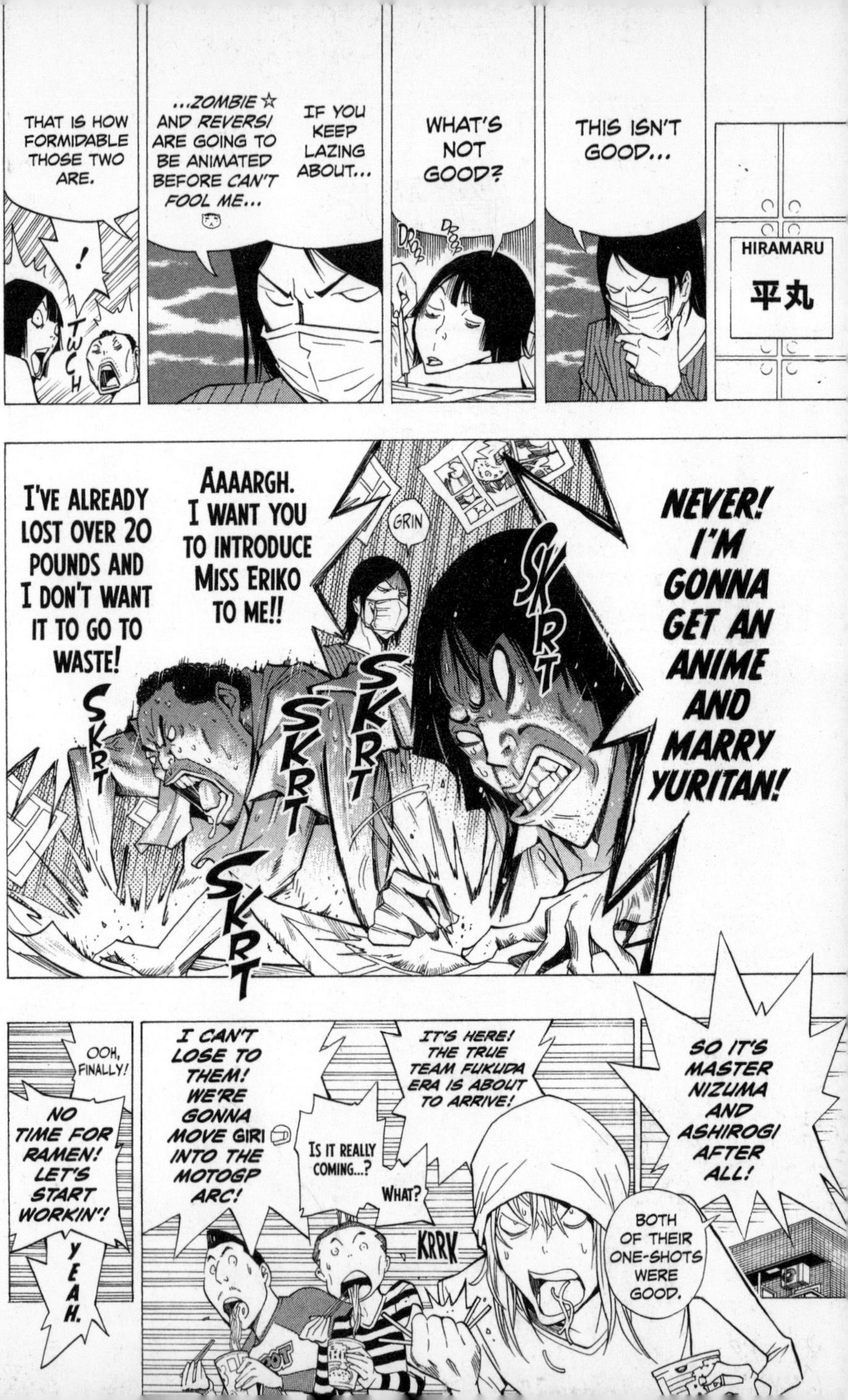
HIRAMARU
平丸
THIS ISN'T GOOD...
WHAT'S NOT GOOD?
DRAW DRAW
IF YOU KEEP LAZING ABOUT...
...ZOMBIE☆ AND REVERSI ARE GOING TO BE ANIMATED BEFORE CAN'T FOOL ME...
THAT IS HOW FORMIDABLE THOSE TWO ARE.
!
TWCH
NEVER! I'M GONNA GET AN ANIME AND MARRY YURITAN!
SKRT
GRIN
AAAARGH. I WANT YOU TO INTRODUCE MISS ERIKO TO ME!!
SKRT
SKRT
I'VE ALREADY LOST OVER 20 POUNDS AND I DON'T WANT IT TO GO TO WASTE!
SKRT
SKRT
SO IT'S MASTER NIZUMA AND ASHIROGI AFTER ALL!
BOTH OF THEIR ONE-SHOTS WERE GOOD.
IT'S HERE! THE TRUE TEAM FUKUDA ERA IS ABOUT TO ARRIVE!
KRRK
WHAT?
IS IT REALLY COMING...?
I CAN'T LOSE TO THEM! WE'RE GONNA MOVE GIRI INTO THE MOTOGP ARC!
OOH, FINALLY!
NO TIME FOR RAMEN! LET'S START WORKIN'!
YEAH.

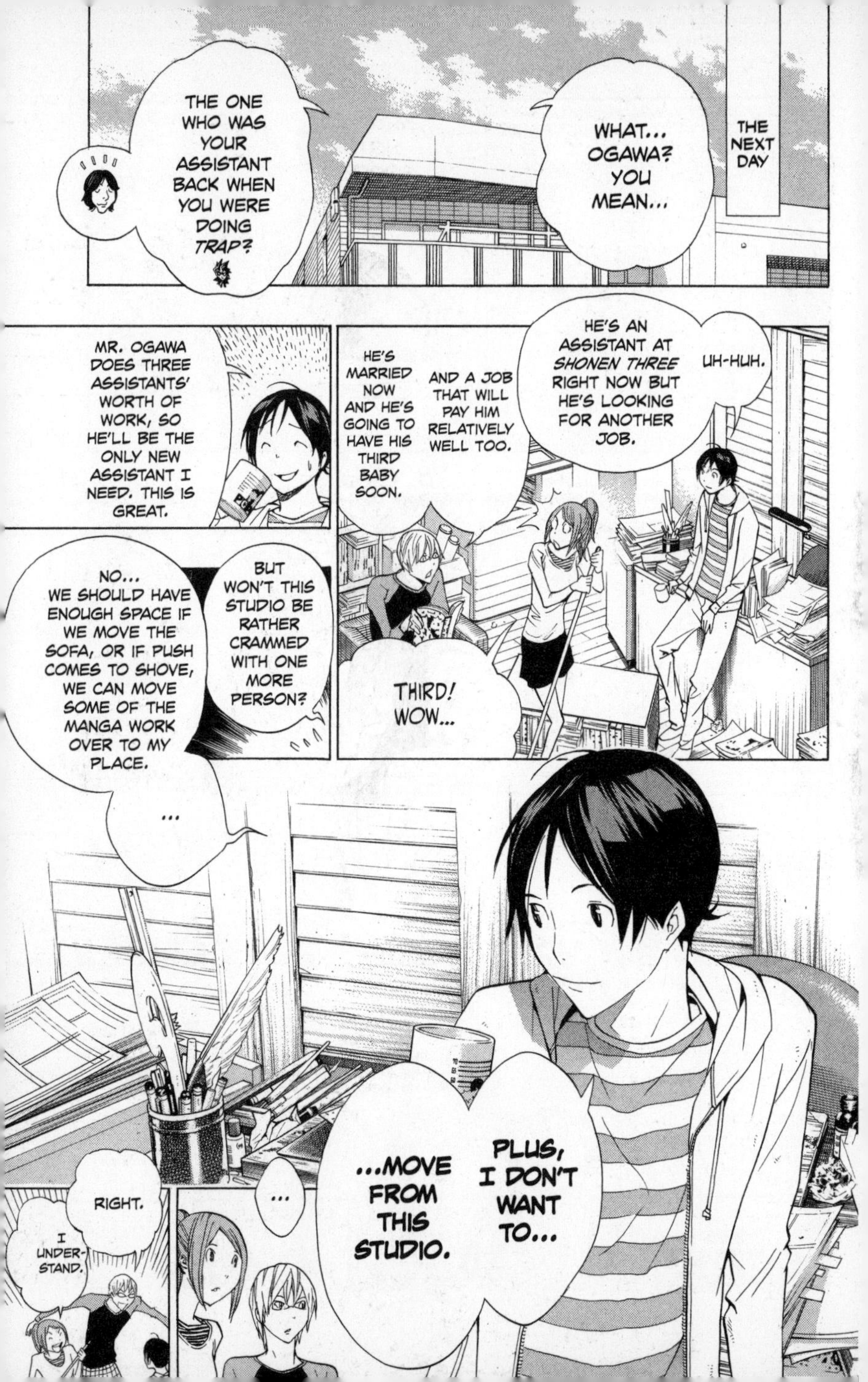
THE NEXT DAY
WHAT... OGAWA? YOU MEAN...
THE ONE WHO WAS YOUR ASSISTANT BACK WHEN YOU WERE DOING *TRAP*?
UH-HUH.
HE'S AN ASSISTANT AT *SHONEN THREE* RIGHT NOW BUT HE'S LOOKING FOR ANOTHER JOB.
AND A JOB THAT WILL PAY HIM RELATIVELY WELL TOO.
HE'S MARRIED NOW AND HE'S GOING TO HAVE HIS THIRD BABY SOON.
THIRD! WOW...
MR. OGAWA DOES THREE ASSISTANTS' WORTH OF WORK, SO HE'LL BE THE ONLY NEW ASSISTANT I NEED. THIS IS GREAT.
BUT WON'T THIS STUDIO BE RATHER CRAMMED WITH ONE MORE PERSON?
NO... WE SHOULD HAVE ENOUGH SPACE IF WE MOVE THE SOFA, OR IF PUSH COMES TO SHOVE, WE CAN MOVE SOME OF THE MANGA WORK OVER TO MY PLACE.
...
PLUS, I DON'T WANT TO...
...MOVE FROM THIS STUDIO.
...
RIGHT.
I UNDER-STAND.

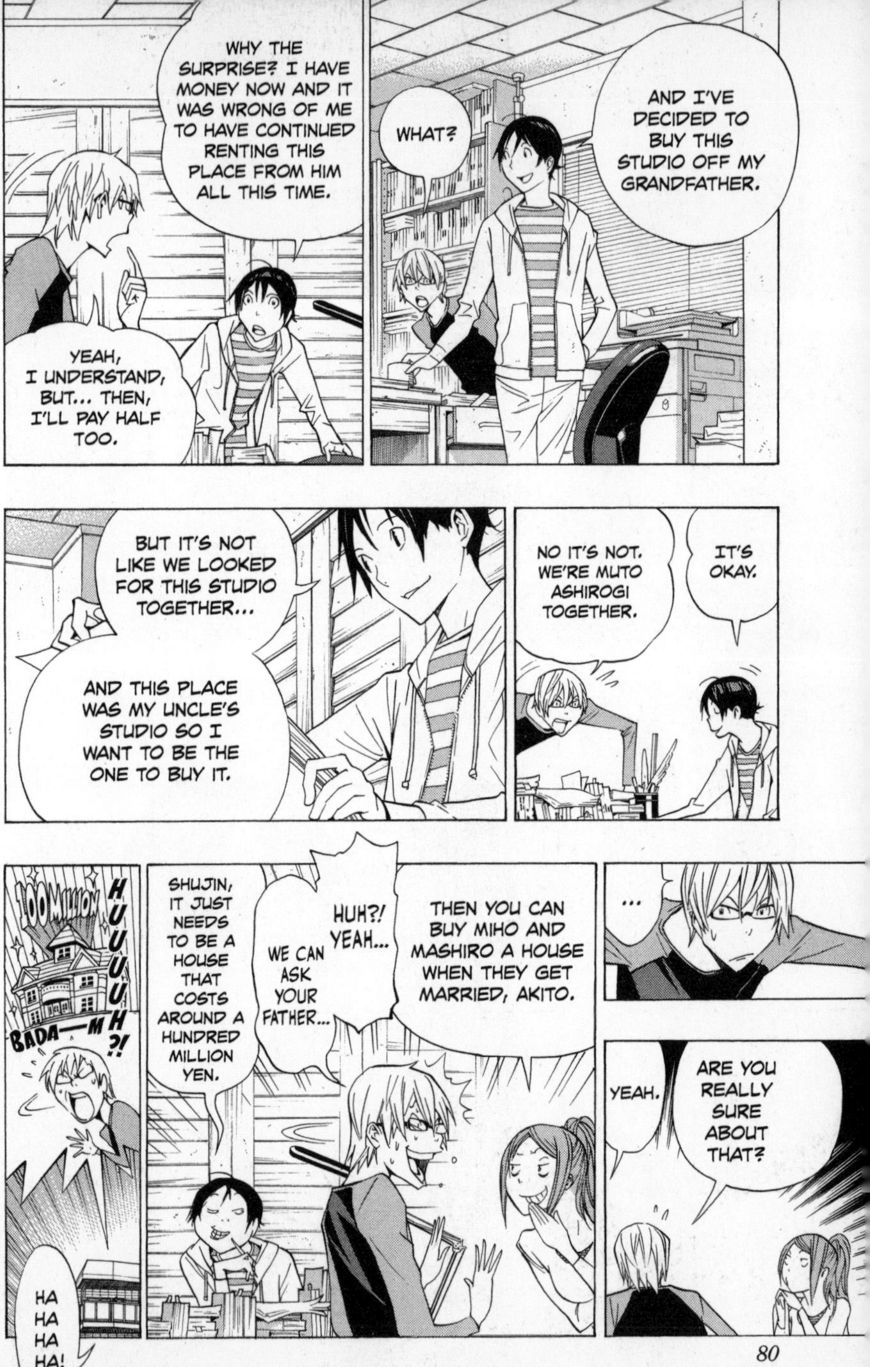
AND I'VE DECIDED TO BUY THIS STUDIO OFF MY GRANDFATHER.
WHAT?
WHY THE SURPRISE? I HAVE MONEY NOW AND IT WAS WRONG OF ME TO HAVE CONTINUED RENTING THIS PLACE FROM HIM ALL THIS TIME.
YEAH, I UNDERSTAND, BUT... THEN, I'LL PAY HALF TOO.
IT'S OKAY.
NO IT'S NOT. WE'RE MUTO ASHIROGI TOGETHER.
BUT IT'S NOT LIKE WE LOOKED FOR THIS STUDIO TOGETHER...
AND THIS PLACE WAS MY UNCLE'S STUDIO SO I WANT TO BE THE ONE TO BUY IT.
...
ARE YOU REALLY SURE ABOUT THAT?
YEAH.
THEN YOU CAN BUY MIHO AND MASHIRO A HOUSE WHEN THEY GET MARRIED, AKITO.
HUH?! YEAH...
WE CAN ASK YOUR FATHER...
SHUJIN, IT JUST NEEDS TO BE A HOUSE THAT COSTS AROUND A HUNDRED MILLION YEN.
HUUUUUH?!
100 MILLION
BADA—M
HA HA HA HA!

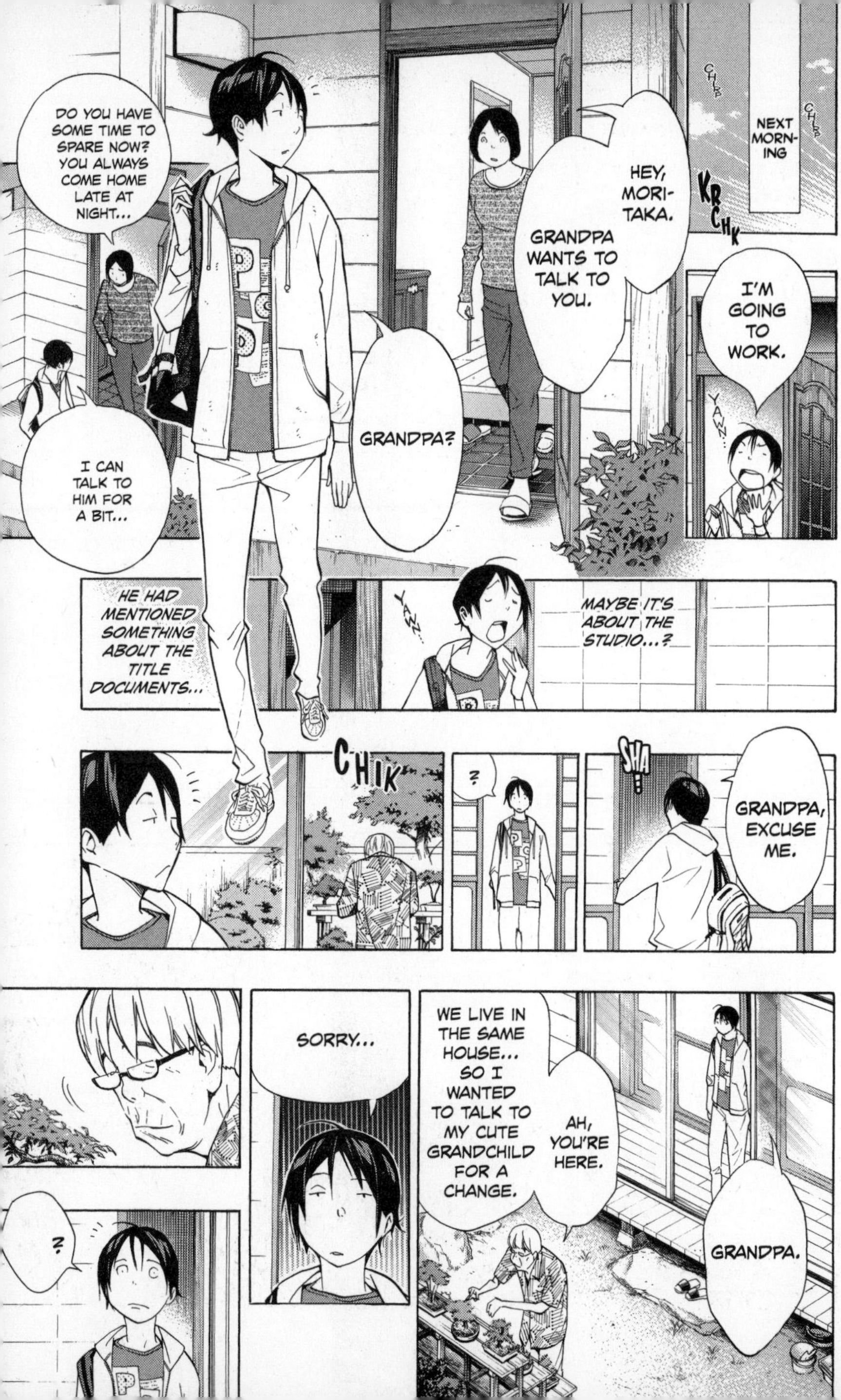

CHIRP
CHIRP
NEXT MORNING
KRCHK
I'M GOING TO WORK.
YAWN...
HEY, MORITAKA.
GRANDPA WANTS TO TALK TO YOU.
GRANDPA?
DO YOU HAVE SOME TIME TO SPARE NOW? YOU ALWAYS COME HOME LATE AT NIGHT...
I CAN TALK TO HIM FOR A BIT...
MAYBE IT'S ABOUT THE STUDIO...?
YAWN...
HE HAD MENTIONED SOMETHING ABOUT THE TITLE DOCUMENTS...
SHA
GRANDPA, EXCUSE ME.
?
CHIK
GRANDPA.
AH, YOU'RE HERE.
WE LIVE IN THE SAME HOUSE... SO I WANTED TO TALK TO MY CUTE GRANDCHILD FOR A CHANGE.
SORRY...
?

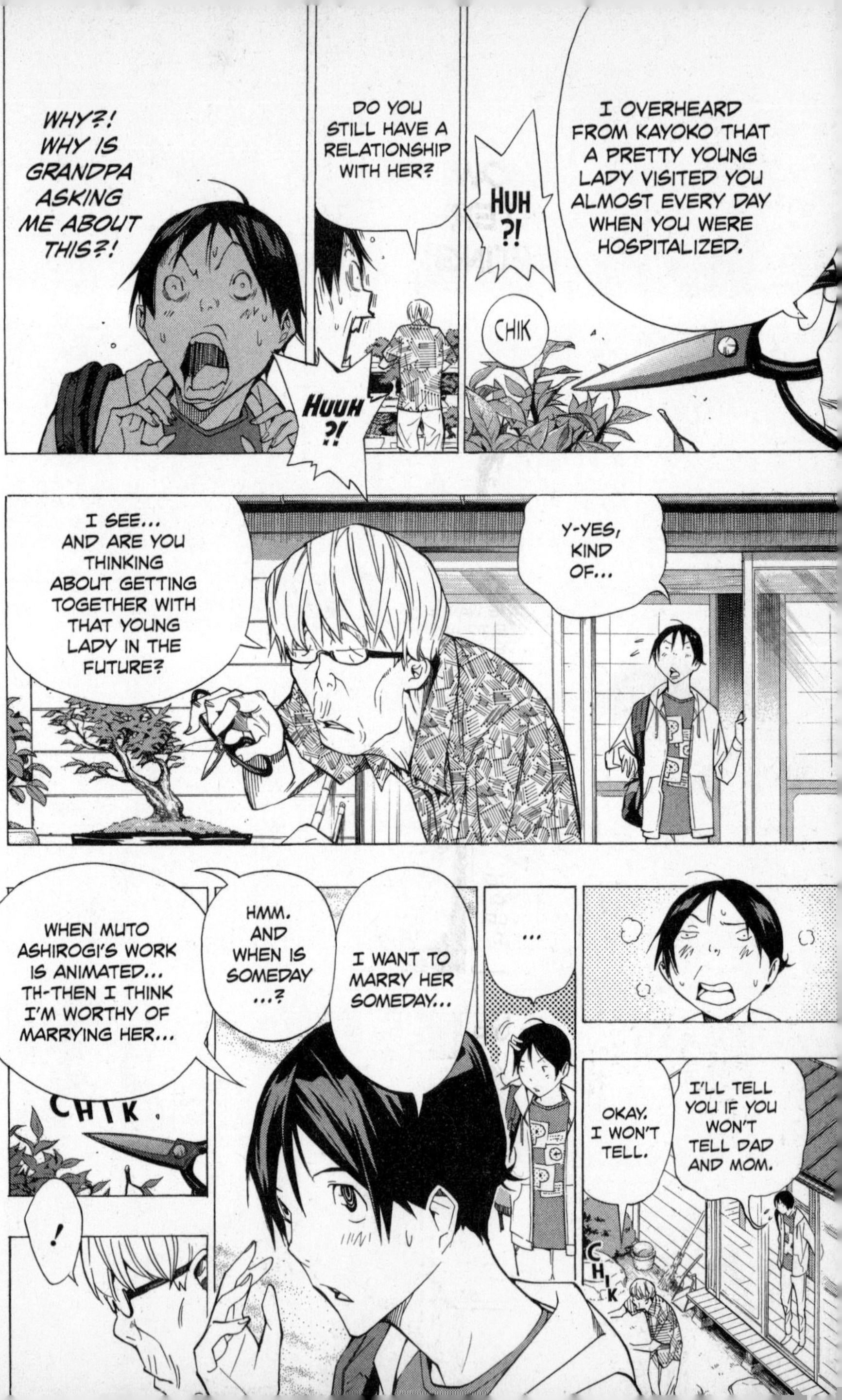
I OVERHEARD FROM KAYOKO THAT A PRETTY YOUNG LADY VISITED YOU ALMOST EVERY DAY WHEN YOU WERE HOSPITALIZED.
HUH ?!
CHIK
DO YOU STILL HAVE A RELATIONSHIP WITH HER?
HUUH ?!
WHY?! WHY IS GRANDPA ASKING ME ABOUT THIS?!
Y-YES, KIND OF...
I SEE... AND ARE YOU THINKING ABOUT GETTING TOGETHER WITH THAT YOUNG LADY IN THE FUTURE?
...
I'LL TELL YOU IF YOU WON'T TELL DAD AND MOM.
OKAY. I WON'T TELL.
CHIK
I WANT TO MARRY HER SOMEDAY...
HMM. AND WHEN IS SOMEDAY...?
WHEN MUTO ASHIROGI'S WORK IS ANIMATED... TH-THEN I THINK I'M WORTHY OF MARRYING HER...
CHIK
!

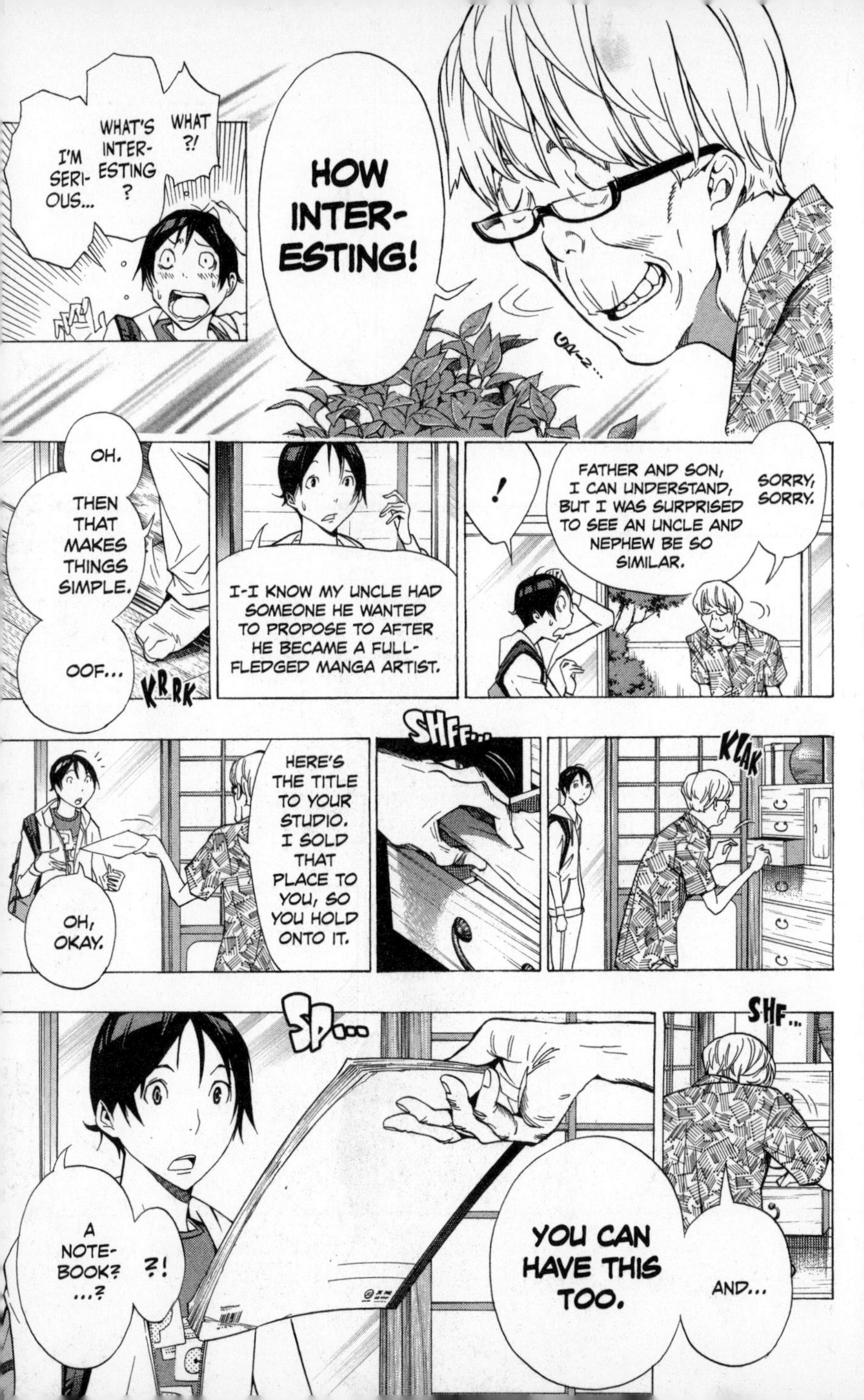
HOW INTER-ESTING!
WHAT ?!
WHAT'S INTER-ESTING ?
I'M SERI-OUS...
SORRY, SORRY.
FATHER AND SON, I CAN UNDERSTAND, BUT I WAS SURPRISED TO SEE AN UNCLE AND NEPHEW BE SO SIMILAR.
!
I-I KNOW MY UNCLE HAD SOMEONE HE WANTED TO PROPOSE TO AFTER HE BECAME A FULL-FLEDGED MANGA ARTIST.
OH.
THEN THAT MAKES THINGS SIMPLE.
OOF...
KRRK
KLAK
SHFF...
HERE'S THE TITLE TO YOUR STUDIO. I SOLD THAT PLACE TO YOU, SO YOU HOLD ONTO IT.
OH, OKAY.
SHF...
AND...
YOU CAN HAVE THIS TOO.
SP...
A NOTE-BOOK? ...?
?!

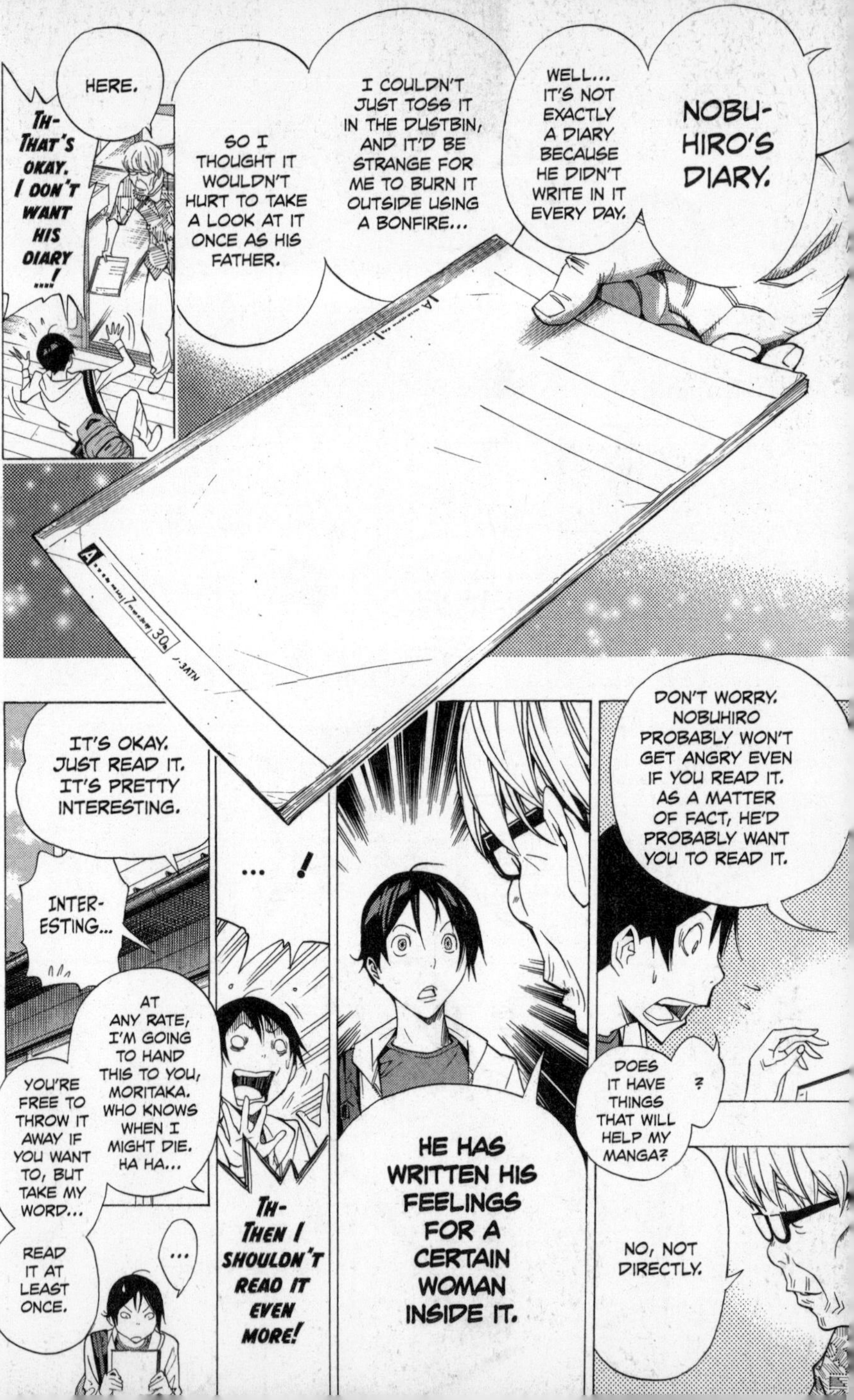
NOBUHIRO'S DIARY.
WELL... IT'S NOT EXACTLY A DIARY BECAUSE HE DIDN'T WRITE IN IT EVERY DAY.
I COULDN'T JUST TOSS IT IN THE DUSTBIN, AND IT'D BE STRANGE FOR ME TO BURN IT OUTSIDE USING A BONFIRE...
SO I THOUGHT IT WOULDN'T HURT TO TAKE A LOOK AT IT ONCE AS HIS FATHER.
HERE.
TH-THAT'S OKAY. I DON'T WANT HIS DIARY...!
DON'T WORRY. NOBUHIRO PROBABLY WON'T GET ANGRY EVEN IF YOU READ IT. AS A MATTER OF FACT, HE'D PROBABLY WANT YOU TO READ IT.
DOES IT HAVE THINGS THAT WILL HELP MY MANGA?
NO, NOT DIRECTLY.
HE HAS WRITTEN HIS FEELINGS FOR A CERTAIN WOMAN INSIDE IT.
... !
TH-THEN I SHOULDN'T READ IT EVEN MORE!
IT'S OKAY. JUST READ IT. IT'S PRETTY INTERESTING.
INTERESTING...
AT ANY RATE, I'M GOING TO HAND THIS TO YOU, MORITAKA. WHO KNOWS WHEN I MIGHT DIE. HA HA...
YOU'RE FREE TO THROW IT AWAY IF YOU WANT TO, BUT TAKE MY WORD...
READ IT AT LEAST ONCE.
...

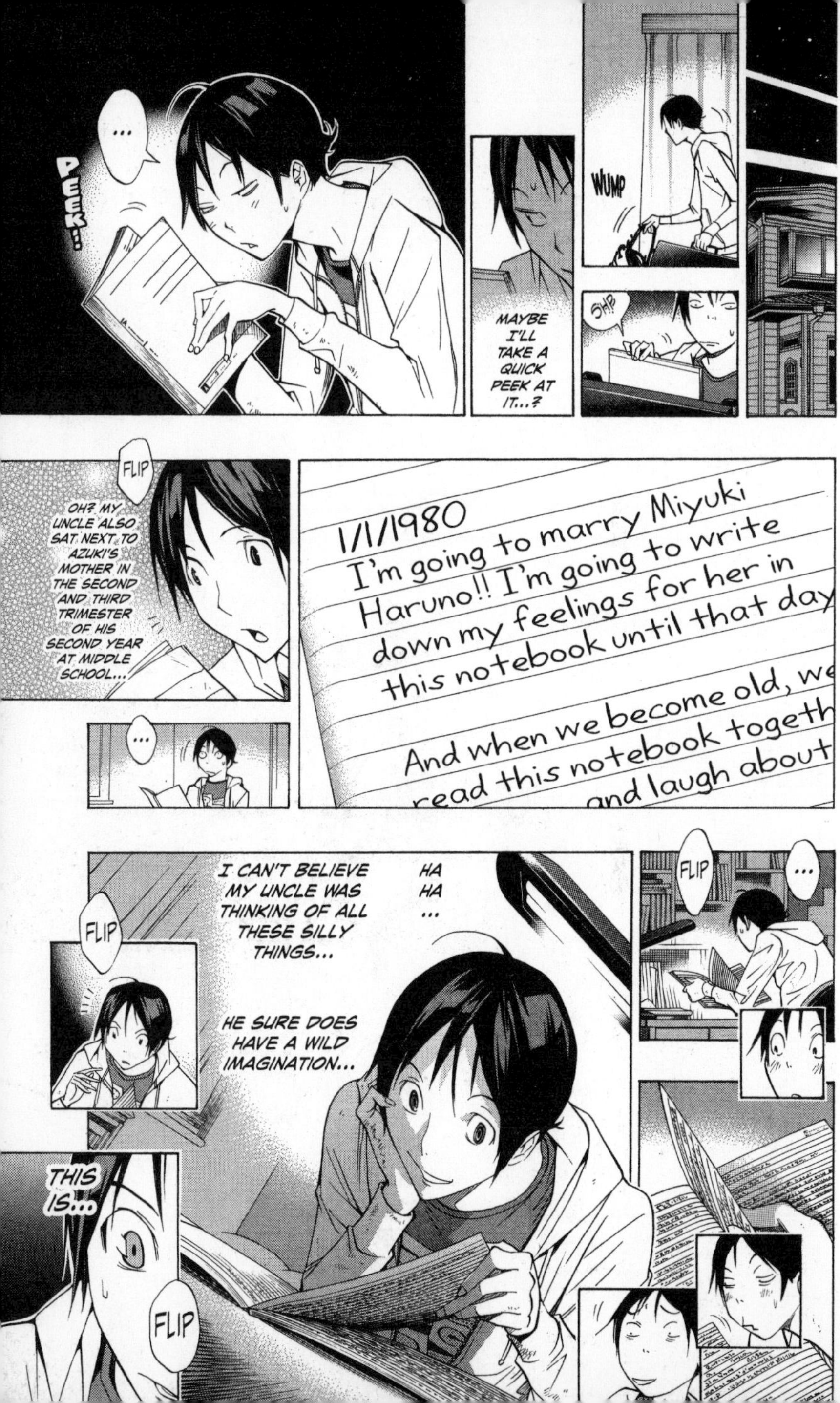
WUMP
SHP
MAYBE I'LL TAKE A QUICK PEEK AT IT...?
...
PEEK!!
1/1/1980
I'm going to marry Miyuki
Haruno!! I'm going to write
down my feelings for her in
this notebook until that day
And when we become old, we
read this notebook togeth
and laugh about
FLIP
OH? MY UNCLE ALSO SAT NEXT TO AZUKI'S MOTHER IN THE SECOND AND THIRD TRIMESTER OF HIS SECOND YEAR AT MIDDLE SCHOOL...
...
...
FLIP
HA HA ...
I CAN'T BELIEVE MY UNCLE WAS THINKING OF ALL THESE SILLY THINGS...
HE SURE DOES HAVE A WILD IMAGINATION...
FLIP
THIS IS...
FLIP

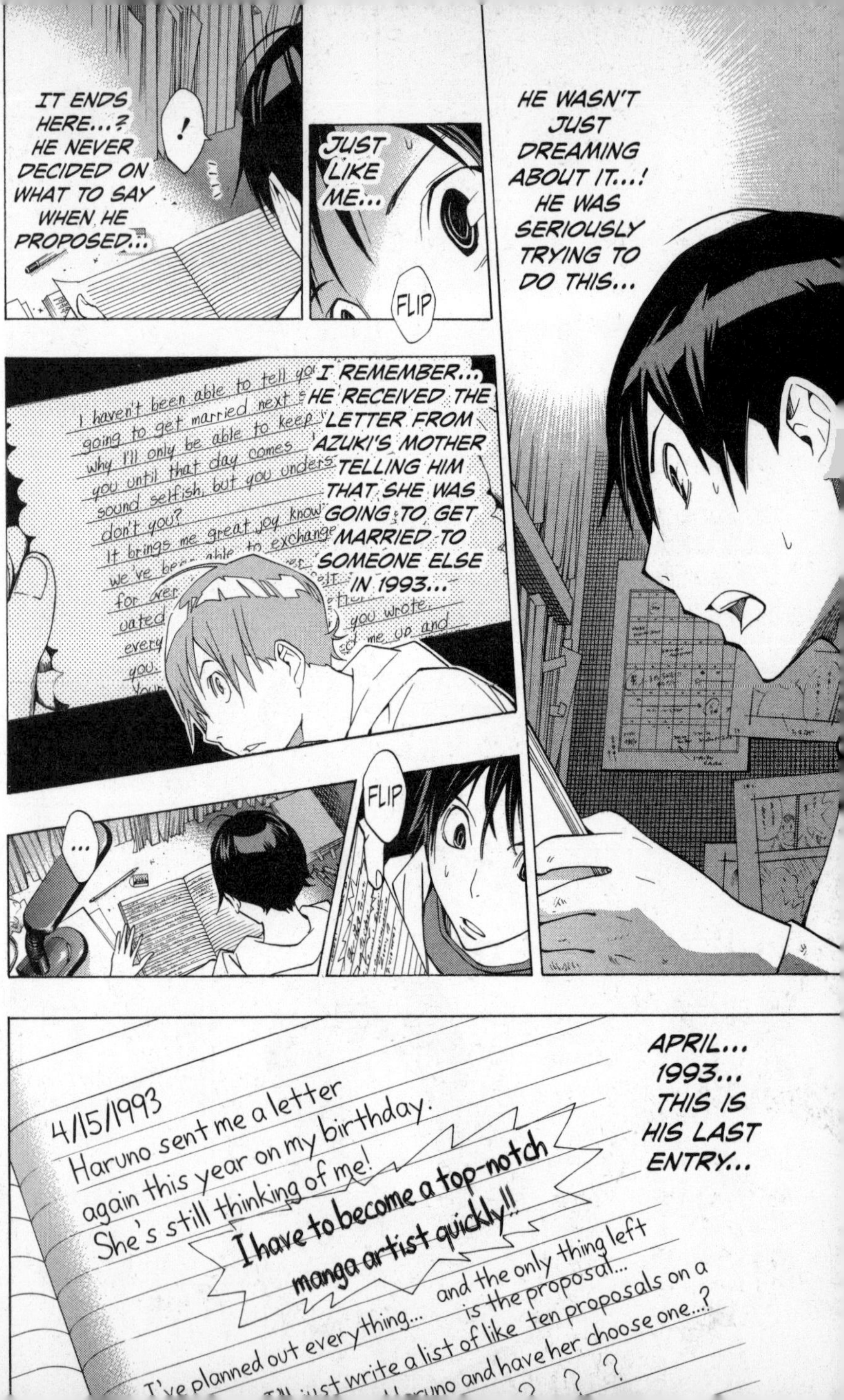
HE WASN'T JUST DREAMING ABOUT IT...! HE WAS SERIOUSLY TRYING TO DO THIS...
JUST LIKE ME...
FLIP
IT ENDS HERE...? HE NEVER DECIDED ON WHAT TO SAY WHEN HE PROPOSED...
!
I REMEMBER... HE RECEIVED THE LETTER FROM AZUKI'S MOTHER TELLING HIM THAT SHE WAS GOING TO GET MARRIED TO SOMEONE ELSE IN 1993...
I haven't been able to tell yo
going to get married next
why I'll only be able to keep
you until that day comes
sound selfish, but you unders
don't you?
It brings me great joy know
FLIP
...
APRIL... 1993... THIS IS HIS LAST ENTRY...
4/15/1993
Haruno sent me a letter
again this year on my birthday.
She's still thinking of me!
I have to become a top-notch manga artist quickly!!
I've planned out everything... and the only thing left is the proposal...
I'll just write a list of like ten proposals on a
Haruno and have her choose one...?
? ? ?

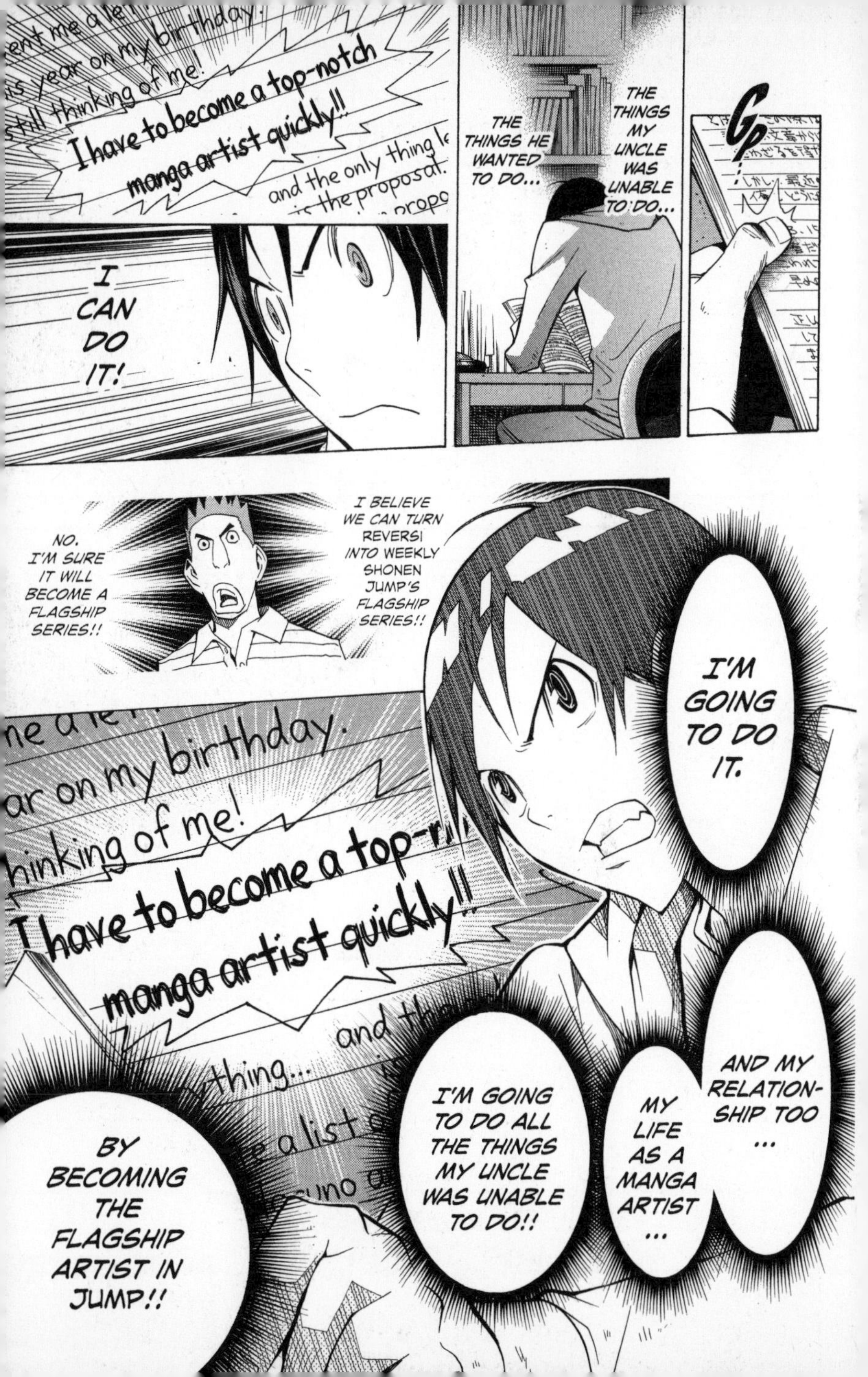
GP
THE THINGS MY UNCLE WAS UNABLE TO DO...
THE THINGS HE WANTED TO DO...
this year on my birthday
still thinking of me!
I have to become a top-notch manga artist quickly!!
and the only thing le
is the proposal.
I CAN DO IT!
I'M GOING TO DO IT.
I BELIEVE WE CAN TURN REVERSI INTO WEEKLY SHONEN JUMP'S FLAGSHIP SERIES!!
NO. I'M SURE IT WILL BECOME A FLAGSHIP SERIES!!
ar on my birthday.
hinking of me!
I have to become a top-
manga artist quickly!!
and the
thing...
a list
AND MY RELATION-SHIP TOO...
MY LIFE AS A MANGA ARTIST...
I'M GOING TO DO ALL THE THINGS MY UNCLE WAS UNABLE TO DO!!
BY BECOMING THE FLAGSHIP ARTIST IN JUMP!!

OHBA'S STORYBOARD

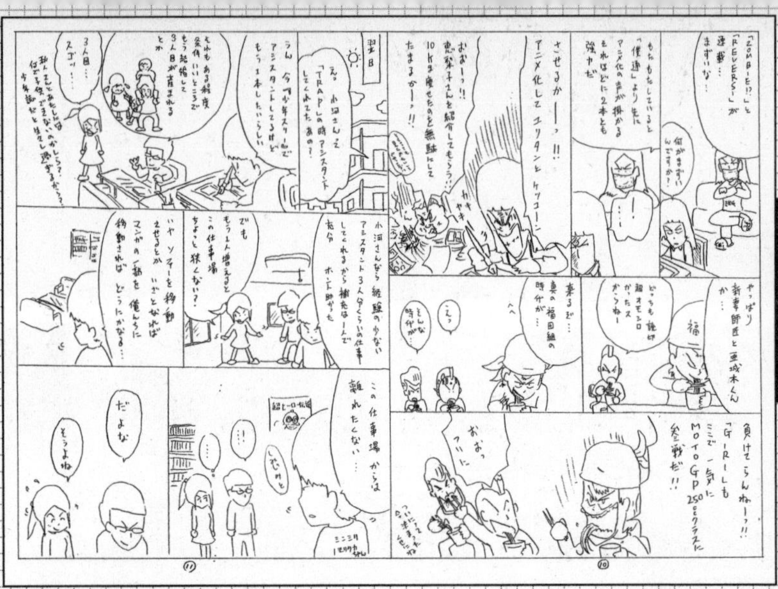

「ZOMBIE!!」と「REVERSI」が連載…
まずいな…
何がまずいんですか？
もたもたしていると「僕道」より先にアニメ化の声が掛かる それほどに2本とも強力だ
させるか——っ!! アニメ化してユリタンとケッコーン
おおーっ!! 恵梨子さんを紹介してもらう!! 10kgも痩せたのを無駄にしてたまるかーっ!!
やっぱり新妻師匠と亜城木くんか…
どっちも読切超オモシロかったスからねー
来るぞ…真の福田組の時代が…
えっ そんな時代が…
負けてらんねーっ!! 「GIRL」もここで一気にMOTOGP250ccクラスに参戦だ!!
おおっ ついに
翌日
え、小河さんって「TRAP」の時アシスタントしてくれた あの？
うん 今少年スクールでアシスタントしてるけどもう1本したいらしい
3人目…スゴッ…
小河さんなら経験の少ないアシスタント3人分くらいの仕事してくれるから補充は1人で充分 ホント助かった
でも もう1人増えるとこの仕事場ちょっと狭くない？
いやソファーを移動させるとかいざとなればマンガの一部を俺んちに移動させればどうにかなる…
この仕事場からは離れたくない…
だよな
そうよね

OBATA'S STORYBOARD

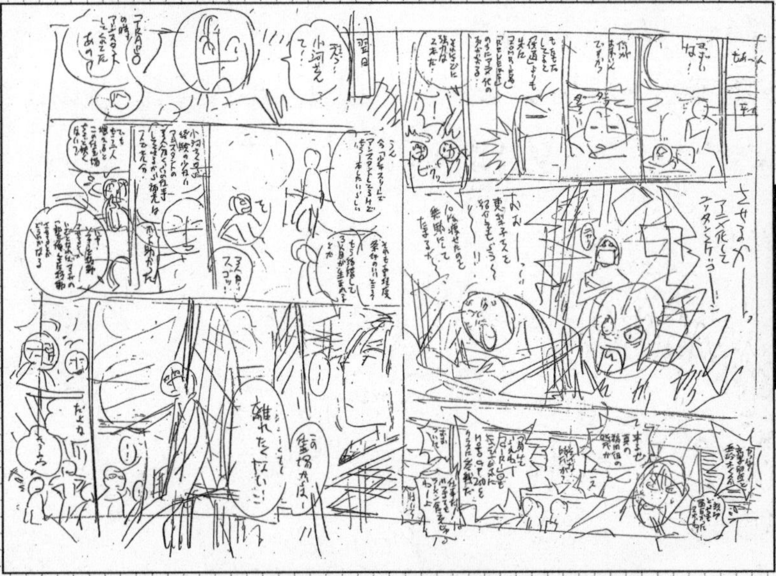

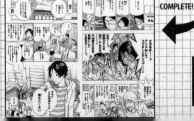

COMPLETE!

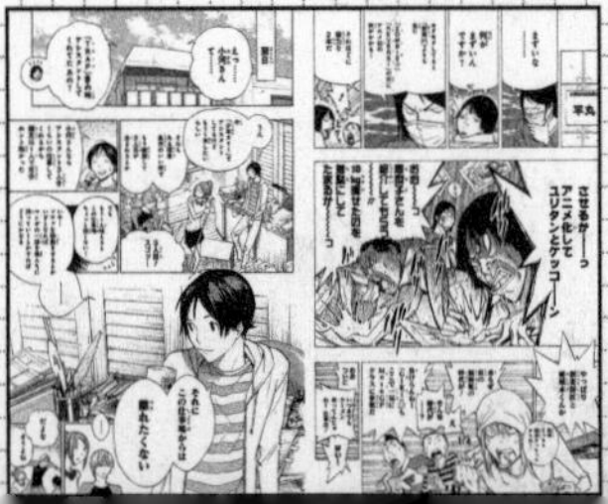

*CREATOR STORYBOARDS AND FINISHED PAGES IN JAPANESE

BAKUMAN。 vol.18

"Until the Final Draft Is Complete"

Chapter 155, pp. 78-79

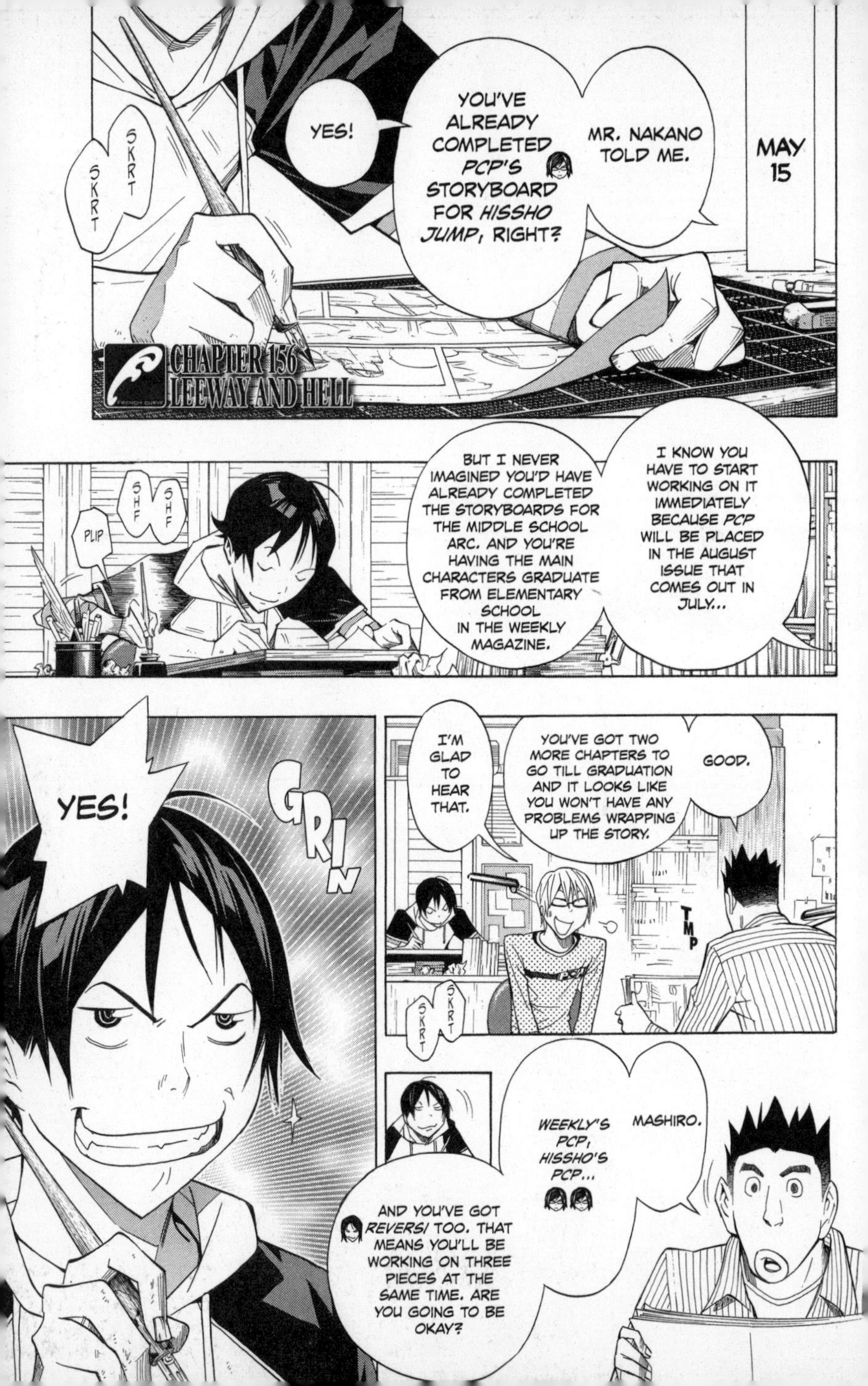
MAY 15
MR. NAKANO TOLD ME.
YOU'VE ALREADY COMPLETED *PCP'S* STORYBOARD FOR *HISSHO JUMP*, RIGHT?
YES!
SKRT SKRT
CHAPTER 156 LEEWAY AND HELL
I KNOW YOU HAVE TO START WORKING ON IT IMMEDIATELY BECAUSE *PCP* WILL BE PLACED IN THE AUGUST ISSUE THAT COMES OUT IN JULY...
BUT I NEVER IMAGINED YOU'D HAVE ALREADY COMPLETED THE STORYBOARDS FOR THE MIDDLE SCHOOL ARC. AND YOU'RE HAVING THE MAIN CHARACTERS GRADUATE FROM ELEMENTARY SCHOOL IN THE WEEKLY MAGAZINE.
SHF SHF
PLIP
GOOD.
YOU'VE GOT TWO MORE CHAPTERS TO GO TILL GRADUATION AND IT LOOKS LIKE YOU WON'T HAVE ANY PROBLEMS WRAPPING UP THE STORY.
I'M GLAD TO HEAR THAT.
TMP
SKRT SKRT
MASHIRO.
WEEKLY'S PCP, HISSHO'S PCP...
AND YOU'VE GOT *REVERSI* TOO. THAT MEANS YOU'LL BE WORKING ON THREE PIECES AT THE SAME TIME. ARE YOU GOING TO BE OKAY?
YES!
GRIN

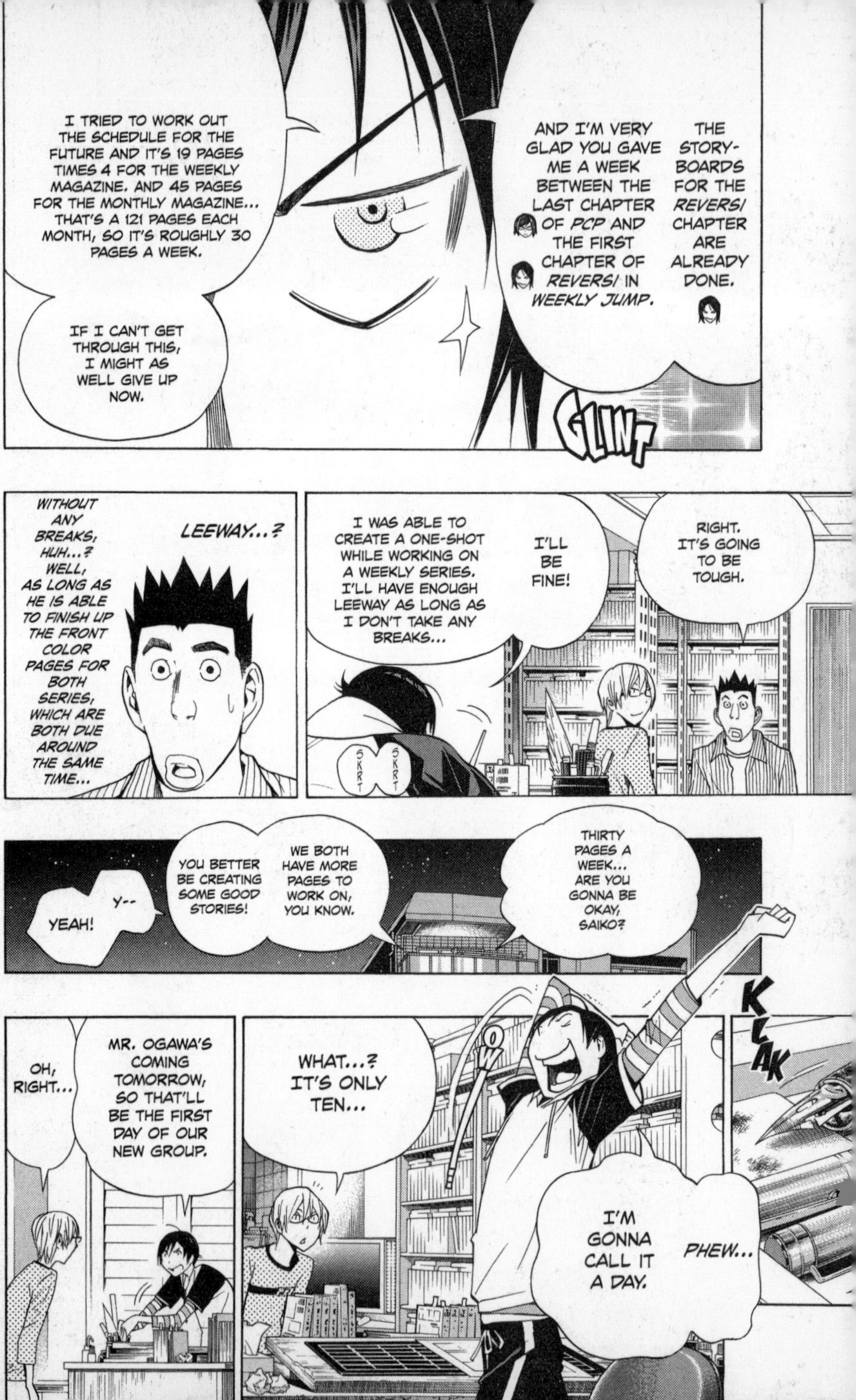
THE STORYBOARDS FOR THE *REVERSI* CHAPTER ARE ALREADY DONE.
AND I'M VERY GLAD YOU GAVE ME A WEEK BETWEEN THE LAST CHAPTER OF *PCP* AND THE FIRST CHAPTER OF *REVERSI* IN *WEEKLY JUMP*.
I TRIED TO WORK OUT THE SCHEDULE FOR THE FUTURE AND IT'S 19 PAGES TIMES 4 FOR THE WEEKLY MAGAZINE. AND 45 PAGES FOR THE MONTHLY MAGAZINE... THAT'S A 121 PAGES EACH MONTH, SO IT'S ROUGHLY 30 PAGES A WEEK.
IF I CAN'T GET THROUGH THIS, I MIGHT AS WELL GIVE UP NOW.
GLINT
RIGHT. IT'S GOING TO BE TOUGH.
I'LL BE FINE!
I WAS ABLE TO CREATE A ONE-SHOT WHILE WORKING ON A WEEKLY SERIES. I'LL HAVE ENOUGH LEEWAY AS LONG AS I DON'T TAKE ANY BREAKS...
SKRT
SKRT
LEEWAY...?
WITHOUT ANY BREAKS, HUH...? WELL, AS LONG AS HE IS ABLE TO FINISH UP THE FRONT COLOR PAGES FOR BOTH SERIES, WHICH ARE BOTH DUE AROUND THE SAME TIME...
THIRTY PAGES A WEEK... ARE YOU GONNA BE OKAY, SAIKO?
WE BOTH HAVE MORE PAGES TO WORK ON, YOU KNOW.
YOU BETTER BE CREATING SOME GOOD STORIES!
Y-- YEAH!
KLAK
PHEW...
I'M GONNA CALL IT A DAY.
OW
WHAT...? IT'S ONLY TEN...
MR. OGAWA'S COMING TOMORROW, SO THAT'LL BE THE FIRST DAY OF OUR NEW GROUP.
OH, RIGHT...

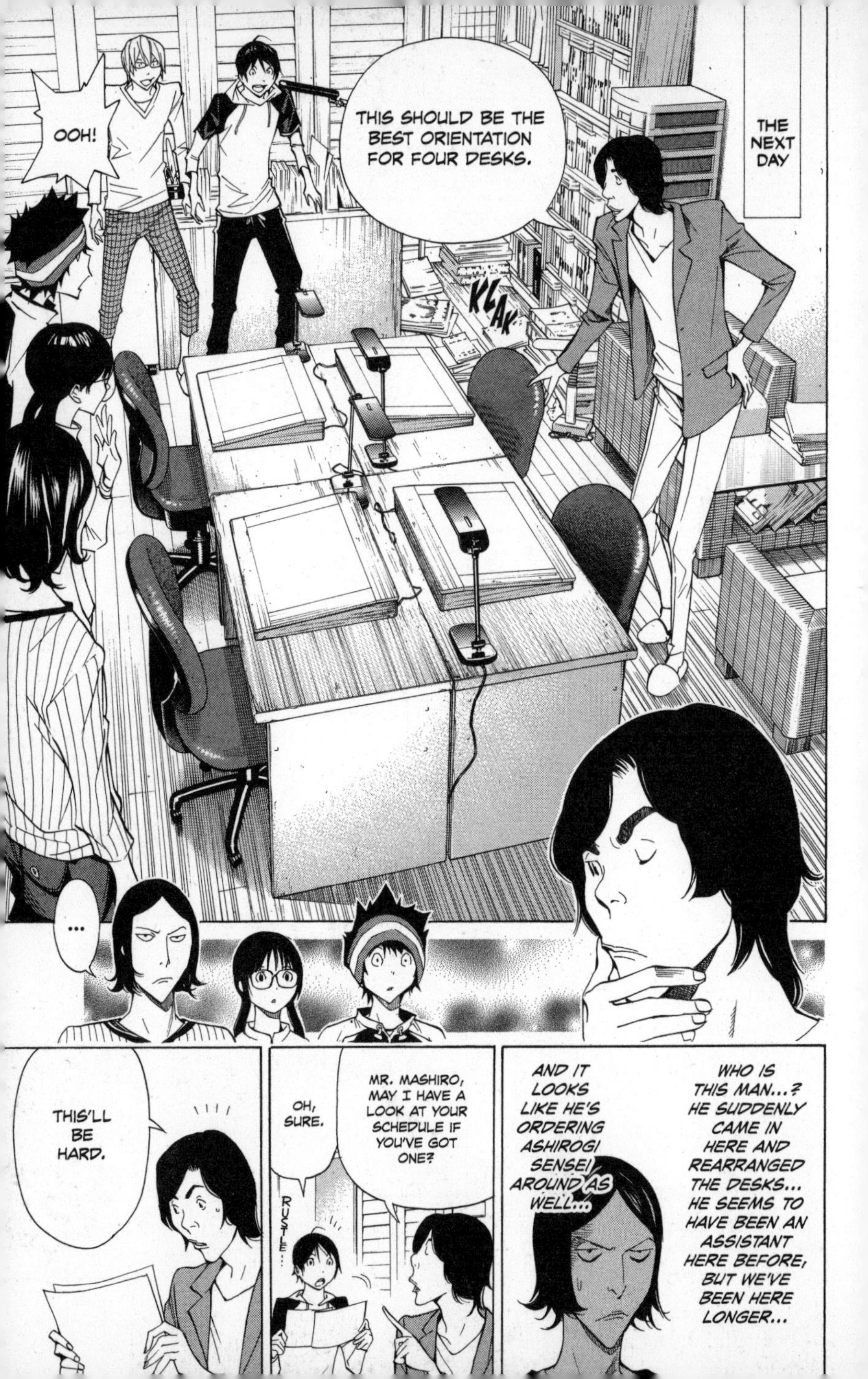
THE NEXT DAY
THIS SHOULD BE THE BEST ORIENTATION FOR FOUR DESKS.
KLAK
OOH!
...
WHO IS THIS MAN...? HE SUDDENLY CAME IN HERE AND REARRANGED THE DESKS... HE SEEMS TO HAVE BEEN AN ASSISTANT HERE BEFORE, BUT WE'VE BEEN HERE LONGER...
AND IT LOOKS LIKE HE'S ORDERING ASHIROGI SENSEI AROUND AS WELL...
MR. MASHIRO, MAY I HAVE A LOOK AT YOUR SCHEDULE IF YOU'VE GOT ONE?
OH, SURE.
RUSTLE...
THIS'LL BE HARD.

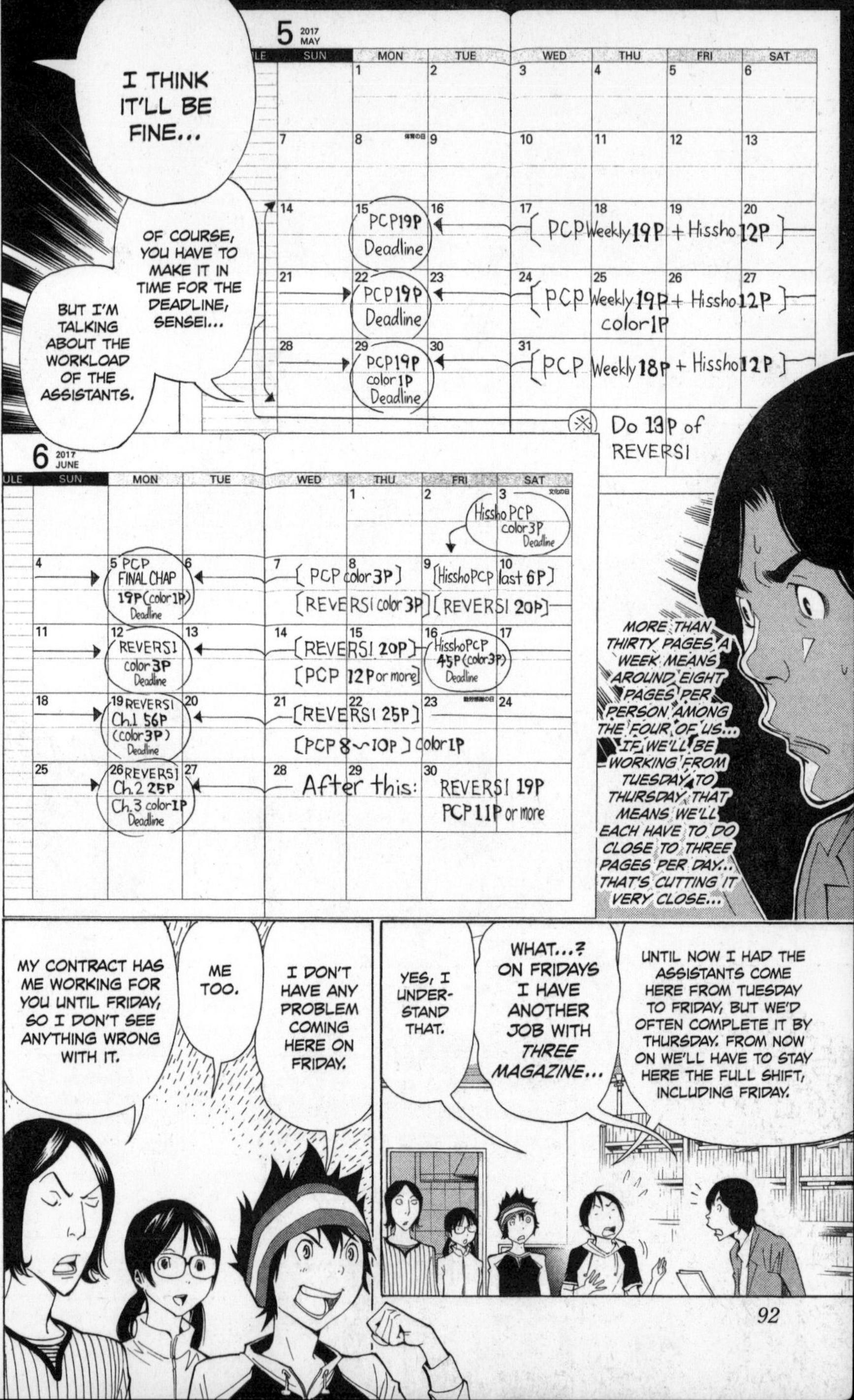

5 2017 MAY
SUN MON TUE WED THU FRI SAT
15 PCP 19P Deadline
[PCP Weekly 19P + Hissho 12P]
22 PCP 19P Deadline
[PCP Weekly 19P + Hissho 12P] color 1P
29 PCP 19P color 1P Deadline
[PCP Weekly 18P + Hissho 12P]
※ Do 13P of REVERSI
I THINK IT'LL BE FINE...
OF COURSE, YOU HAVE TO MAKE IT IN TIME FOR THE DEADLINE, SENSEI...
BUT I'M TALKING ABOUT THE WORKLOAD OF THE ASSISTANTS.
6 2017 JUNE
SUN MON TUE WED THU FRI SAT
3 Hissho PCP color 3P Deadline
5 PCP FINAL CHAP 19P (color 1P) Deadline
[PCP color 3P] [Hissho PCP last 6P]
[REVERSI color 3P] [REVERSI 20P]
12 REVERSI color 3P Deadline
[REVERSI 20P] [PCP 12P or more]
16 Hissho PCP 45P (color 3P) Deadline
19 REVERSI Ch.1 56P (color 3P) Deadline
[REVERSI 25P] [PCP 8~10P] color 1P
26 REVERSI Ch.2 25P Ch.3 color 1P Deadline
After this: REVERSI 19P PCP 11P or more
MORE THAN THIRTY PAGES A WEEK MEANS AROUND EIGHT PAGES PER PERSON AMONG THE FOUR OF US... IF WE'LL BE WORKING FROM TUESDAY TO THURSDAY THAT MEANS WE'LL EACH HAVE TO DO CLOSE TO THREE PAGES PER DAY... THAT'S CUTTING IT VERY CLOSE...
UNTIL NOW I HAD THE ASSISTANTS COME HERE FROM TUESDAY TO FRIDAY, BUT WE'D OFTEN COMPLETE IT BY THURSDAY. FROM NOW ON WE'LL HAVE TO STAY HERE THE FULL SHIFT, INCLUDING FRIDAY.
WHAT...? ON FRIDAYS I HAVE ANOTHER JOB WITH THREE MAGAZINE...
YES, I UNDERSTAND THAT.
I DON'T HAVE ANY PROBLEM COMING HERE ON FRIDAY.
ME TOO.
MY CONTRACT HAS ME WORKING FOR YOU UNTIL FRIDAY, SO I DON'T SEE ANYTHING WRONG WITH IT.

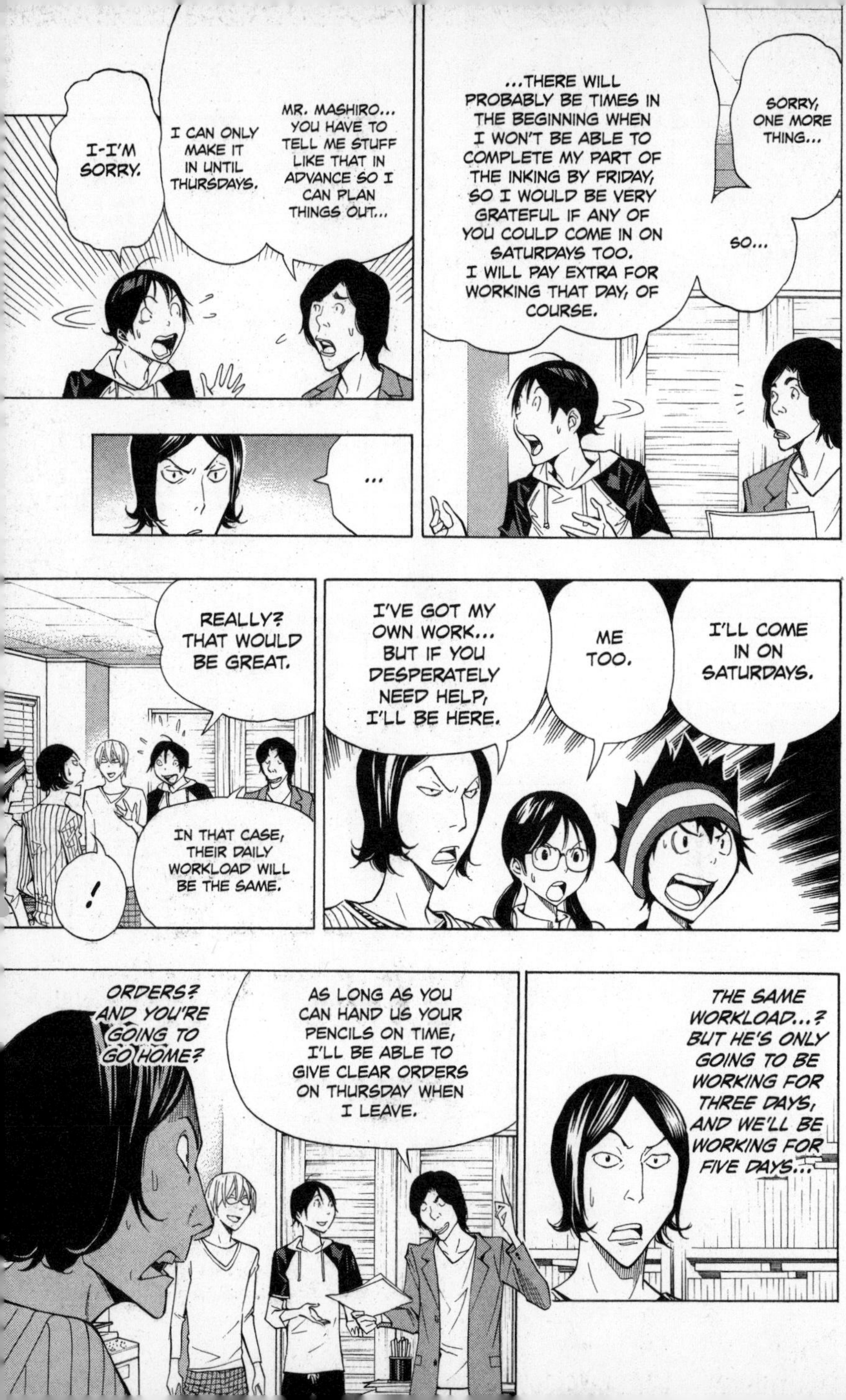
SORRY, ONE MORE THING...
SO...
...THERE WILL PROBABLY BE TIMES IN THE BEGINNING WHEN I WON'T BE ABLE TO COMPLETE MY PART OF THE INKING BY FRIDAY, SO I WOULD BE VERY GRATEFUL IF ANY OF YOU COULD COME IN ON SATURDAYS TOO. I WILL PAY EXTRA FOR WORKING THAT DAY, OF COURSE.
MR. MASHIRO... YOU HAVE TO TELL ME STUFF LIKE THAT IN ADVANCE SO I CAN PLAN THINGS OUT...
I CAN ONLY MAKE IT IN UNTIL THURSDAYS.
I-I'M SORRY.
...
I'LL COME IN ON SATURDAYS.
ME TOO.
I'VE GOT MY OWN WORK... BUT IF YOU DESPERATELY NEED HELP, I'LL BE HERE.
REALLY? THAT WOULD BE GREAT.
IN THAT CASE, THEIR DAILY WORKLOAD WILL BE THE SAME.
!
THE SAME WORKLOAD...? BUT HE'S ONLY GOING TO BE WORKING FOR THREE DAYS, AND WE'LL BE WORKING FOR FIVE DAYS...
AS LONG AS YOU CAN HAND US YOUR PENCILS ON TIME, I'LL BE ABLE TO GIVE CLEAR ORDERS ON THURSDAY WHEN I LEAVE.
ORDERS? AND YOU'RE GOING TO GO HOME?

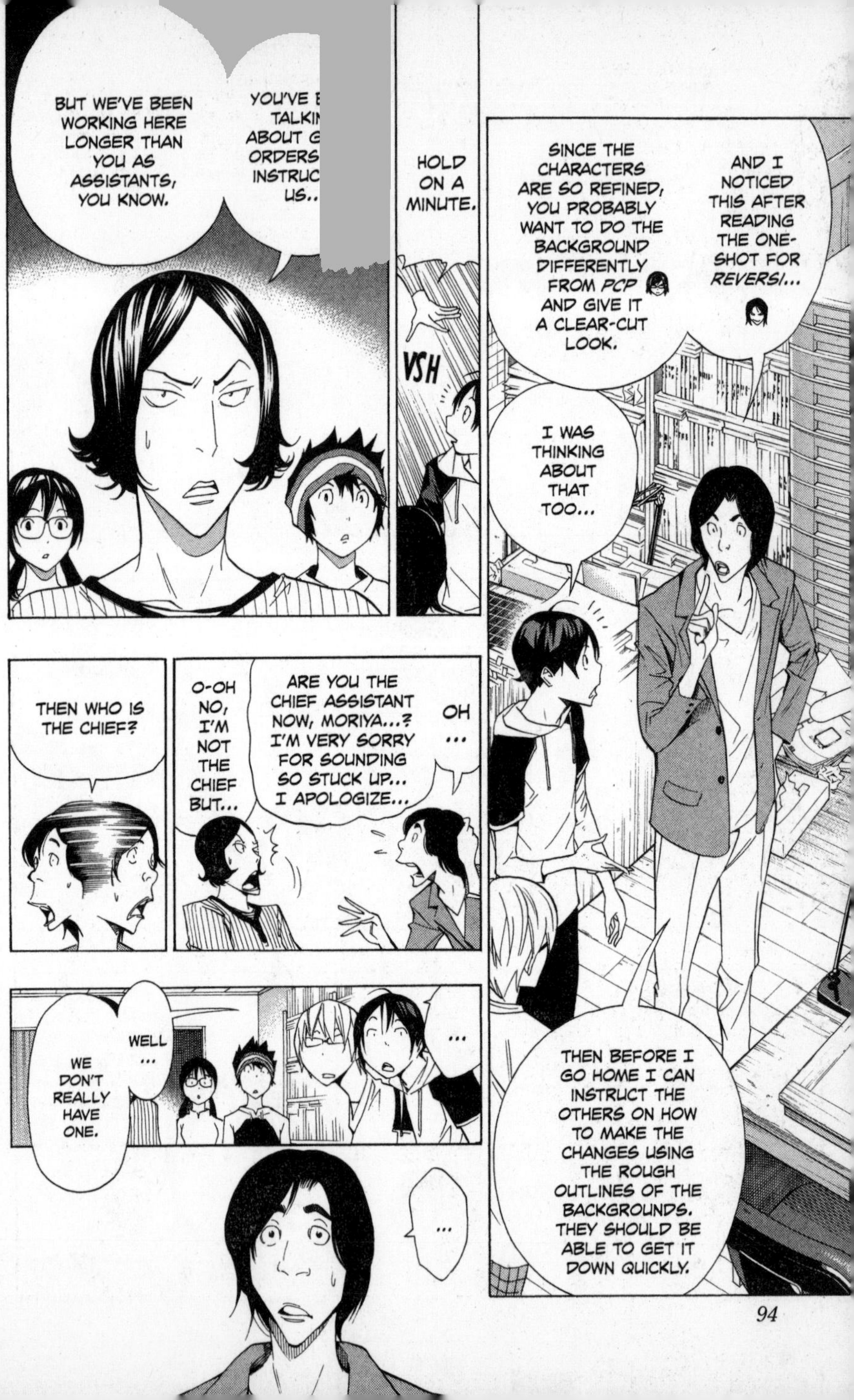

YOU'VE B TALKIN ABOUT G ORDERS INSTRUC US..
BUT WE'VE BEEN WORKING HERE LONGER THAN YOU AS ASSISTANTS, YOU KNOW.
HOLD ON A MINUTE.
VSH
AND I NOTICED THIS AFTER READING THE ONE-SHOT FOR *REVERSI*...
SINCE THE CHARACTERS ARE SO REFINED, YOU PROBABLY WANT TO DO THE BACKGROUND DIFFERENTLY FROM *PCP* AND GIVE IT A CLEAR-CUT LOOK.
I WAS THINKING ABOUT THAT TOO...
THEN BEFORE I GO HOME I CAN INSTRUCT THE OTHERS ON HOW TO MAKE THE CHANGES USING THE ROUGH OUTLINES OF THE BACKGROUNDS. THEY SHOULD BE ABLE TO GET IT DOWN QUICKLY.
OH ...
ARE YOU THE CHIEF ASSISTANT NOW, MORIYA...? I'M VERY SORRY FOR SOUNDING SO STUCK UP... I APOLOGIZE...
O-OH NO, I'M NOT THE CHIEF BUT...
THEN WHO IS THE CHIEF?
...
WELL ...
WE DON'T REALLY HAVE ONE.
...

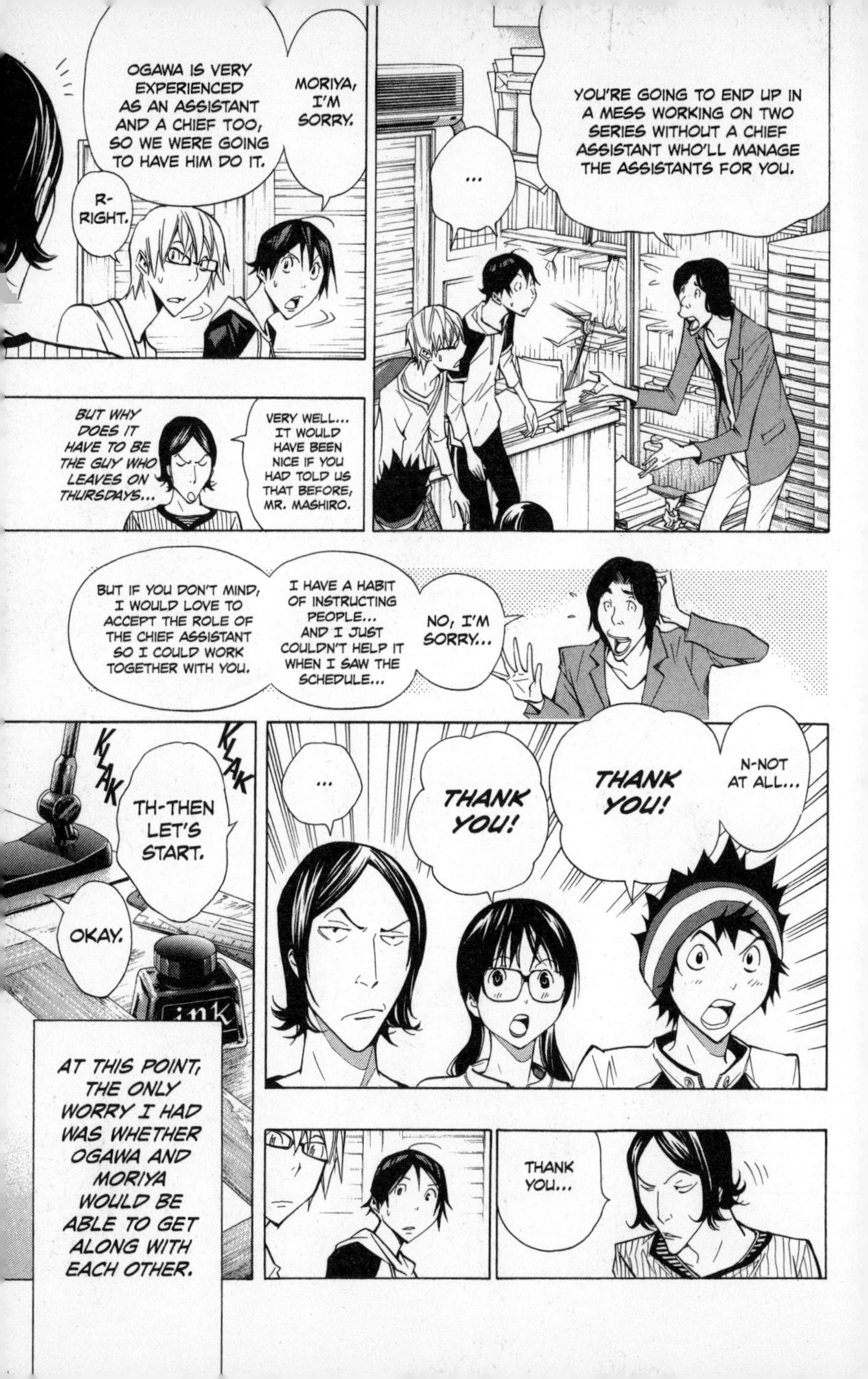

MORIYA, I'M SORRY.
OGAWA IS VERY EXPERIENCED AS AN ASSISTANT AND A CHIEF TOO, SO WE WERE GOING TO HAVE HIM DO IT.
R-RIGHT.
YOU'RE GOING TO END UP IN A MESS WORKING ON TWO SERIES WITHOUT A CHIEF ASSISTANT WHO'LL MANAGE THE ASSISTANTS FOR YOU.
...
VERY WELL... IT WOULD HAVE BEEN NICE IF YOU HAD TOLD US THAT BEFORE, MR. MASHIRO.
BUT WHY DOES IT HAVE TO BE THE GUY WHO LEAVES ON THURSDAYS...
NO, I'M SORRY...
I HAVE A HABIT OF INSTRUCTING PEOPLE... AND I JUST COULDN'T HELP IT WHEN I SAW THE SCHEDULE...
BUT IF YOU DON'T MIND, I WOULD LOVE TO ACCEPT THE ROLE OF THE CHIEF ASSISTANT SO I COULD WORK TOGETHER WITH YOU.
N-NOT AT ALL...
THANK YOU!
THANK YOU!
...
KLAK
KLAK
TH-THEN LET'S START.
OKAY.
THANK YOU...
AT THIS POINT, THE ONLY WORRY I HAD WAS WHETHER OGAWA AND MORIYA WOULD BE ABLE TO GET ALONG WITH EACH OTHER.

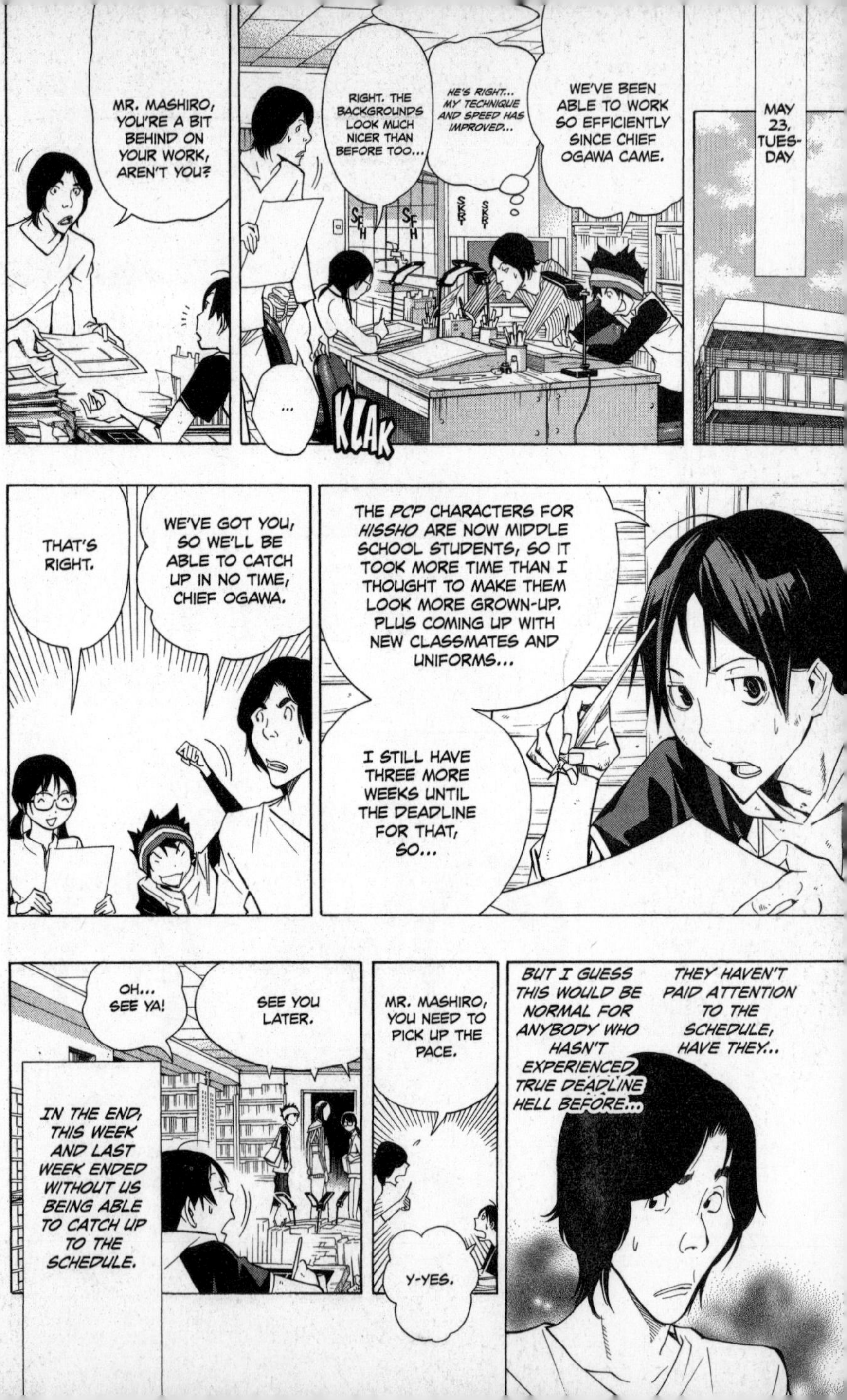
MAY 23, TUESDAY
WE'VE BEEN ABLE TO WORK SO EFFICIENTLY SINCE CHIEF OGAWA CAME.
HE'S RIGHT... MY TECHNIQUE AND SPEED HAS IMPROVED...
RIGHT. THE BACKGROUNDS LOOK MUCH NICER THAN BEFORE TOO...
SKRT
SKRT
SFH
SFH
...
KLAK
MR. MASHIRO, YOU'RE A BIT BEHIND ON YOUR WORK, AREN'T YOU?
THE PCP CHARACTERS FOR HISSHO ARE NOW MIDDLE SCHOOL STUDENTS, SO IT TOOK MORE TIME THAN I THOUGHT TO MAKE THEM LOOK MORE GROWN-UP. PLUS COMING UP WITH NEW CLASSMATES AND UNIFORMS...
I STILL HAVE THREE MORE WEEKS UNTIL THE DEADLINE FOR THAT, SO...
WE'VE GOT YOU, SO WE'LL BE ABLE TO CATCH UP IN NO TIME, CHIEF OGAWA.
THAT'S RIGHT.
THEY HAVEN'T PAID ATTENTION TO THE SCHEDULE, HAVE THEY...
BUT I GUESS THIS WOULD BE NORMAL FOR ANYBODY WHO HASN'T EXPERIENCED TRUE DEADLINE HELL BEFORE...
MR. MASHIRO, YOU NEED TO PICK UP THE PACE.
Y-YES.
SEE YOU LATER.
OH... SEE YA!
IN THE END, THIS WEEK AND LAST WEEK ENDED WITHOUT US BEING ABLE TO CATCH UP TO THE SCHEDULE.

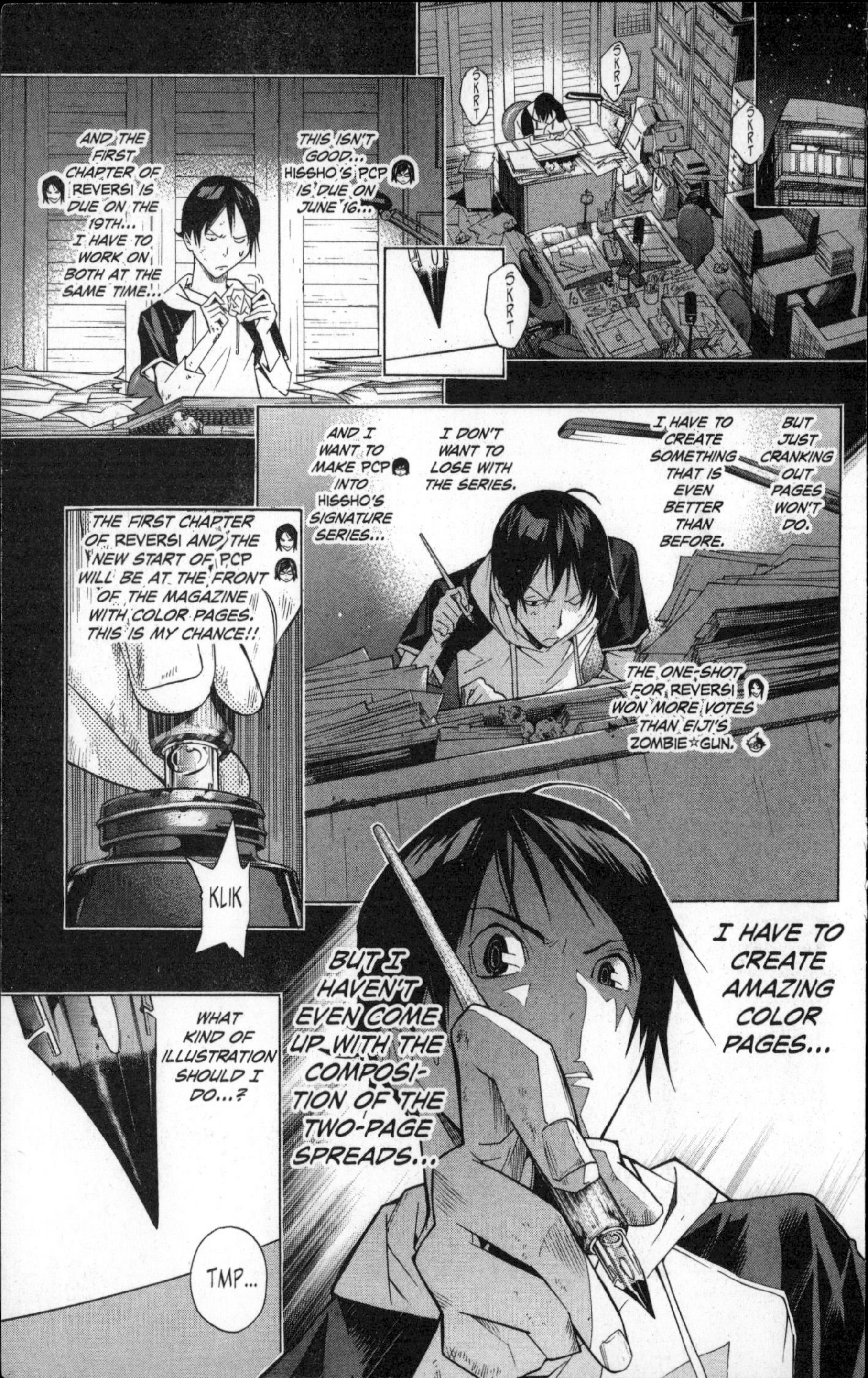

SKRT
SKRT
SKRT
SKRT
THIS ISN'T GOOD... HISSHO'S PCP IS DUE ON JUNE 16...
AND THE FIRST CHAPTER OF REVERSI IS DUE ON THE 19TH... I HAVE TO WORK ON BOTH AT THE SAME TIME...
BUT JUST CRANKING OUT PAGES WON'T DO.
I HAVE TO CREATE SOMETHING THAT IS EVEN BETTER THAN BEFORE.
I DON'T WANT TO LOSE WITH THE SERIES.
AND I WANT TO MAKE PCP INTO HISSHO'S SIGNATURE SERIES...
THE ONE-SHOT FOR REVERSI WON MORE VOTES THAN EIJI'S ZOMBIE☆GUN.
THE FIRST CHAPTER OF REVERSI AND THE NEW START OF PCP WILL BE AT THE FRONT OF THE MAGAZINE WITH COLOR PAGES. THIS IS MY CHANCE!!
KLIK
I HAVE TO CREATE AMAZING COLOR PAGES...
BUT I HAVEN'T EVEN COME UP WITH THE COMPOSITION OF THE TWO-PAGE SPREADS...
WHAT KIND OF ILLUSTRATION SHOULD I DO...?
TMP...

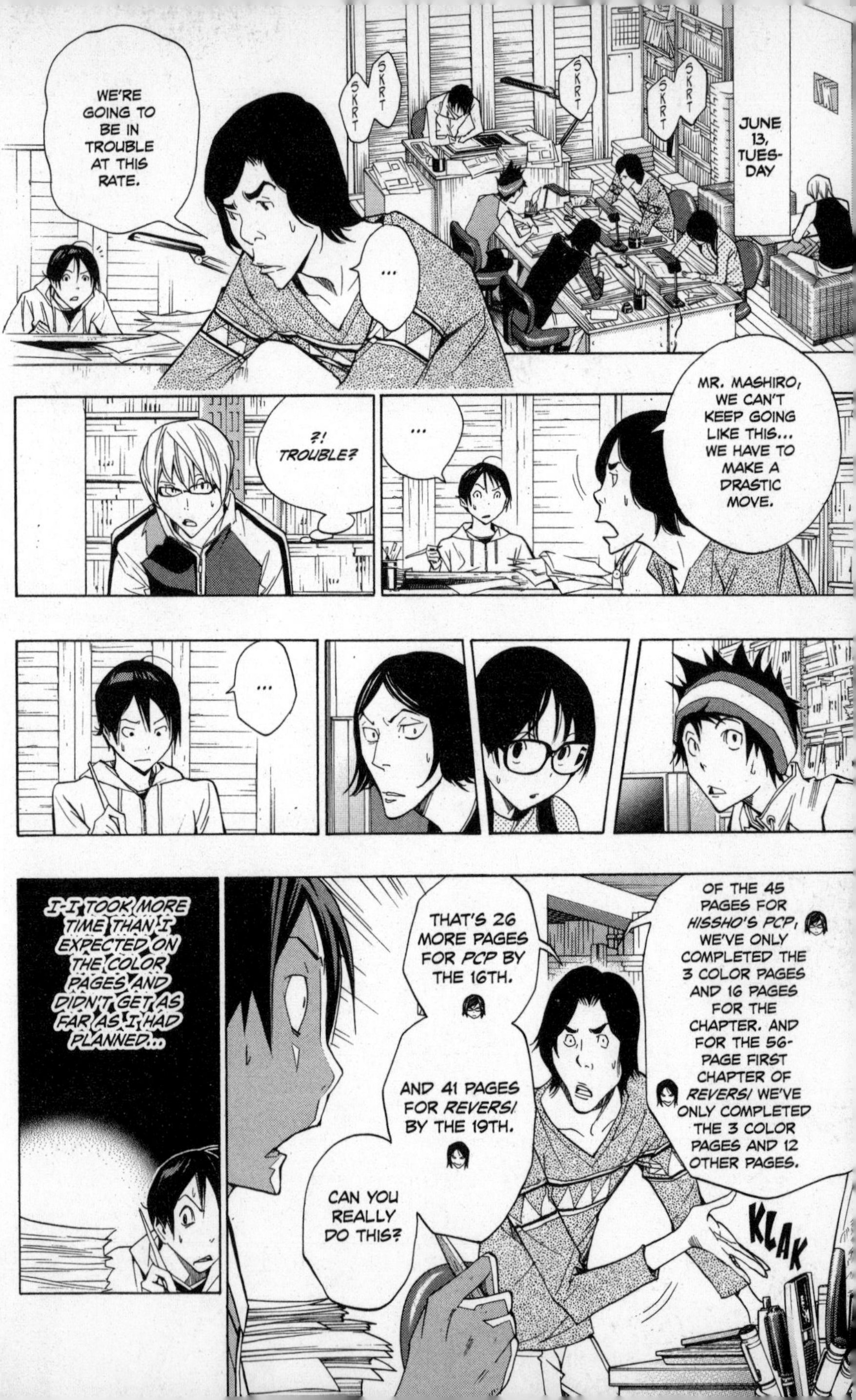
JUNE 13, TUESDAY
SKRT
SKRT
SKRT
SKRT
WE'RE GOING TO BE IN TROUBLE AT THIS RATE.
...
MR. MASHIRO, WE CAN'T KEEP GOING LIKE THIS... WE HAVE TO MAKE A DRASTIC MOVE.
...
?! TROUBLE?
...
OF THE 45 PAGES FOR HISSHO'S PCP, WE'VE ONLY COMPLETED THE 3 COLOR PAGES AND 16 PAGES FOR THE CHAPTER. AND FOR THE 56-PAGE FIRST CHAPTER OF REVERSI WE'VE ONLY COMPLETED THE 3 COLOR PAGES AND 12 OTHER PAGES.
KLAK
THAT'S 26 MORE PAGES FOR PCP BY THE 16TH.
AND 41 PAGES FOR REVERSI BY THE 19TH.
CAN YOU REALLY DO THIS?
I-I TOOK MORE TIME THAN I EXPECTED ON THE COLOR PAGES AND DIDN'T GET AS FAR AS I HAD PLANNED...

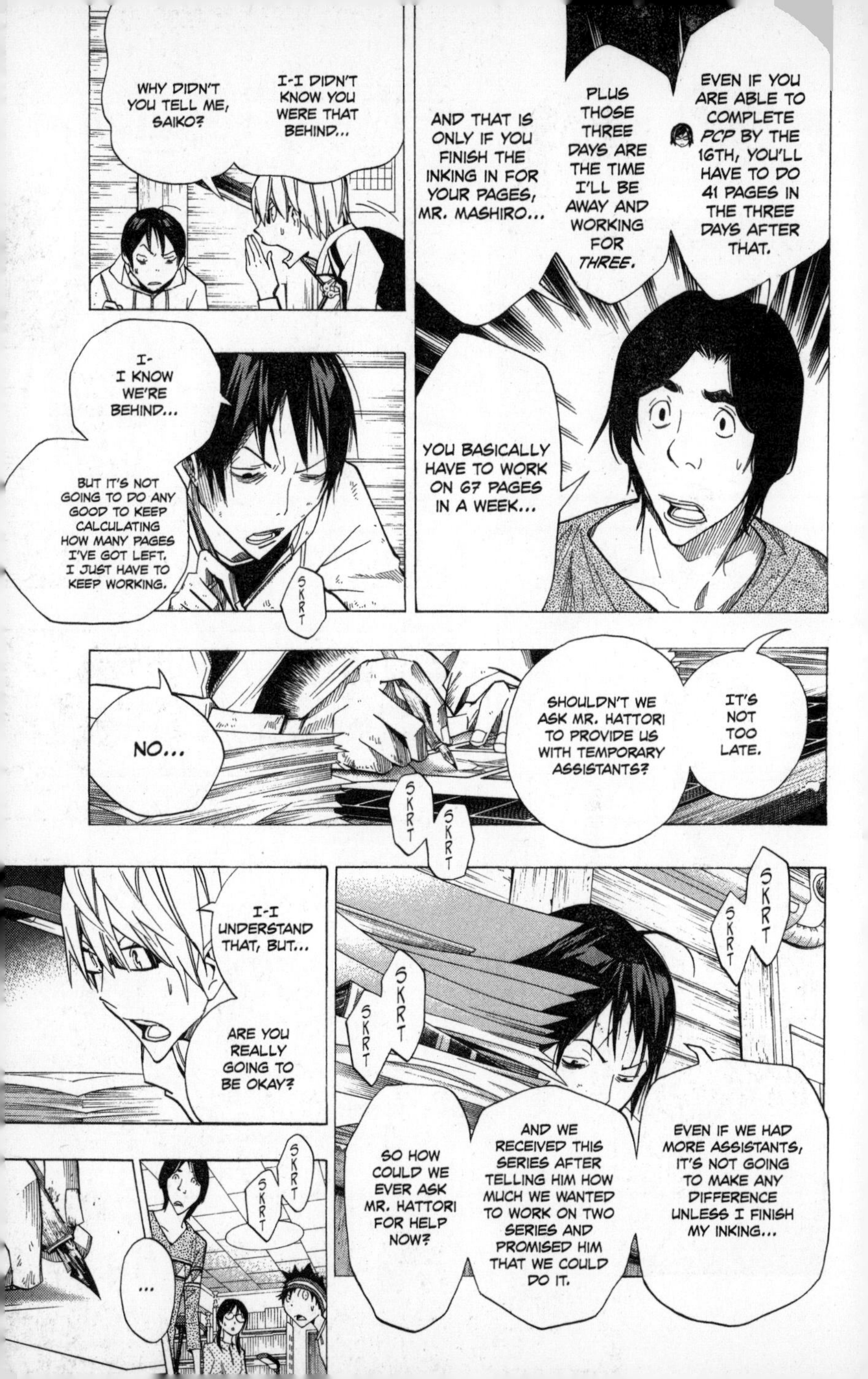

EVEN IF YOU ARE ABLE TO COMPLETE *PCP* BY THE 16TH, YOU'LL HAVE TO DO 41 PAGES IN THE THREE DAYS AFTER THAT.
PLUS THOSE THREE DAYS ARE THE TIME I'LL BE AWAY AND WORKING FOR *THREE*.
AND THAT IS ONLY IF YOU FINISH THE INKING IN FOR YOUR PAGES, MR. MASHIRO...
YOU BASICALLY HAVE TO WORK ON 67 PAGES IN A WEEK...
I-I DIDN'T KNOW YOU WERE THAT BEHIND...
WHY DIDN'T YOU TELL ME, SAIKO?
I- I KNOW WE'RE BEHIND...
BUT IT'S NOT GOING TO DO ANY GOOD TO KEEP CALCULATING HOW MANY PAGES I'VE GOT LEFT. I JUST HAVE TO KEEP WORKING.
SKRT
IT'S NOT TOO LATE.
SHOULDN'T WE ASK MR. HATTORI TO PROVIDE US WITH TEMPORARY ASSISTANTS?
SKRT
SKRT
NO...
SKRT
SKRT
EVEN IF WE HAD MORE ASSISTANTS, IT'S NOT GOING TO MAKE ANY DIFFERENCE UNLESS I FINISH MY INKING...
AND WE RECEIVED THIS SERIES AFTER TELLING HIM HOW MUCH WE WANTED TO WORK ON TWO SERIES AND PROMISED HIM THAT WE COULD DO IT.
SO HOW COULD WE EVER ASK MR. HATTORI FOR HELP NOW?
SKRT
SKRT
I-I UNDERSTAND THAT, BUT...
ARE YOU REALLY GOING TO BE OKAY?
SKRT
SKRT
...

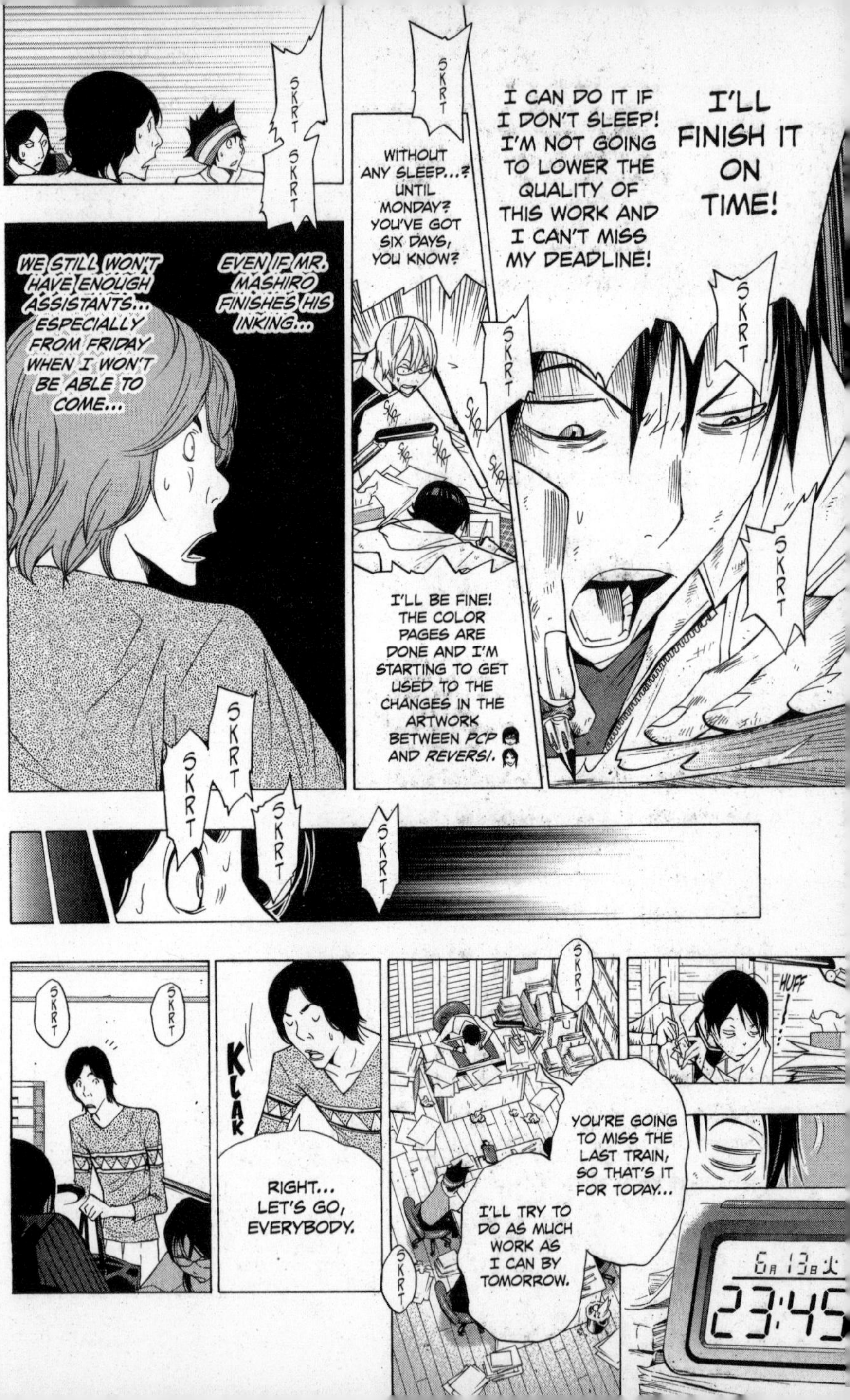
I'LL FINISH IT ON TIME!
SKRT
SKRT
I CAN DO IT IF I DON'T SLEEP! I'M NOT GOING TO LOWER THE QUALITY OF THIS WORK AND I CAN'T MISS MY DEADLINE!
SKRT
WITHOUT ANY SLEEP...? UNTIL MONDAY? YOU'VE GOT SIX DAYS, YOU KNOW?
SKRT
I'LL BE FINE! THE COLOR PAGES ARE DONE AND I'M STARTING TO GET USED TO THE CHANGES IN THE ARTWORK BETWEEN *PCP* AND *REVERSI*.
SKRT SKRT SKRT
EVEN IF MR. MASHIRO FINISHES HIS INKING...
WE STILL WON'T HAVE ENOUGH ASSISTANTS... ESPECIALLY FROM FRIDAY WHEN I WON'T BE ABLE TO COME...
SKRT
SKRT
SKRT
SKRT
6月13日火
23:45
HUFF
YOU'RE GOING TO MISS THE LAST TRAIN, SO THAT'S IT FOR TODAY...
I'LL TRY TO DO AS MUCH WORK AS I CAN BY TOMORROW.
SKRT
SKRT
KLAK
RIGHT... LET'S GO, EVERYBODY.
SKRT
SKRT

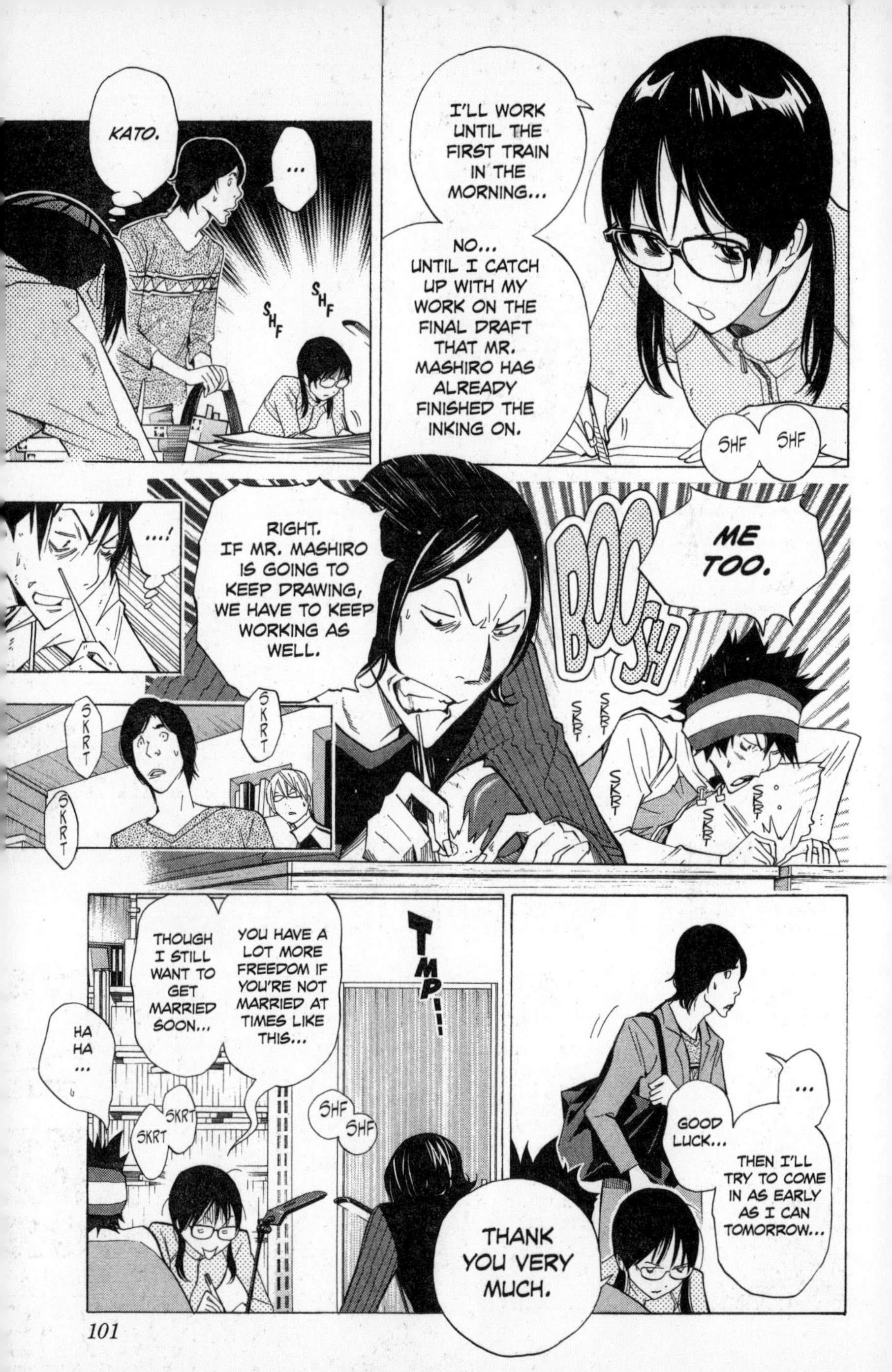
I'LL WORK UNTIL THE FIRST TRAIN IN THE MORNING...
NO... UNTIL I CATCH UP WITH MY WORK ON THE FINAL DRAFT THAT MR. MASHIRO HAS ALREADY FINISHED THE INKING ON.
SHF SHF
KATO.
...
SHF SHF
ME TOO.
BOOSH
SKRT SKRT
SKRT SKRT SKRT
RIGHT. IF MR. MASHIRO IS GOING TO KEEP DRAWING, WE HAVE TO KEEP WORKING AS WELL.
...!
SKRT SKRT SKRT
...
THEN I'LL TRY TO COME IN AS EARLY AS I CAN TOMORROW...
GOOD LUCK...
THANK YOU VERY MUCH.
TMP!!
YOU HAVE A LOT MORE FREEDOM IF YOU'RE NOT MARRIED AT TIMES LIKE THIS...
THOUGH I STILL WANT TO GET MARRIED SOON...
HA HA ...
SHF SHF
SKRT SKRT

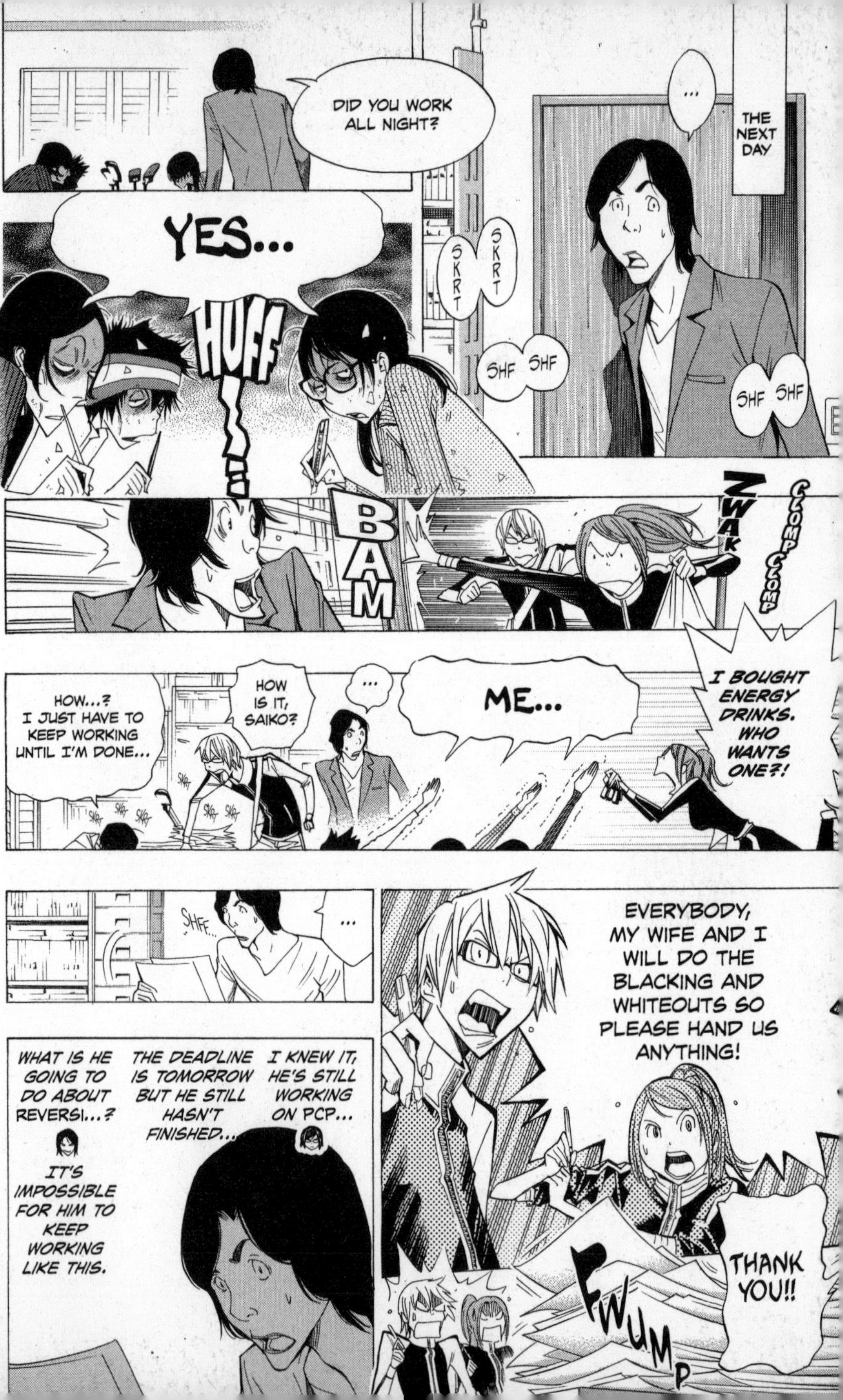
THE NEXT DAY
...
SKRT SKRT
SHF SHF
SHF SHF
DID YOU WORK ALL NIGHT?
YES...
HUFF
ZWAK
CLOMP CLOMP
BAM
I BOUGHT ENERGY DRINKS. WHO WANTS ONE?!
ME...
...
HOW IS IT, SAIKO?
HOW...? I JUST HAVE TO KEEP WORKING UNTIL I'M DONE...
EVERYBODY, MY WIFE AND I WILL DO THE BLACKING AND WHITEOUTS SO PLEASE HAND US ANYTHING!
THANK YOU!!
FWUMP
SHFF...
...
I KNEW IT, HE'S STILL WORKING ON PCP...
THE DEADLINE IS TOMORROW BUT HE STILL HASN'T FINISHED...
WHAT IS HE GOING TO DO ABOUT REVERSI...?
IT'S IMPOSSIBLE FOR HIM TO KEEP WORKING LIKE THIS.

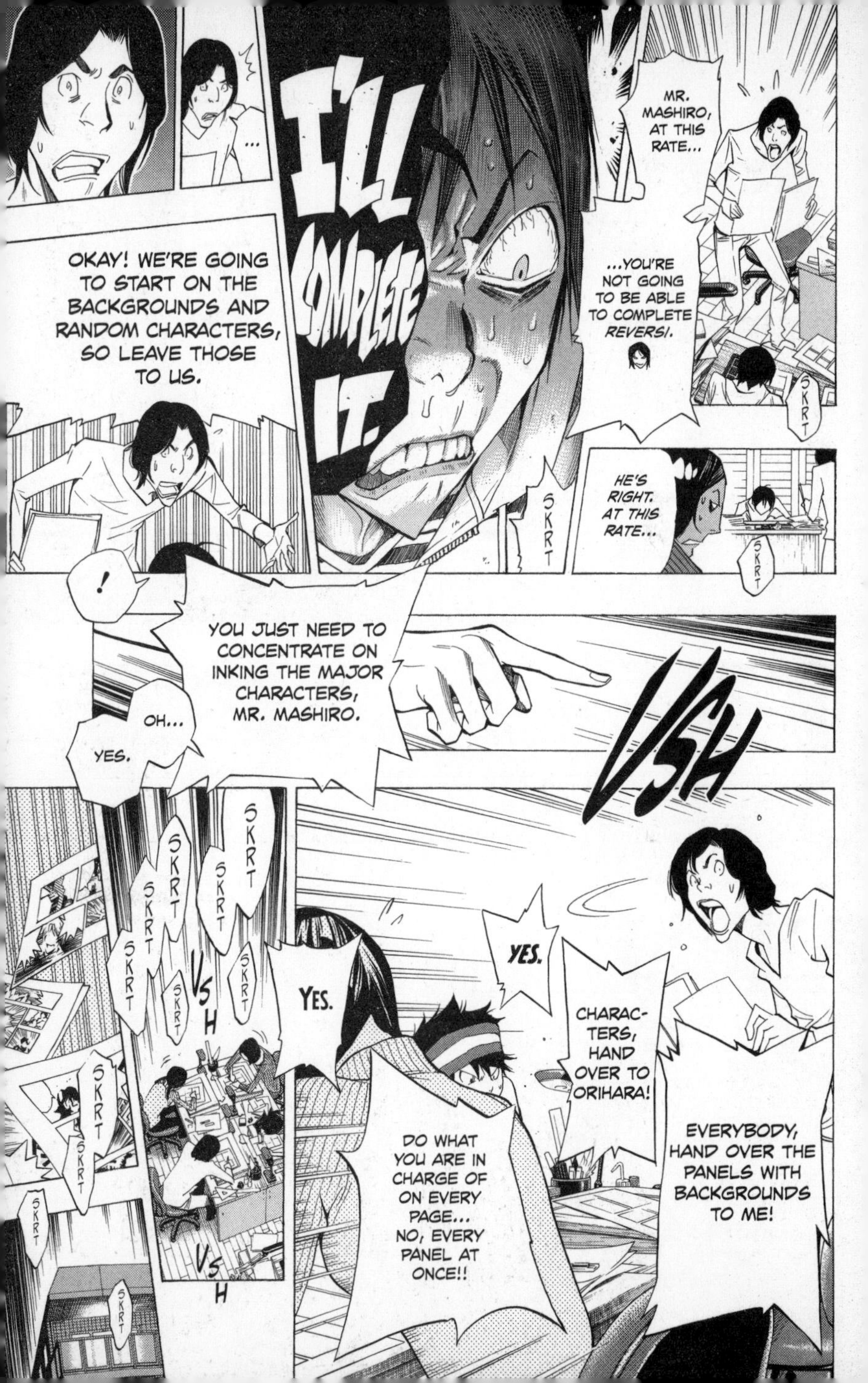

MR. MASHIRO, AT THIS RATE...
...YOU'RE NOT GOING TO BE ABLE TO COMPLETE *REVERSI*.
SKRT
HE'S RIGHT. AT THIS RATE...
SKRT
I'LL COMPLETE IT.
SKRT
...
OKAY! WE'RE GOING TO START ON THE BACKGROUNDS AND RANDOM CHARACTERS, SO LEAVE THOSE TO US.
!
VSH
YOU JUST NEED TO CONCENTRATE ON INKING THE MAJOR CHARACTERS, MR. MASHIRO.
OH...
YES.
EVERYBODY, HAND OVER THE PANELS WITH BACKGROUNDS TO ME!
CHARACTERS, HAND OVER TO ORIHARA!
YES.
YES.
DO WHAT YOU ARE IN CHARGE OF ON EVERY PAGE... NO, EVERY PANEL AT ONCE!!
SKRT
SKRT
SKRT
SKRT
VSH
SKRT
SKRT
SKRT
SKRT
SKRT
VSH
SKRT

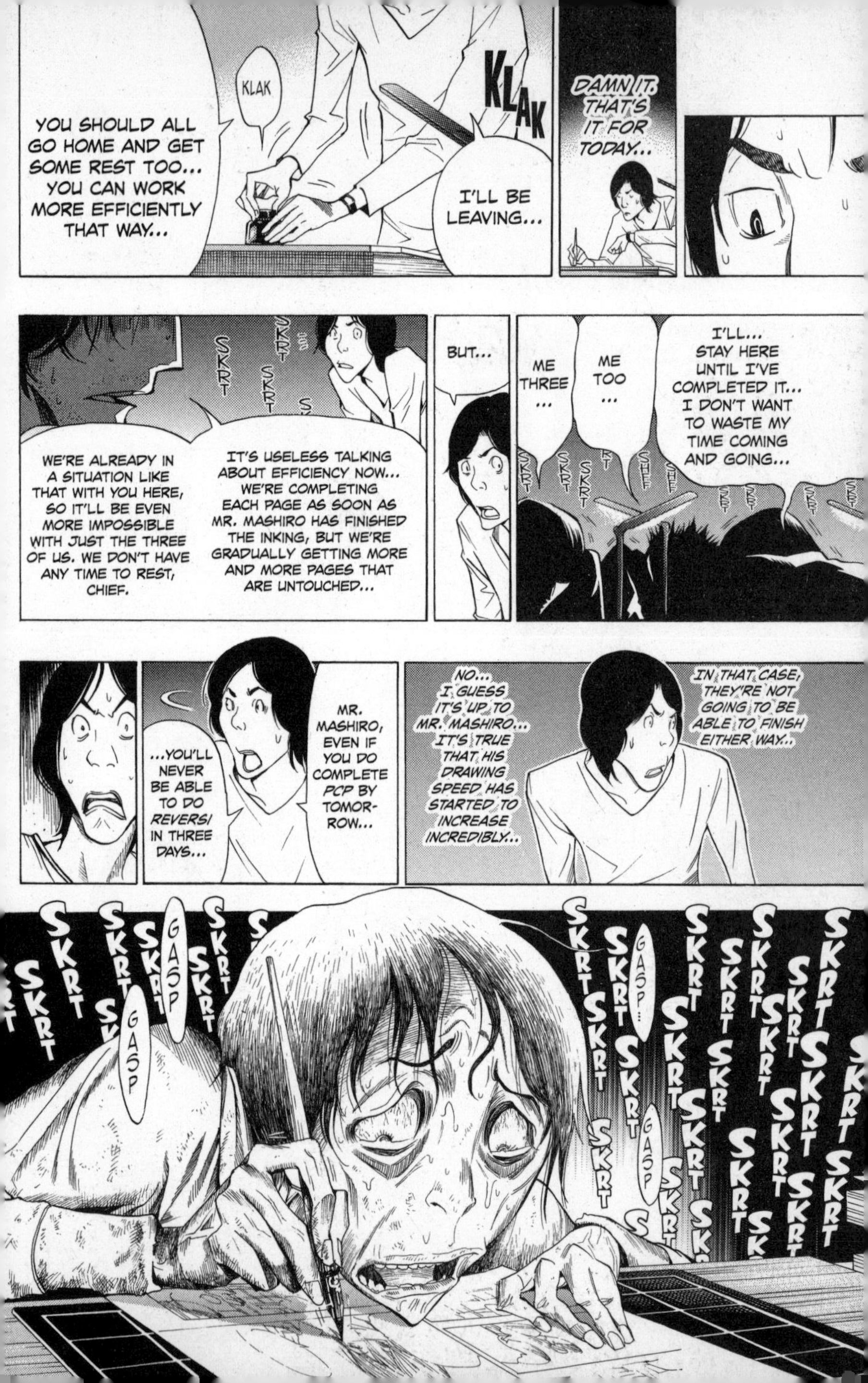

DAMN IT. THAT'S IT FOR TODAY...
KLAK
I'LL BE LEAVING...
KLAK
YOU SHOULD ALL GO HOME AND GET SOME REST TOO... YOU CAN WORK MORE EFFICIENTLY THAT WAY...
I'LL... STAY HERE UNTIL I'VE COMPLETED IT... I DON'T WANT TO WASTE MY TIME COMING AND GOING...
ME TOO ...
ME THREE ...
SKRT SKRT SHFF SHFF SKRT SKRT
BUT...
SKRT SKRT SKRT
IT'S USELESS TALKING ABOUT EFFICIENCY NOW... WE'RE COMPLETING EACH PAGE AS SOON AS MR. MASHIRO HAS FINISHED THE INKING, BUT WE'RE GRADUALLY GETTING MORE AND MORE PAGES THAT ARE UNTOUCHED...
WE'RE ALREADY IN A SITUATION LIKE THAT WITH YOU HERE, SO IT'LL BE EVEN MORE IMPOSSIBLE WITH JUST THE THREE OF US. WE DON'T HAVE ANY TIME TO REST, CHIEF.
IN THAT CASE, THEY'RE NOT GOING TO BE ABLE TO FINISH EITHER WAY...
NO... I GUESS IT'S UP TO MR. MASHIRO... IT'S TRUE THAT HIS DRAWING SPEED HAS STARTED TO INCREASE INCREDIBLY...
MR. MASHIRO, EVEN IF YOU DO COMPLETE *PCP* BY TOMORROW...
...YOU'LL NEVER BE ABLE TO DO *REVERSI* IN THREE DAYS...
SKRT SKRT SKRT SKRT SKRT
GASP...
GASP
SKRT SKRT SKRT SKRT
GASP
GASP

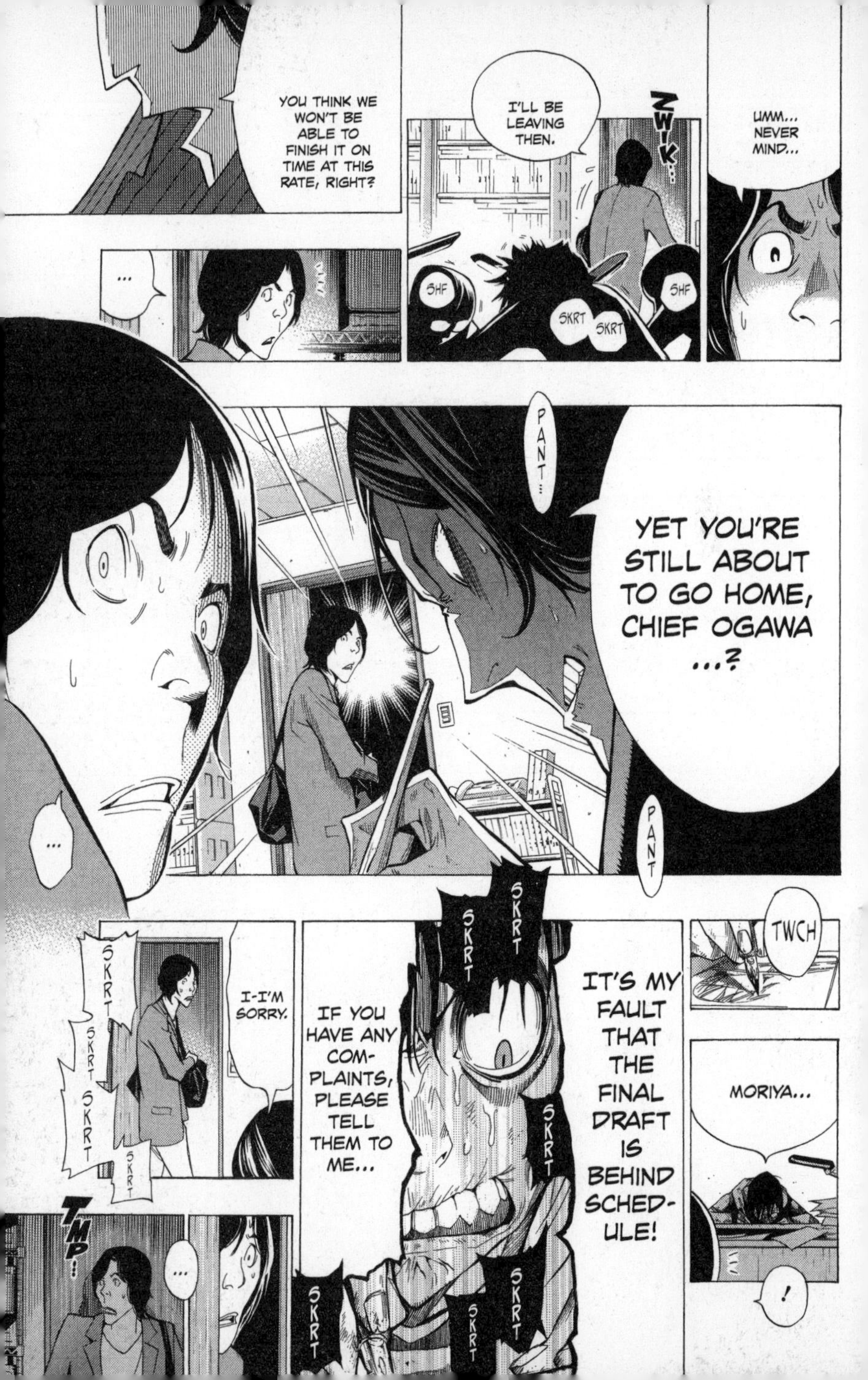
UMM... NEVER MIND...
ZWIK...
I'LL BE LEAVING THEN.
SHF
SKRT
SKRT
SHF
YOU THINK WE WON'T BE ABLE TO FINISH IT ON TIME AT THIS RATE, RIGHT?
...
PANT...
YET YOU'RE STILL ABOUT TO GO HOME, CHIEF OGAWA ...?
PANT
PANT
...
TWCH
MORIYA...
!
SKRT
SKRT
IT'S MY FAULT THAT THE FINAL DRAFT IS BEHIND SCHED-ULE!
SKRT
IF YOU HAVE ANY COM-PLAINTS, PLEASE TELL THEM TO ME...
SKRT
SKRT
SKRT
I-I'M SORRY.
SKRT
SKRT
SKRT
SKRT
SKRT
TMP!!
...

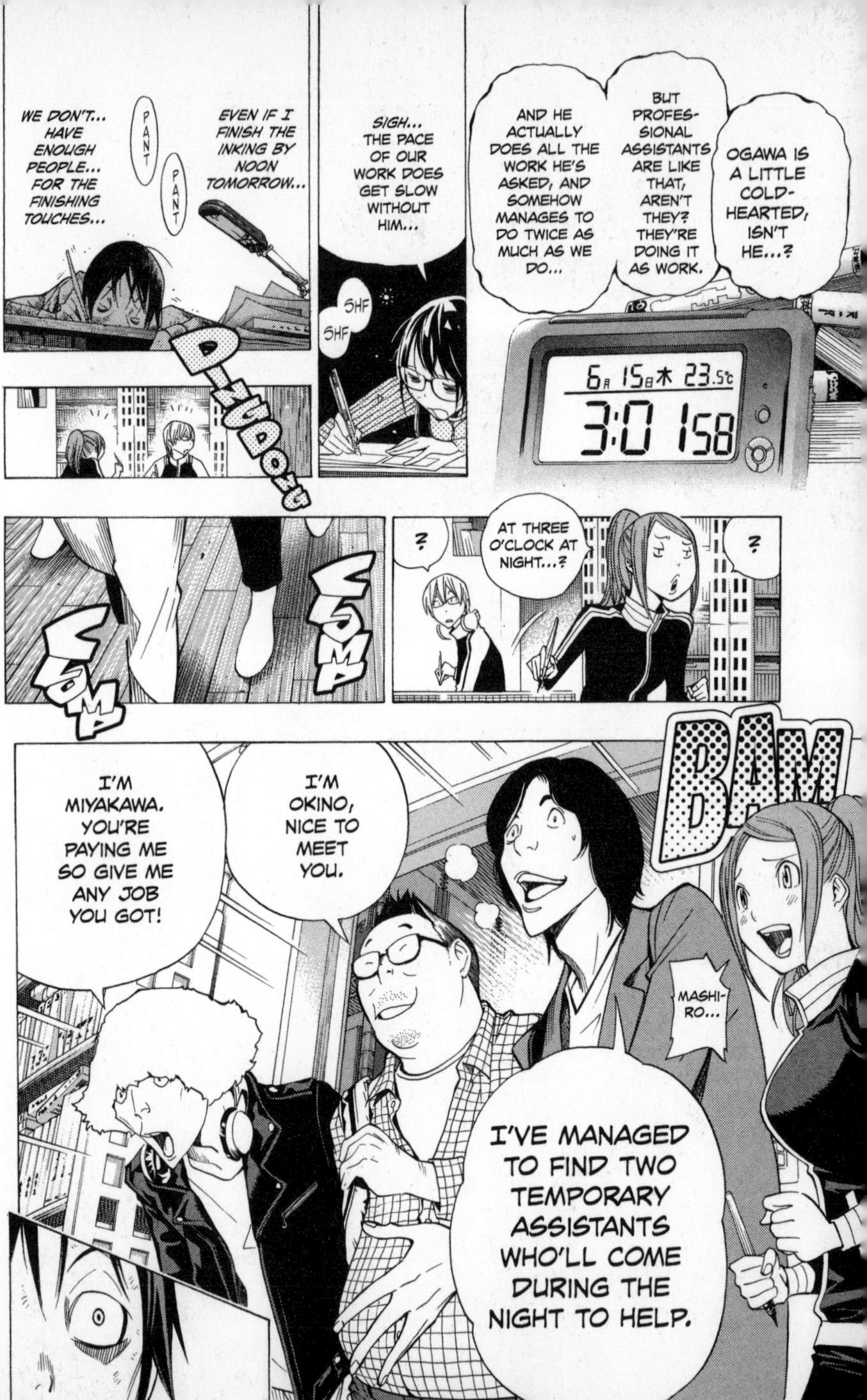

OGAWA IS A LITTLE COLD-HEARTED, ISN'T HE...?
BUT PROFES-SIONAL ASSISTANTS ARE LIKE THAT, AREN'T THEY? THEY'RE DOING IT AS WORK.
AND HE ACTUALLY DOES ALL THE WORK HE'S ASKED, AND SOMEHOW MANAGES TO DO TWICE AS MUCH AS WE DO...
6月 15日 木 23.5℃
3:01 58
SIGH... THE PACE OF OUR WORK DOES GET SLOW WITHOUT HIM...
SHF
SHF
EVEN IF I FINISH THE INKING BY NOON TOMORROW...
PANT
PANT
WE DON'T... HAVE ENOUGH PEOPLE... FOR THE FINISHING TOUCHES...
DINGDONG
?
AT THREE O'CLOCK AT NIGHT...?
?
CLOMP
CLOMP
BAM
MASHIRO...
I'VE MANAGED TO FIND TWO TEMPORARY ASSISTANTS WHO'LL COME DURING THE NIGHT TO HELP.
I'M OKINO, NICE TO MEET YOU.
I'M MIYAKAWA. YOU'RE PAYING ME SO GIVE ME ANY JOB YOU GOT!

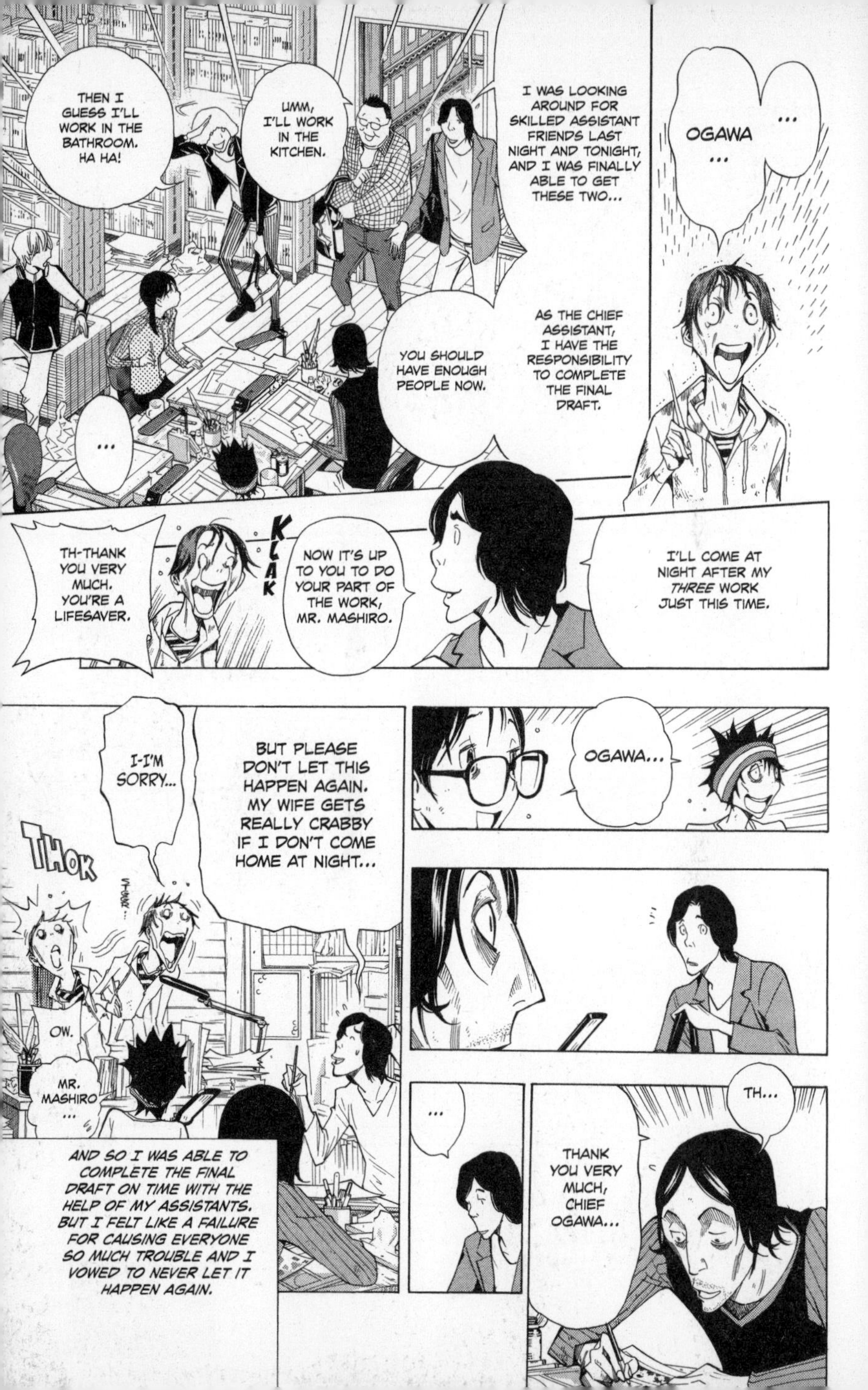

OGAWA ... ...
I WAS LOOKING AROUND FOR SKILLED ASSISTANT FRIENDS LAST NIGHT AND TONIGHT, AND I WAS FINALLY ABLE TO GET THESE TWO...
UMM, I'LL WORK IN THE KITCHEN.
THEN I GUESS I'LL WORK IN THE BATHROOM. HA HA!
AS THE CHIEF ASSISTANT, I HAVE THE RESPONSIBILITY TO COMPLETE THE FINAL DRAFT.
YOU SHOULD HAVE ENOUGH PEOPLE NOW.
...
I'LL COME AT NIGHT AFTER MY *THREE* WORK JUST THIS TIME.
NOW IT'S UP TO YOU TO DO YOUR PART OF THE WORK, MR. MASHIRO.
KLAK
TH-THANK YOU VERY MUCH. YOU'RE A LIFESAVER.
OGAWA...
TH...
THANK YOU VERY MUCH, CHIEF OGAWA...
...
BUT PLEASE DON'T LET THIS HAPPEN AGAIN. MY WIFE GETS REALLY CRABBY IF I DON'T COME HOME AT NIGHT...
I-I'M SORRY...
THOK
OW.
MR. MASHIRO ...
AND SO I WAS ABLE TO COMPLETE THE FINAL DRAFT ON TIME WITH THE HELP OF MY ASSISTANTS. BUT I FELT LIKE A FAILURE FOR CAUSING EVERYONE SO MUCH TROUBLE AND I VOWED TO NEVER LET IT HAPPEN AGAIN.

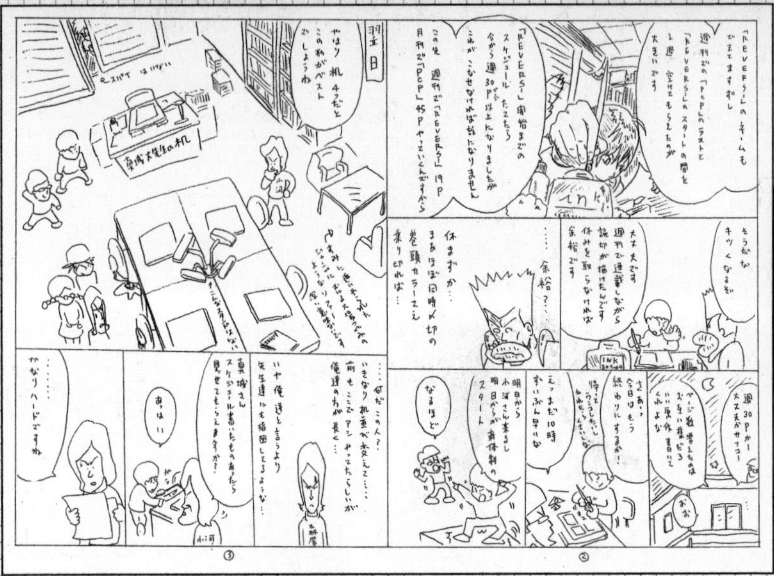
「REVERSI」のネームもできてますし
週刊での「PCP」のラストと「REVERSI」のスタートの間を1週空けてもらえたのが大きいです
「REVERSI」開始までのスケジュールたてたら今から週30P以上になりましたがこれがこなせなければ話になりません
この先週刊で「REVERSI」19P月刊で「PCP」45Pやっていくんですから
そうだなキツくなるぞ
大丈夫です週刊で連載しながら読切が描けたんです休みを取らなければ余裕です
……余裕?
休まずか…まあほぼ同時〆切で巻頭カラーさえ乗り切れば…
週30Pかー大丈夫かサイコー
ページ数増えたのはお互い様だろいい原作書いてくれよ
おお
さあ…今日はもう終わりにするか!
えっまだ10時ずいぶん早いな
明日から小河さん来るし明日からが新体制のスタート
なるほど
翌日
やはり机4つだとこの形がベストかしょうね
東城大先生の机
……何だこの人?いきなり机並べ変えて…前もここでアシやってたらしいが俺達の方が長く…
いや俺達と言うより先生達にも指図してるような…
東城さんスケジュール書いたもの見せてもらえますか?
あっはい
……かなりハードですね

OHBA'S STORYBOARD

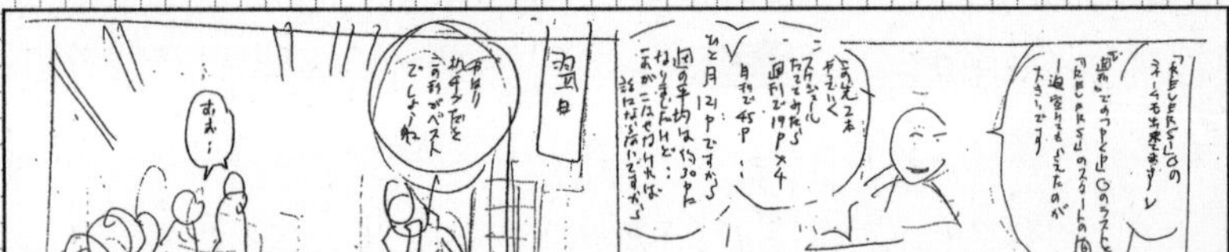

OBATA'S STORYBOARD

COMPLETE!

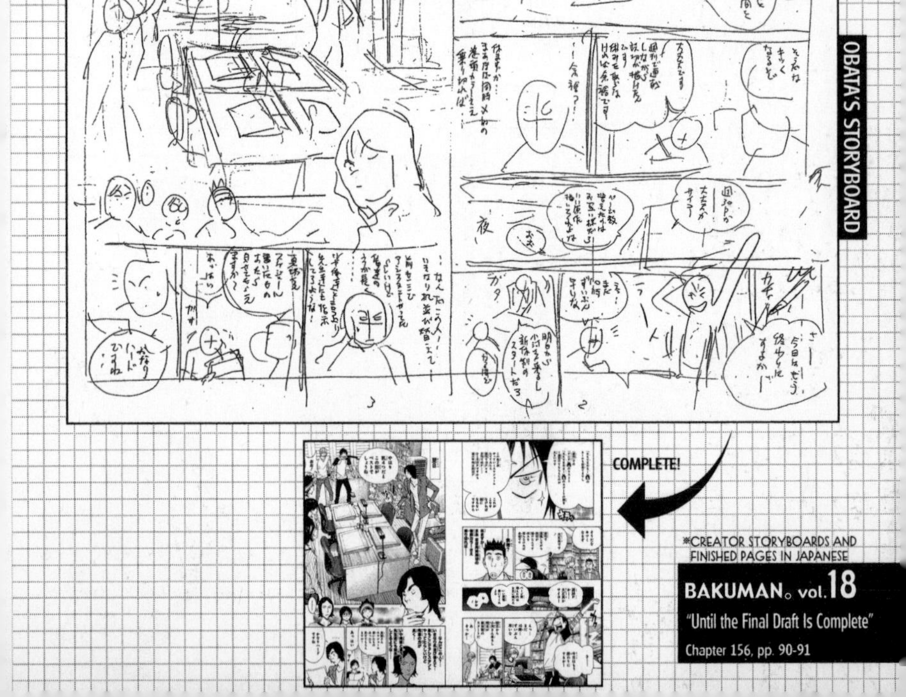

※CREATOR STORYBOARDS AND FINISHED PAGES IN JAPANESE

BAKUMAN。 vol.18

"Until the Final Draft Is Complete"

Chapter 156, pp. 90-91

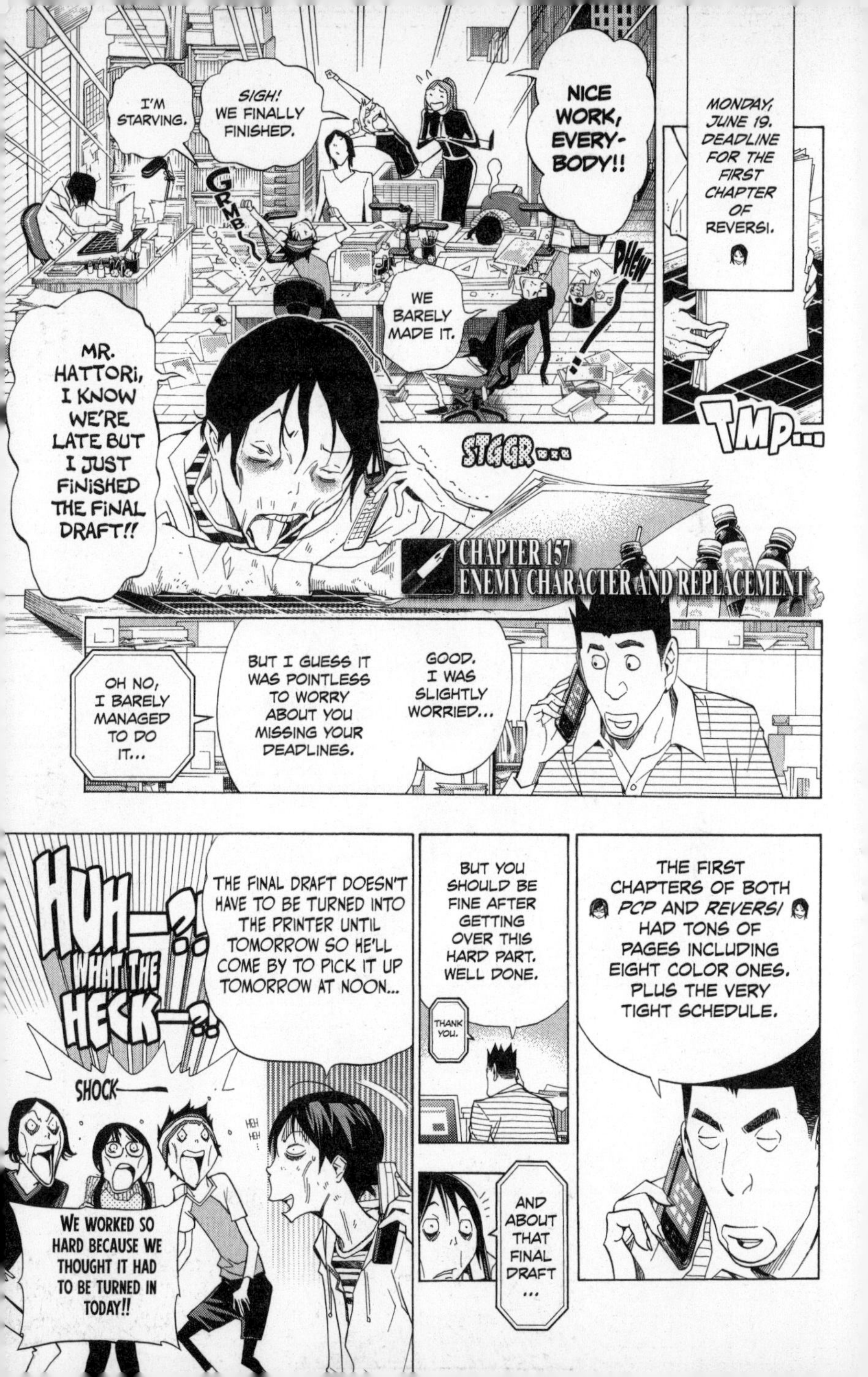
MONDAY, JUNE 19. DEADLINE FOR THE FIRST CHAPTER OF REVERSI.
TMP...
NICE WORK, EVERY-BODY!!
SIGH! WE FINALLY FINISHED.
I'M STARVING.
GRMBL
PHEW
WE BARELY MADE IT.
STGGR...
MR. HATTORI, I KNOW WE'RE LATE BUT I JUST FINISHED THE FINAL DRAFT!!
CHAPTER 157
ENEMY CHARACTER AND REPLACEMENT
GOOD. I WAS SLIGHTLY WORRIED...
BUT I GUESS IT WAS POINTLESS TO WORRY ABOUT YOU MISSING YOUR DEADLINES.
OH NO, I BARELY MANAGED TO DO IT...
THE FIRST CHAPTERS OF BOTH PCP AND REVERSI HAD TONS OF PAGES INCLUDING EIGHT COLOR ONES. PLUS THE VERY TIGHT SCHEDULE.
BUT YOU SHOULD BE FINE AFTER GETTING OVER THIS HARD PART. WELL DONE.
THANK YOU.
AND ABOUT THAT FINAL DRAFT...
THE FINAL DRAFT DOESN'T HAVE TO BE TURNED INTO THE PRINTER UNTIL TOMORROW SO HE'LL COME BY TO PICK IT UP TOMORROW AT NOON...
HUH—?!
WHAT THE HECK—?!
SHOCK
HEH HEH
WE WORKED SO HARD BECAUSE WE THOUGHT IT HAD TO BE TURNED IN TODAY!!

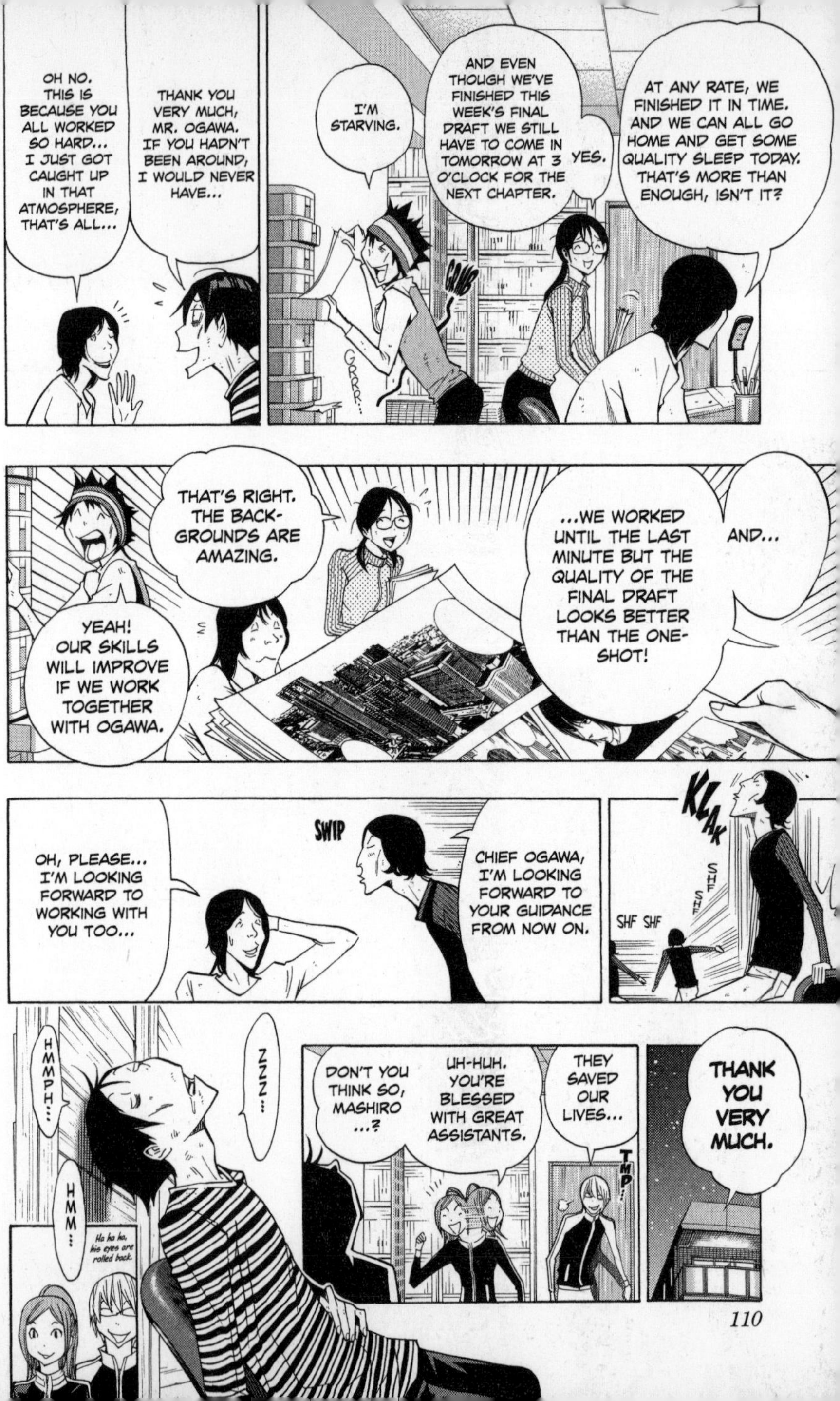
AT ANY RATE, WE FINISHED IT IN TIME. AND WE CAN ALL GO HOME AND GET SOME QUALITY SLEEP TODAY. THAT'S MORE THAN ENOUGH, ISN'T IT?
YES.
AND EVEN THOUGH WE'VE FINISHED THIS WEEK'S FINAL DRAFT WE STILL HAVE TO COME IN TOMORROW AT 3 O'CLOCK FOR THE NEXT CHAPTER.
I'M STARVING.
GRMB
GRRRR...
THANK YOU VERY MUCH, MR. OGAWA. IF YOU HADN'T BEEN AROUND, I WOULD NEVER HAVE...
OH NO. THIS IS BECAUSE YOU ALL WORKED SO HARD... I JUST GOT CAUGHT UP IN THAT ATMOSPHERE, THAT'S ALL...
AND...
...WE WORKED UNTIL THE LAST MINUTE BUT THE QUALITY OF THE FINAL DRAFT LOOKS BETTER THAN THE ONE-SHOT!
THAT'S RIGHT. THE BACK-GROUNDS ARE AMAZING.
YEAH! OUR SKILLS WILL IMPROVE IF WE WORK TOGETHER WITH OGAWA.
KLAK
SHF SHF
SHF SHF
CHIEF OGAWA, I'M LOOKING FORWARD TO YOUR GUIDANCE FROM NOW ON.
SWIP
OH, PLEASE... I'M LOOKING FORWARD TO WORKING WITH YOU TOO...
THANK YOU VERY MUCH.
THEY SAVED OUR LIVES...
TMP...
UH-HUH. YOU'RE BLESSED WITH GREAT ASSISTANTS.
DON'T YOU THINK SO, MASHIRO...?
ZZZ...
HMMPH...
HMM...
Ha ho ho, his eyes are rolled back.

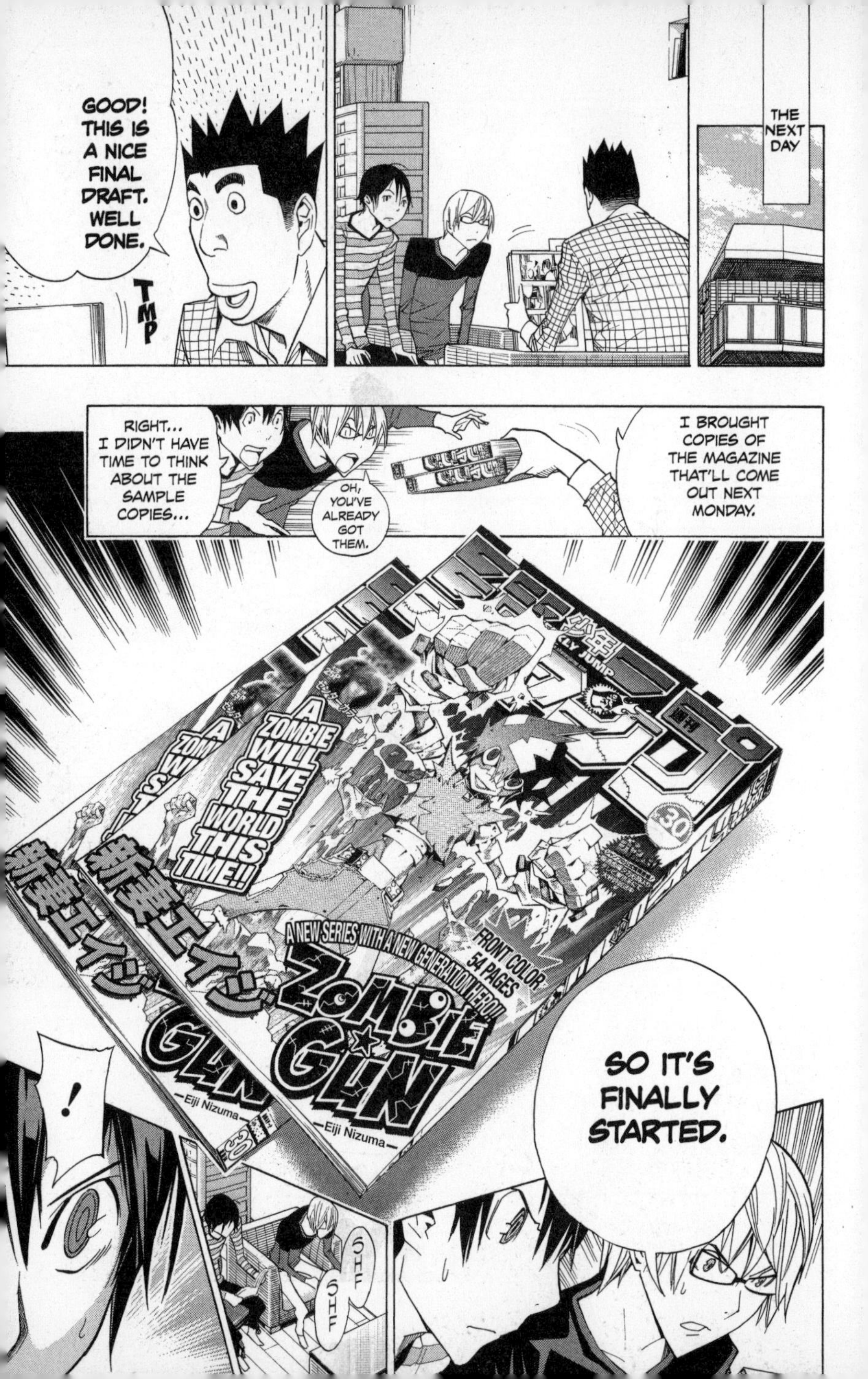
THE NEXT DAY
GOOD! THIS IS A NICE FINAL DRAFT. WELL DONE.
TMP
I BROUGHT COPIES OF THE MAGAZINE THAT'LL COME OUT NEXT MONDAY.
OH, YOU'VE ALREADY GOT THEM.
RIGHT... I DIDN'T HAVE TIME TO THINK ABOUT THE SAMPLE COPIES...
A ZOMBIE WILL SAVE THE WORLD THIS TIME!!
FRONT COLOR 54 PAGES
A NEW SERIES WITH A NEW GENERATION HERO!!
ZOMBIE☆GUN
—Eiji Nizuma—
30
SO IT'S FINALLY STARTED.
!
SHF
SHF

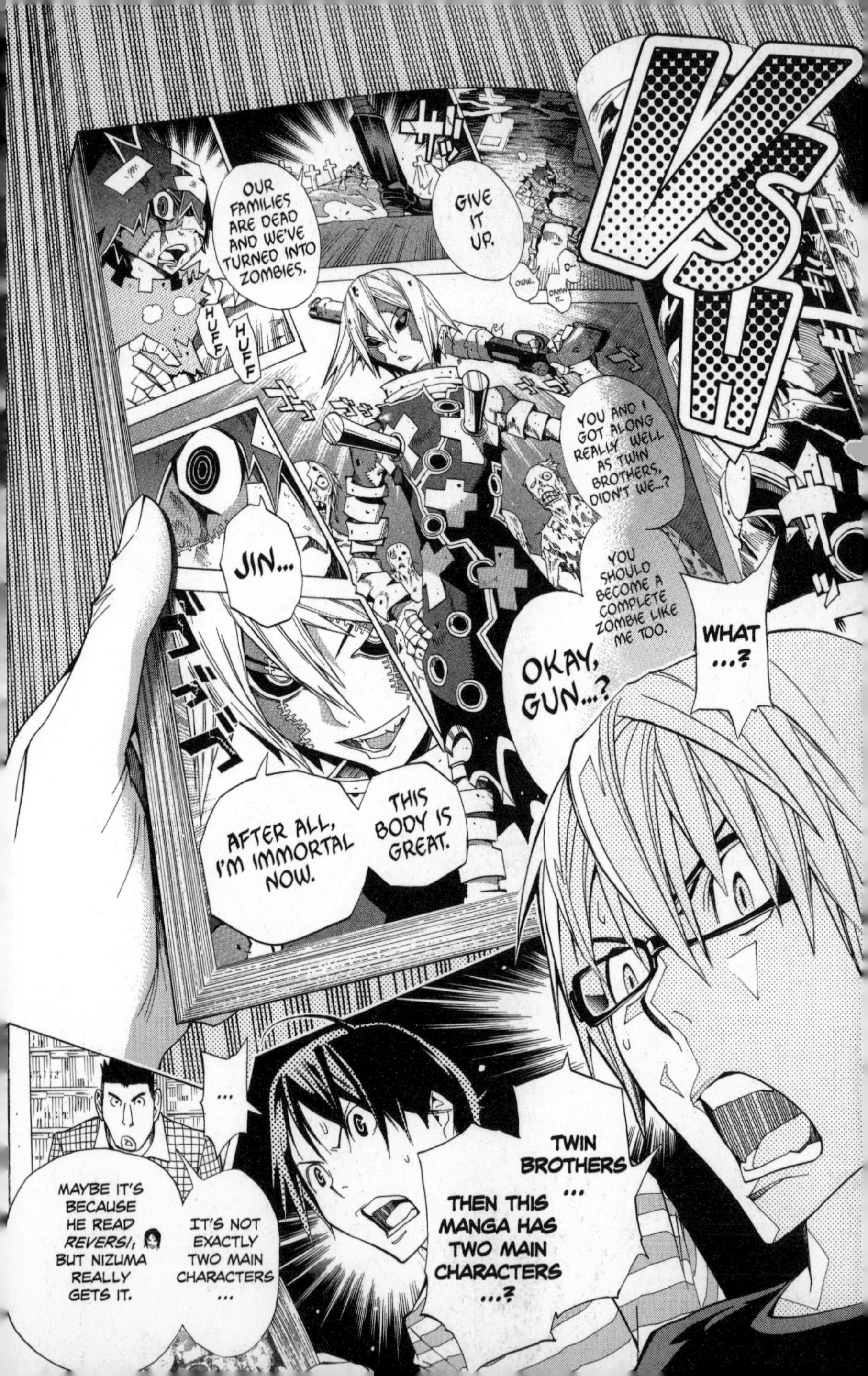
VSH
D-...
DAMN IT...
OWW...
GIVE IT UP.
OUR FAMILIES ARE DEAD AND WE'VE TURNED INTO ZOMBIES.
HUFF HUFF
YOU AND I GOT ALONG REALLY WELL AS TWIN BROTHERS, DIDN'T WE...?
YOU SHOULD BECOME A COMPLETE ZOMBIE LIKE ME TOO.
JIN...
THIS BODY IS GREAT.
AFTER ALL, I'M IMMORTAL NOW.
WHAT ...?
OKAY, GUN...?
TWIN BROTHERS ...
THEN THIS MANGA HAS TWO MAIN CHARACTERS ...?
...
IT'S NOT EXACTLY TWO MAIN CHARACTERS ...
MAYBE IT'S BECAUSE HE READ *REVERSI*, BUT NIZUMA REALLY GETS IT.

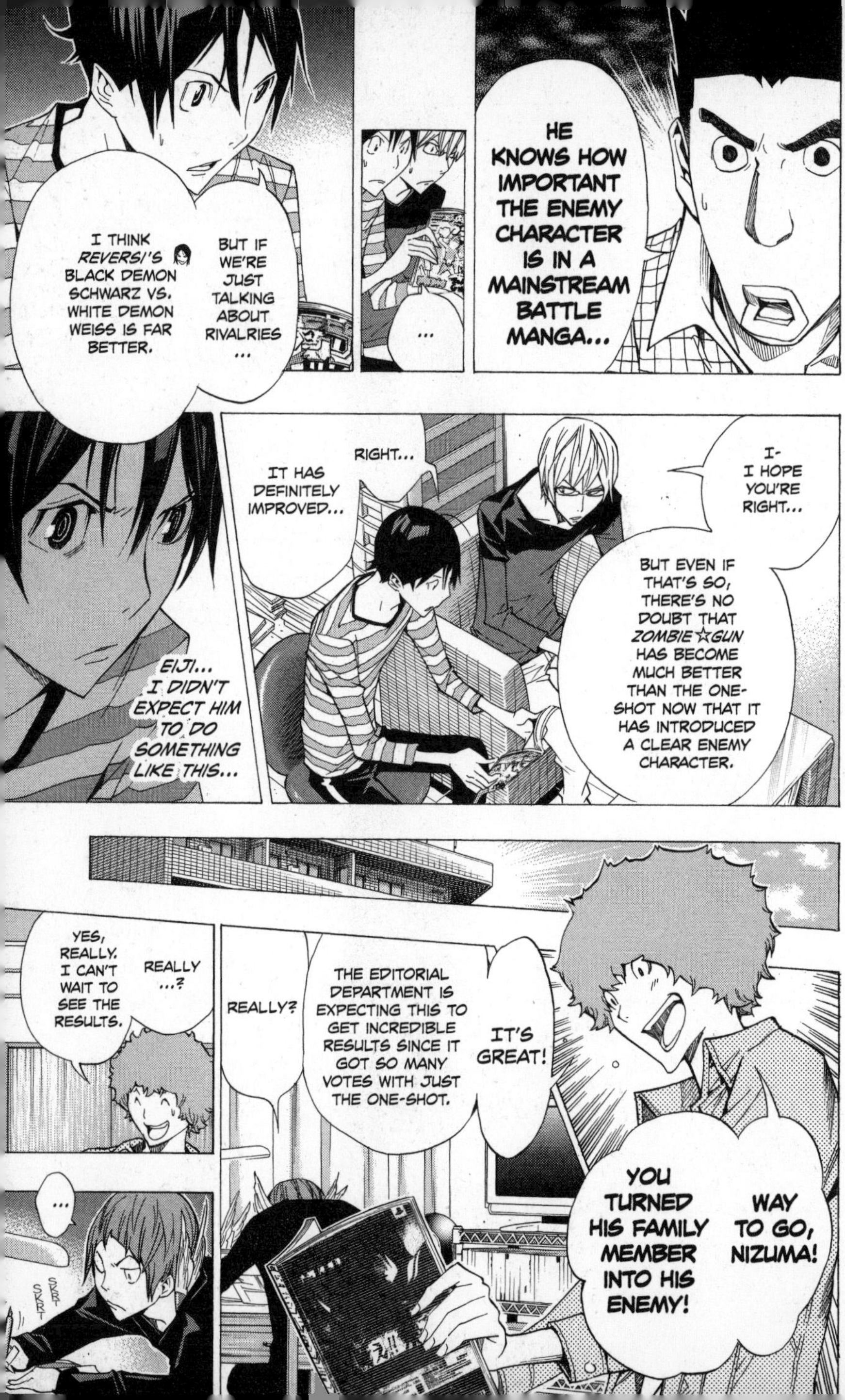
HE KNOWS HOW IMPORTANT THE ENEMY CHARACTER IS IN A MAINSTREAM BATTLE MANGA...
...
BUT IF WE'RE JUST TALKING ABOUT RIVALRIES...
I THINK *REVERSI*'S BLACK DEMON SCHWARZ VS. WHITE DEMON WEISS IS FAR BETTER.
I- I HOPE YOU'RE RIGHT...
BUT EVEN IF THAT'S SO, THERE'S NO DOUBT THAT *ZOMBIE☆GUN* HAS BECOME MUCH BETTER THAN THE ONE-SHOT NOW THAT IT HAS INTRODUCED A CLEAR ENEMY CHARACTER.
RIGHT...
IT HAS DEFINITELY IMPROVED...
EIJI... I DIDN'T EXPECT HIM TO DO SOMETHING LIKE THIS...
WAY TO GO, NIZUMA!
YOU TURNED HIS FAMILY MEMBER INTO HIS ENEMY!
IT'S GREAT!
THE EDITORIAL DEPARTMENT IS EXPECTING THIS TO GET INCREDIBLE RESULTS SINCE IT GOT SO MANY VOTES WITH JUST THE ONE-SHOT.
REALLY?
REALLY...?
YES, REALLY. I CAN'T WAIT TO SEE THE RESULTS.
...
SKRT
SKRT

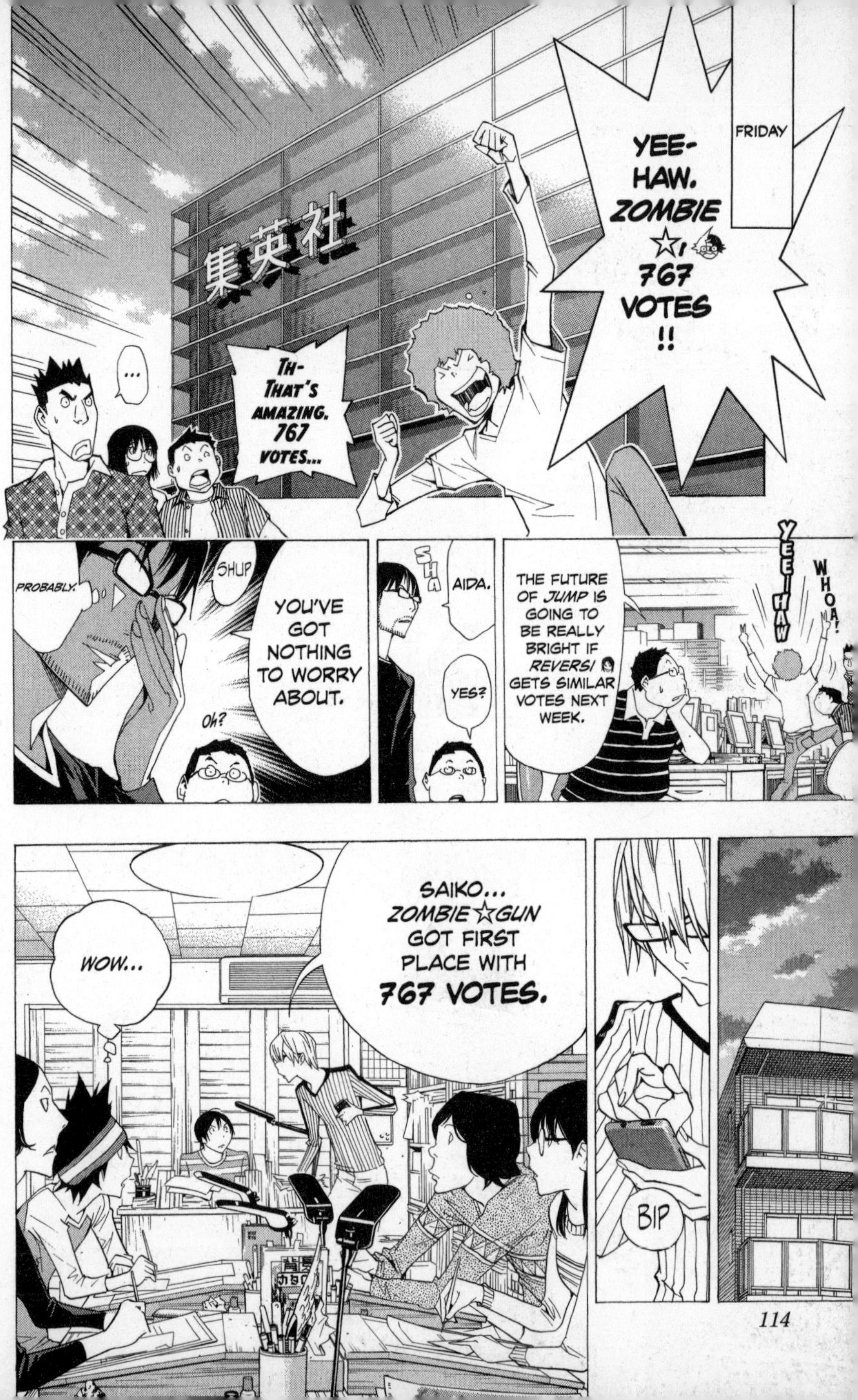

FRIDAY
YEE-HAW. ZOMBIE☆, 767 VOTES!!
TH-THAT'S AMAZING. 767 VOTES...
...
YEE-HAW
WHOA!
THE FUTURE OF JUMP IS GOING TO BE REALLY BRIGHT IF REVERSI GETS SIMILAR VOTES NEXT WEEK.
SHA
AIDA.
YES?
SHUP
YOU'VE GOT NOTHING TO WORRY ABOUT.
Oh?
PROBABLY.
BIP
SAIKO... ZOMBIE☆GUN GOT FIRST PLACE WITH 767 VOTES.
WOW...

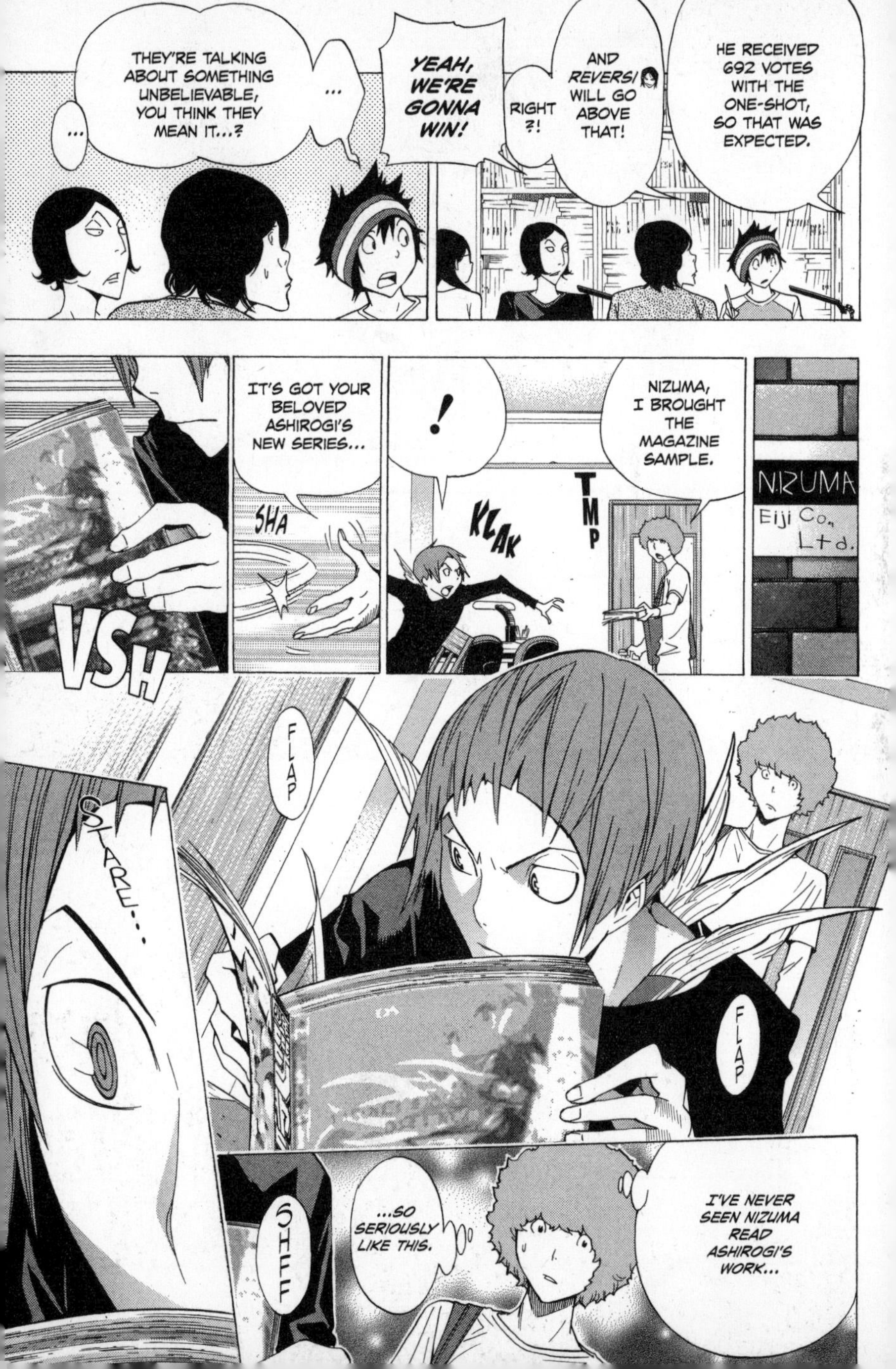
HE RECEIVED 692 VOTES WITH THE ONE-SHOT, SO THAT WAS EXPECTED.
AND REVERSI WILL GO ABOVE THAT!
RIGHT ?!
YEAH, WE'RE GONNA WIN!
...
THEY'RE TALKING ABOUT SOMETHING UNBELIEVABLE, YOU THINK THEY MEAN IT...?
...
NIZUMA Eiji Co., Ltd.
NIZUMA, I BROUGHT THE MAGAZINE SAMPLE.
TMP
!
KLAK
IT'S GOT YOUR BELOVED ASHIROGI'S NEW SERIES...
SHA
VSH
FLAP
FLAP
STARE...
I'VE NEVER SEEN NIZUMA READ ASHIROGI'S WORK...
...SO SERIOUSLY LIKE THIS.
SHFF

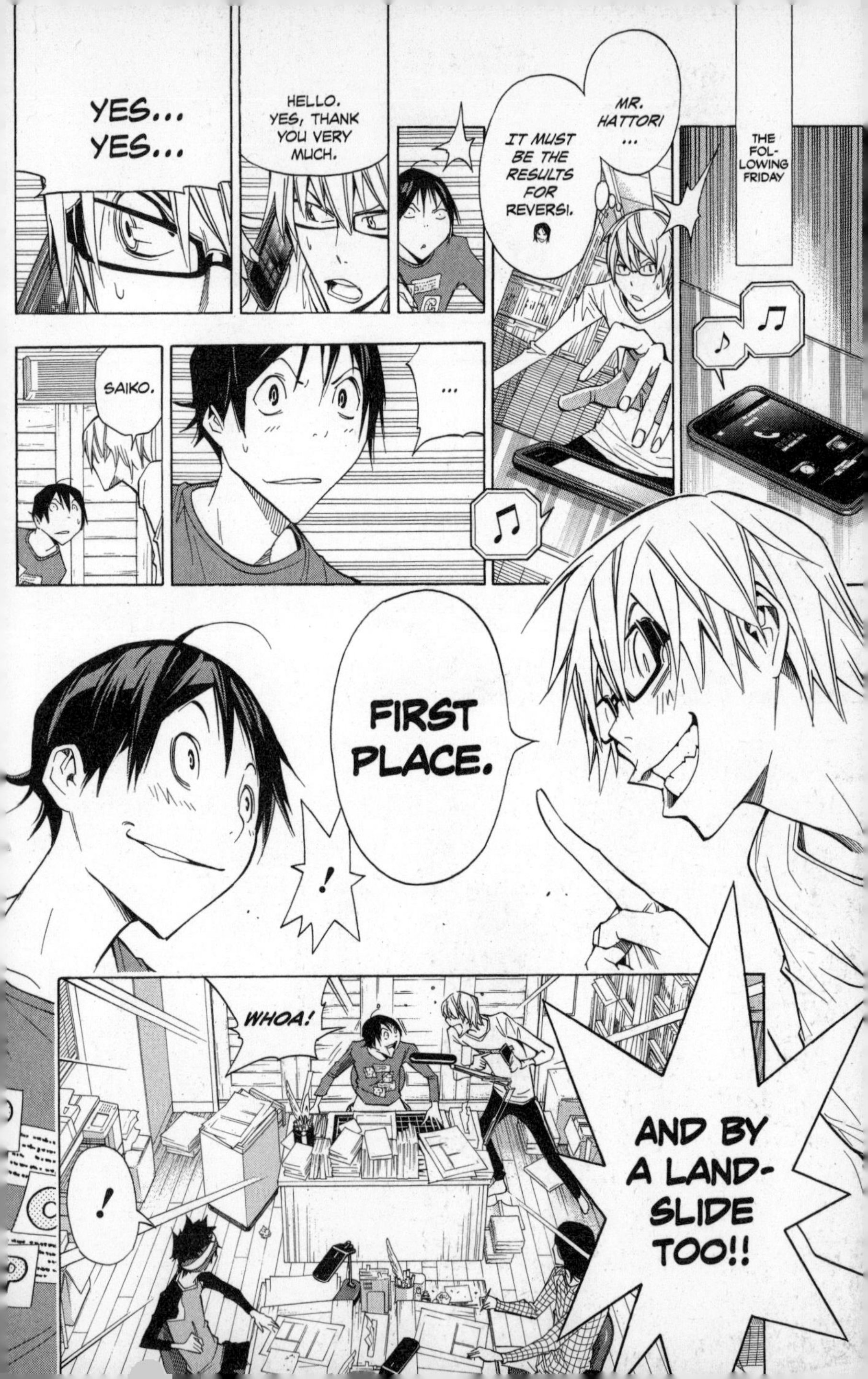
THE FOL-LOWING FRIDAY
♪ ♫
♫
MR. HATTORI ...
IT MUST BE THE RESULTS FOR REVERSI.
HELLO. YES, THANK YOU VERY MUCH.
YES... YES...
...
SAIKO.
FIRST PLACE.
!
AND BY A LAND-SLIDE TOO!!
WHOA!
!

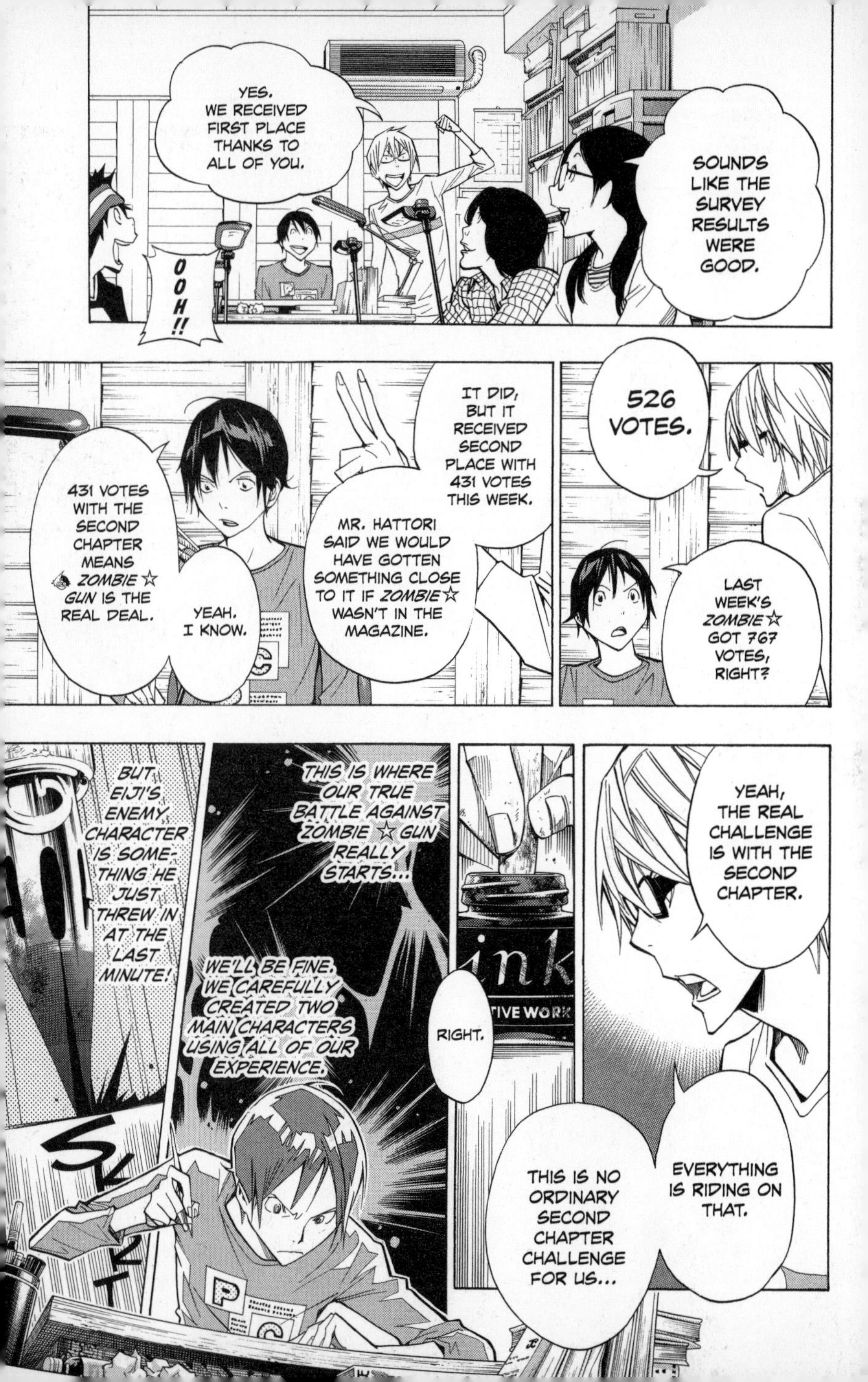
SOUNDS LIKE THE SURVEY RESULTS WERE GOOD.
YES. WE RECEIVED FIRST PLACE THANKS TO ALL OF YOU.
OOOH!!
526 VOTES.
LAST WEEK'S ZOMBIE☆ GOT 767 VOTES, RIGHT?
IT DID, BUT IT RECEIVED SECOND PLACE WITH 431 VOTES THIS WEEK.
MR. HATTORI SAID WE WOULD HAVE GOTTEN SOMETHING CLOSE TO IT IF ZOMBIE☆ WASN'T IN THE MAGAZINE.
YEAH. I KNOW.
431 VOTES WITH THE SECOND CHAPTER MEANS ZOMBIE☆GUN IS THE REAL DEAL.
YEAH, THE REAL CHALLENGE IS WITH THE SECOND CHAPTER.
EVERYTHING IS RIDING ON THAT.
THIS IS NO ORDINARY SECOND CHAPTER CHALLENGE FOR US...
ink
RIGHT.
THIS IS WHERE OUR TRUE BATTLE AGAINST ZOMBIE☆GUN REALLY STARTS...
BUT EIJI'S ENEMY CHARACTER IS SOMETHING HE JUST THREW IN AT THE LAST MINUTE!
WE'LL BE FINE. WE CAREFULLY CREATED TWO MAIN CHARACTERS USING ALL OF OUR EXPERIENCE.

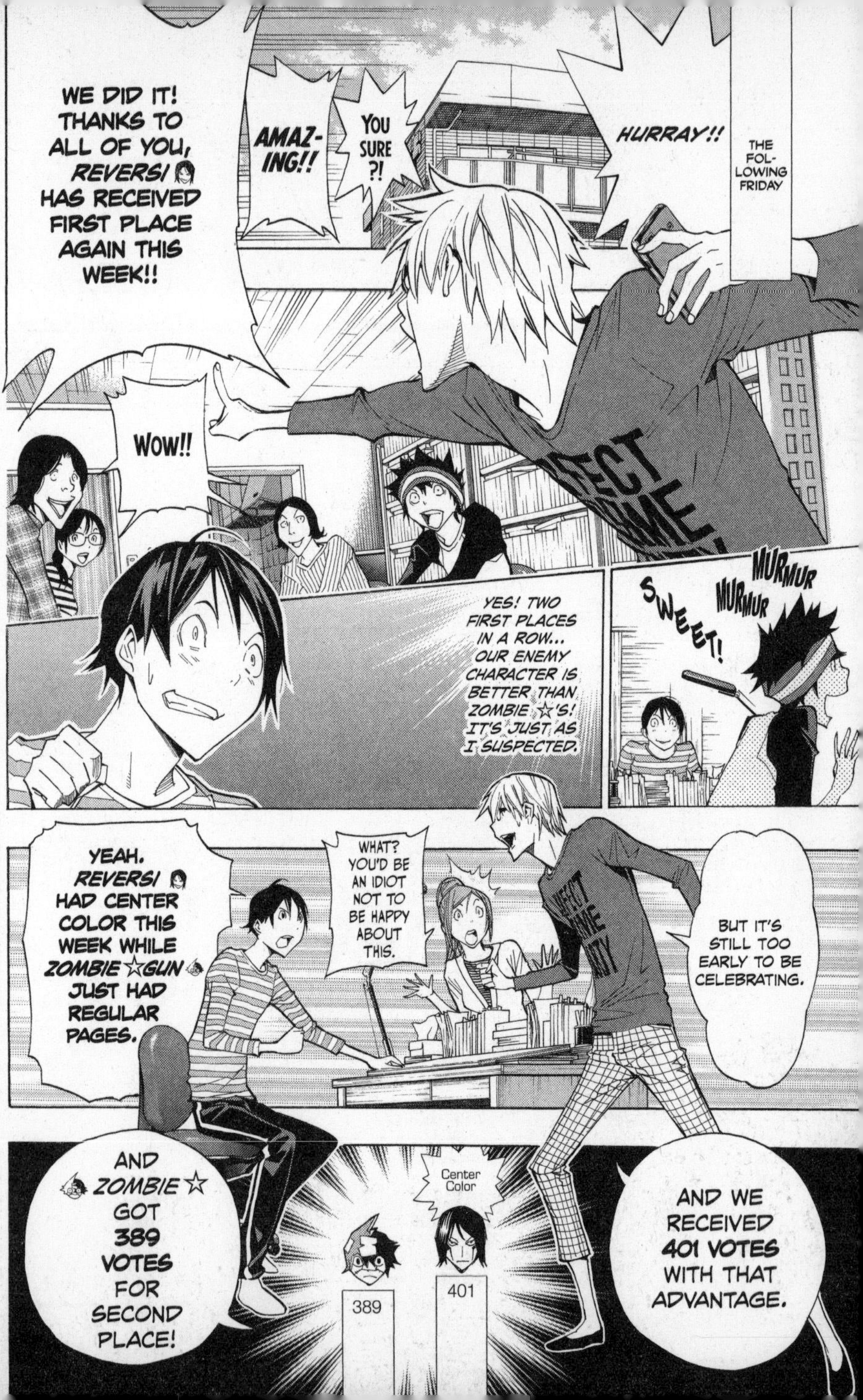
THE FOLLOWING FRIDAY
HURRAY!!
YOU SURE?!
AMAZING!!
WE DID IT! THANKS TO ALL OF YOU, REVERSI HAS RECEIVED FIRST PLACE AGAIN THIS WEEK!!
WOW!!
MURMUR MURMUR
SWEET!
YES! TWO FIRST PLACES IN A ROW... OUR ENEMY CHARACTER IS BETTER THAN ZOMBIE☆'S! IT'S JUST AS I SUSPECTED.
BUT IT'S STILL TOO EARLY TO BE CELEBRATING.
WHAT? YOU'D BE AN IDIOT NOT TO BE HAPPY ABOUT THIS.
YEAH. REVERSI HAD CENTER COLOR THIS WEEK WHILE ZOMBIE☆GUN JUST HAD REGULAR PAGES.
AND WE RECEIVED 401 VOTES WITH THAT ADVANTAGE.
Center Color
401
389
AND ZOMBIE☆ GOT 389 VOTES FOR SECOND PLACE!

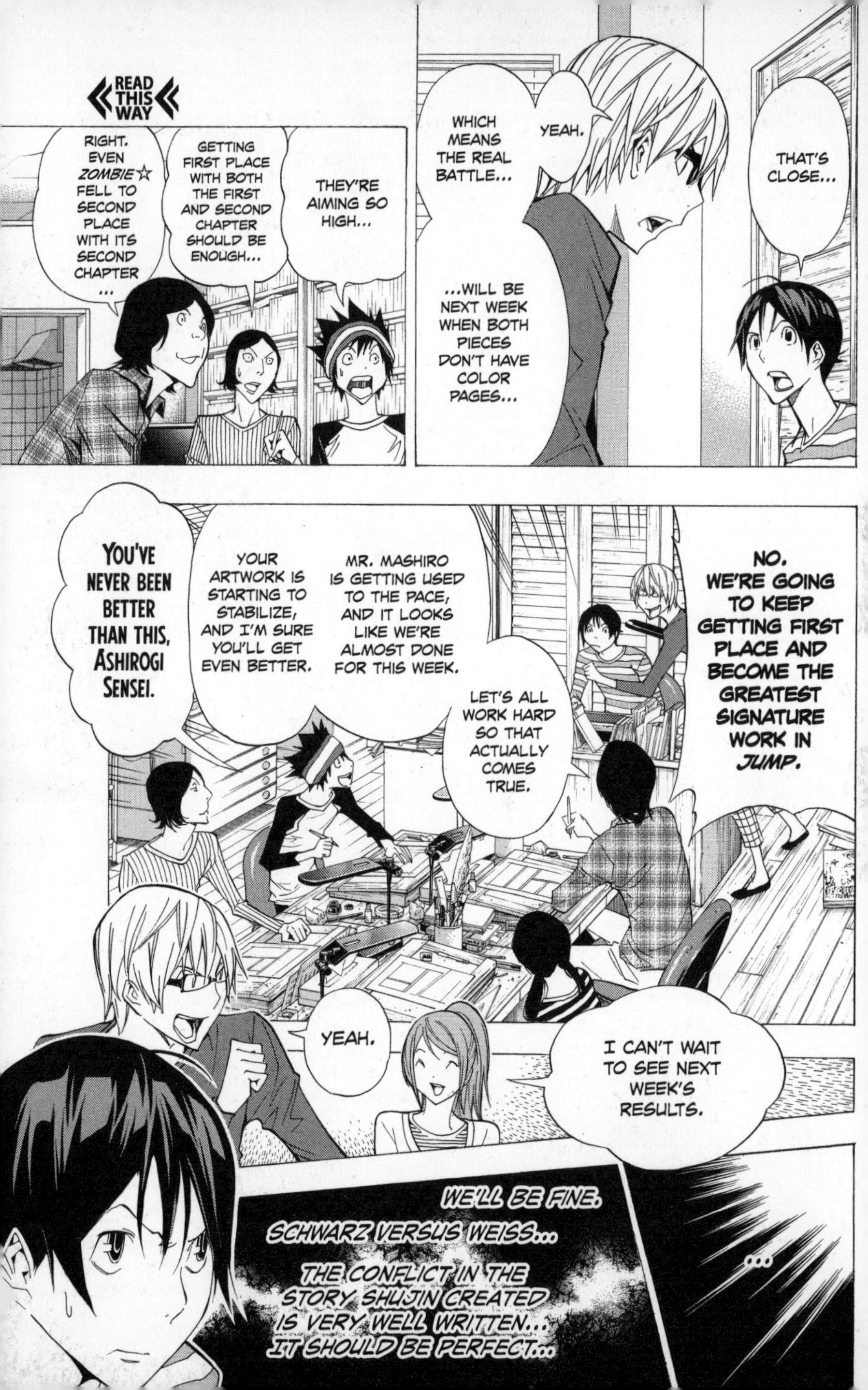
READ THIS WAY
THAT'S CLOSE...
YEAH.
WHICH MEANS THE REAL BATTLE...
...WILL BE NEXT WEEK WHEN BOTH PIECES DON'T HAVE COLOR PAGES...
THEY'RE AIMING SO HIGH...
GETTING FIRST PLACE WITH BOTH THE FIRST AND SECOND CHAPTER SHOULD BE ENOUGH...
RIGHT. EVEN *ZOMBIE*☆ FELL TO SECOND PLACE WITH ITS SECOND CHAPTER...
NO. WE'RE GOING TO KEEP GETTING FIRST PLACE AND BECOME THE GREATEST SIGNATURE WORK IN *JUMP*.
LET'S ALL WORK HARD SO THAT ACTUALLY COMES TRUE.
MR. MASHIRO IS GETTING USED TO THE PACE, AND IT LOOKS LIKE WE'RE ALMOST DONE FOR THIS WEEK.
YOUR ARTWORK IS STARTING TO STABILIZE, AND I'M SURE YOU'LL GET EVEN BETTER.
YOU'VE NEVER BEEN BETTER THAN THIS, ASHIROGI SENSEI.
I CAN'T WAIT TO SEE NEXT WEEK'S RESULTS.
YEAH.
...
WE'LL BE FINE.
SCHWARZ VERSUS WEISS...
THE CONFLICT IN THE STORY SHUJIN CREATED IS VERY WELL WRITTEN...
IT SHOULD BE PERFECT...

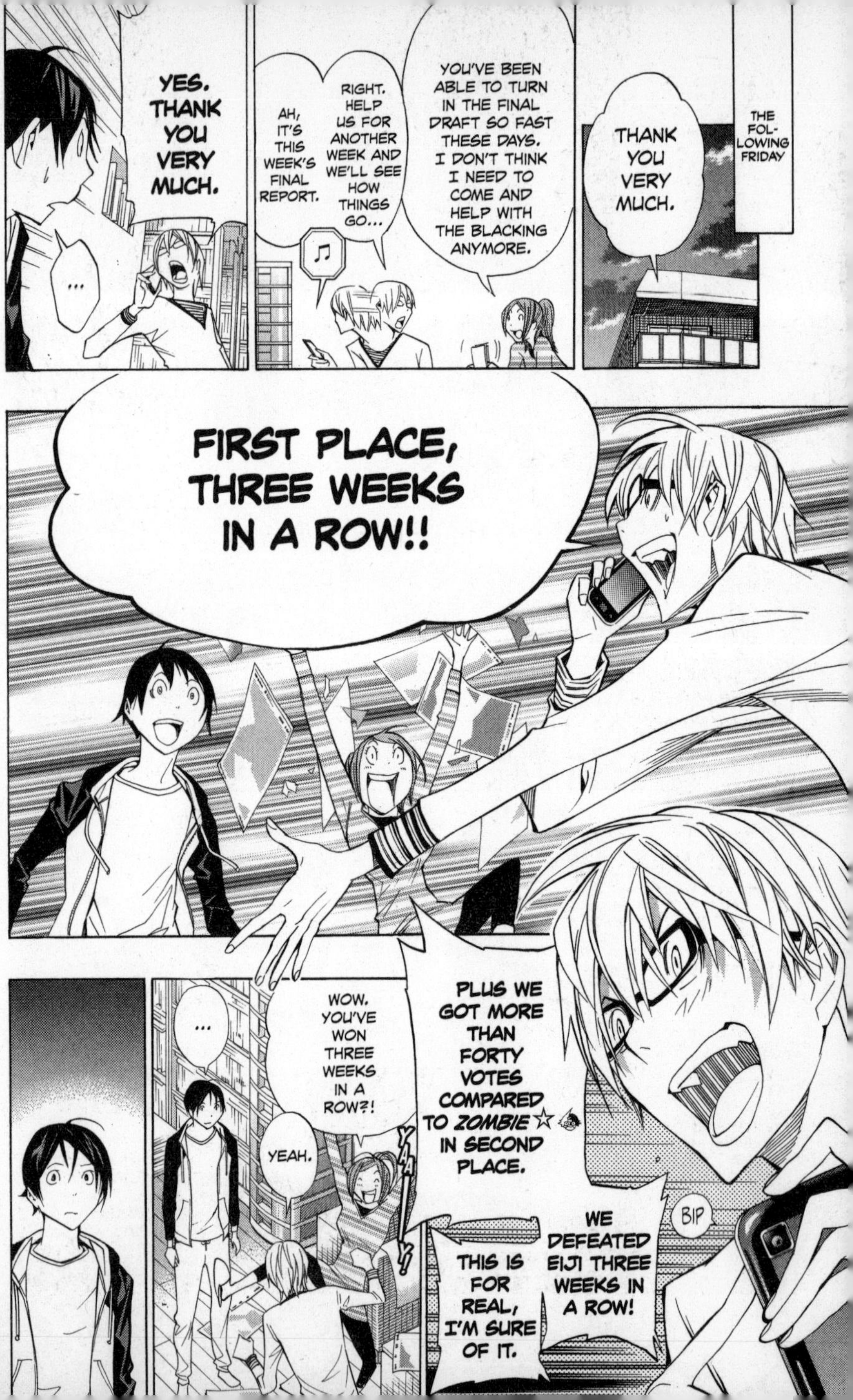
THE FOLLOWING FRIDAY
THANK YOU VERY MUCH.
YOU'VE BEEN ABLE TO TURN IN THE FINAL DRAFT SO FAST THESE DAYS. I DON'T THINK I NEED TO COME AND HELP WITH THE BLACKING ANYMORE.
RIGHT. HELP US FOR ANOTHER WEEK AND WE'LL SEE HOW THINGS GO...
AH, IT'S THIS WEEK'S FINAL REPORT.
♫
YES. THANK YOU VERY MUCH.
...
FIRST PLACE, THREE WEEKS IN A ROW!!
PLUS WE GOT MORE THAN FORTY VOTES COMPARED TO *ZOMBIE*☆ IN SECOND PLACE.
BIP
WE DEFEATED EIJI THREE WEEKS IN A ROW!
THIS IS FOR REAL, I'M SURE OF IT.
WOW. YOU'VE WON THREE WEEKS IN A ROW?!
YEAH.
YAAAY!
...

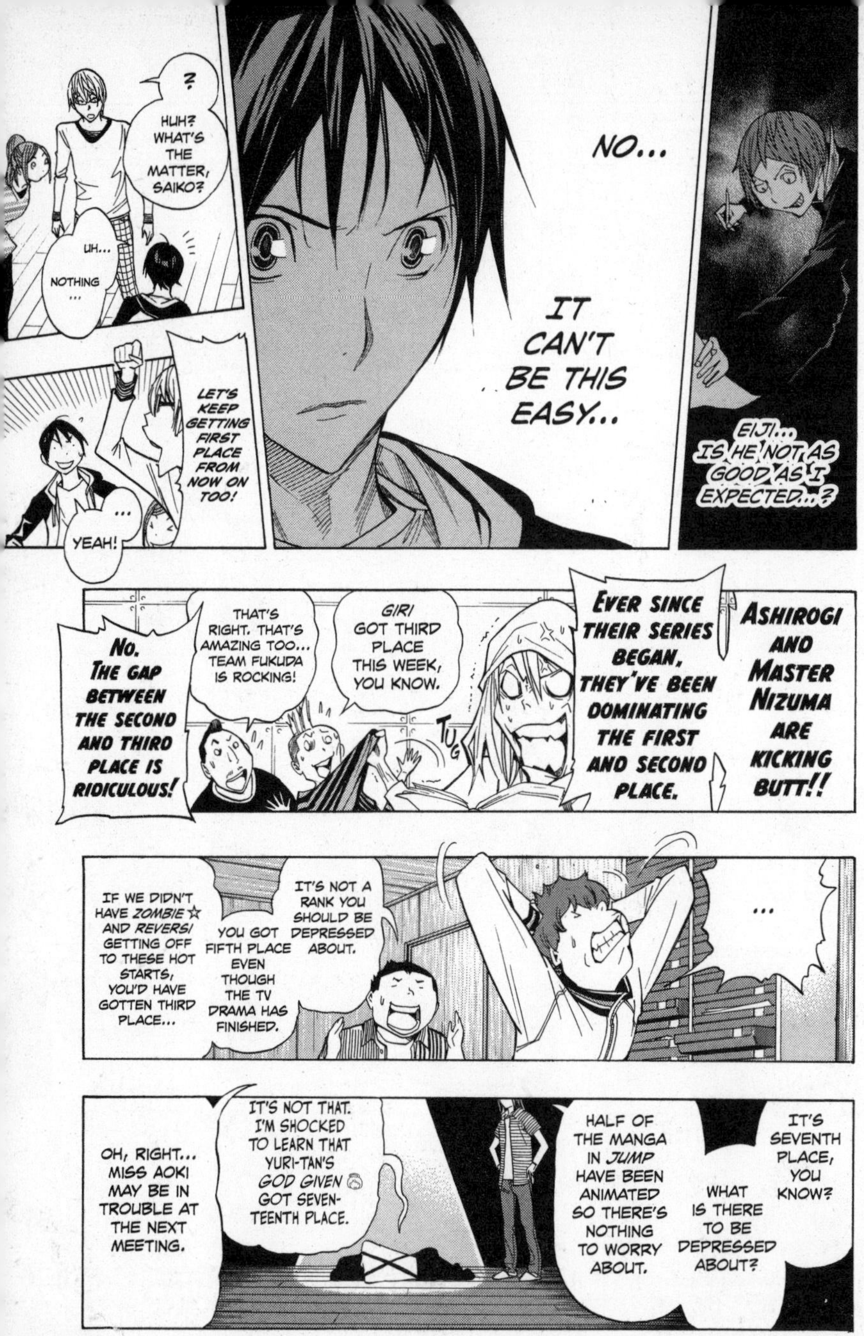
EIJI... IS HE NOT AS GOOD AS I EXPECTED...?
NO...
IT CAN'T BE THIS EASY...
?
HUH? WHAT'S THE MATTER, SAIKO?
UH...
NOTHING...
LET'S KEEP GETTING FIRST PLACE FROM NOW ON TOO!
...
YEAH!
ASHIROGI AND MASTER NIZUMA ARE KICKING BUTT!!
EVER SINCE THEIR SERIES BEGAN, THEY'VE BEEN DOMINATING THE FIRST AND SECOND PLACE.
TUG
GIRI GOT THIRD PLACE THIS WEEK, YOU KNOW.
THAT'S RIGHT. THAT'S AMAZING TOO... TEAM FUKUDA IS ROCKING!
NO. THE GAP BETWEEN THE SECOND AND THIRD PLACE IS RIDICULOUS!
...
IT'S NOT A RANK YOU SHOULD BE DEPRESSED ABOUT.
YOU GOT FIFTH PLACE EVEN THOUGH THE TV DRAMA HAS FINISHED.
IF WE DIDN'T HAVE *ZOMBIE☆* AND *REVERSI* GETTING OFF TO THESE HOT STARTS, YOU'D HAVE GOTTEN THIRD PLACE...
IT'S SEVENTH PLACE, YOU KNOW?
WHAT IS THERE TO BE DEPRESSED ABOUT?
HALF OF THE MANGA IN *JUMP* HAVE BEEN ANIMATED SO THERE'S NOTHING TO WORRY ABOUT.
IT'S NOT THAT. I'M SHOCKED TO LEARN THAT YURI-TAN'S *GOD GIVEN* GOT SEVENTEENTH PLACE.
OH, RIGHT... MISS AOKI MAY BE IN TROUBLE AT THE NEXT MEETING.

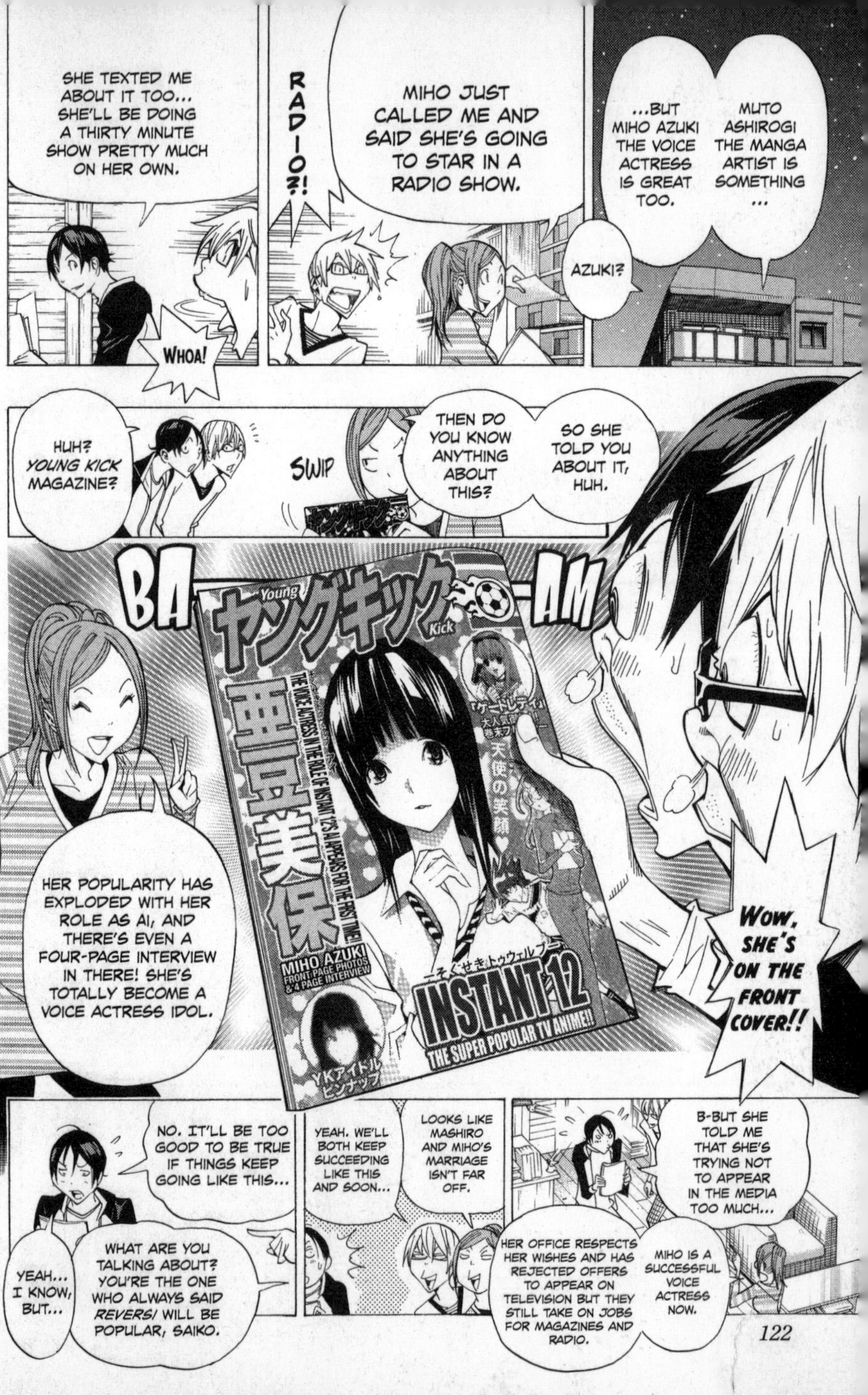
MUTO ASHIROGI THE MANGA ARTIST IS SOMETHING...
...BUT MIHO AZUKI THE VOICE ACTRESS IS GREAT TOO.
AZUKI?
MIHO JUST CALLED ME AND SAID SHE'S GOING TO STAR IN A RADIO SHOW.
RADIO?!
SHE TEXTED ME ABOUT IT TOO... SHE'LL BE DOING A THIRTY MINUTE SHOW PRETTY MUCH ON HER OWN.
WHOA!
SO SHE TOLD YOU ABOUT IT, HUH.
THEN DO YOU KNOW ANYTHING ABOUT THIS?
SWIP
HUH? *YOUNG KICK* MAGAZINE?
WOW, SHE'S ON THE FRONT COVER!!
BA—AM
Young ヤングキック Kick
THE VOICE ACTRESS IN THE ROLE OF INSTANT 12'S AI APPEARS FOR THE FIRST TIME!
亜豆美保
MIHO AZUKI FRONT PAGE PHOTOS & 4 PAGE INTERVIEW
天使の笑顔
そくせき トゥウェルブ
INSTANT 12
THE SUPER POPULAR TV ANIME!!
YKアイドル ピンナップ
HER POPULARITY HAS EXPLODED WITH HER ROLE AS AI, AND THERE'S EVEN A FOUR-PAGE INTERVIEW IN THERE! SHE'S TOTALLY BECOME A VOICE ACTRESS IDOL.
B-BUT SHE TOLD ME THAT SHE'S TRYING NOT TO APPEAR IN THE MEDIA TOO MUCH...
MIHO IS A SUCCESSFUL VOICE ACTRESS NOW.
HER OFFICE RESPECTS HER WISHES AND HAS REJECTED OFFERS TO APPEAR ON TELEVISION BUT THEY STILL TAKE ON JOBS FOR MAGAZINES AND RADIO.
LOOKS LIKE MASHIRO AND MIHO'S MARRIAGE ISN'T FAR OFF.
YEAH. WE'LL BOTH KEEP SUCCEEDING LIKE THIS AND SOON...
NO. IT'LL BE TOO GOOD TO BE TRUE IF THINGS KEEP GOING LIKE THIS...
WHAT ARE YOU TALKING ABOUT? YOU'RE THE ONE WHO ALWAYS SAID *REVERSI* WILL BE POPULAR, SAIKO.
YEAH... I KNOW, BUT...

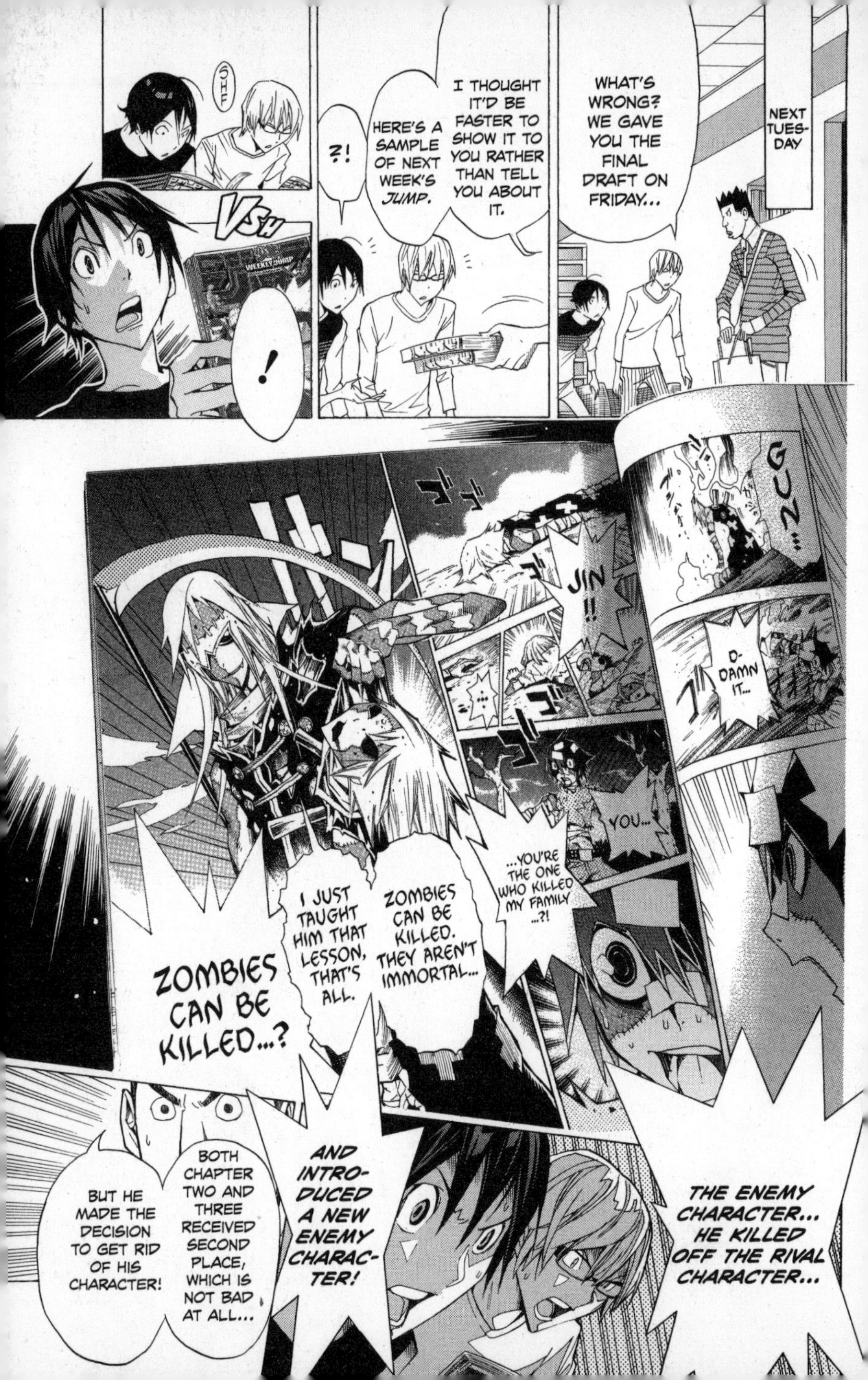
NEXT TUESDAY
WHAT'S WRONG? WE GAVE YOU THE FINAL DRAFT ON FRIDAY...
I THOUGHT IT'D BE FASTER TO SHOW IT TO YOU RATHER THAN TELL YOU ABOUT IT.
HERE'S A SAMPLE OF NEXT WEEK'S *JUMP*.
?!
SHF
VSH
WEEKLY JUMP
!
GUN...
D-DAMN IT...
JIN!!
YOU...
...YOU'RE THE ONE WHO KILLED MY FAMILY ...?!
ZOMBIES CAN BE KILLED. THEY AREN'T IMMORTAL...
I JUST TAUGHT HIM THAT LESSON, THAT'S ALL.
ZOMBIES CAN BE KILLED...?
THE ENEMY CHARACTER... HE KILLED OFF THE RIVAL CHARACTER...
AND INTRODUCED A NEW ENEMY CHARACTER!
BOTH CHAPTER TWO AND THREE RECEIVED SECOND PLACE, WHICH IS NOT BAD AT ALL...
BUT HE MADE THE DECISION TO GET RID OF HIS CHARACTER!

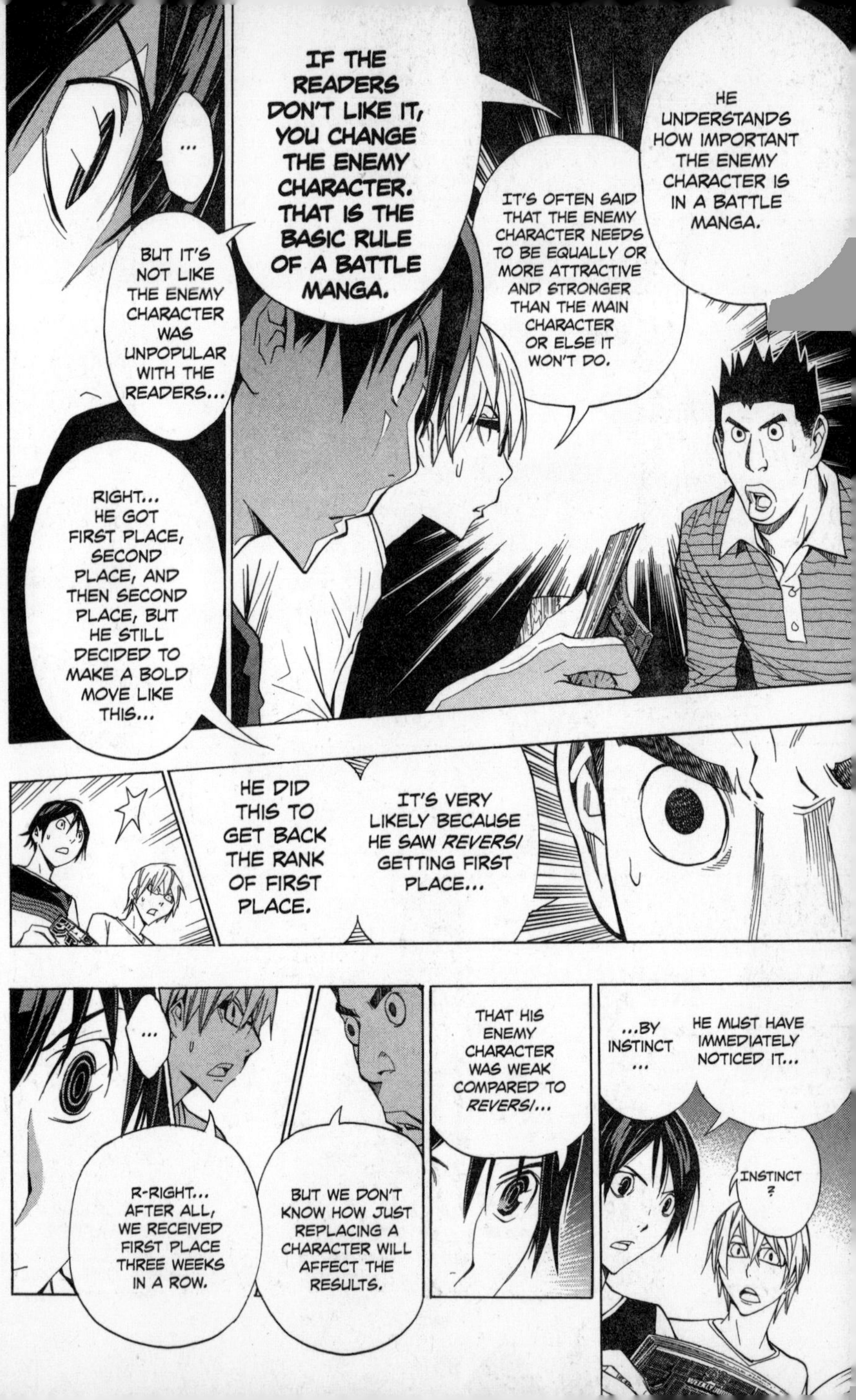
HE UNDERSTANDS HOW IMPORTANT THE ENEMY CHARACTER IS IN A BATTLE MANGA.
IT'S OFTEN SAID THAT THE ENEMY CHARACTER NEEDS TO BE EQUALLY OR MORE ATTRACTIVE AND STRONGER THAN THE MAIN CHARACTER OR ELSE IT WON'T DO.
IF THE READERS DON'T LIKE IT, YOU CHANGE THE ENEMY CHARACTER. THAT IS THE BASIC RULE OF A BATTLE MANGA.
...
BUT IT'S NOT LIKE THE ENEMY CHARACTER WAS UNPOPULAR WITH THE READERS...
RIGHT... HE GOT FIRST PLACE, SECOND PLACE, AND THEN SECOND PLACE, BUT HE STILL DECIDED TO MAKE A BOLD MOVE LIKE THIS...
IT'S VERY LIKELY BECAUSE HE SAW *REVERSI* GETTING FIRST PLACE...
HE DID THIS TO GET BACK THE RANK OF FIRST PLACE.
HE MUST HAVE IMMEDIATELY NOTICED IT...
...BY INSTINCT...
INSTINCT?
THAT HIS ENEMY CHARACTER WAS WEAK COMPARED TO *REVERSI*...
BUT WE DON'T KNOW HOW JUST REPLACING A CHARACTER WILL AFFECT THE RESULTS.
...
R-RIGHT... AFTER ALL, WE RECEIVED FIRST PLACE THREE WEEKS IN A ROW.

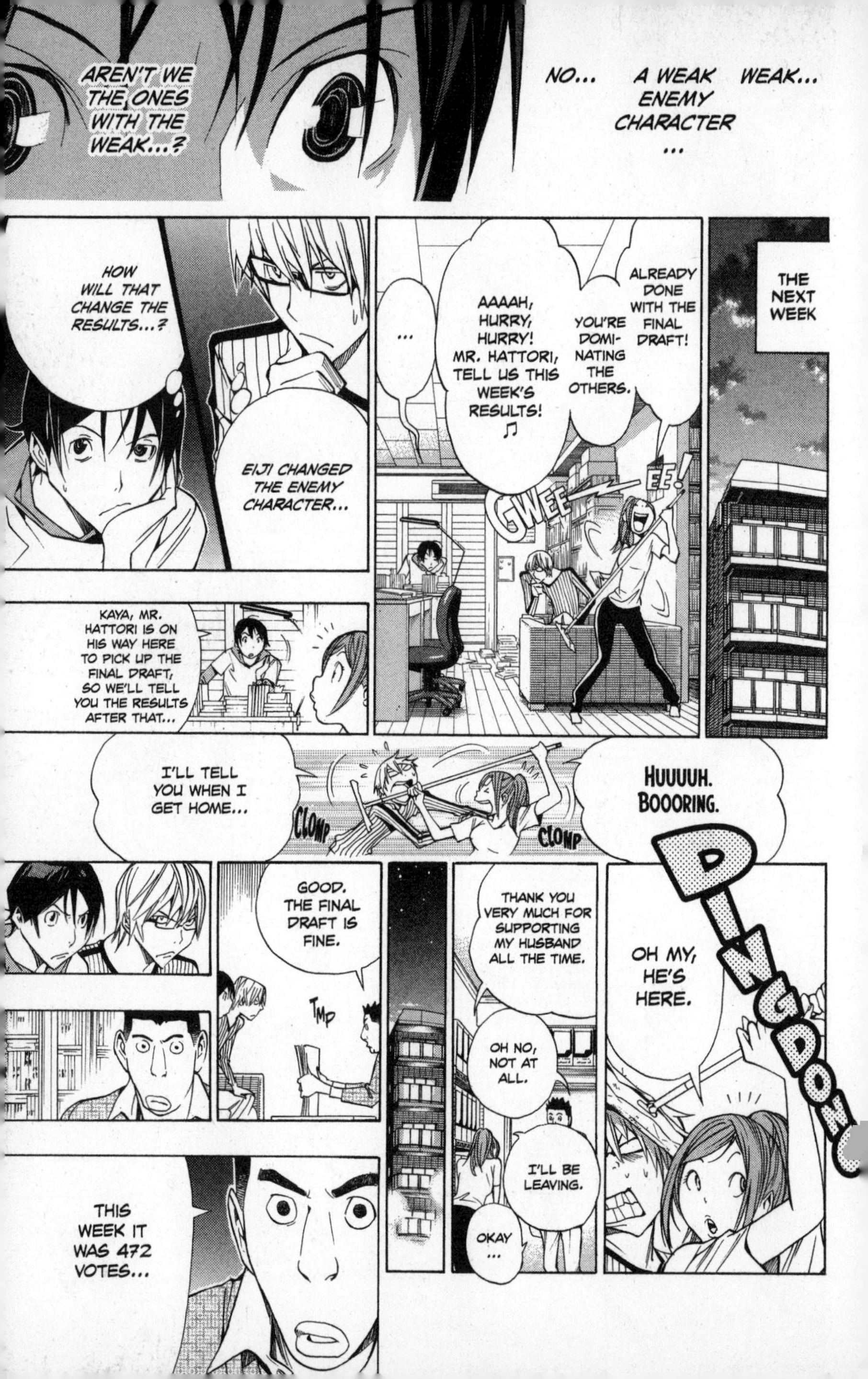
WEAK...
A WEAK ENEMY CHARACTER ...
NO...
AREN'T WE THE ONES WITH THE WEAK...?
THE NEXT WEEK
ALREADY DONE WITH THE FINAL DRAFT!
YOU'RE DOMI-NATING THE OTHERS.
AAAAH, HURRY, HURRY! MR. HATTORI, TELL US THIS WEEK'S RESULTS! ♫
GWEEEE!
...
HOW WILL THAT CHANGE THE RESULTS...?
EIJI CHANGED THE ENEMY CHARACTER...
KAYA, MR. HATTORI IS ON HIS WAY HERE TO PICK UP THE FINAL DRAFT, SO WE'LL TELL YOU THE RESULTS AFTER THAT...
HUUUUH. BOOORING.
CLOMP
CLOMP
I'LL TELL YOU WHEN I GET HOME...
DINGDON
OH MY, HE'S HERE.
THANK YOU VERY MUCH FOR SUPPORTING MY HUSBAND ALL THE TIME.
OH NO, NOT AT ALL.
I'LL BE LEAVING.
OKAY ...
GOOD. THE FINAL DRAFT IS FINE.
TMP
THIS WEEK IT WAS 472 VOTES...

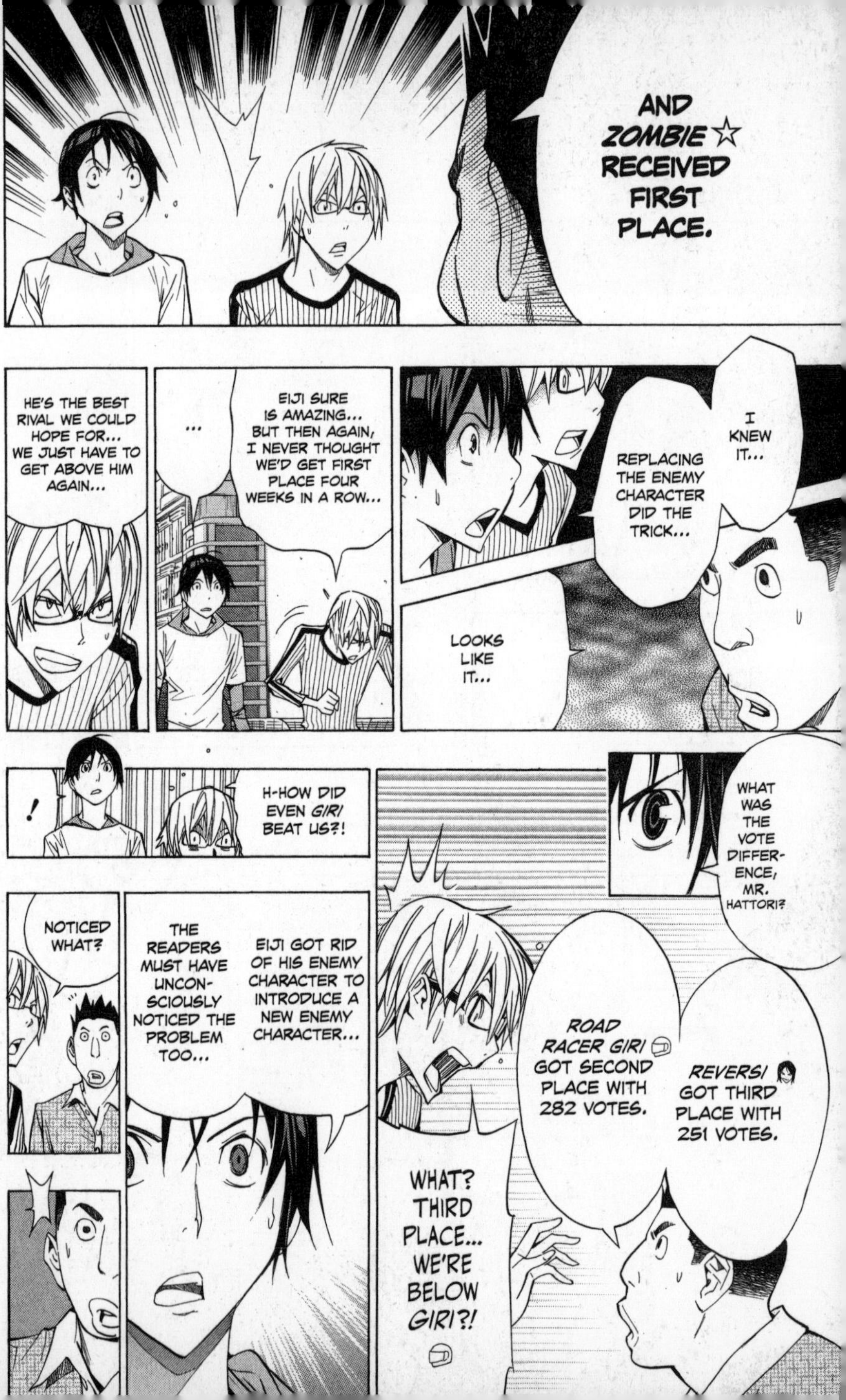
AND ZOMBIE☆ RECEIVED FIRST PLACE.
I KNEW IT...
REPLACING THE ENEMY CHARACTER DID THE TRICK...
LOOKS LIKE IT...
EIJI SURE IS AMAZING... BUT THEN AGAIN, I NEVER THOUGHT WE'D GET FIRST PLACE FOUR WEEKS IN A ROW...
...
HE'S THE BEST RIVAL WE COULD HOPE FOR... WE JUST HAVE TO GET ABOVE HIM AGAIN...
WHAT WAS THE VOTE DIFFERENCE, MR. HATTORI?
ROAD RACER GIRI GOT SECOND PLACE WITH 282 VOTES.
REVERSI GOT THIRD PLACE WITH 251 VOTES.
WHAT? THIRD PLACE... WE'RE BELOW GIRI?!
!
H-HOW DID EVEN GIRI BEAT US?!
EIJI GOT RID OF HIS ENEMY CHARACTER TO INTRODUCE A NEW ENEMY CHARACTER...
THE READERS MUST HAVE UNCONSCIOUSLY NOTICED THE PROBLEM TOO...
NOTICED WHAT?

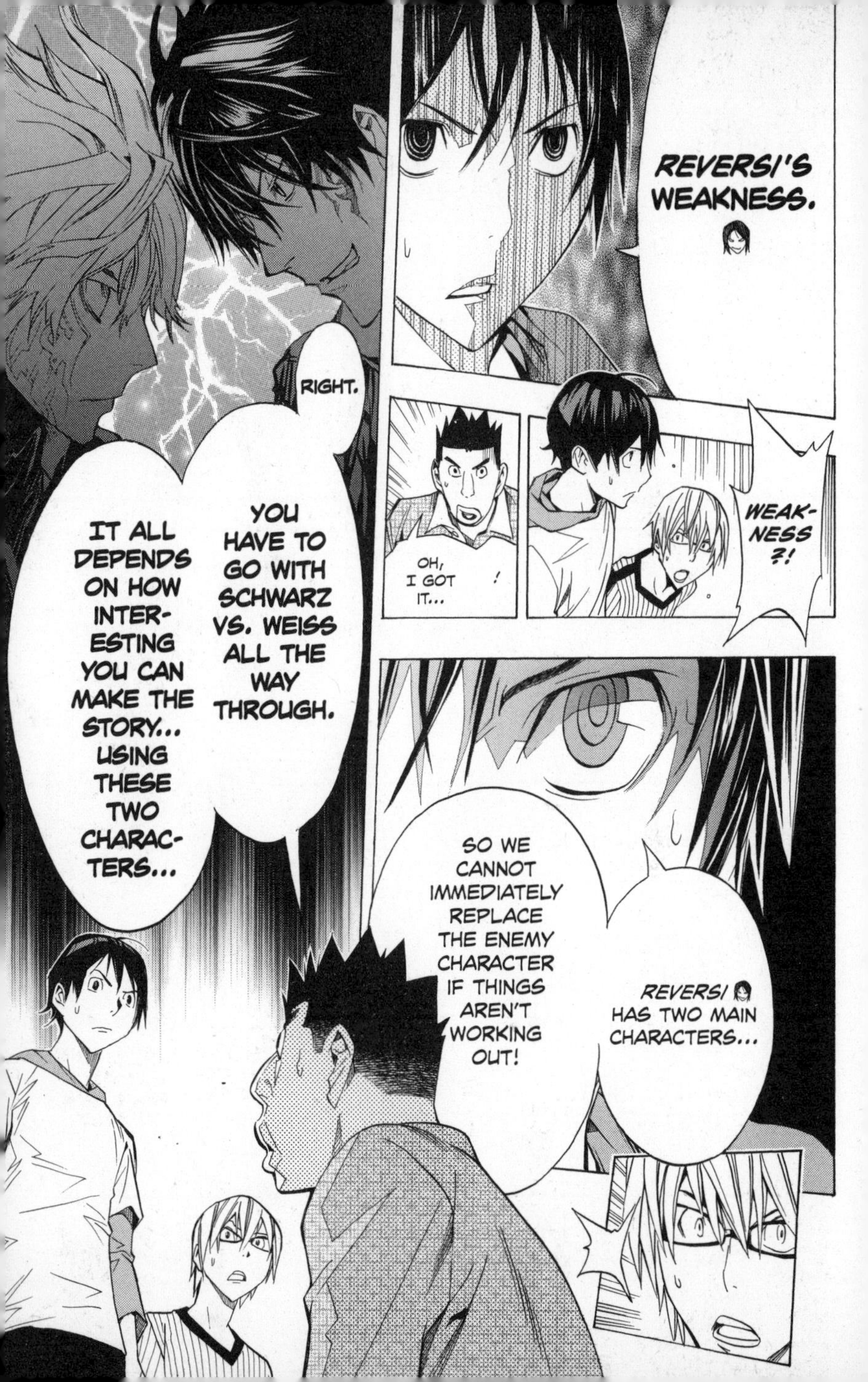
REVERSI'S WEAKNESS.
WEAK-NESS?!
OH, I GOT IT...
REVERSI HAS TWO MAIN CHARACTERS...
SO WE CANNOT IMMEDIATELY REPLACE THE ENEMY CHARACTER IF THINGS AREN'T WORKING OUT!
RIGHT.
YOU HAVE TO GO WITH SCHWARZ VS. WEISS ALL THE WAY THROUGH.
IT ALL DEPENDS ON HOW INTER-ESTING YOU CAN MAKE THE STORY... USING THESE TWO CHARAC-TERS...

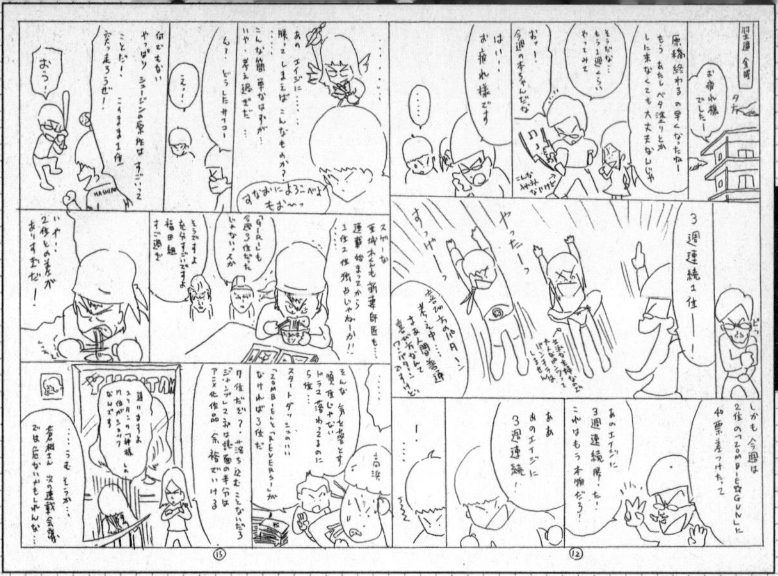

OHBA'S STORYBOARD
翌週 金曜
お疲れ様でしたー
原稿終わるの早くなったねー もう あたし ベタ塗りとか しに来なくても大丈夫なんじゃ
そうだな… もう1週くらい やってみて
おっ! 今週の本ちゃんだな
はい… お疲れ様です
……
3週連続1位ーー!
やったーっ
すっげーっ
しかも今週は2位の「ZOMBIE☆GUN」に 4票差つけたって
あのエイジに 3週連続勝った! これはもう本物だろ!
ああ あのエイジに 3週連続…
…!
あのエイジに…… 勝ってしまえばこんなものか? …こんな簡単なはずが… いや… 考え過ぎだ…
すなおによろこべよ もお〜っ
ん? どうしたサイコー
え…
何でもない やっぱりシュージンの原作はすごいってことだ! 突っ走ろうぜ! このまま1位
おう…
スゲーな 亜城木くんも新妻師匠も… 連載始まってから1位2位独占じゃねーか!!
「PCP」さんも今週3位だったじゃないっスか
そうっすよ 充分すごいですよ 福田組すご過ぎ
いや… 2位との差がありすぎだ!
そんな肩を落とす順位じゃない ドラマ落ちてるのに5位…
スタートダッシュのいい「ZOMBIE☆GUN」と「REVERSI」がなければ3位だ
7位だぞ? 落ち込むことないだろ
…うむ そうか… では危ないかもしれんな…

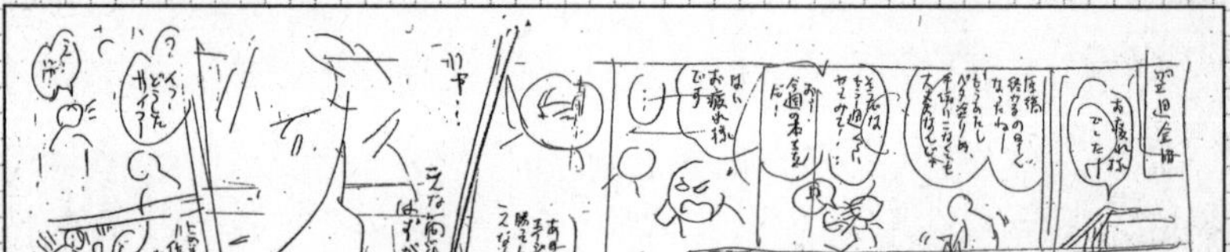

OBATA'S STORYBOARD
3週連続 1位

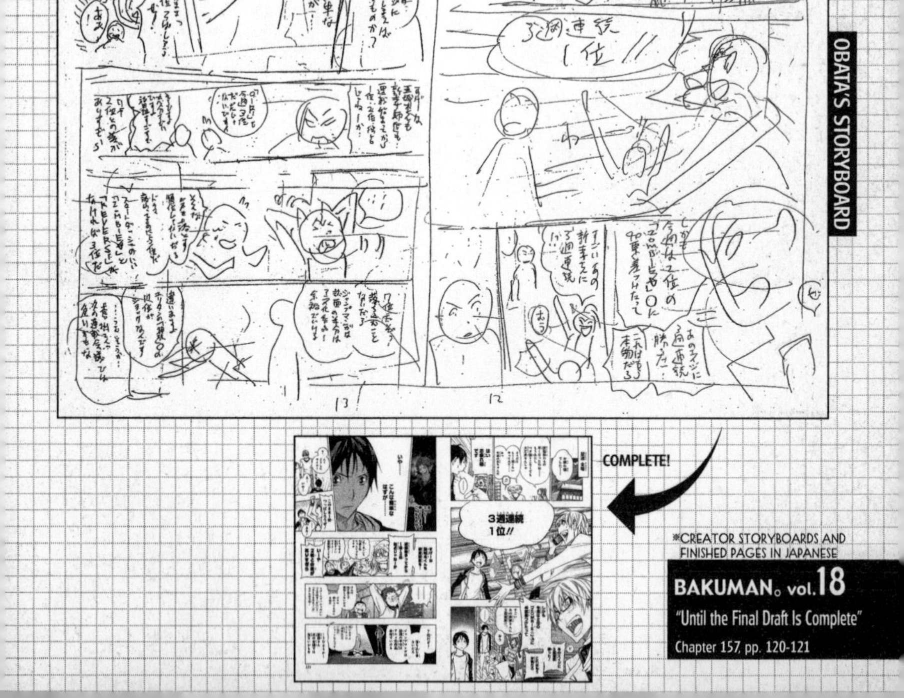

3週連続 1位!!

COMPLETE!

※CREATOR STORYBOARDS AND FINISHED PAGES IN JAPANESE

BAKUMAN。vol.18

"Until the Final Draft Is Complete"

Chapter 157, pp. 120-121

CHAPTER 158 DRAGGING ON AND TOP SPEED

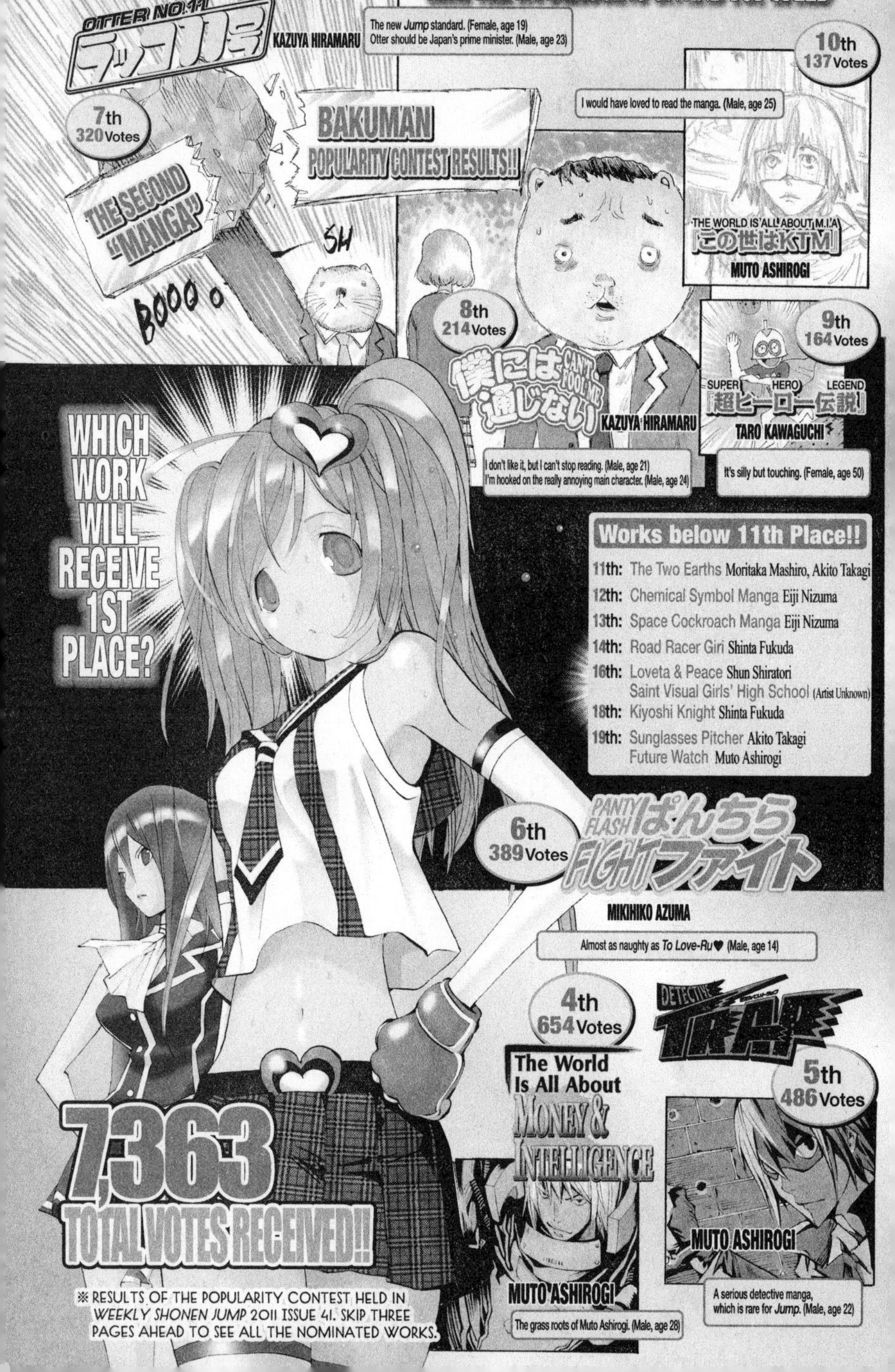
BAKUMAN
POPULARITY CONTEST RESULTS!!
10th
137 Votes
THE WORLD IS ALL ABOUT M.I.A
『この世はKTM』
MUTO ASHIROGI
I would have loved to read the manga. (Male, age 25)
OTTER NO.11
ラッコ11号
KAZUYA HIRAMARU
The new Jump standard. (Female, age 19)
Otter should be Japan's prime minister. (Male, age 23)
7th
320 Votes
THE SECOND "MANGA"
SH
BOOQ o
9th
164 Votes
SUPER HERO LEGEND
『超ヒーロー伝説』
TARO KAWAGUCHI
It's silly but touching. (Female, age 50)
8th
214 Votes
CAN'T FOOL ME
僕には通じない
KAZUYA HIRAMARU
I don't like it, but I can't stop reading. (Male, age 21)
I'm hooked on the really annoying main character. (Male, age 24)
WHICH WORK WILL RECEIVE 1ST PLACE?
Works below 11th Place!!
11th: The Two Earths Moritaka Mashiro, Akito Takagi
12th: Chemical Symbol Manga Eiji Nizuma
13th: Space Cockroach Manga Eiji Nizuma
14th: Road Racer Giri Shinta Fukuda
16th: Loveta & Peace Shun Shiratori
Saint Visual Girls' High School (Artist Unknown)
18th: Kiyoshi Knight Shinta Fukuda
19th: Sunglasses Pitcher Akito Takagi
Future Watch Muto Ashirogi
6th
389 Votes
PANTY FLASH FIGHT
ぱんちらファイト
MIKIHIKO AZUMA
Almost as naughty as To Love-Ru♥ (Male, age 14)
5th
486 Votes
DETECTIVE TRAP
MUTO ASHIROGI
A serious detective manga, which is rare for Jump. (Male, age 22)
4th
654 Votes
The World Is All About MONEY & INTELLIGENCE
MUTO ASHIROGI
The grass roots of Muto Ashirogi. (Male, age 28)
7,363
TOTAL VOTES RECEIVED!!
※ RESULTS OF THE POPULARITY CONTEST HELD IN WEEKLY SHONEN JUMP 2011 ISSUE 41. SKIP THREE PAGES AHEAD TO SEE ALL THE NOMINATED WORKS.

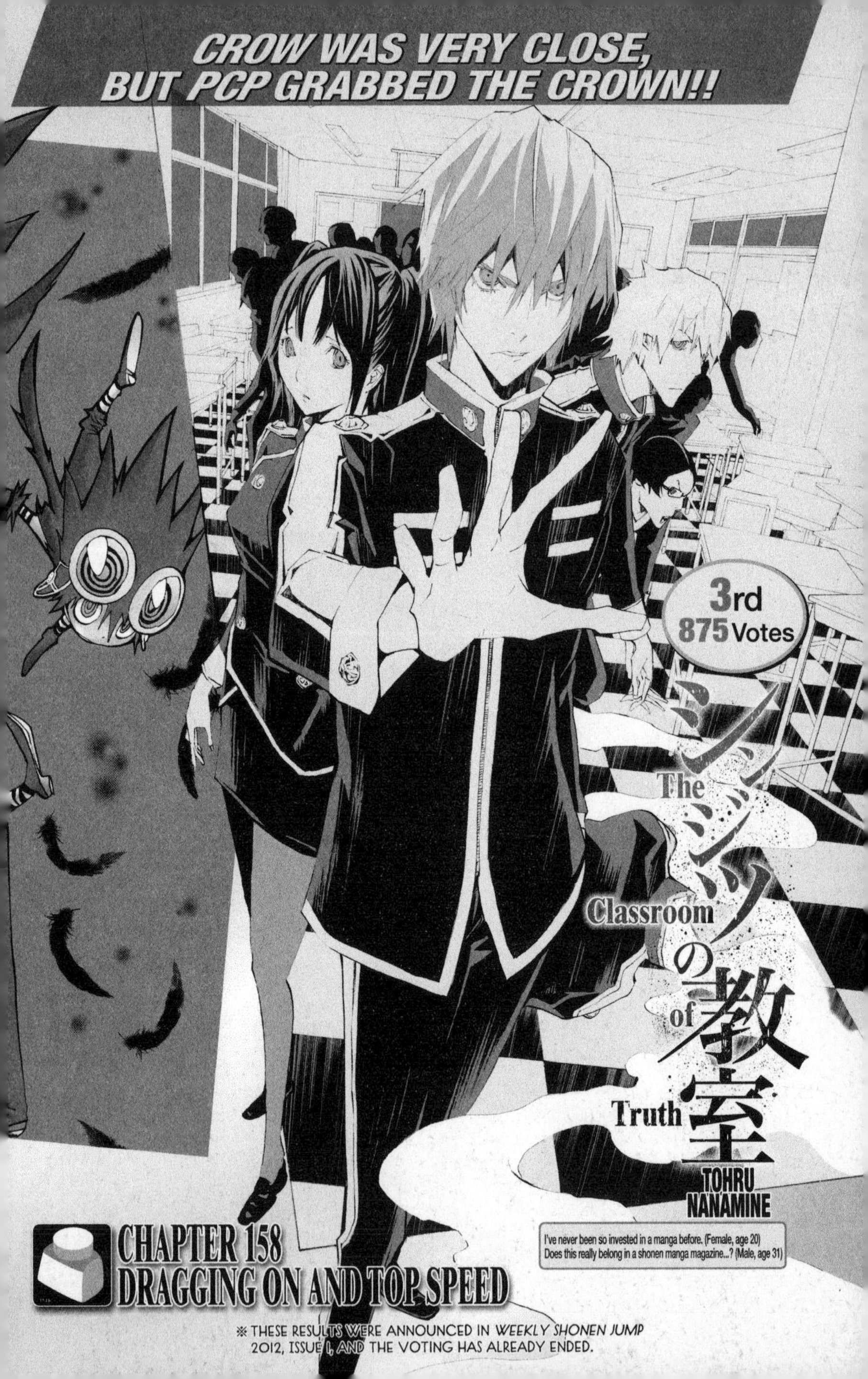
CROW WAS VERY CLOSE, BUT PCP GRABBED THE CROWN!!
3rd
875 Votes
The Classroom of Truth
ミツの教室
TOHRU NANAMINE
I've never been so invested in a manga before. (Female, age 20)
Does this really belong in a shonen manga magazine...? (Male, age 31)
CHAPTER 158
DRAGGING ON AND TOP SPEED
※ THESE RESULTS WERE ANNOUNCED IN WEEKLY SHONEN JUMP 2012, ISSUE 1, AND THE VOTING HAS ALREADY ENDED.

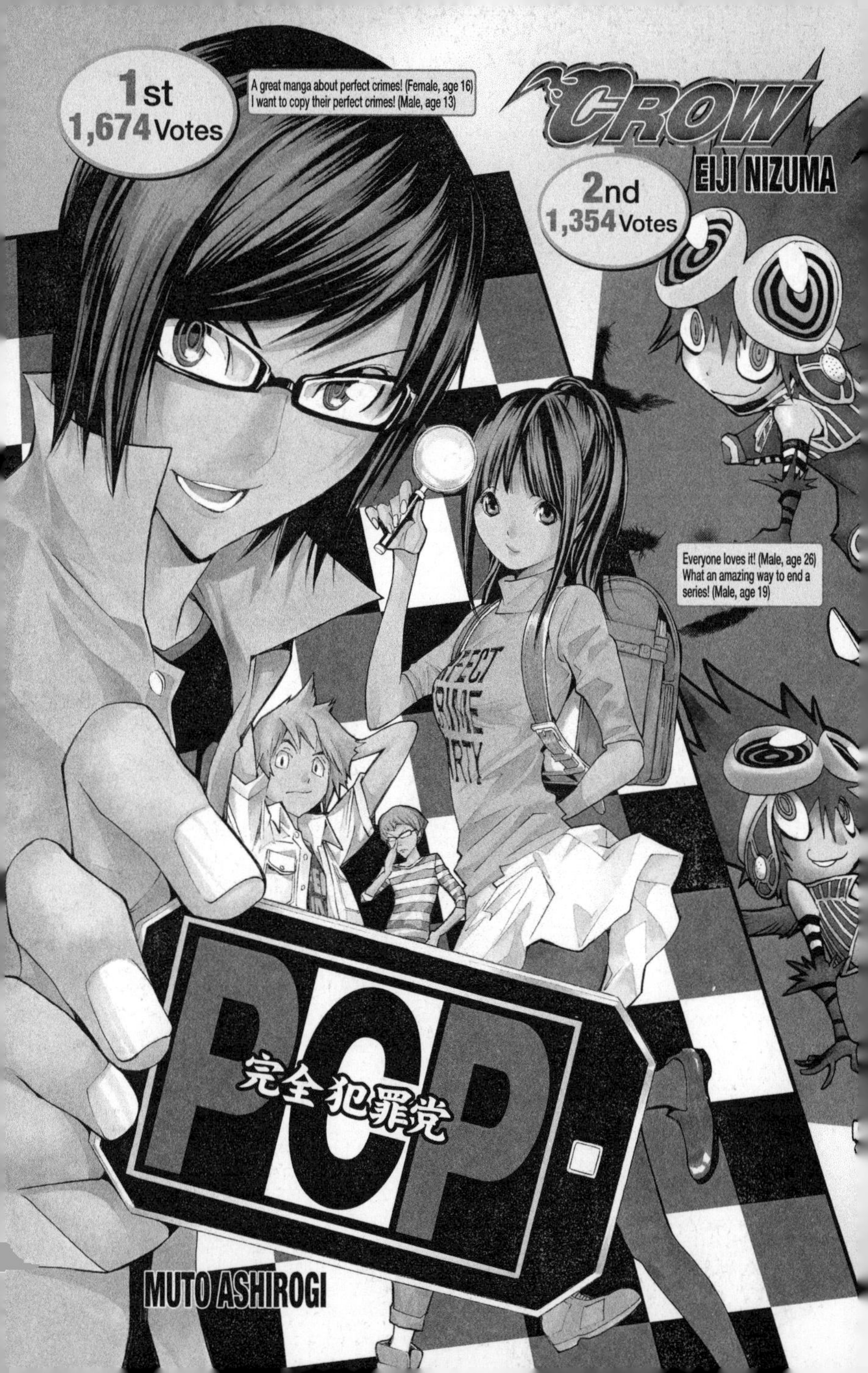
1st
1,674 Votes
A great manga about perfect crimes! (Female, age 16)
I want to copy their perfect crimes! (Male, age 13)
CROW
EIJI NIZUMA
2nd
1,354 Votes
Everyone loves it! (Male, age 26)
What an amazing way to end a series! (Male, age 19)
PCP
完全犯罪党
MUTO ASHIROGI

THE SECOND Bakuman "Manga" Popularity Contest Nominees!!

All Eighty-one nominees are listed here!! And there's more to come!!

#	Title	Author
1	The Two Earths	Moritaka Mashiro / Akito Takagi
2	Sunglasses Pitcher	Akito Takagi
3	The Camera and the Hare	Akito Takagi
4	One Hundred Millionth	Moritaka Mashiro / Akito Takagi
5	The World Is All About Money and Intelligence	Muto Ashirogi
6	Demon Dragon Legend	Muto Ashirogi
7	Angel Days	Muto Ashirogi
8	Overconfidence Hero Super-Confidence Man	Moritaka Mashiro
9	The Shadiest Man in the World	Moritaka Mashiro
10	Con-Detective Hikake	Moritaka Mashiro
11	Invisible Detective Skeleton	Akito Takagi
12	Detective Trap	Muto Ashirogi
13	Me Two	Muto Ashirogi
14	Future Watch	Muto Ashirogi
15	Ten	Muto Ashirogi
16	Vroom, Tanto Daihatsu	Muto Ashirogi
17	The World Is All About M.I.A	Muto Ashirogi
18	Stopper of Magma	Muto Ashirogi
19	PCP -Perfect Crime Party-	Muto Ashirogi
20	A Fleeting Moment	Muto Ashirogi
21	Large Bander	Eiji Nizuma
22	Haitenpepoo	Eiji Nizuma
23	Dogamiberon	Eiji Nizuma
24	Crow	Eiji Nizuma
25	Yellow Hit	Eiji Nizuma
26	Love Power A to Z	Eiji Nizuma
27	Chemical Symbol Manga	Eiji Nizuma
28	Space Cockroach Manga	Eiji Nizuma
29	U-400	Shinta Fukuda
30	Diligent Delinquent	Shinta Fukuda
31	Kiyoshi Knight	Shinta Fukuda
32	Road Racer Giri	Shinta Fukuda
33	Killer Yui	Shinta Fukuda
34	hideout door	Ko Aoki / Takuro Nakai
35	Time of Greenery	Kn Aoki
36	God Given...	Kn Aoki
37	Otter No.11	Kazuya Hiramaru
38	Can't Fool Me	Kazuya Hiramaru
39	Business Boy Kenichi	Shoyo Takahama
40	Mikata's Justice	Shoyo Takahama
41	+Natural	Aiko Iwase / Eiji Nizuma
42	Adolescents	Aiko Akina / Hachiro Happongi
43	Super Hero Legend	Taro Kawaguchi
44	Happy Ranger	Taro Kawaguchi
45	A Hero's Tragedy	Taro Kawaguchi
46	Shapon (The End of Japan)	Ryu Shizuka
47	True Human	Ryu Shizuka
48	The Classroom of Truth	Tohru Nanamine
49	Nerves and the Accompanying Vapor	Tohru Nanamine
50	What You Need for a Meaningful School Life	Tohru Nanamine
51	Loveta & Peace	Shun Shiratori
52	Phantom Thief Cheater	Kyotaro Hibiki
53	Nande?!	Kyotaro Hibiki
54	Love Me Do?	Mikihiko Azuma
55	Panty Flash Fight	Mikihiko Azuma
56	Cheese Crackers	Kisaku Arai
57	Hustlemin A	Kisaku Arai
58	Boy E & Girl B	Kisaku Arai
59	Tournament & School	Kisaku Arai
60	Colorfusical	Koji Makaino
61	Samurai Batter Kil	Nangoku
62	The Sword That Surpasses Time	Shigure Yanagi
63	Wandering about Hollow Town	Shuichi Moriya
64	Chain Gold	Kono
65	Tank Top	Orihara
66	John, the God of Catalog Requests	Shigeo Amada
67	How to Make Good Pot-Stickers	Nikumi Hino
68	Detective Gosuke Akechi	Kyoichi Murasaki / Shun Hanasaki
69	Strawberry Shoot	Ayuto Bori
70	Silent Thunder	Kazuki Kimura
71	Space Yellow Gate	Tetsuya Yanagihara
72	I Am Jump-King	Akina Minami
73	Blackbelt Nine!!	Yoshiyuki Hirai
74	Tatsuya of Tsutaya	Kazuhiro Ozawa
75	+ β	Ibaraki
76	Taracone	(Artist Unknown)
77	What Do You Think About This Shot?	(Artist Unknown)
78	Scoutman Joss	(Artist Unknown)
79	4.8 Foot Goalie	(Artist Unknown)
80	Bloody Table Tennis	(Artist Unknown)
81	Saint Visual Girls' High School	(Artist Unknown)

※ THIS NOMINEE LIST RAN IN *WEEKLY SHONEN JUMP* ISSUE 41 IN 2011.

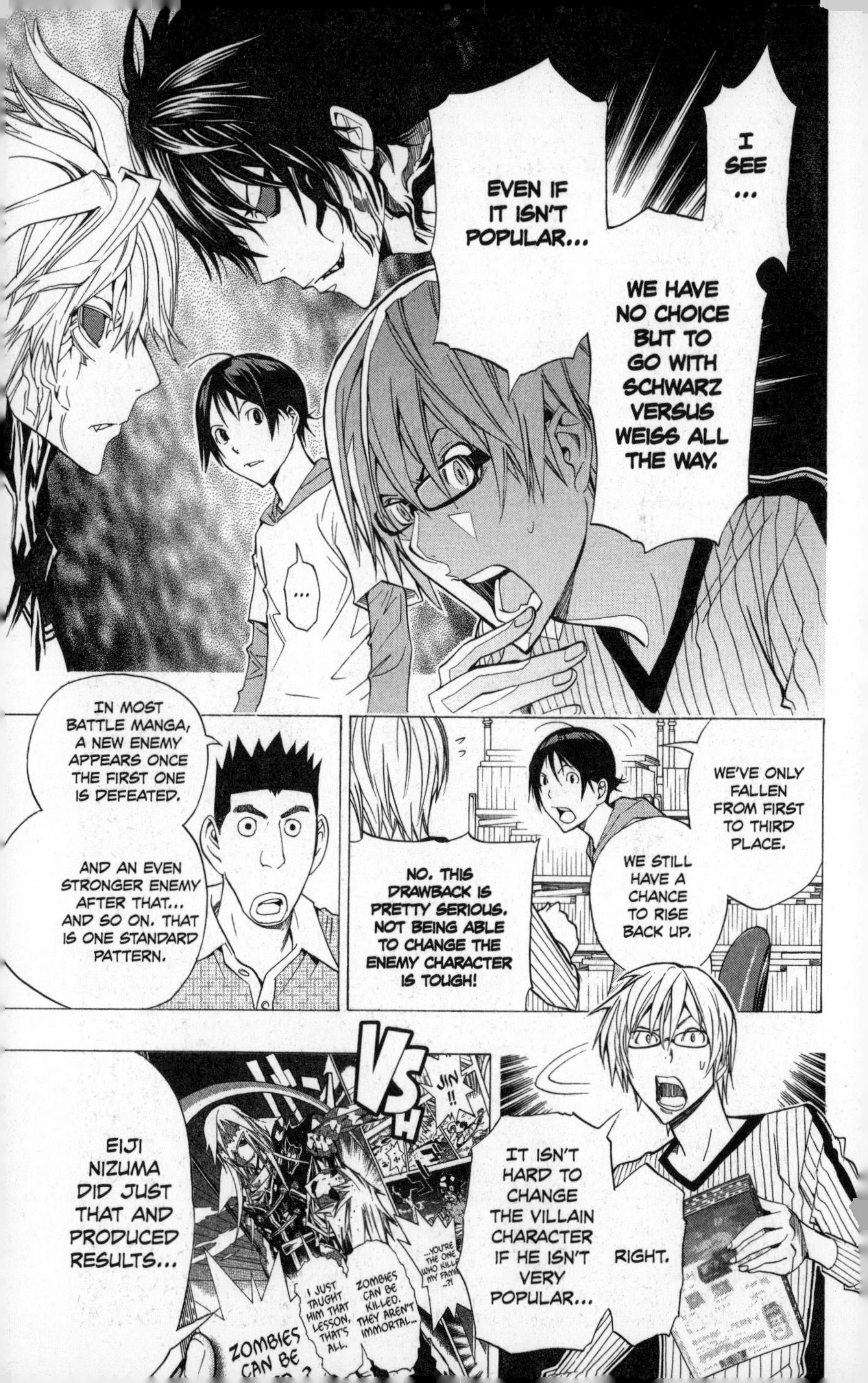
I SEE...
EVEN IF IT ISN'T POPULAR...
WE HAVE NO CHOICE BUT TO GO WITH SCHWARZ VERSUS WEISS ALL THE WAY.
...
WE'VE ONLY FALLEN FROM FIRST TO THIRD PLACE.
WE STILL HAVE A CHANCE TO RISE BACK UP.
NO. THIS DRAWBACK IS PRETTY SERIOUS. NOT BEING ABLE TO CHANGE THE ENEMY CHARACTER IS TOUGH!
IN MOST BATTLE MANGA, A NEW ENEMY APPEARS ONCE THE FIRST ONE IS DEFEATED.
AND AN EVEN STRONGER ENEMY AFTER THAT... AND SO ON. THAT IS ONE STANDARD PATTERN.
RIGHT.
IT ISN'T HARD TO CHANGE THE VILLAIN CHARACTER IF HE ISN'T VERY POPULAR...
EIJI NIZUMA DID JUST THAT AND PRODUCED RESULTS...
VS
JIN!!
ZOMBIES CAN BE KILLED. THEY AREN'T IMMORTAL...
I JUST TAUGHT HIM THAT LESSON, THAT'S ALL.

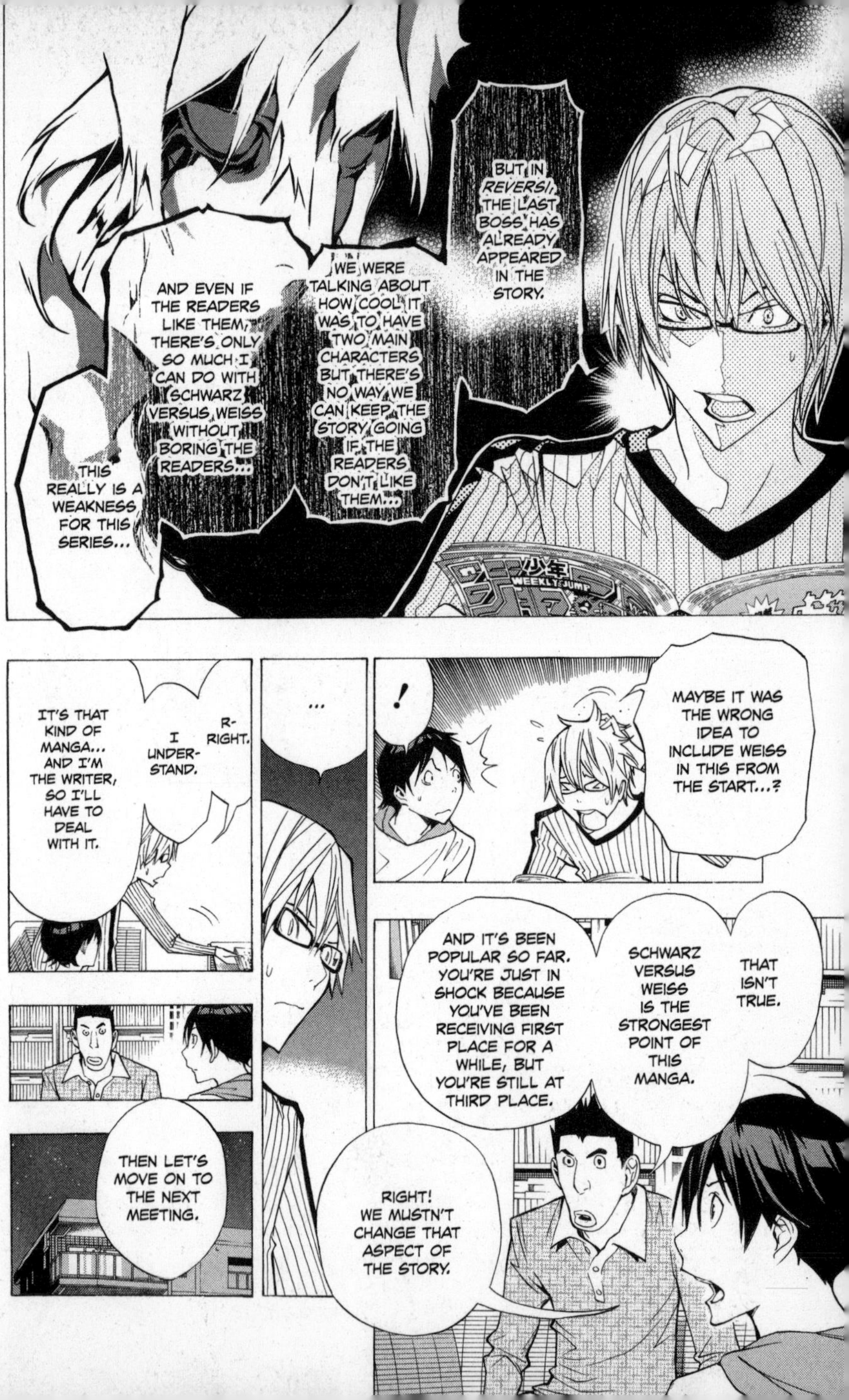
BUT IN *REVERSI*, THE LAST BOSS HAS ALREADY APPEARED IN THE STORY.
WE WERE TALKING ABOUT HOW COOL IT WAS TO HAVE TWO MAIN CHARACTERS BUT THERE'S NO WAY WE CAN KEEP THE STORY GOING IF THE READERS DON'T LIKE THEM...
AND EVEN IF THE READERS LIKE THEM, THERE'S ONLY SO MUCH I CAN DO WITH SCHWARZ VERSUS WEISS WITHOUT BORING THE READERS...
THIS REALLY IS A WEAKNESS FOR THIS SERIES...
MAYBE IT WAS THE WRONG IDEA TO INCLUDE WEISS IN THIS FROM THE START...?
!
THAT ISN'T TRUE.
SCHWARZ VERSUS WEISS IS THE STRONGEST POINT OF THIS MANGA.
AND IT'S BEEN POPULAR SO FAR. YOU'RE JUST IN SHOCK BECAUSE YOU'VE BEEN RECEIVING FIRST PLACE FOR A WHILE, BUT YOU'RE STILL AT THIRD PLACE.
RIGHT! WE MUSTN'T CHANGE THAT ASPECT OF THE STORY.
...
R-RIGHT.
I UNDERSTAND.
IT'S THAT KIND OF MANGA... AND I'M THE WRITER, SO I'LL HAVE TO DEAL WITH IT.
THEN LET'S MOVE ON TO THE NEXT MEETING.

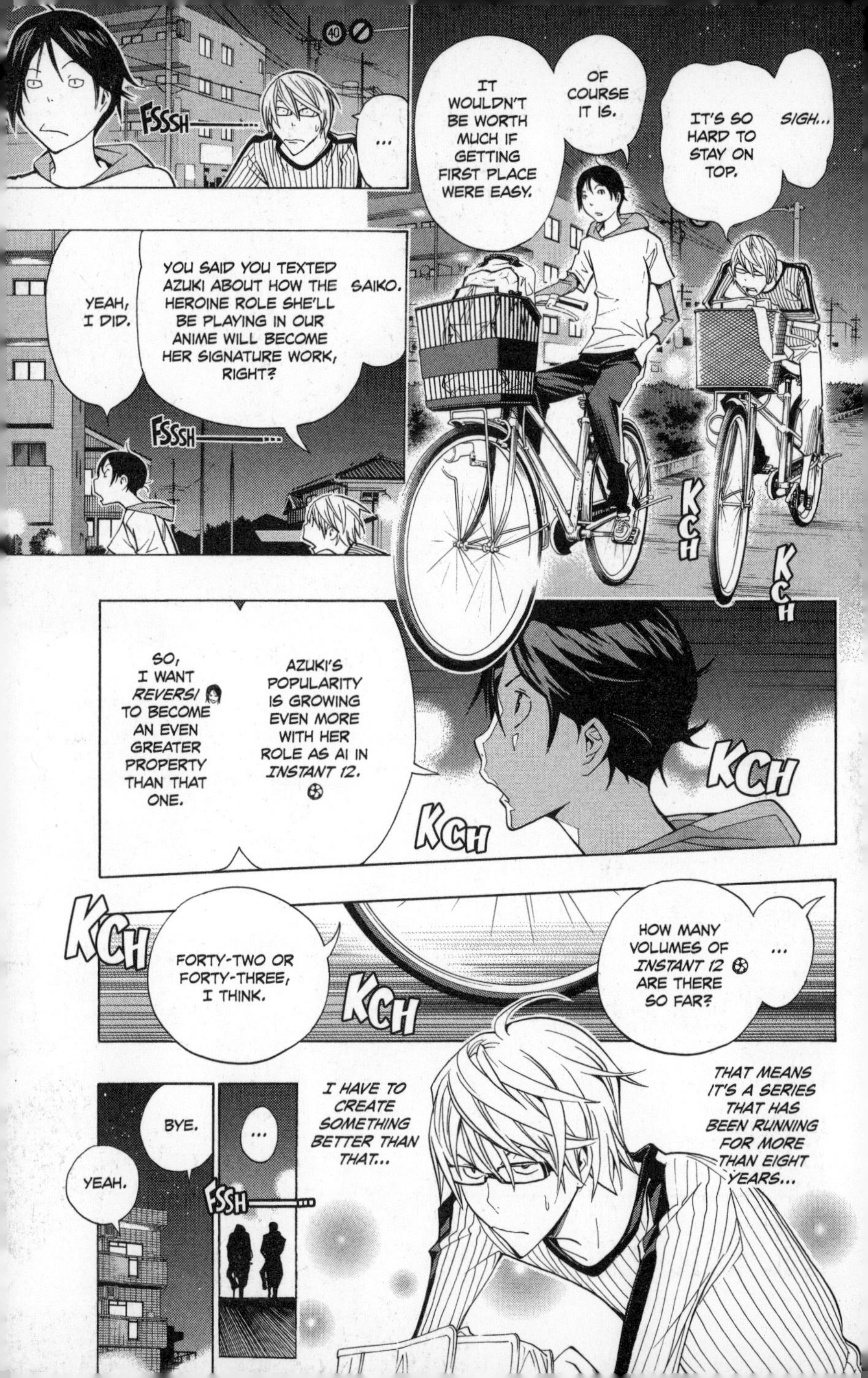
SIGH...
IT'S SO HARD TO STAY ON TOP.
OF COURSE IT IS.
IT WOULDN'T BE WORTH MUCH IF GETTING FIRST PLACE WERE EASY.
KCH
KCH
...
FSSSH
SAIKO.
YOU SAID YOU TEXTED AZUKI ABOUT HOW THE HEROINE ROLE SHE'LL BE PLAYING IN OUR ANIME WILL BECOME HER SIGNATURE WORK, RIGHT?
YEAH, I DID.
FSSSH
KCH
AZUKI'S POPULARITY IS GROWING EVEN MORE WITH HER ROLE AS AI IN *INSTANT 12*.
SO, I WANT *REVERSI* TO BECOME AN EVEN GREATER PROPERTY THAN THAT ONE.
KCH
...
HOW MANY VOLUMES OF *INSTANT 12* ARE THERE SO FAR?
KCH
FORTY-TWO OR FORTY-THREE, I THINK.
KCH
THAT MEANS IT'S A SERIES THAT HAS BEEN RUNNING FOR MORE THAN EIGHT YEARS...
I HAVE TO CREATE SOMETHING BETTER THAN THAT...
...
FSSH
BYE.
YEAH.

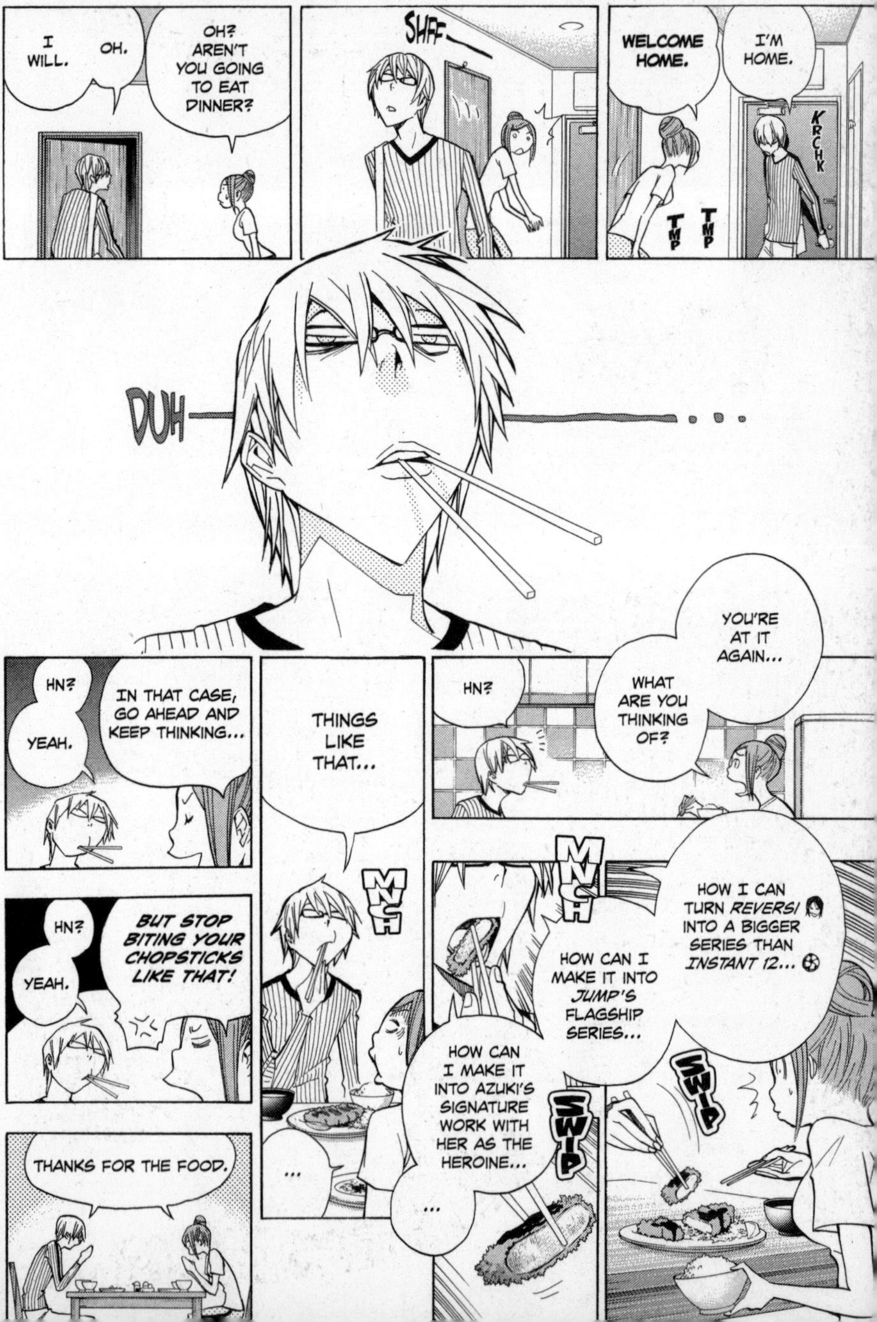
I'M HOME.
KRCHK
WELCOME HOME.
TMP TMP
SHFF
OH? AREN'T YOU GOING TO EAT DINNER?
OH.
I WILL.
DUH...
YOU'RE AT IT AGAIN...
WHAT ARE YOU THINKING OF?
HN?
MNCH
HOW I CAN TURN *REVERSI* INTO A BIGGER SERIES THAN *INSTANT 12*...
HOW CAN I MAKE IT INTO *JUMP'S* FLAGSHIP SERIES...
SWIP
HOW CAN I MAKE IT INTO AZUKI'S SIGNATURE WORK WITH HER AS THE HEROINE...
SWIP
...
THINGS LIKE THAT...
MNCH
...
IN THAT CASE, GO AHEAD AND KEEP THINKING...
HN?
YEAH.
BUT STOP BITING YOUR CHOPSTICKS LIKE THAT!
HN?
YEAH.
THANKS FOR THE FOOD.

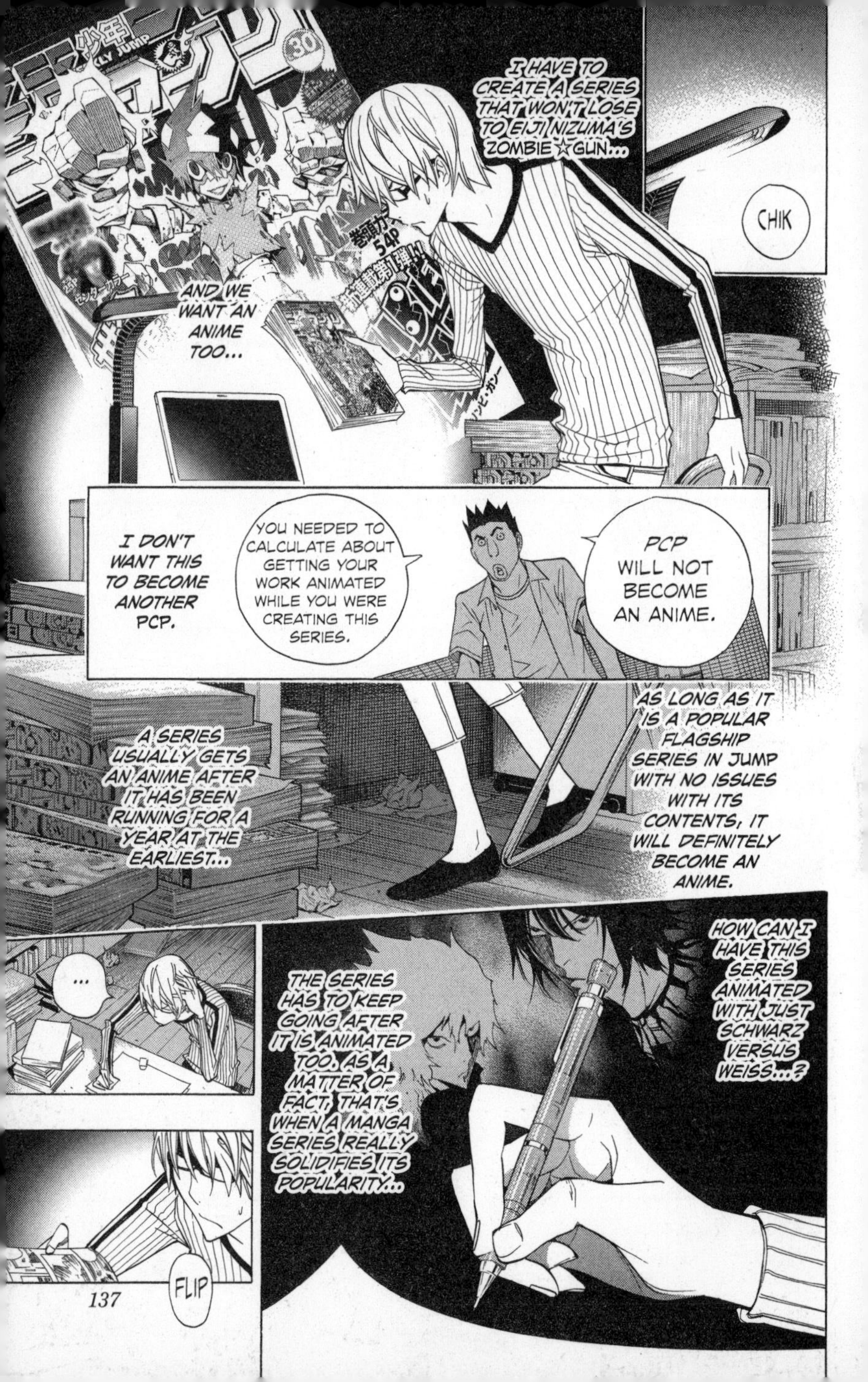
CHIK
I HAVE TO CREATE A SERIES THAT WON'T LOSE TO EIJI NIZUMA'S ZOMBIE☆GUN...
AND WE WANT AN ANIME TOO...
PCP WILL NOT BECOME AN ANIME.
YOU NEEDED TO CALCULATE ABOUT GETTING YOUR WORK ANIMATED WHILE YOU WERE CREATING THIS SERIES.
I DON'T WANT THIS TO BECOME ANOTHER PCP.
AS LONG AS IT IS A POPULAR FLAGSHIP SERIES IN JUMP WITH NO ISSUES WITH ITS CONTENTS, IT WILL DEFINITELY BECOME AN ANIME.
A SERIES USUALLY GETS AN ANIME AFTER IT HAS BEEN RUNNING FOR A YEAR AT THE EARLIEST...
HOW CAN I HAVE THIS SERIES ANIMATED WITH JUST SCHWARZ VERSUS WEISS...?
THE SERIES HAS TO KEEP GOING AFTER IT IS ANIMATED TOO. AS A MATTER OF FACT, THAT'S WHEN A MANGA SERIES REALLY SOLIDIFIES ITS POPULARITY...
...
FLIP

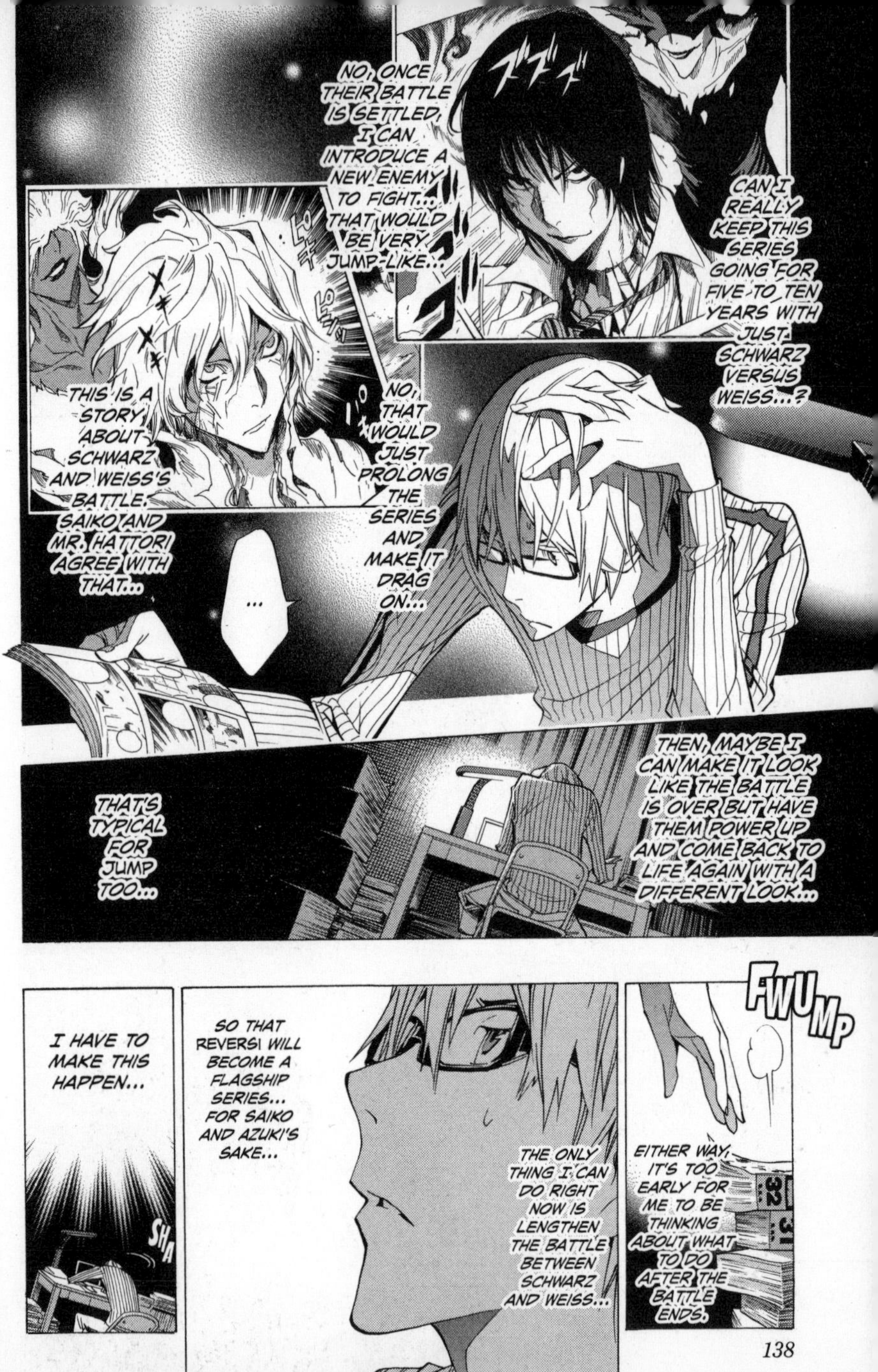
CAN I REALLY KEEP THIS SERIES GOING FOR FIVE TO TEN YEARS WITH JUST SCHWARZ VERSUS WEISS...?
NO, ONCE THEIR BATTLE IS SETTLED, I CAN INTRODUCE A NEW ENEMY TO FIGHT... THAT WOULD BE VERY JUMP-LIKE...
NO, THAT WOULD JUST PROLONG THE SERIES AND MAKE IT DRAG ON...
THIS IS A STORY ABOUT SCHWARZ AND WEISS'S BATTLE. SAIKO AND MR. HATTORI AGREE WITH THAT...
...
THEN, MAYBE I CAN MAKE IT LOOK LIKE THE BATTLE IS OVER BUT HAVE THEM POWER UP AND COME BACK TO LIFE AGAIN WITH A DIFFERENT LOOK...
THAT'S TYPICAL FOR JUMP TOO...
FWUMP
EITHER WAY, IT'S TOO EARLY FOR ME TO BE THINKING ABOUT WHAT TO DO AFTER THE BATTLE ENDS.
THE ONLY THING I CAN DO RIGHT NOW IS LENGTHEN THE BATTLE BETWEEN SCHWARZ AND WEISS...
SO THAT REVERSI WILL BECOME A FLAGSHIP SERIES... FOR SAIKO AND AZUKI'S SAKE...
I HAVE TO MAKE THIS HAPPEN...
SHA

READ THIS WAY

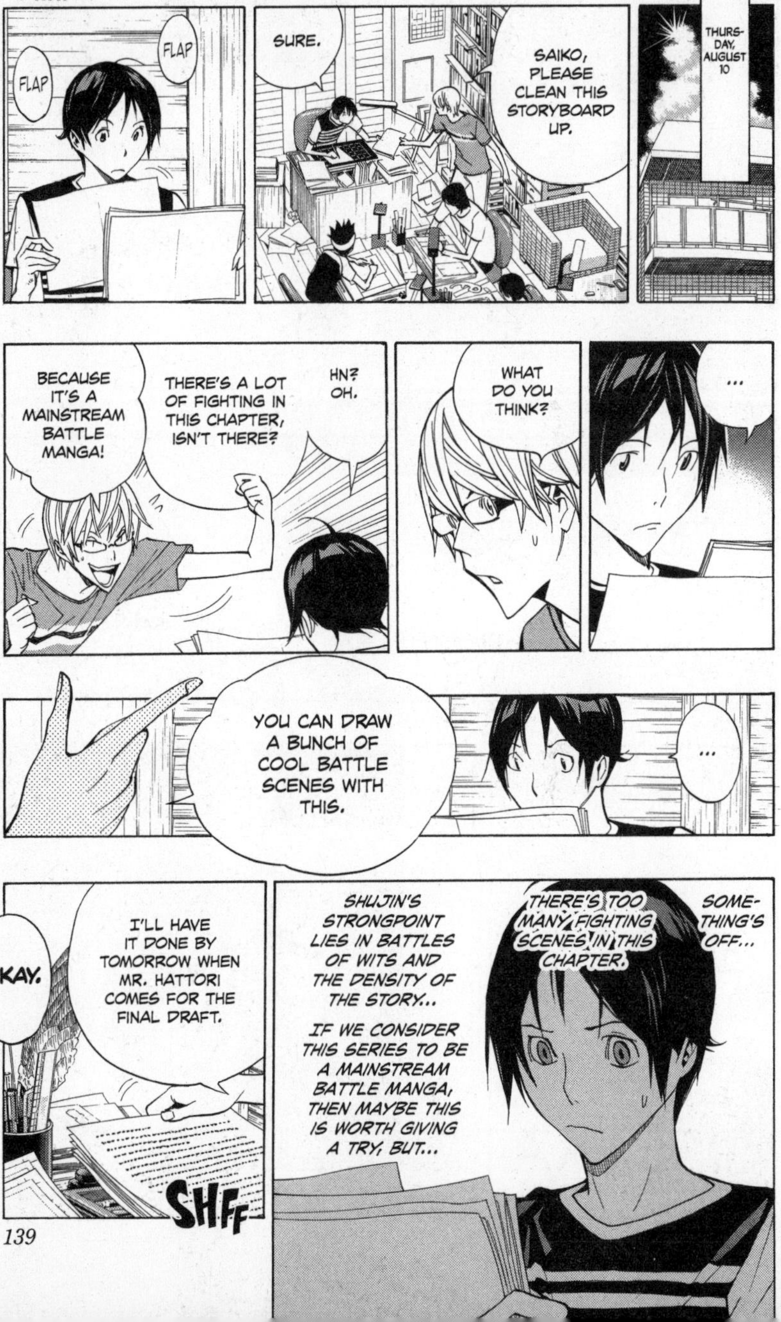

THURS-DAY, AUGUST 10
SAIKO, PLEASE CLEAN THIS STORYBOARD UP.
SURE.
FLAP
FLAP
...
WHAT DO YOU THINK?
HN? OH.
THERE'S A LOT OF FIGHTING IN THIS CHAPTER, ISN'T THERE?
BECAUSE IT'S A MAINSTREAM BATTLE MANGA!
...
YOU CAN DRAW A BUNCH OF COOL BATTLE SCENES WITH THIS.
SOME-THING'S OFF...
THERE'S TOO MANY FIGHTING SCENES IN THIS CHAPTER.
SHUJIN'S STRONGPOINT LIES IN BATTLES OF WITS AND THE DENSITY OF THE STORY...
IF WE CONSIDER THIS SERIES TO BE A MAINSTREAM BATTLE MANGA, THEN MAYBE THIS IS WORTH GIVING A TRY, BUT...
I'LL HAVE IT DONE BY TOMORROW WHEN MR. HATTORI COMES FOR THE FINAL DRAFT.
OKAY.
SHFF

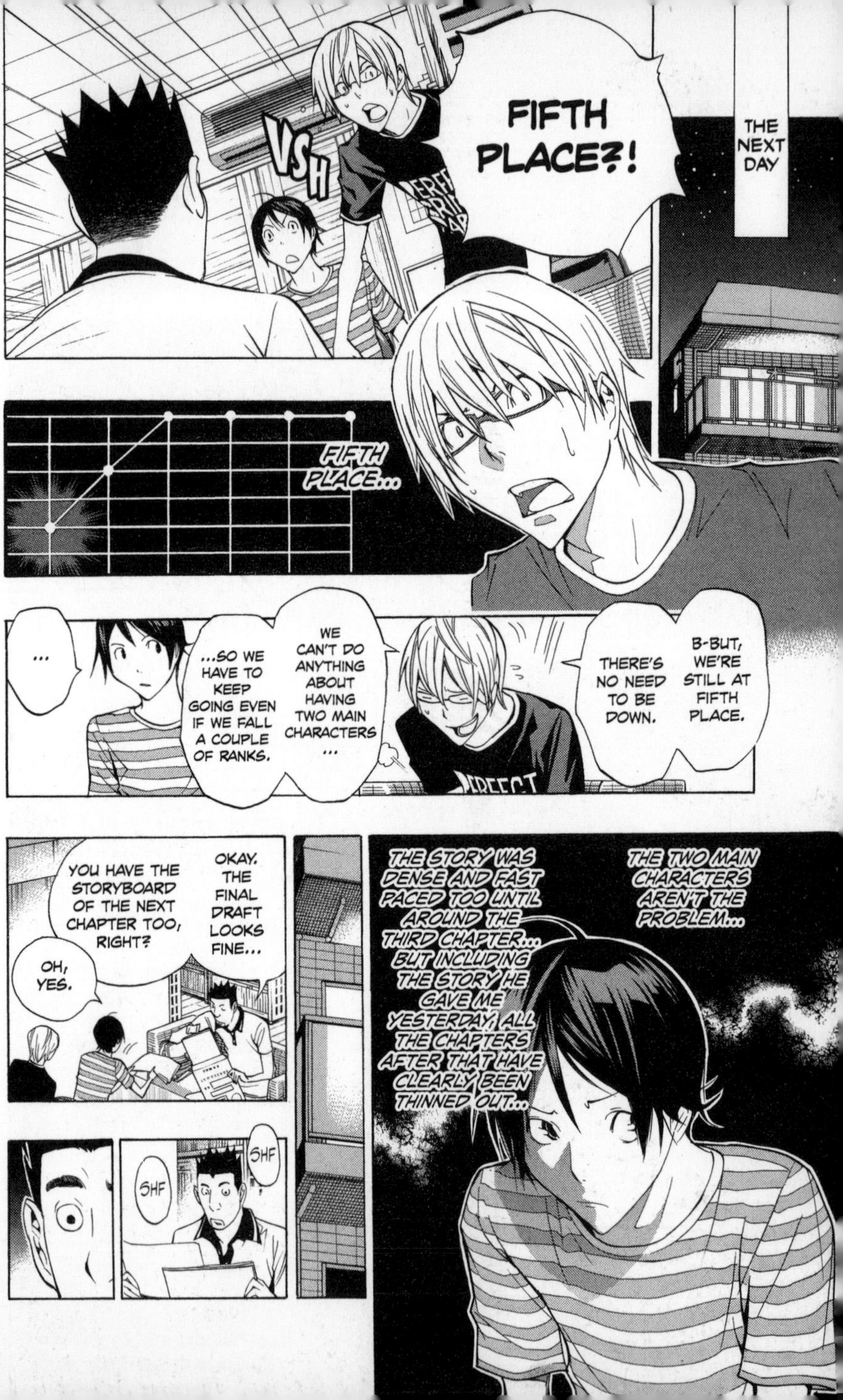
THE NEXT DAY
FIFTH PLACE?!
VSH
FIFTH PLACE...
B-BUT, WE'RE STILL AT FIFTH PLACE.
THERE'S NO NEED TO BE DOWN.
WE CAN'T DO ANYTHING ABOUT HAVING TWO MAIN CHARACTERS...
...SO WE HAVE TO KEEP GOING EVEN IF WE FALL A COUPLE OF RANKS.
...
THE TWO MAIN CHARACTERS AREN'T THE PROBLEM...
THE STORY WAS DENSE AND FAST PACED TOO UNTIL AROUND THE THIRD CHAPTER... BUT INCLUDING THE STORY HE GAVE ME YESTERDAY, ALL THE CHAPTERS AFTER THAT HAVE CLEARLY BEEN THINNED OUT...
OKAY. THE FINAL DRAFT LOOKS FINE...
YOU HAVE THE STORYBOARD OF THE NEXT CHAPTER TOO, RIGHT?
OH, YES.
SHF
SHF

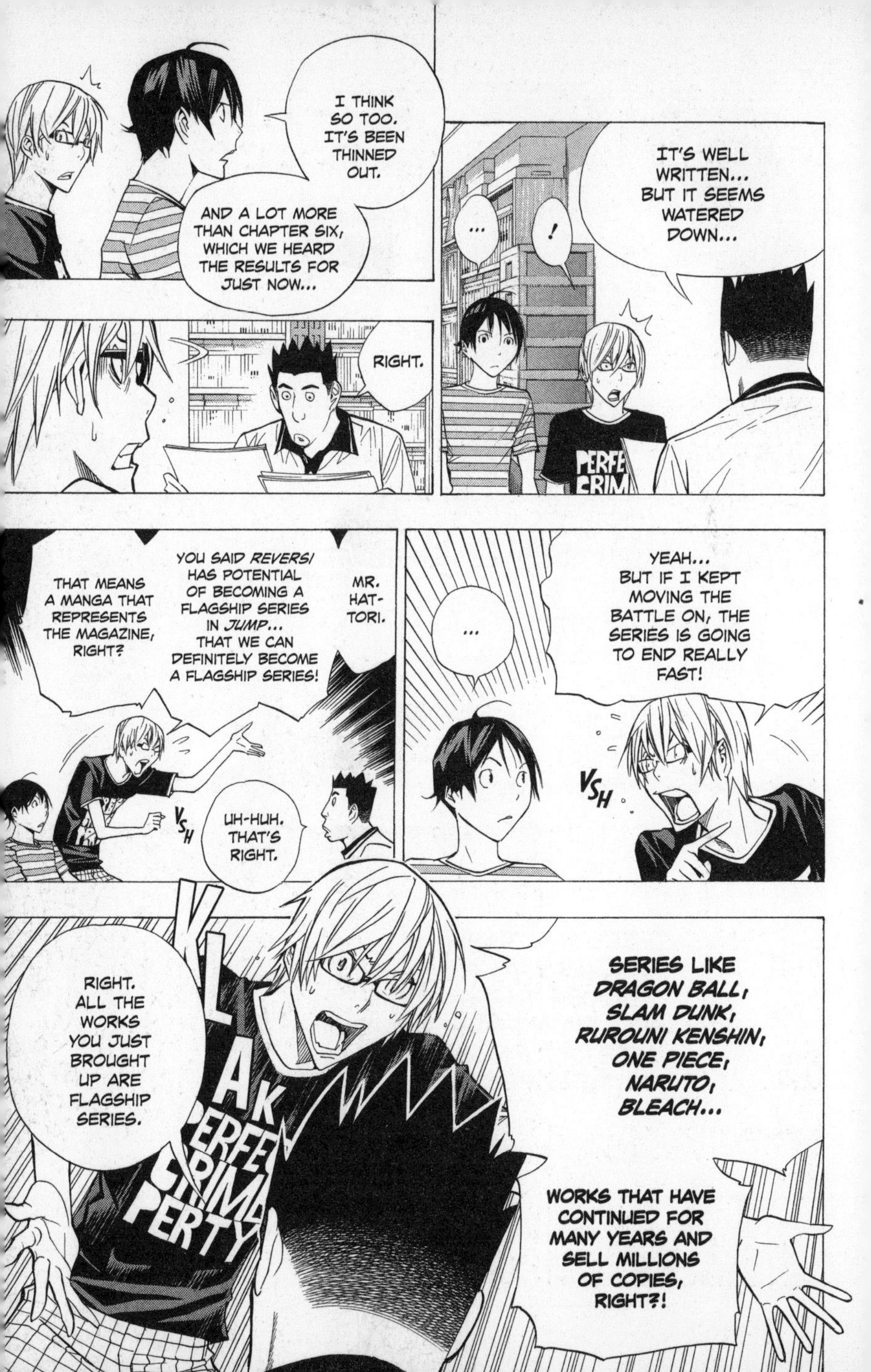

IT'S WELL WRITTEN... BUT IT SEEMS WATERED DOWN...
!
...
I THINK SO TOO. IT'S BEEN THINNED OUT.
AND A LOT MORE THAN CHAPTER SIX, WHICH WE HEARD THE RESULTS FOR JUST NOW...
RIGHT.
YEAH... BUT IF I KEPT MOVING THE BATTLE ON, THE SERIES IS GOING TO END REALLY FAST!
...
VSH
MR. HATTORI.
YOU SAID *REVERSI* HAS POTENTIAL OF BECOMING A FLAGSHIP SERIES IN *JUMP*... THAT WE CAN DEFINITELY BECOME A FLAGSHIP SERIES!
THAT MEANS A MANGA THAT REPRESENTS THE MAGAZINE, RIGHT?
VSH
UH-HUH. THAT'S RIGHT.
SERIES LIKE *DRAGON BALL*, *SLAM DUNK*, *RUROUNI KENSHIN*, *ONE PIECE*, *NARUTO*, *BLEACH*...
WORKS THAT HAVE CONTINUED FOR MANY YEARS AND SELL MILLIONS OF COPIES, RIGHT?!
RIGHT. ALL THE WORKS YOU JUST BROUGHT UP ARE FLAGSHIP SERIES.

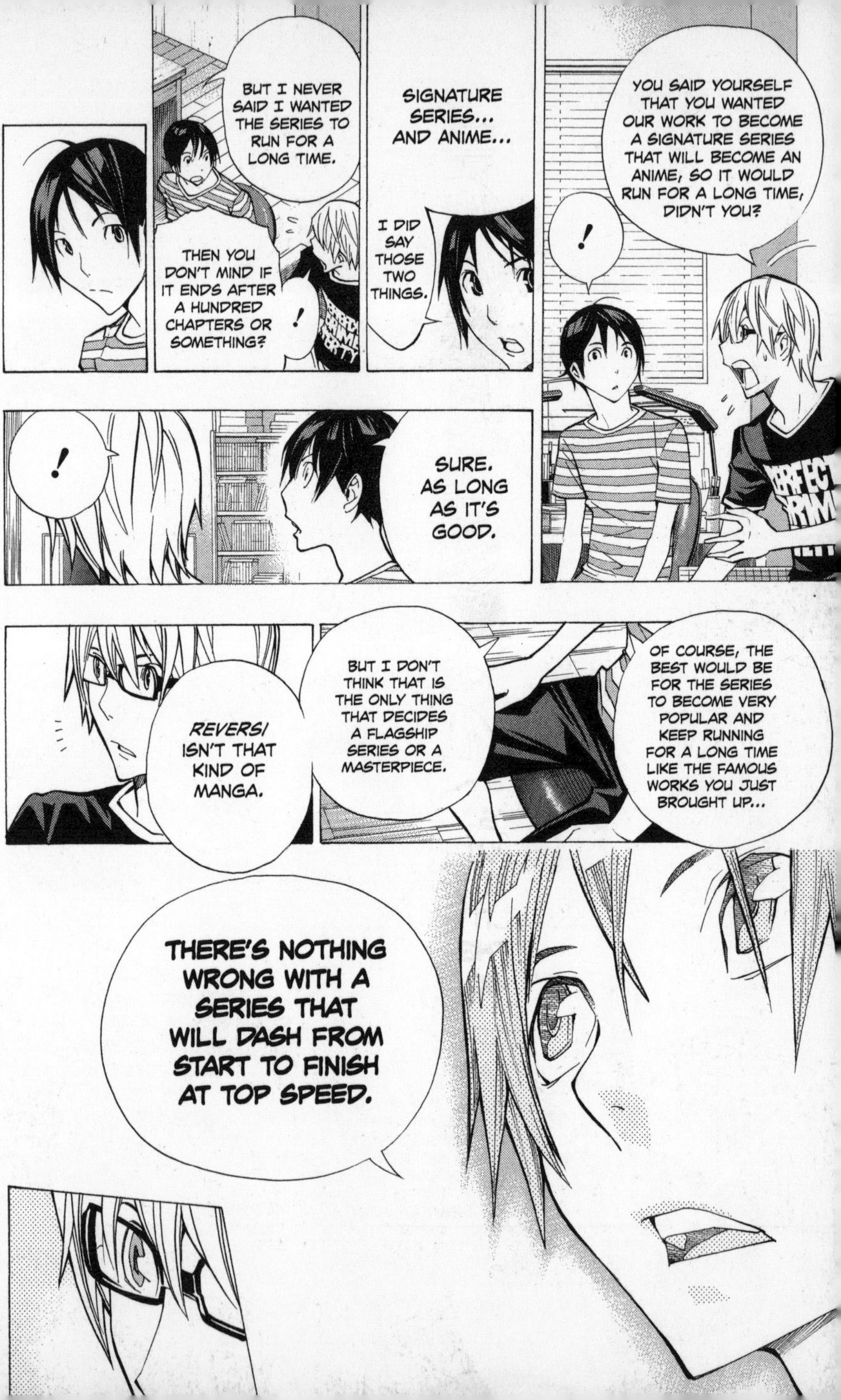
YOU SAID YOURSELF THAT YOU WANTED OUR WORK TO BECOME A SIGNATURE SERIES THAT WILL BECOME AN ANIME, SO IT WOULD RUN FOR A LONG TIME, DIDN'T YOU?
!
SIGNATURE SERIES... AND ANIME...
I DID SAY THOSE TWO THINGS.
BUT I NEVER SAID I WANTED THE SERIES TO RUN FOR A LONG TIME.
THEN YOU DON'T MIND IF IT ENDS AFTER A HUNDRED CHAPTERS OR SOMETHING?
!
SURE. AS LONG AS IT'S GOOD.
!
OF COURSE, THE BEST WOULD BE FOR THE SERIES TO BECOME VERY POPULAR AND KEEP RUNNING FOR A LONG TIME LIKE THE FAMOUS WORKS YOU JUST BROUGHT UP...
BUT I DON'T THINK THAT IS THE ONLY THING THAT DECIDES A FLAGSHIP SERIES OR A MASTERPIECE.
REVERSI ISN'T THAT KIND OF MANGA.
THERE'S NOTHING WRONG WITH A SERIES THAT WILL DASH FROM START TO FINISH AT TOP SPEED.

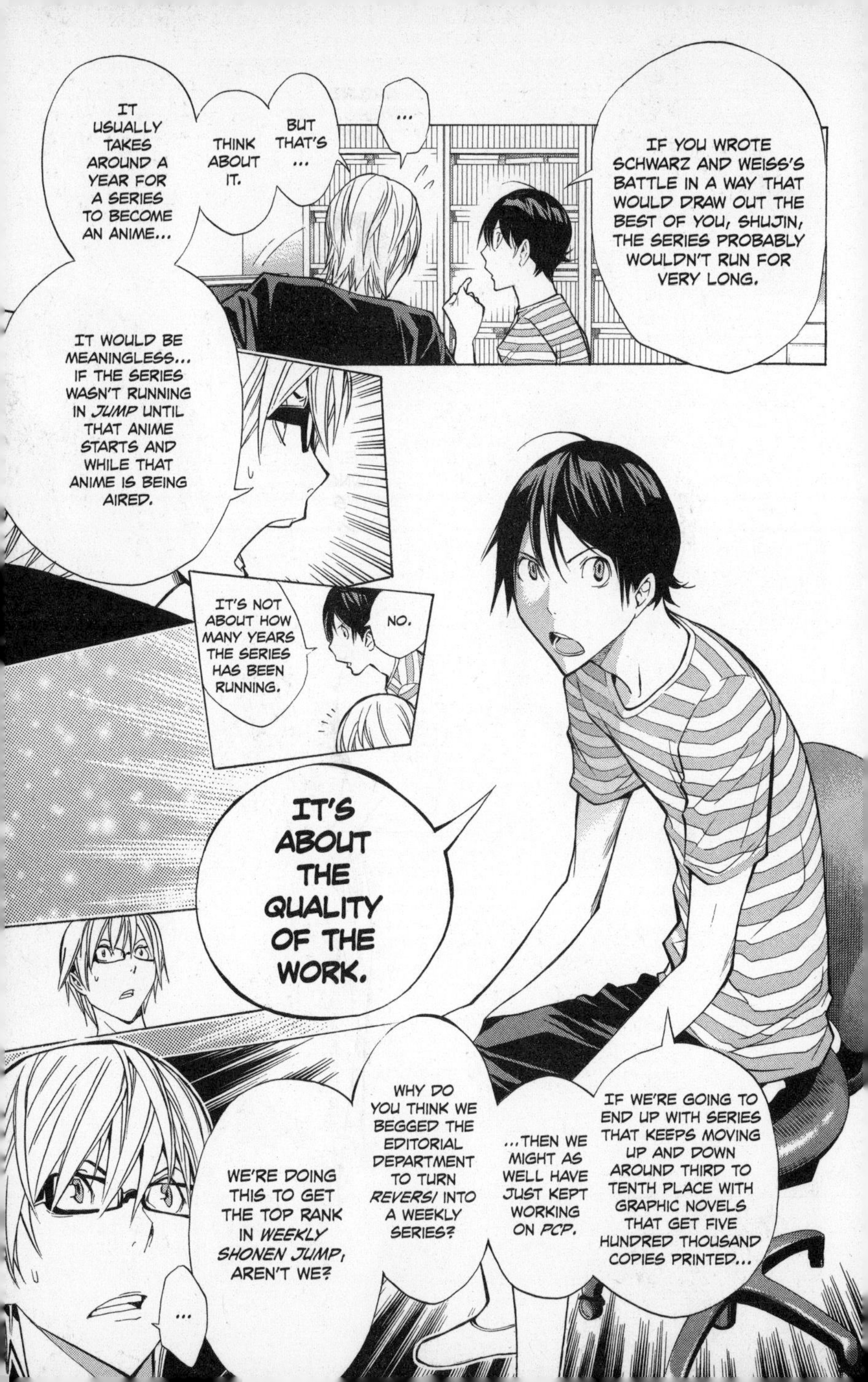
IF YOU WROTE SCHWARZ AND WEISS'S BATTLE IN A WAY THAT WOULD DRAW OUT THE BEST OF YOU, SHUJIN, THE SERIES PROBABLY WOULDN'T RUN FOR VERY LONG.
...
BUT THAT'S ...
THINK ABOUT IT.
IT USUALLY TAKES AROUND A YEAR FOR A SERIES TO BECOME AN ANIME...
IT WOULD BE MEANINGLESS... IF THE SERIES WASN'T RUNNING IN *JUMP* UNTIL THAT ANIME STARTS AND WHILE THAT ANIME IS BEING AIRED.
NO.
IT'S NOT ABOUT HOW MANY YEARS THE SERIES HAS BEEN RUNNING.
IT'S ABOUT THE QUALITY OF THE WORK.
IF WE'RE GOING TO END UP WITH SERIES THAT KEEPS MOVING UP AND DOWN AROUND THIRD TO TENTH PLACE WITH GRAPHIC NOVELS THAT GET FIVE HUNDRED THOUSAND COPIES PRINTED...
...THEN WE MIGHT AS WELL HAVE JUST KEPT WORKING ON *PCP*.
WHY DO YOU THINK WE BEGGED THE EDITORIAL DEPARTMENT TO TURN *REVERSI* INTO A WEEKLY SERIES?
WE'RE DOING THIS TO GET THE TOP RANK IN *WEEKLY SHONEN JUMP*, AREN'T WE?
...

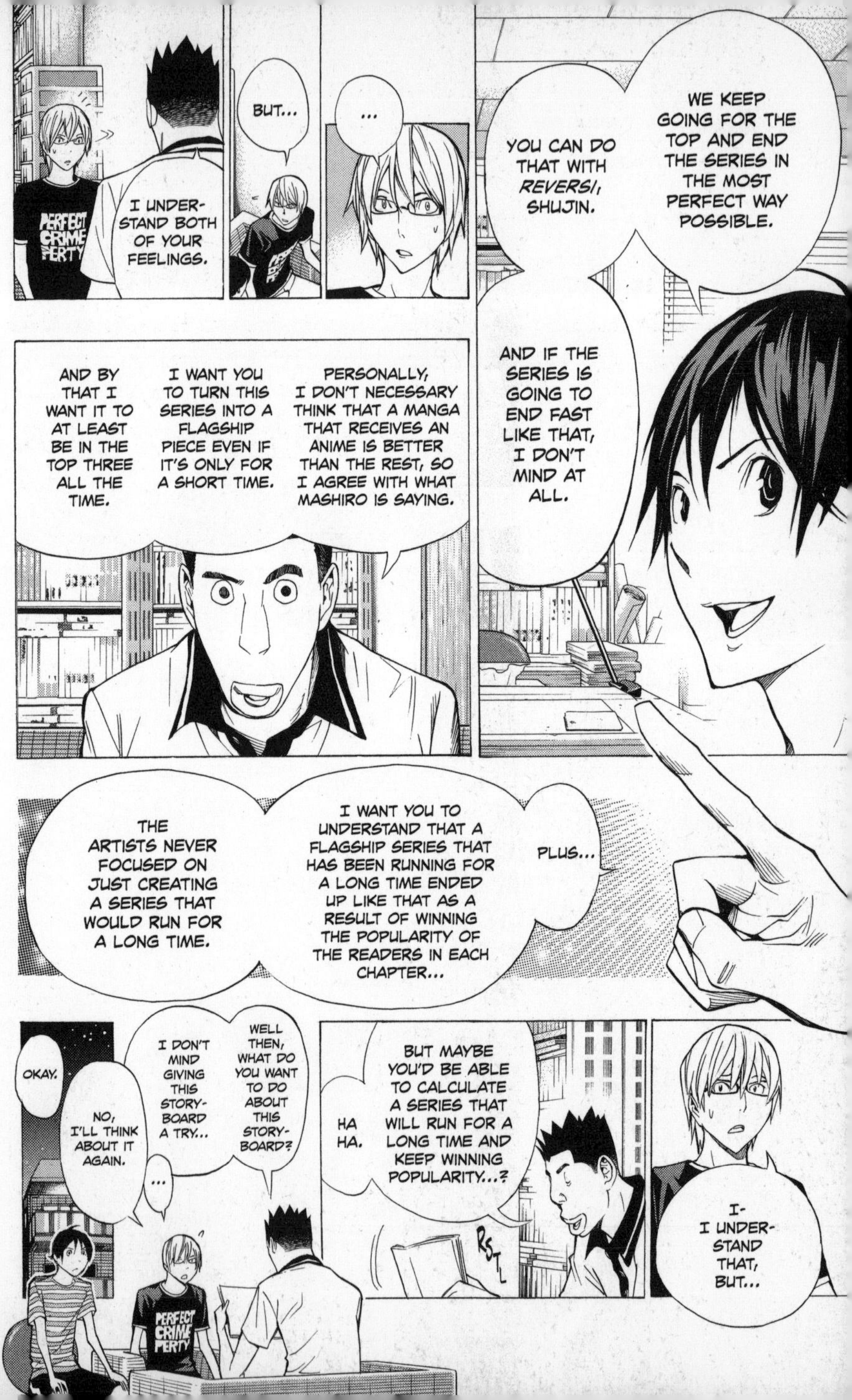
WE KEEP GOING FOR THE TOP AND END THE SERIES IN THE MOST PERFECT WAY POSSIBLE.
YOU CAN DO THAT WITH *REVERSI*, SHUJIN.
AND IF THE SERIES IS GOING TO END FAST LIKE THAT, I DON'T MIND AT ALL.
...
BUT...
I UNDER-STAND BOTH OF YOUR FEELINGS.
PERFECT CRIME PERTY
PERSONALLY, I DON'T NECESSARY THINK THAT A MANGA THAT RECEIVES AN ANIME IS BETTER THAN THE REST, SO I AGREE WITH WHAT MASHIRO IS SAYING.
I WANT YOU TO TURN THIS SERIES INTO A FLAGSHIP PIECE EVEN IF IT'S ONLY FOR A SHORT TIME.
AND BY THAT I WANT IT TO AT LEAST BE IN THE TOP THREE ALL THE TIME.
PLUS...
I WANT YOU TO UNDERSTAND THAT A FLAGSHIP SERIES THAT HAS BEEN RUNNING FOR A LONG TIME ENDED UP LIKE THAT AS A RESULT OF WINNING THE POPULARITY OF THE READERS IN EACH CHAPTER...
THE ARTISTS NEVER FOCUSED ON JUST CREATING A SERIES THAT WOULD RUN FOR A LONG TIME.
I- I UNDER-STAND THAT, BUT...
BUT MAYBE YOU'D BE ABLE TO CALCULATE A SERIES THAT WILL RUN FOR A LONG TIME AND KEEP WINNING POPULARITY...?
HA HA.
RSTL
WELL THEN, WHAT DO YOU WANT TO DO ABOUT THIS STORY-BOARD?
I DON'T MIND GIVING THIS STORY-BOARD A TRY...
OKAY.
NO, I'LL THINK ABOUT IT AGAIN.
...
PERFECT CRIME PERTY

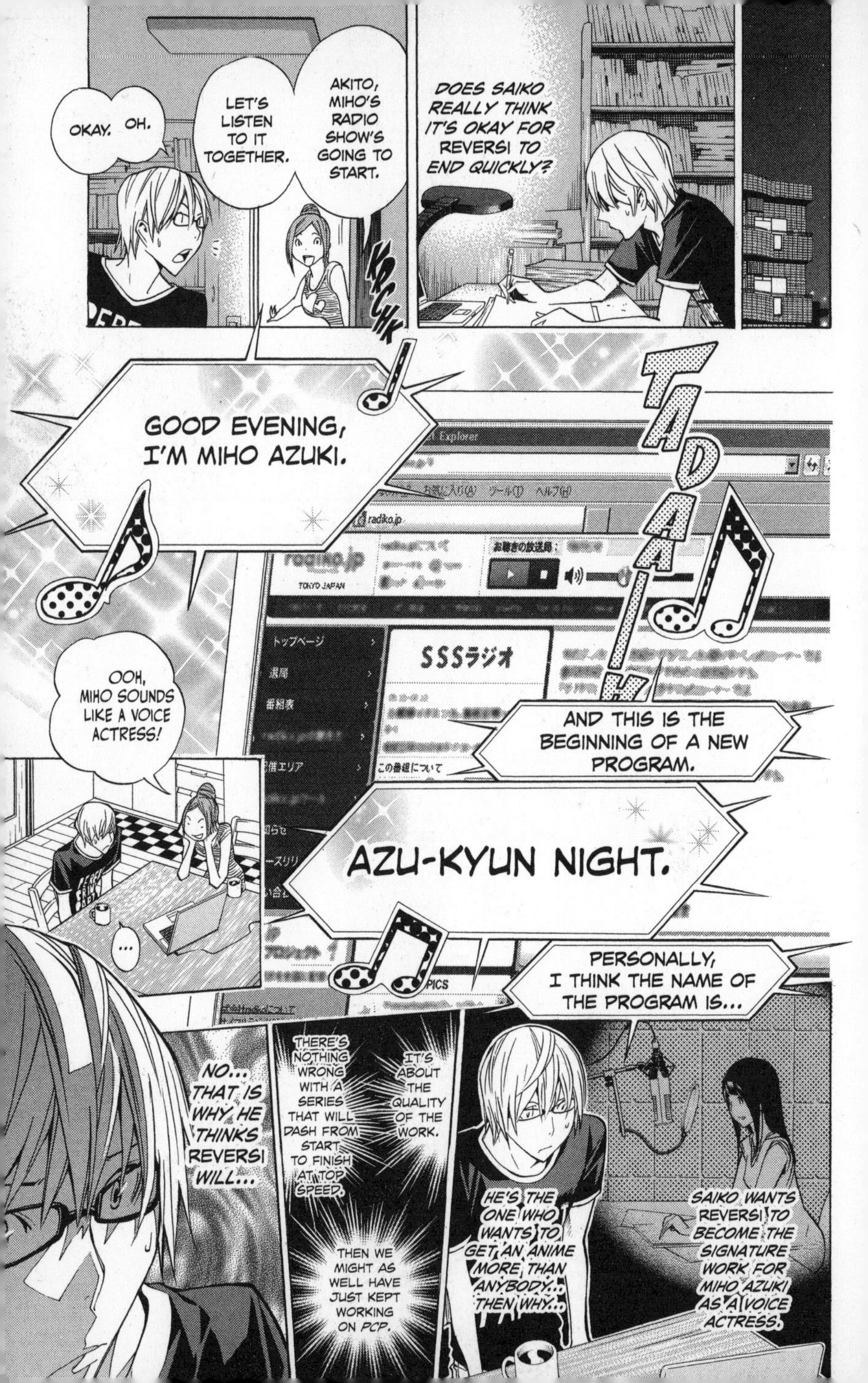
DOES SAIKO REALLY THINK IT'S OKAY FOR REVERSI TO END QUICKLY?
AKITO, MIHO'S RADIO SHOW'S GOING TO START.
LET'S LISTEN TO IT TOGETHER.
OKAY. OH.
KRCHK
TADAAAH
GOOD EVENING, I'M MIHO AZUKI.
radiko.jp
SSSラジオ
AND THIS IS THE BEGINNING OF A NEW PROGRAM.
OOH, MIHO SOUNDS LIKE A VOICE ACTRESS!
AZU-KYUN NIGHT.
...
PERSONALLY, I THINK THE NAME OF THE PROGRAM IS...
SAIKO WANTS REVERSI TO BECOME THE SIGNATURE WORK FOR MIHO AZUKI AS A VOICE ACTRESS.
HE'S THE ONE WHO WANTS TO GET AN ANIME MORE THAN ANYBODY... THEN WHY...
IT'S ABOUT THE QUALITY OF THE WORK.
THERE'S NOTHING WRONG WITH A SERIES THAT WILL DASH FROM START TO FINISH AT TOP SPEED.
THEN WE MIGHT AS WELL HAVE JUST KEPT WORKING ON PCP.
NO... THAT IS WHY HE THINKS REVERSI WILL...

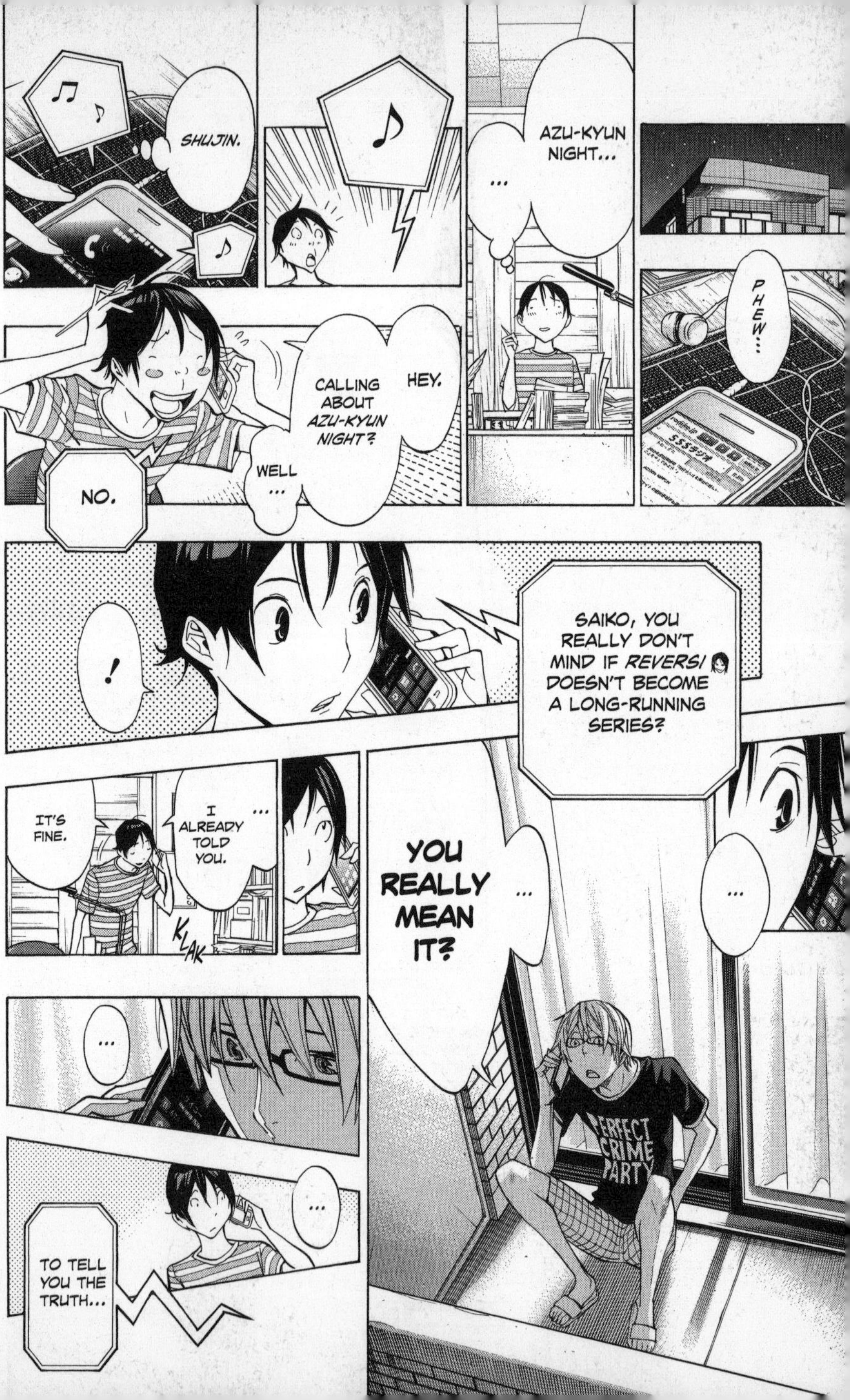
PHEW...
AZU-KYUN NIGHT...
...
♪
♫ ♪
SHUJIN.
♪
HEY.
CALLING ABOUT AZU-KYUN NIGHT?
WELL ...
NO.
SAIKO, YOU REALLY DON'T MIND IF REVERSI DOESN'T BECOME A LONG-RUNNING SERIES?
!
...
...
I ALREADY TOLD YOU.
IT'S FINE.
KLAK
...
YOU REALLY MEAN IT?
...
...
TO TELL YOU THE TRUTH...

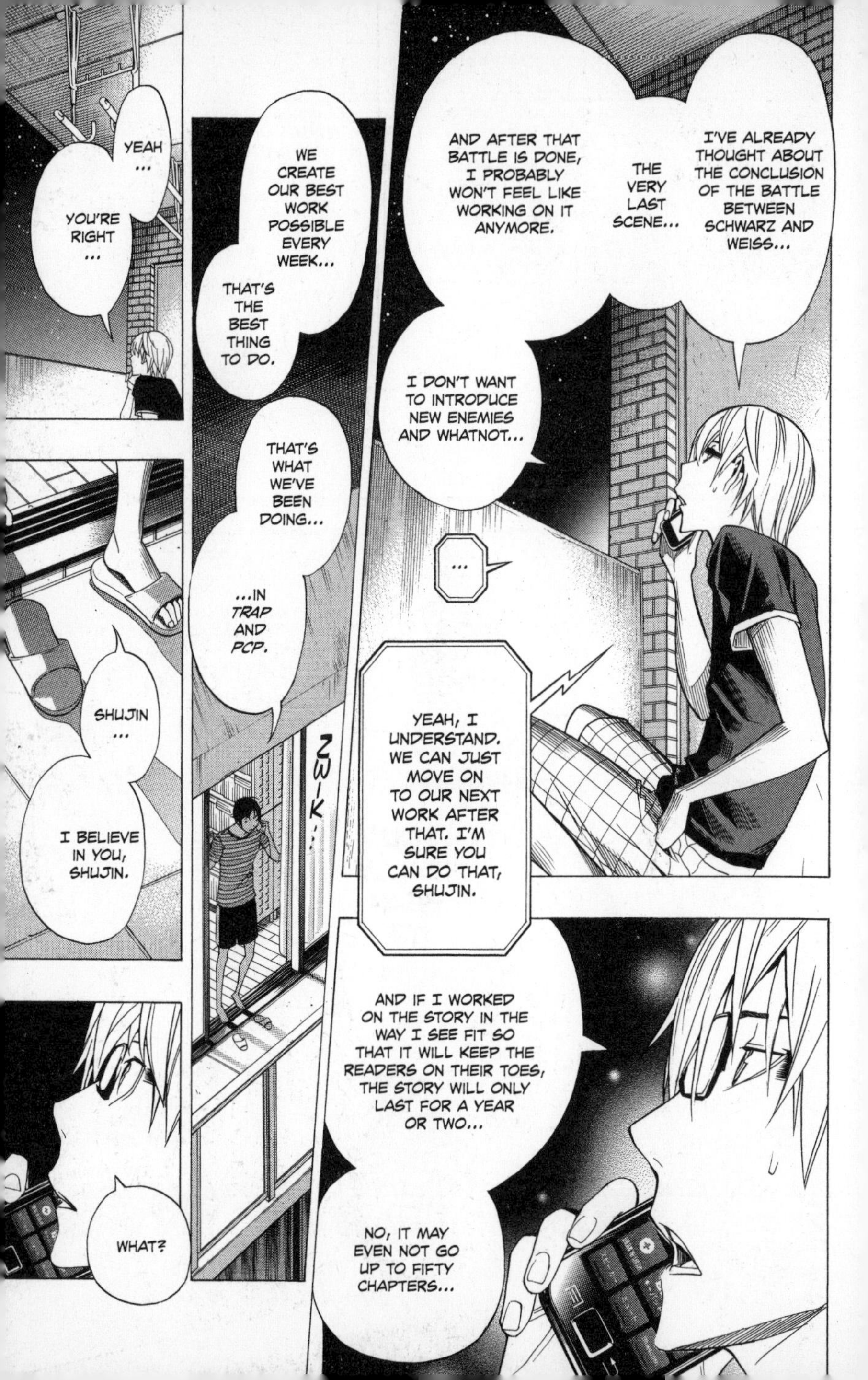

I'VE ALREADY THOUGHT ABOUT THE CONCLUSION OF THE BATTLE BETWEEN SCHWARZ AND WEISS...
THE VERY LAST SCENE...
AND AFTER THAT BATTLE IS DONE, I PROBABLY WON'T FEEL LIKE WORKING ON IT ANYMORE.
I DON'T WANT TO INTRODUCE NEW ENEMIES AND WHATNOT...
...
YEAH, I UNDERSTAND. WE CAN JUST MOVE ON TO OUR NEXT WORK AFTER THAT. I'M SURE YOU CAN DO THAT, SHUJIN.
AND IF I WORKED ON THE STORY IN THE WAY I SEE FIT SO THAT IT WILL KEEP THE READERS ON THEIR TOES, THE STORY WILL ONLY LAST FOR A YEAR OR TWO...
NO, IT MAY EVEN NOT GO UP TO FIFTY CHAPTERS...
WE CREATE OUR BEST WORK POSSIBLE EVERY WEEK...
THAT'S THE BEST THING TO DO.
THAT'S WHAT WE'VE BEEN DOING...
...IN *TRAP* AND *PCP*.
ZWIK...
YEAH...
YOU'RE RIGHT...
SHUJIN...
I BELIEVE IN YOU, SHUJIN.
WHAT?

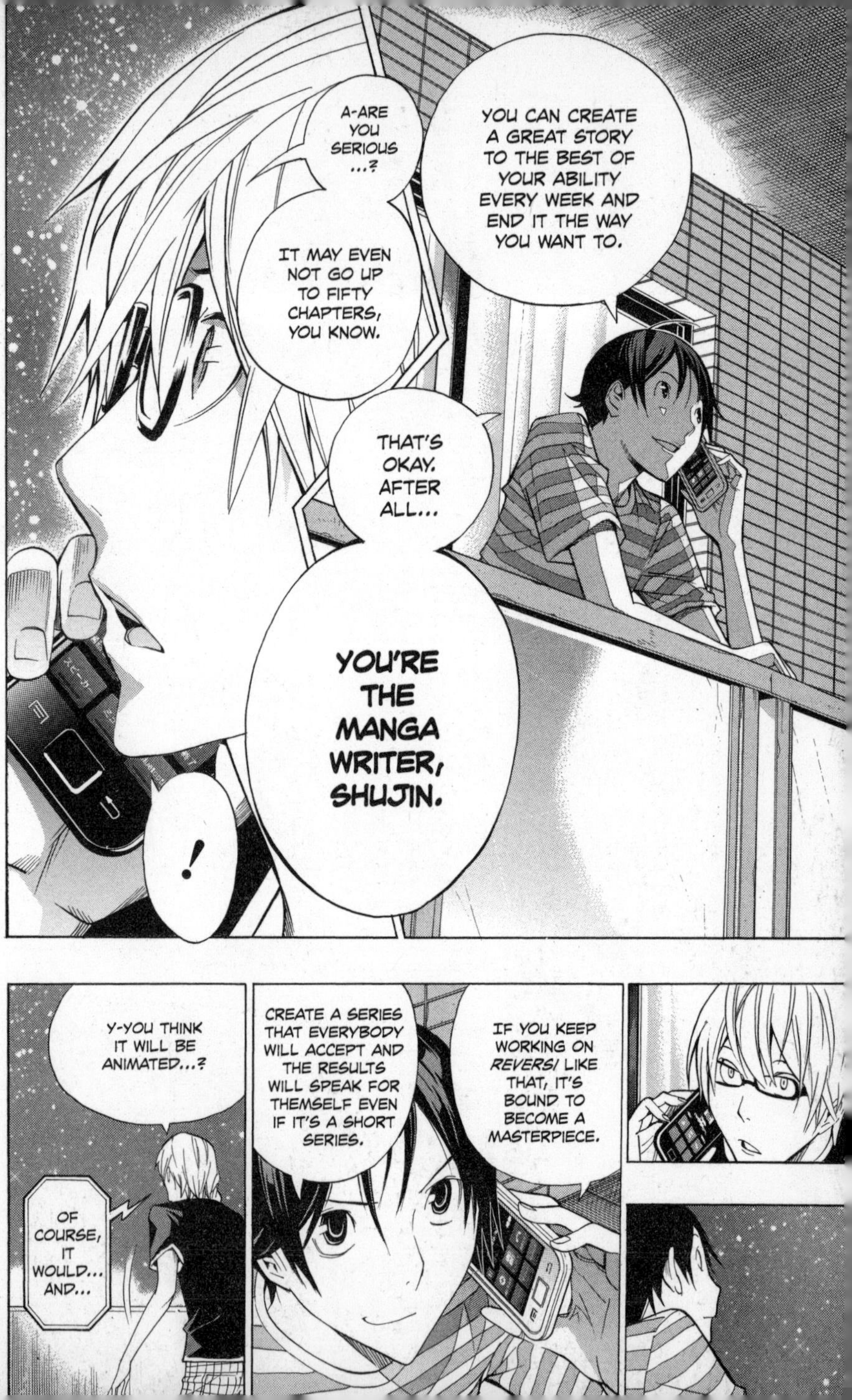
YOU CAN CREATE A GREAT STORY TO THE BEST OF YOUR ABILITY EVERY WEEK AND END IT THE WAY YOU WANT TO.
A-ARE YOU SERIOUS ...?
IT MAY EVEN NOT GO UP TO FIFTY CHAPTERS, YOU KNOW.
THAT'S OKAY. AFTER ALL...
YOU'RE THE MANGA WRITER, SHUJIN.
!
IF YOU KEEP WORKING ON *REVERSI* LIKE THAT, IT'S BOUND TO BECOME A MASTERPIECE.
CREATE A SERIES THAT EVERYBODY WILL ACCEPT AND THE RESULTS WILL SPEAK FOR THEMSELF EVEN IF IT'S A SHORT SERIES.
Y-YOU THINK IT WILL BE ANIMATED...?
OF COURSE, IT WOULD... AND...

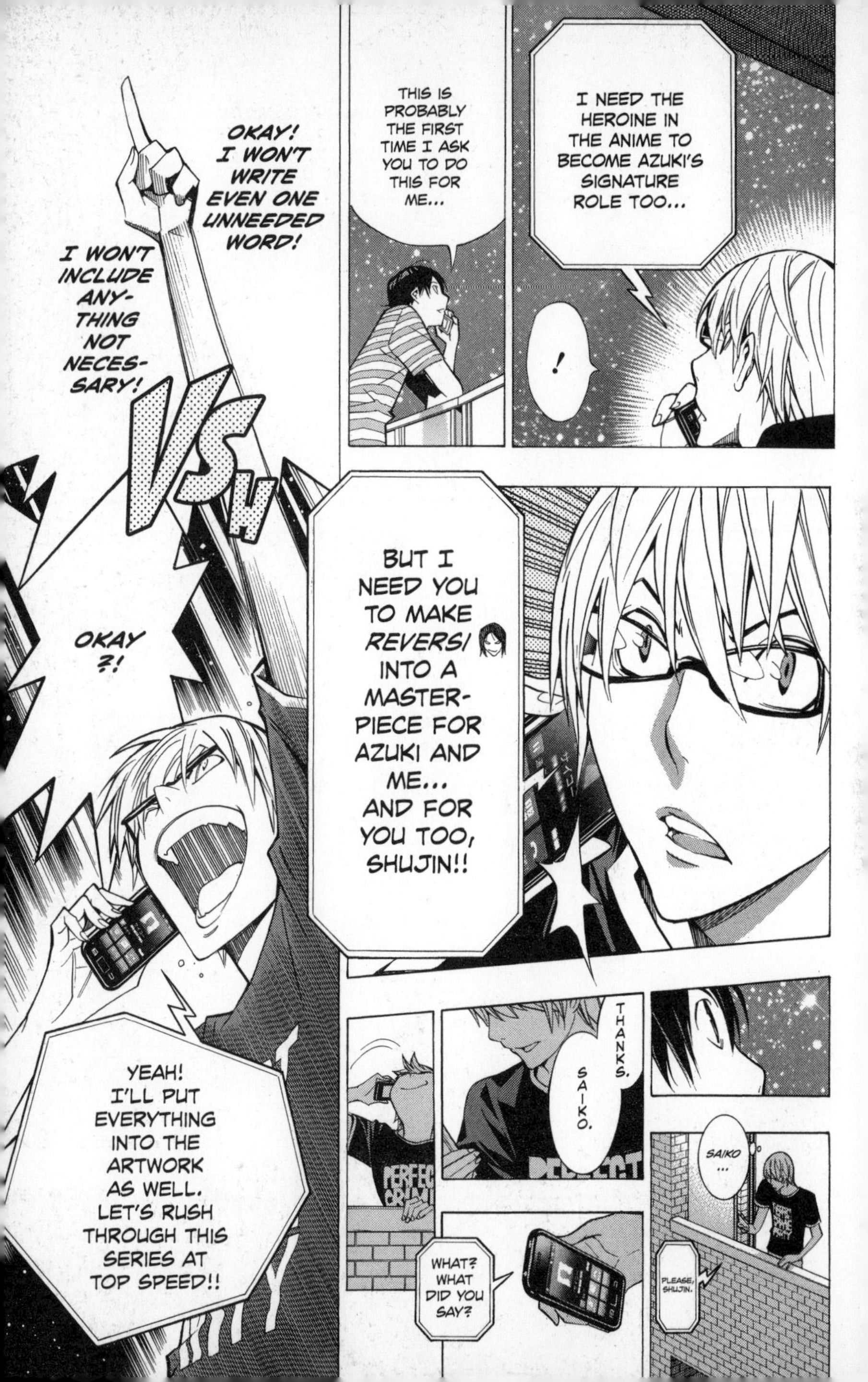

I NEED THE HEROINE IN THE ANIME TO BECOME AZUKI'S SIGNATURE ROLE TOO...
!
THIS IS PROBABLY THE FIRST TIME I ASK YOU TO DO THIS FOR ME...
BUT I NEED YOU TO MAKE *REVERSI* INTO A MASTERPIECE FOR AZUKI AND ME... AND FOR YOU TOO, SHUJIN!!
THANKS. SAIKO.
SAIKO...
PLEASE, SHUJIN.
WHAT? WHAT DID YOU SAY?
OKAY! I WON'T WRITE EVEN ONE UNNEEDED WORD!
I WON'T INCLUDE ANYTHING NOT NECESSARY!
VSH
OKAY?!
YEAH! I'LL PUT EVERYTHING INTO THE ARTWORK AS WELL. LET'S RUSH THROUGH THIS SERIES AT TOP SPEED!!

OHBA'S STORYBOARD

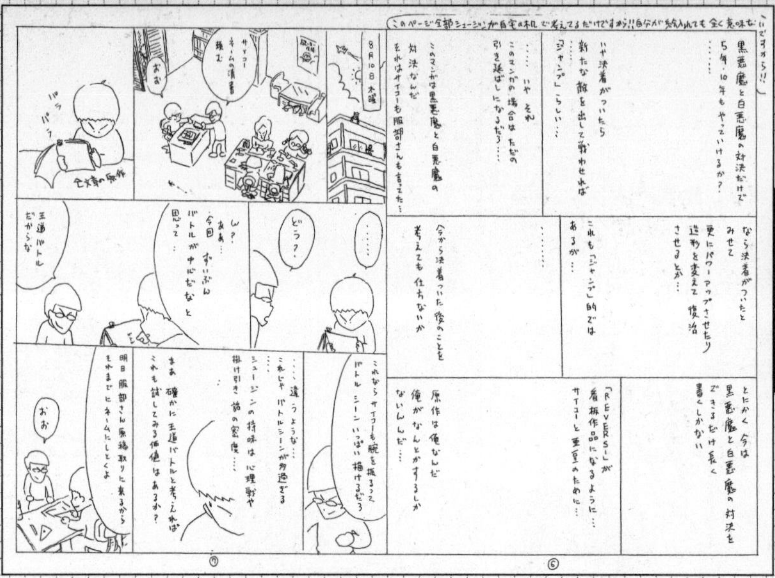
このページ全部シュージンが自宅の机で考えてるだけですから!!自分が絵入れても全く意味ないですから!!
黒悪魔と白悪魔の対決だけで 5年・10年もやっていけるか?
……
いや決着がついたら 新たな敵を出して戦わせれば 「ジャンプ」らしい…
……いや それ このマンガの場合は ただの引き延ばしになるだろ……
このマンガは黒悪魔と白悪魔の対決なんだ それはサイコーも服部さんも言ってた…
なら決着がついたとみせて 更にパワーアップさせたり 造形を変えて 復活させるとか…
これも「ジャンプ」的では あるが…
……
今から決着ついた後のことを 考えても仕方ないか
とにかく今は 黒悪魔と白悪魔の対決を できるだけ長く 書くしかない
「REVERSI」が 看板作品になるように… サイコーと亜豆のために…
原作は俺なんだ 俺がなんとかするしかないんだ…
⑥
8月10日 木曜
サイコー ネームの清書 頼む
おお
パラ パラ
全文章の原作
……
どう?
ん? ああ… 今回 ずいぶんバトルが中心だなと 思って…
王道バトルだからな
これならサイコーも腕を振るって バトルシーンいっぱい描けるだろ
……違うような…… これじゃバトルシーンが多過ぎる…… シュージンの持ち味は 心理戦や 掛け引き 話の密度……
まあ 確かに王道バトルと考えれば これも試してみる価値はあるか?
明日服部さん原稿取りに来るから それまでにネームにしとくよ
おお
⑦

OBATA'S STORYBOARD

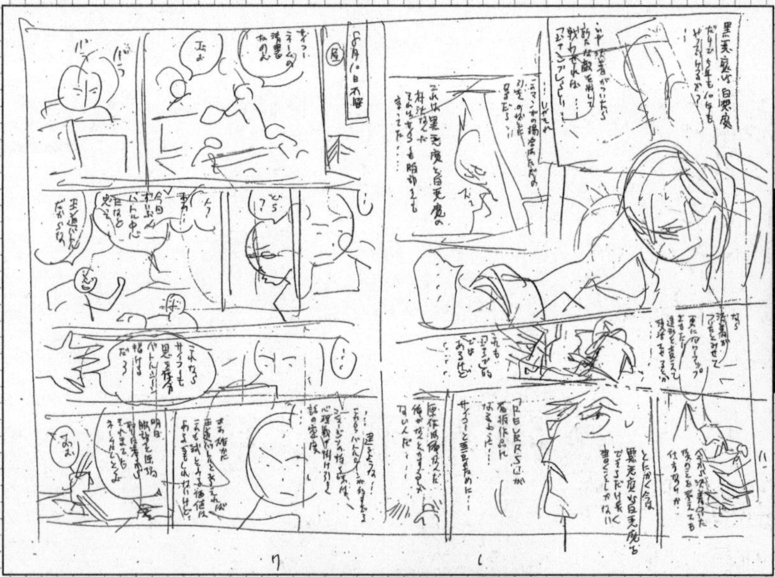

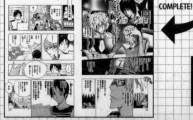

COMPLETE!

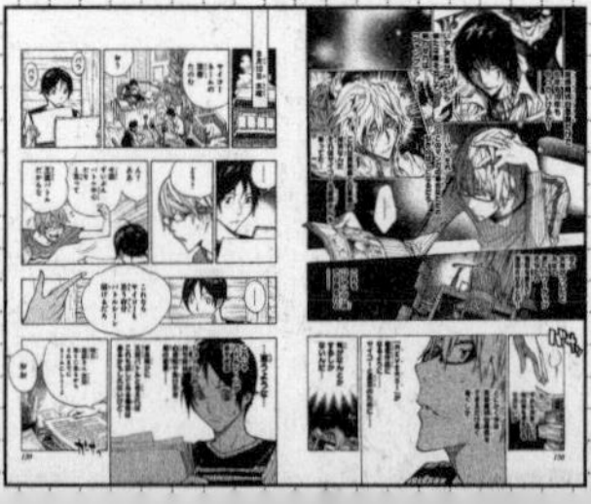

※CREATOR STORYBOARDS AND FINISHED PAGES IN JAPANESE

BAKUMAN。vol.18

"Until the Final Draft Is Complete"

Chapter 158, pp. 138-139

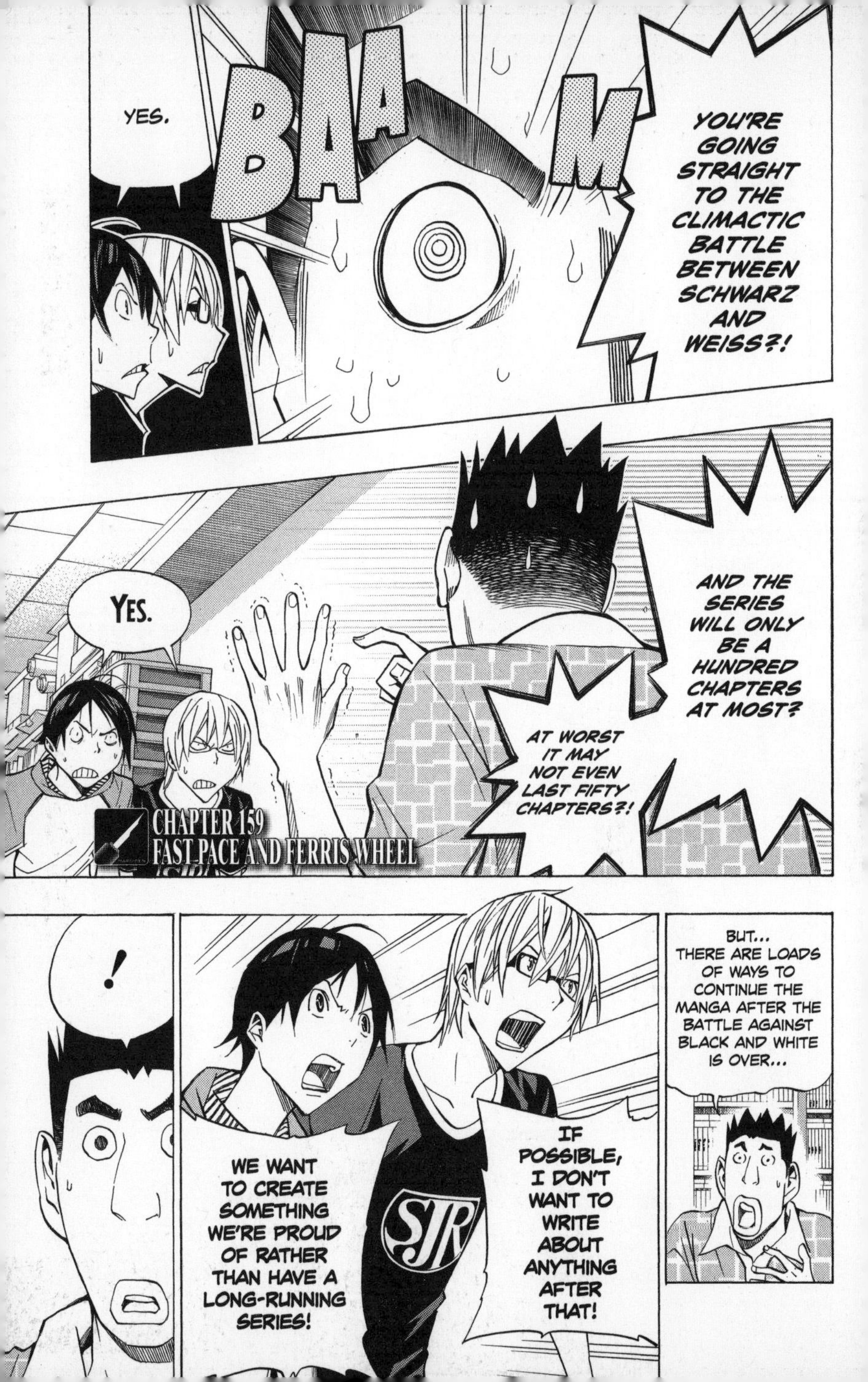
YOU'RE GOING STRAIGHT TO THE CLIMACTIC BATTLE BETWEEN SCHWARZ AND WEISS?!
BAAM
YES.
AND THE SERIES WILL ONLY BE A HUNDRED CHAPTERS AT MOST?
AT WORST IT MAY NOT EVEN LAST FIFTY CHAPTERS?!
YES.
CHAPTER 159
FAST PACE AND FERRIS WHEEL
BUT... THERE ARE LOADS OF WAYS TO CONTINUE THE MANGA AFTER THE BATTLE AGAINST BLACK AND WHITE IS OVER...
IF POSSIBLE, I DON'T WANT TO WRITE ABOUT ANYTHING AFTER THAT!
WE WANT TO CREATE SOMETHING WE'RE PROUD OF RATHER THAN HAVE A LONG-RUNNING SERIES!
!

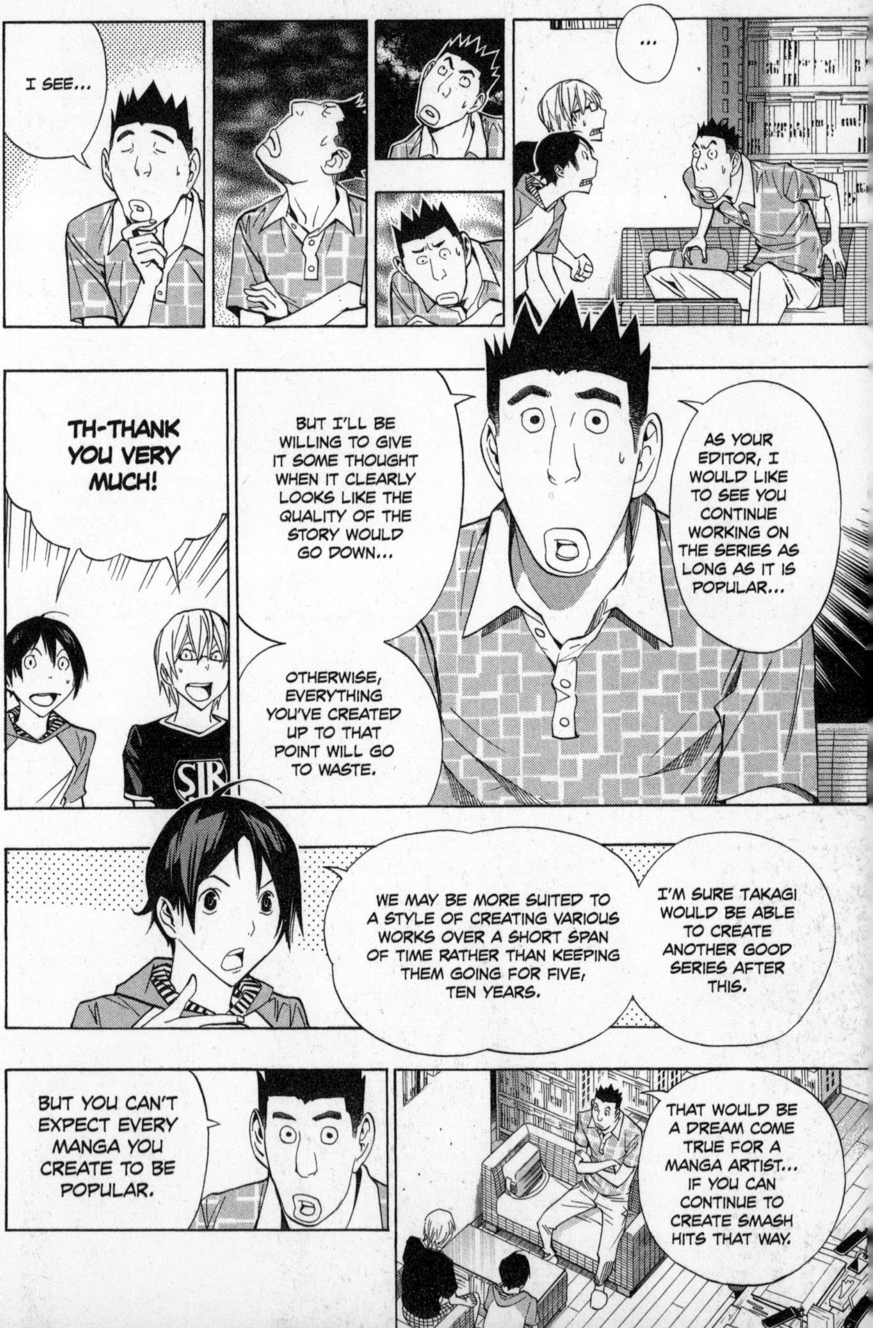
...
I SEE...
AS YOUR EDITOR, I WOULD LIKE TO SEE YOU CONTINUE WORKING ON THE SERIES AS LONG AS IT IS POPULAR...
BUT I'LL BE WILLING TO GIVE IT SOME THOUGHT WHEN IT CLEARLY LOOKS LIKE THE QUALITY OF THE STORY WOULD GO DOWN...
OTHERWISE, EVERYTHING YOU'VE CREATED UP TO THAT POINT WILL GO TO WASTE.
TH-THANK YOU VERY MUCH!
I'M SURE TAKAGI WOULD BE ABLE TO CREATE ANOTHER GOOD SERIES AFTER THIS.
WE MAY BE MORE SUITED TO A STYLE OF CREATING VARIOUS WORKS OVER A SHORT SPAN OF TIME RATHER THAN KEEPING THEM GOING FOR FIVE, TEN YEARS.
THAT WOULD BE A DREAM COME TRUE FOR A MANGA ARTIST... IF YOU CAN CONTINUE TO CREATE SMASH HITS THAT WAY.
BUT YOU CAN'T EXPECT EVERY MANGA YOU CREATE TO BE POPULAR.

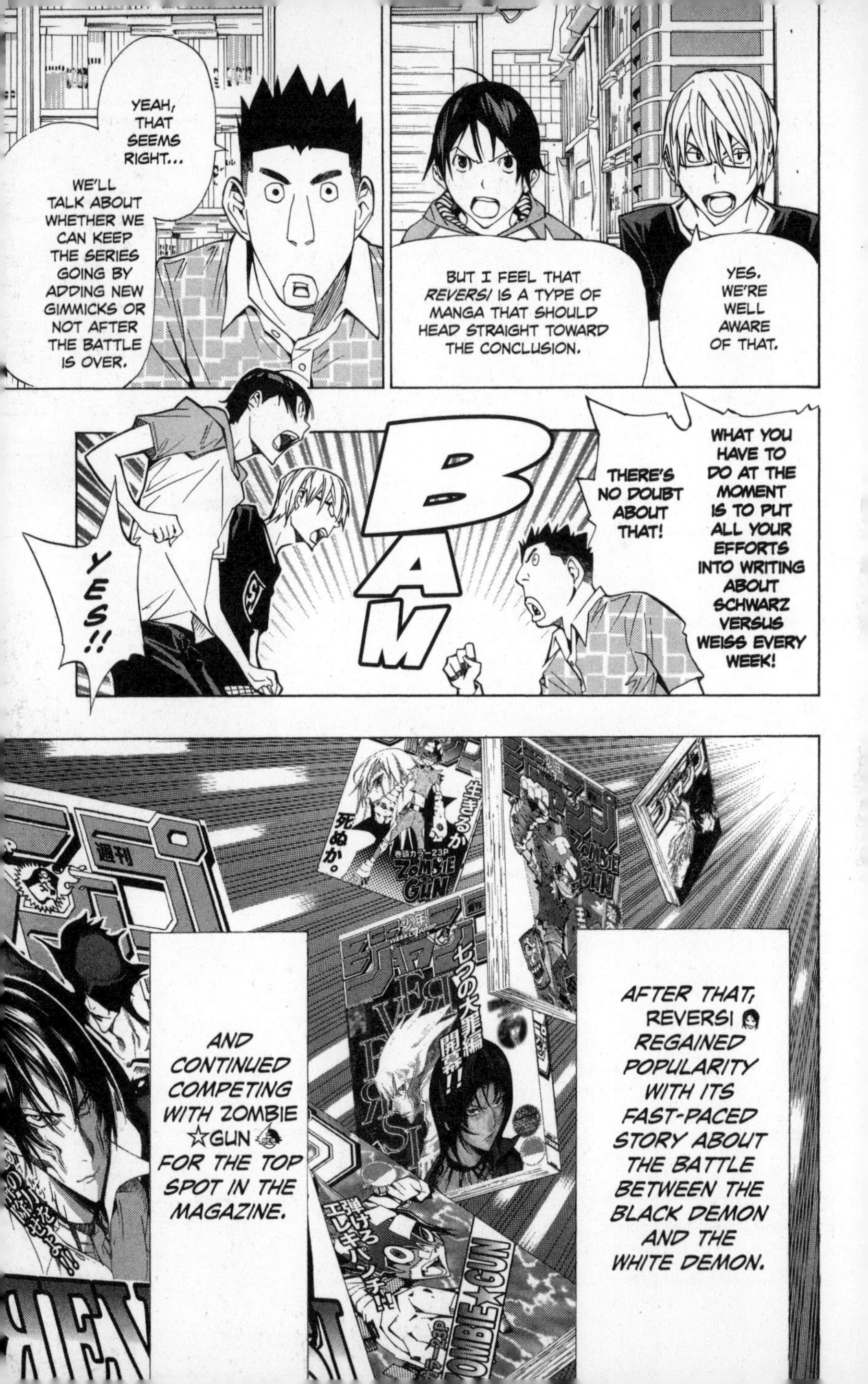
YES. WE'RE WELL AWARE OF THAT.
BUT I FEEL THAT *REVERSI* IS A TYPE OF MANGA THAT SHOULD HEAD STRAIGHT TOWARD THE CONCLUSION.
YEAH, THAT SEEMS RIGHT...
WE'LL TALK ABOUT WHETHER WE CAN KEEP THE SERIES GOING BY ADDING NEW GIMMICKS OR NOT AFTER THE BATTLE IS OVER.
WHAT YOU HAVE TO DO AT THE MOMENT IS TO PUT ALL YOUR EFFORTS INTO WRITING ABOUT SCHWARZ VERSUS WEISS EVERY WEEK!
THERE'S NO DOUBT ABOUT THAT!
BAM
YES!!
AFTER THAT, REVERSI REGAINED POPULARITY WITH ITS FAST-PACED STORY ABOUT THE BATTLE BETWEEN THE BLACK DEMON AND THE WHITE DEMON.
生きるか死ぬか。
巻頭カラー23P
ZOMBIE GUN
七つの大罪編開幕!!
弾けろエレキパンチ!!
ZOMBIE☆GUN
AND CONTINUED COMPETING WITH ZOMBIE☆GUN FOR THE TOP SPOT IN THE MAGAZINE.

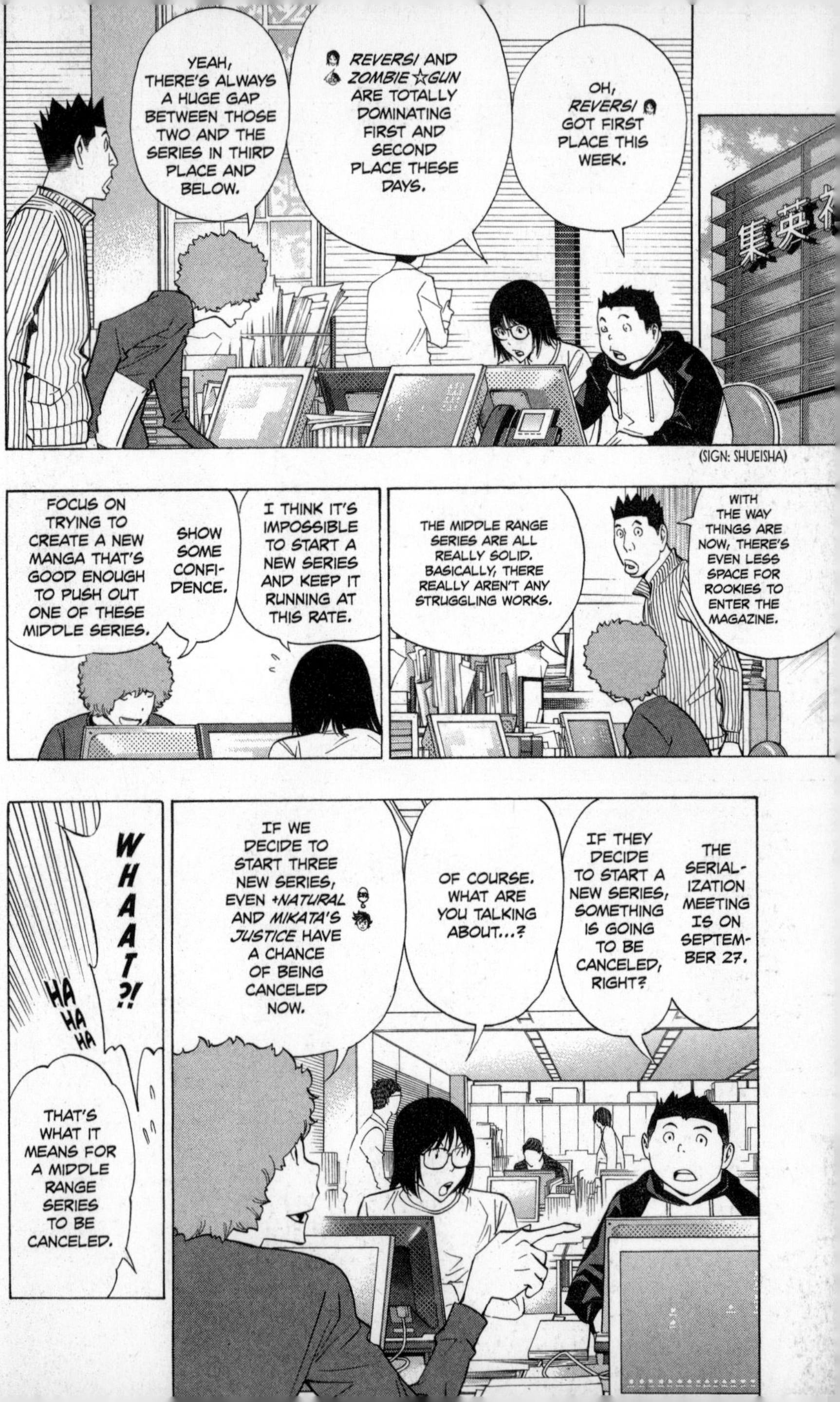
OH, REVERSI GOT FIRST PLACE THIS WEEK.
REVERSI AND ZOMBIE☆GUN ARE TOTALLY DOMINATING FIRST AND SECOND PLACE THESE DAYS.
YEAH, THERE'S ALWAYS A HUGE GAP BETWEEN THOSE TWO AND THE SERIES IN THIRD PLACE AND BELOW.
(SIGN: SHUEISHA)
WITH THE WAY THINGS ARE NOW, THERE'S EVEN LESS SPACE FOR ROOKIES TO ENTER THE MAGAZINE.
THE MIDDLE RANGE SERIES ARE ALL REALLY SOLID. BASICALLY, THERE REALLY AREN'T ANY STRUGGLING WORKS.
I THINK IT'S IMPOSSIBLE TO START A NEW SERIES AND KEEP IT RUNNING AT THIS RATE.
SHOW SOME CONFI-DENCE.
FOCUS ON TRYING TO CREATE A NEW MANGA THAT'S GOOD ENOUGH TO PUSH OUT ONE OF THESE MIDDLE SERIES.
THE SERIAL-IZATION MEETING IS ON SEPTEM-BER 27.
IF THEY DECIDE TO START A NEW SERIES, SOMETHING IS GOING TO BE CANCELED, RIGHT?
OF COURSE. WHAT ARE YOU TALKING ABOUT...?
IF WE DECIDE TO START THREE NEW SERIES, EVEN +NATURAL AND MIKATA'S JUSTICE HAVE A CHANCE OF BEING CANCELED NOW.
WHAAAT?!
HA HA HA
THAT'S WHAT IT MEANS FOR A MIDDLE RANGE SERIES TO BE CANCELED.

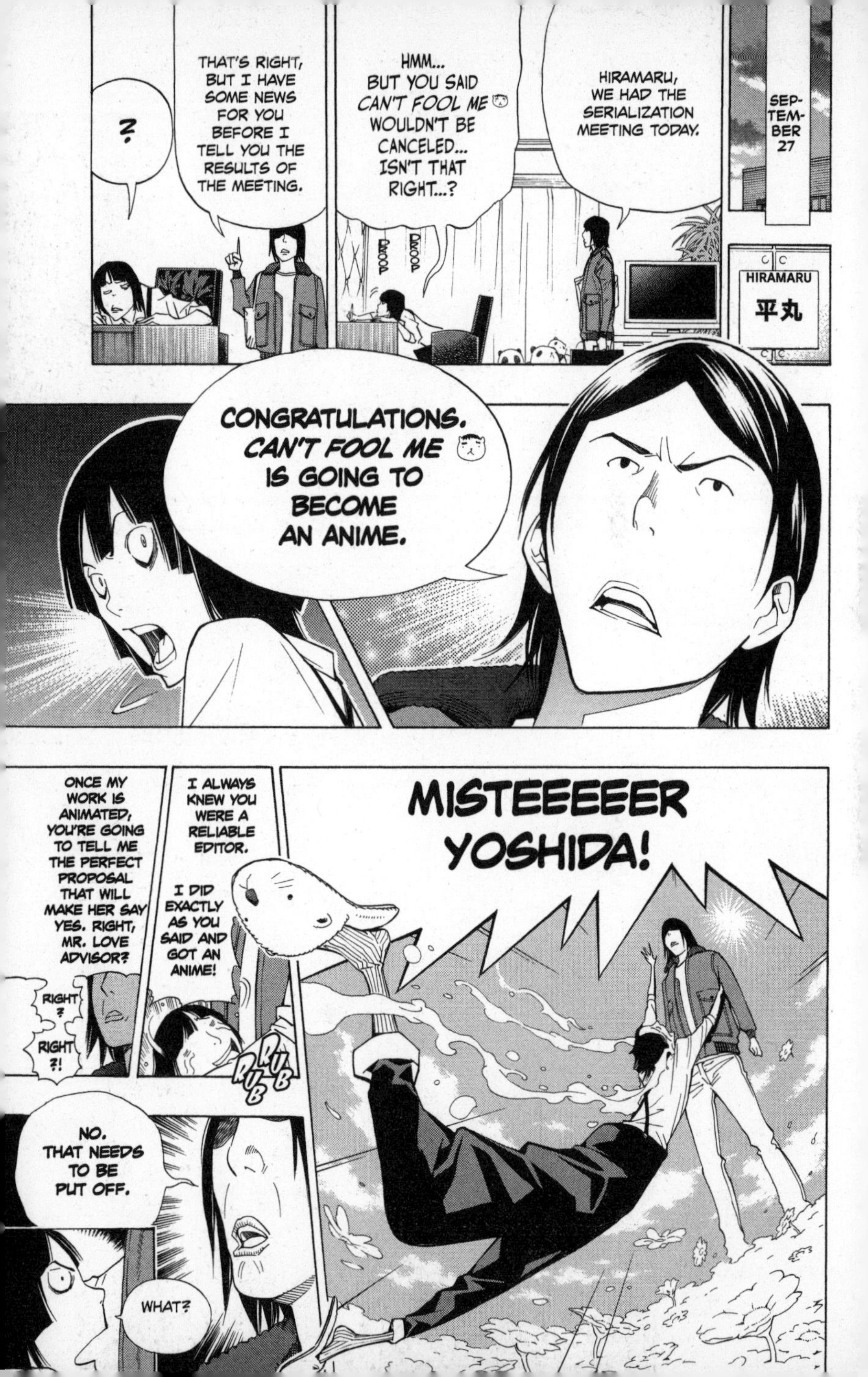
SEP-TEM-BER 27
HIRAMARU
平丸
HIRAMARU, WE HAD THE SERIALIZATION MEETING TODAY.
HMM... BUT YOU SAID CAN'T FOOL ME WOULDN'T BE CANCELED... ISN'T THAT RIGHT...?
DROOP
DROOP
THAT'S RIGHT, BUT I HAVE SOME NEWS FOR YOU BEFORE I TELL YOU THE RESULTS OF THE MEETING.
?
CONGRATULATIONS. CAN'T FOOL ME IS GOING TO BECOME AN ANIME.
MISTEEEEEER YOSHIDA!
I ALWAYS KNEW YOU WERE A RELIABLE EDITOR.
ONCE MY WORK IS ANIMATED, YOU'RE GOING TO TELL ME THE PERFECT PROPOSAL THAT WILL MAKE HER SAY YES. RIGHT, MR. LOVE ADVISOR?
I DID EXACTLY AS YOU SAID AND GOT AN ANIME!
RIGHT?
RIGHT?!
RUB RUB
NO. THAT NEEDS TO BE PUT OFF.
WHAT?

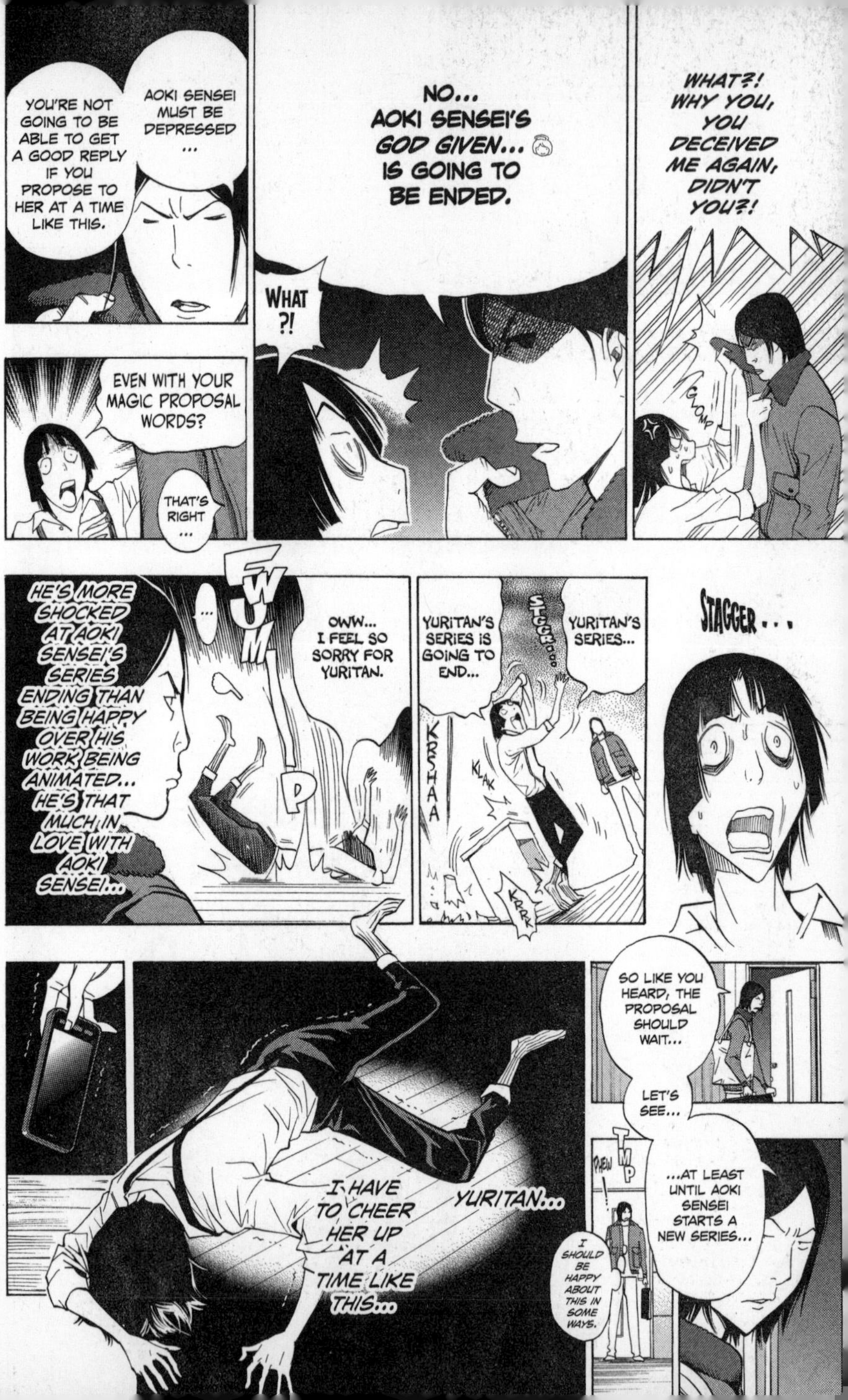
WHAT?! WHY YOU, YOU DECEIVED ME AGAIN, DIDN'T YOU?!
GLOMP
NO... AOKI SENSEI'S GOD GIVEN... IS GOING TO BE ENDED.
WHAT ?!
AOKI SENSEI MUST BE DEPRESSED...
YOU'RE NOT GOING TO BE ABLE TO GET A GOOD REPLY IF YOU PROPOSE TO HER AT A TIME LIKE THIS.
EVEN WITH YOUR MAGIC PROPOSAL WORDS?
THAT'S RIGHT...
STAGGER...
YURITAN'S SERIES...
STGGR...
YURITAN'S SERIES IS GOING TO END...
KRSHAA
KLAK
KRRK
OWW... I FEEL SO SORRY FOR YURITAN.
FWUMP
...
HE'S MORE SHOCKED AT AOKI SENSEI'S SERIES ENDING THAN BEING HAPPY OVER HIS WORK BEING ANIMATED... HE'S THAT MUCH IN LOVE WITH AOKI SENSEI...
SO LIKE YOU HEARD, THE PROPOSAL SHOULD WAIT...
LET'S SEE...
...AT LEAST UNTIL AOKI SENSEI STARTS A NEW SERIES...
TMP
PHEW!
I SHOULD BE HAPPY ABOUT THIS IN SOME WAYS.
YURITAN...
I HAVE TO CHEER HER UP AT A TIME LIKE THIS...

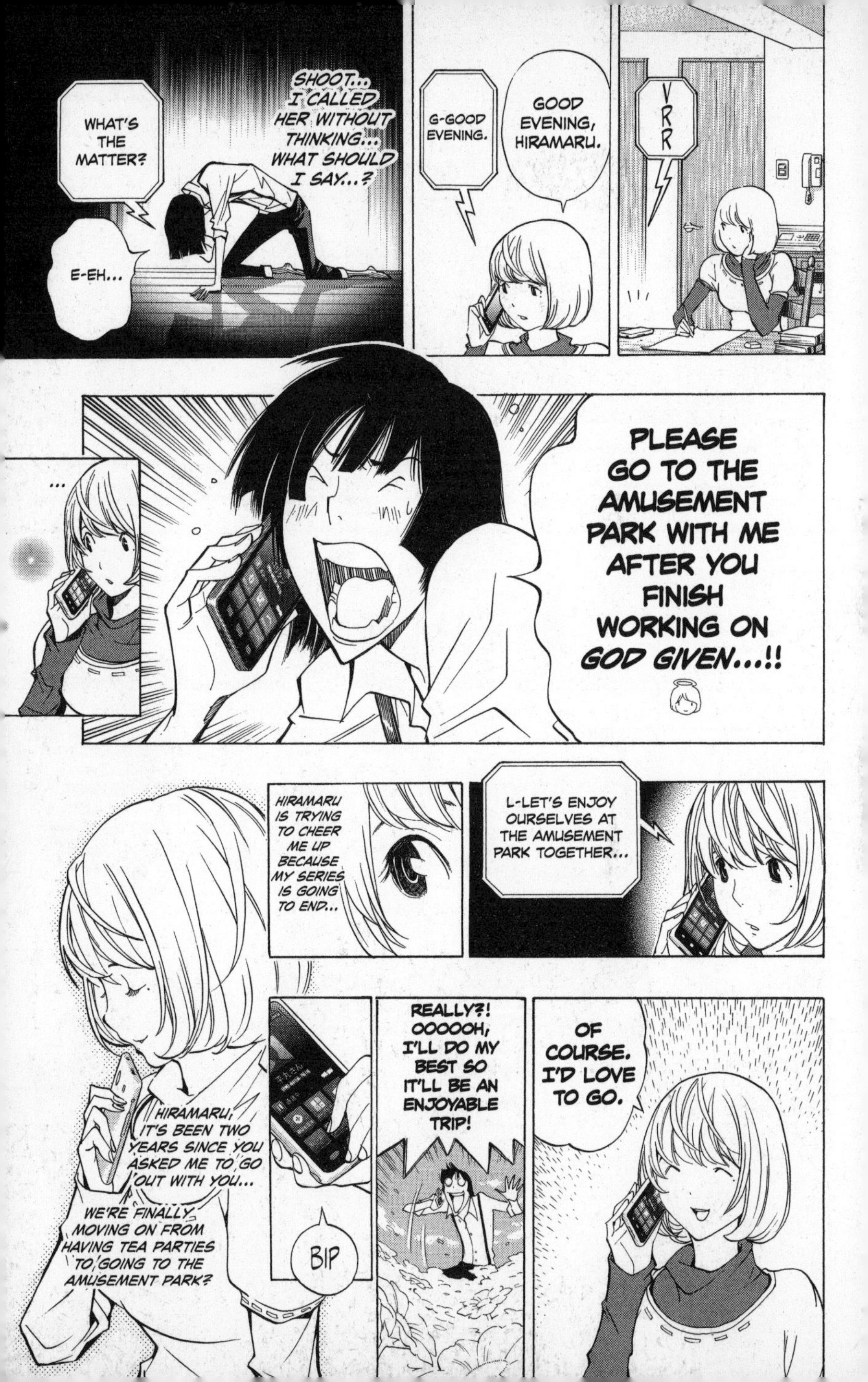
VRR
GOOD EVENING, HIRAMARU.
G-GOOD EVENING.
SHOOT... I CALLED HER WITHOUT THINKING... WHAT SHOULD I SAY...?
WHAT'S THE MATTER?
E-EH...
PLEASE GO TO THE AMUSEMENT PARK WITH ME AFTER YOU FINISH WORKING ON GOD GIVEN...!!
...
L-LET'S ENJOY OURSELVES AT THE AMUSEMENT PARK TOGETHER...
HIRAMARU IS TRYING TO CHEER ME UP BECAUSE MY SERIES IS GOING TO END...
OF COURSE. I'D LOVE TO GO.
REALLY?! OOOOOH, I'LL DO MY BEST SO IT'LL BE AN ENJOYABLE TRIP!
BIP
HIRAMARU, IT'S BEEN TWO YEARS SINCE YOU ASKED ME TO GO OUT WITH YOU...
WE'RE FINALLY MOVING ON FROM HAVING TEA PARTIES TO GOING TO THE AMUSEMENT PARK?

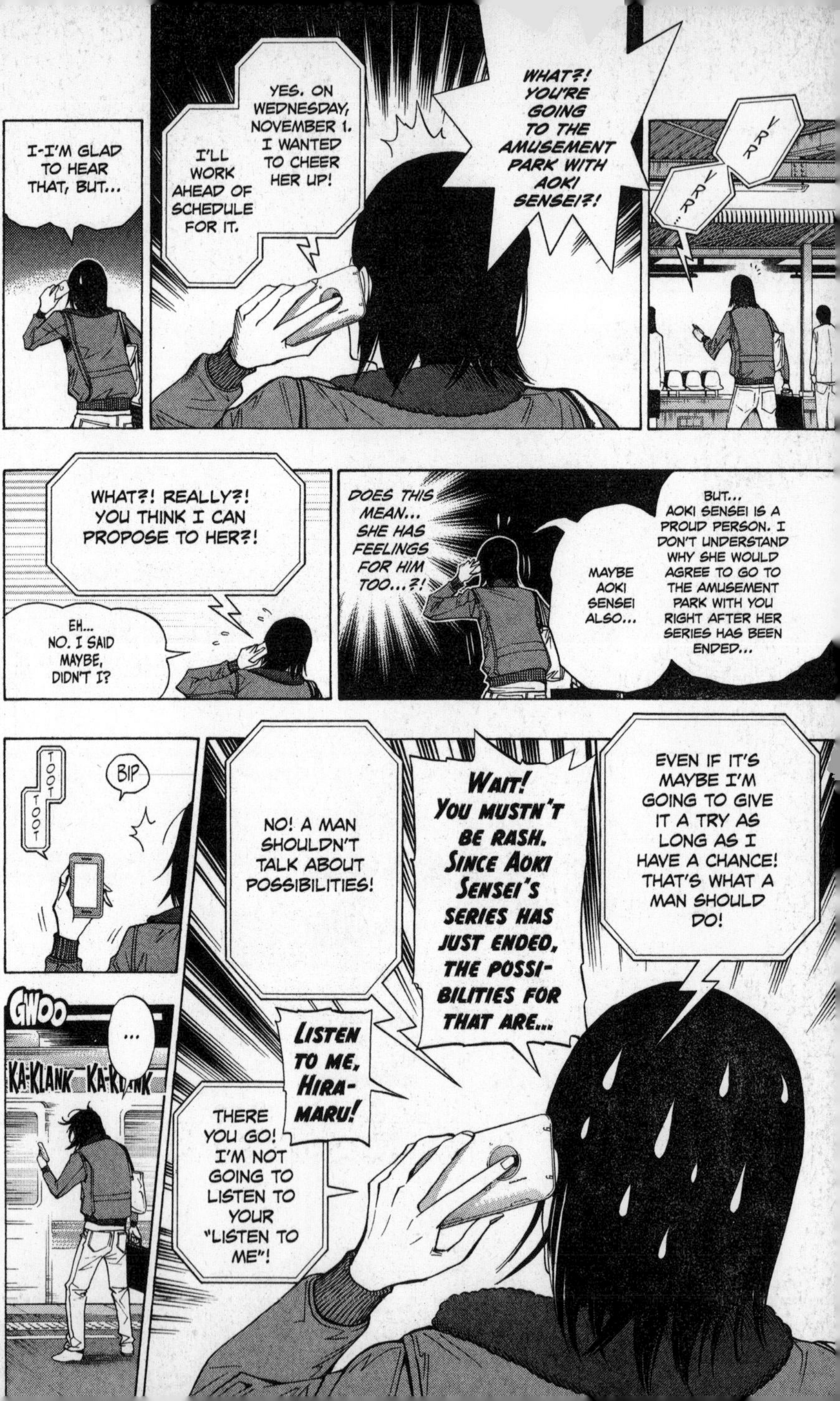
VRR
VRR...
WHAT?! YOU'RE GOING TO THE AMUSEMENT PARK WITH AOKI SENSEI?!
YES. ON WEDNESDAY, NOVEMBER 1. I WANTED TO CHEER HER UP!
I'LL WORK AHEAD OF SCHEDULE FOR IT.
I-I'M GLAD TO HEAR THAT, BUT...
BUT... AOKI SENSEI IS A PROUD PERSON. I DON'T UNDERSTAND WHY SHE WOULD AGREE TO GO TO THE AMUSEMENT PARK WITH YOU RIGHT AFTER HER SERIES HAS BEEN ENDED...
MAYBE AOKI SENSEI ALSO...
DOES THIS MEAN... SHE HAS FEELINGS FOR HIM TOO...?!
WHAT?! REALLY?! YOU THINK I CAN PROPOSE TO HER?!
EH... NO. I SAID MAYBE, DIDN'T I?
EVEN IF IT'S MAYBE I'M GOING TO GIVE IT A TRY AS LONG AS I HAVE A CHANCE! THAT'S WHAT A MAN SHOULD DO!
WAIT! YOU MUSTN'T BE RASH. SINCE AOKI SENSEI'S SERIES HAS JUST ENDED, THE POSSI-BILITIES FOR THAT ARE...
NO! A MAN SHOULDN'T TALK ABOUT POSSIBILITIES!
LISTEN TO ME, HIRA-MARU!
THERE YOU GO! I'M NOT GOING TO LISTEN TO YOUR "LISTEN TO ME"!
TOOT TOOT
BIP
GWOO
...
KA-KLANK KA-KLANK

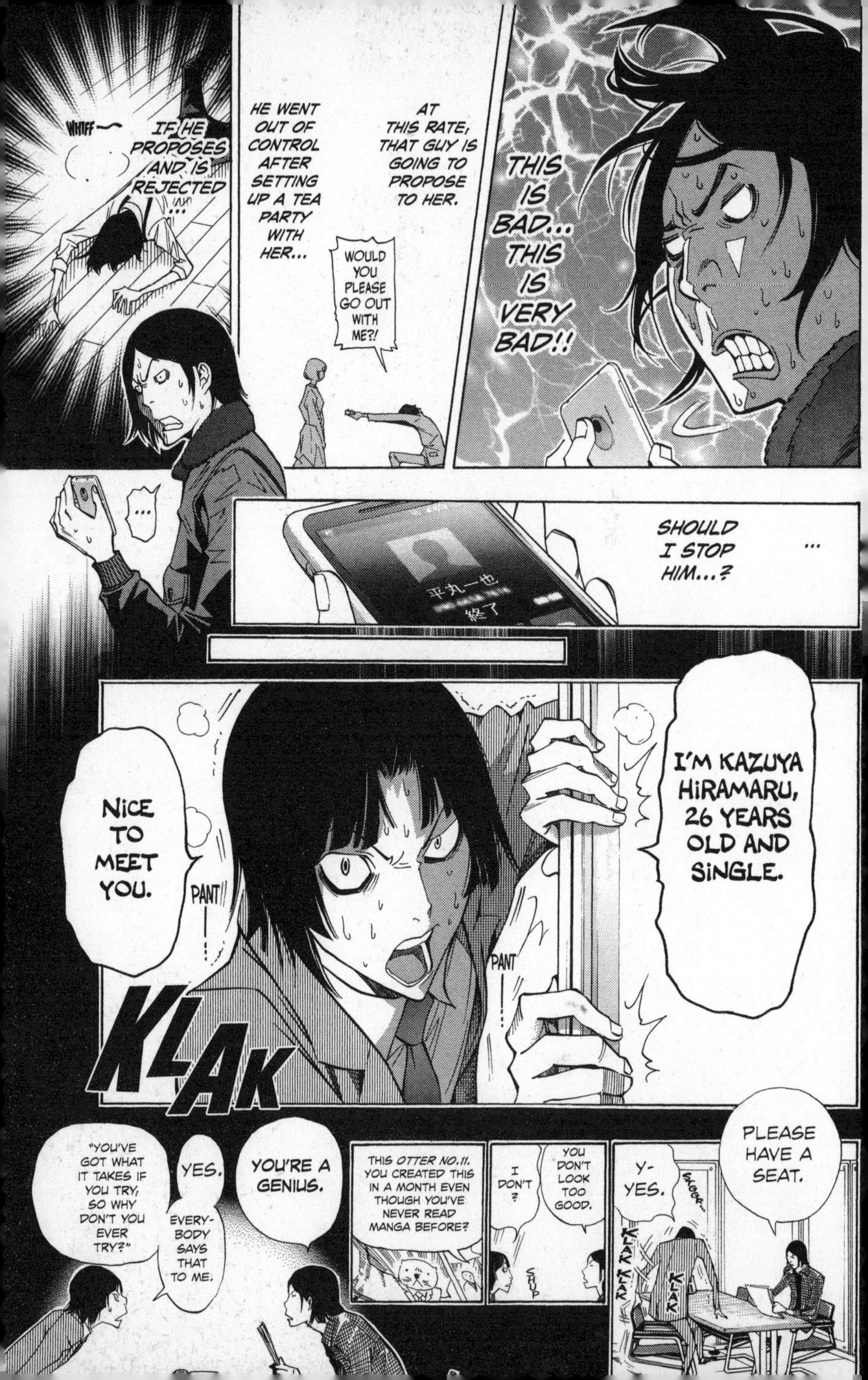
THIS IS BAD... THIS IS VERY BAD!!
AT THIS RATE, THAT GUY IS GOING TO PROPOSE TO HER.
HE WENT OUT OF CONTROL AFTER SETTING UP A TEA PARTY WITH HER...
WOULD YOU PLEASE GO OUT WITH ME?!
WHIFF~
IF HE PROPOSES AND IS REJECTED
...
...
...
SHOULD I STOP HIM...?
平丸一也
終了
I'M KAZUYA HIRAMARU, 26 YEARS OLD AND SINGLE.
PANT
NICE TO MEET YOU.
PANT
KLAK
PLEASE HAVE A SEAT.
Y-YES.
SKGGR...
KLAK KLAK
KLAK
YOU DON'T LOOK TOO GOOD.
I DON'T ?
SHUP
THIS OTTER NO.11. YOU CREATED THIS IN A MONTH EVEN THOUGH YOU'VE NEVER READ MANGA BEFORE?
YOU'RE A GENIUS.
YES.
EVERY-BODY SAYS THAT TO ME.
"YOU'VE GOT WHAT IT TAKES IF YOU TRY, SO WHY DON'T YOU EVER TRY?"

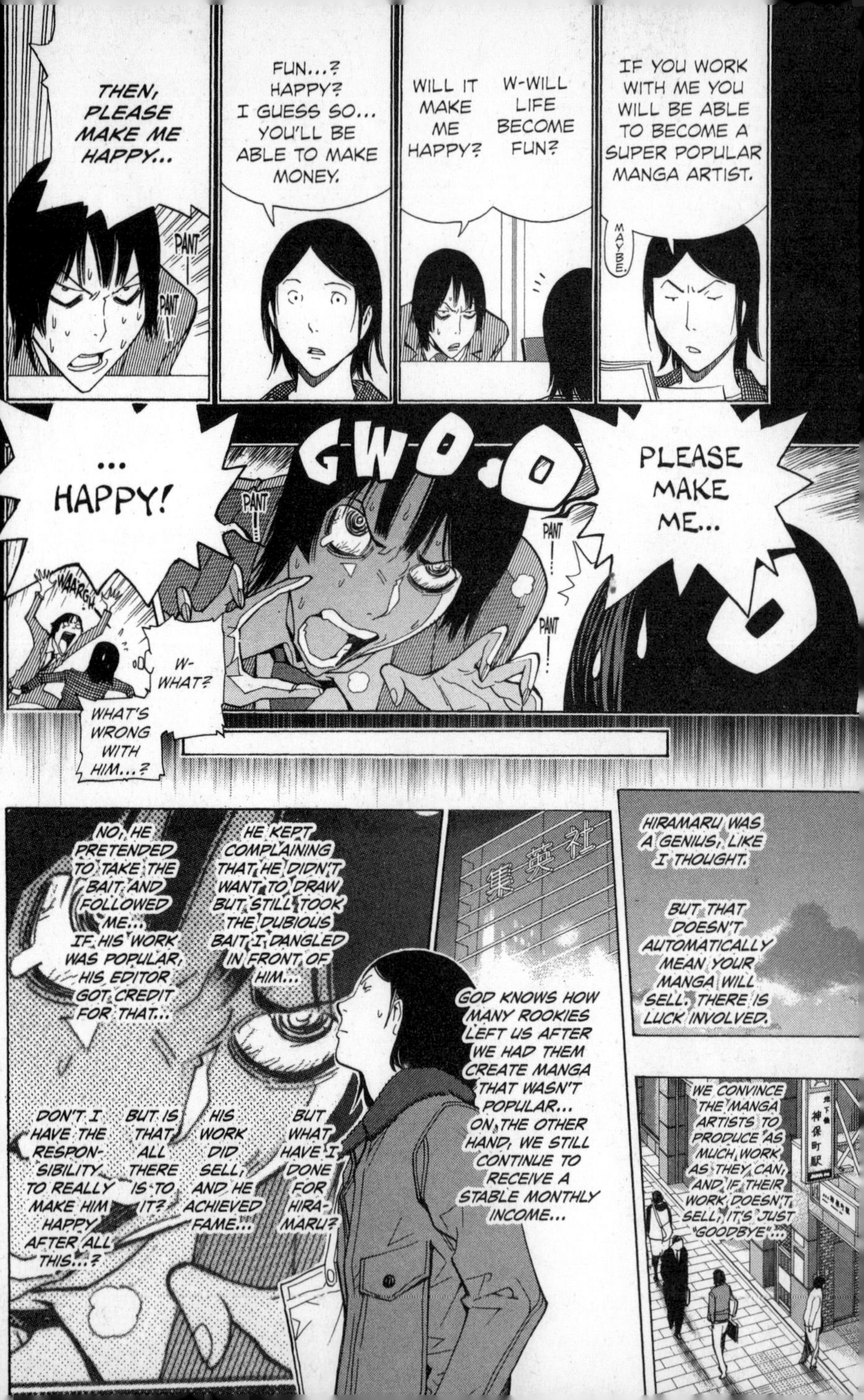
IF YOU WORK WITH ME YOU WILL BE ABLE TO BECOME A SUPER POPULAR MANGA ARTIST.
MAYBE.
W-WILL LIFE BECOME FUN?
WILL IT MAKE ME HAPPY?
FUN...? HAPPY? I GUESS SO... YOU'LL BE ABLE TO MAKE MONEY.
THEN, PLEASE MAKE ME HAPPY...
PANT
PANT
PLEASE MAKE ME...
GWO O
PANT
PANT
PANT
... HAPPY!
WAARGH
W-WHAT?
WHAT'S WRONG WITH HIM...?
HIRAMARU WAS A GENIUS, LIKE I THOUGHT.
BUT THAT DOESN'T AUTOMATICALLY MEAN YOUR MANGA WILL SELL. THERE IS LUCK INVOLVED.
集英社
WE CONVINCE THE MANGA ARTISTS TO PRODUCE AS MUCH WORK AS THEY CAN, AND IF THEIR WORK DOESN'T SELL, IT'S JUST "GOODBYE"...
神保町駅
GOD KNOWS HOW MANY ROOKIES LEFT US AFTER WE HAD THEM CREATE MANGA THAT WASN'T POPULAR... ON THE OTHER HAND, WE STILL CONTINUE TO RECEIVE A STABLE MONTHLY INCOME...
HE KEPT COMPLAINING THAT HE DIDN'T WANT TO DRAW BUT STILL TOOK THE DUBIOUS BAIT I DANGLED IN FRONT OF HIM...
NO, HE PRETENDED TO TAKE THE BAIT AND FOLLOWED ME... IF HIS WORK WAS POPULAR, HIS EDITOR GOT CREDIT FOR THAT...
BUT WHAT HAVE I DONE FOR HIRAMARU?
HIS WORK DID SELL, AND HE ACHIEVED FAME...
BUT IS THAT ALL THERE IS TO IT?
DON'T I HAVE THE RESPONSIBILITY TO REALLY MAKE HIM HAPPY AFTER ALL THIS...?

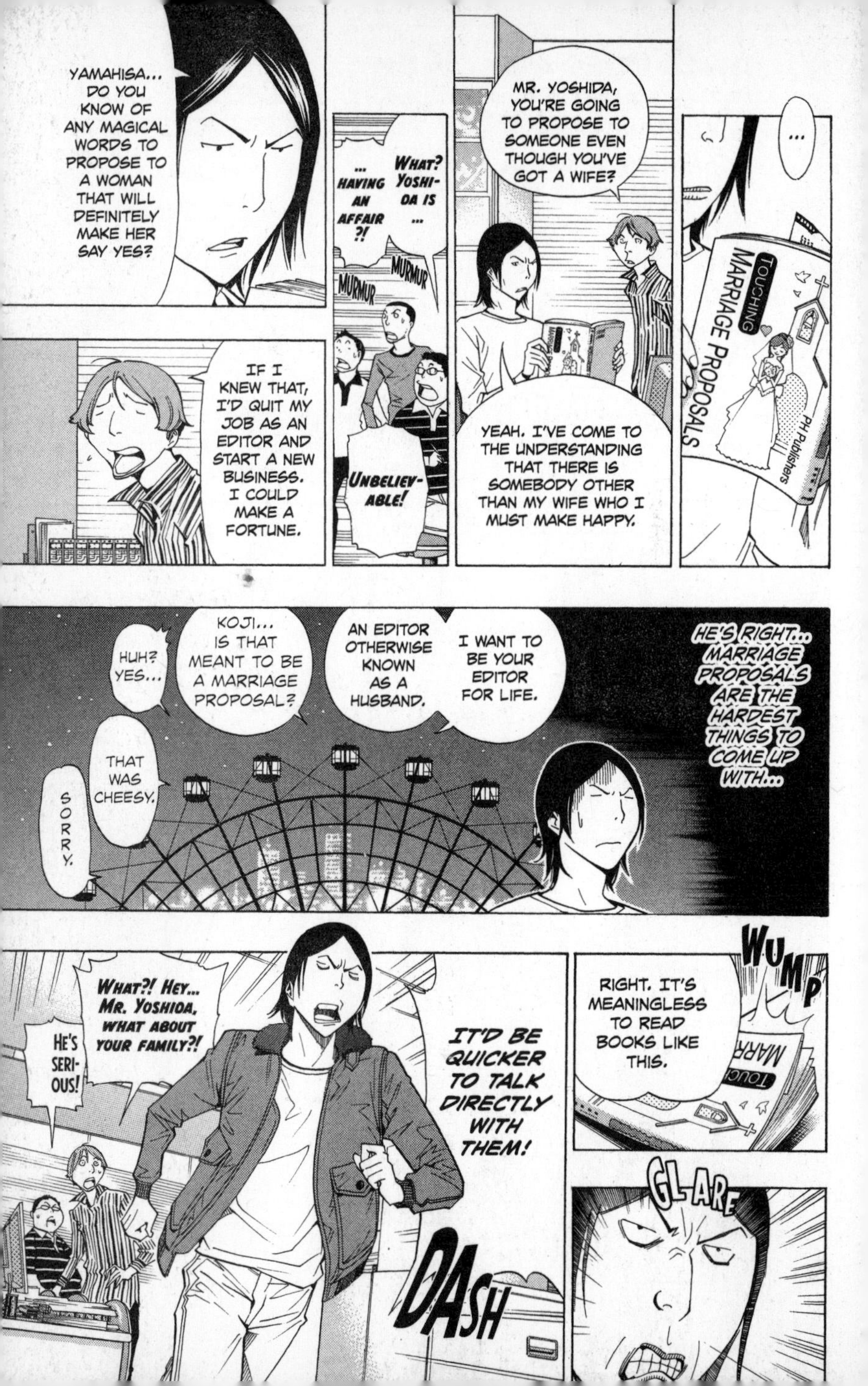
TOUCHING
MARRIAGE PROPOSALS
PH Publishers
...
MR. YOSHIDA, YOU'RE GOING TO PROPOSE TO SOMEONE EVEN THOUGH YOU'VE GOT A WIFE?
YEAH. I'VE COME TO THE UNDERSTANDING THAT THERE IS SOMEBODY OTHER THAN MY WIFE WHO I MUST MAKE HAPPY.
WHAT? YOSHI-OA IS ...
... HAVING AN AFFAIR ?!
MURMUR
MURMUR
UNBELIEV-ABLE!
YAMAHISA... DO YOU KNOW OF ANY MAGICAL WORDS TO PROPOSE TO A WOMAN THAT WILL DEFINITELY MAKE HER SAY YES?
IF I KNEW THAT, I'D QUIT MY JOB AS AN EDITOR AND START A NEW BUSINESS. I COULD MAKE A FORTUNE.
HE'S RIGHT... MARRIAGE PROPOSALS ARE THE HARDEST THINGS TO COME UP WITH...
I WANT TO BE YOUR EDITOR FOR LIFE.
AN EDITOR OTHERWISE KNOWN AS A HUSBAND.
KOJI... IS THAT MEANT TO BE A MARRIAGE PROPOSAL?
HUH? YES...
THAT WAS CHEESY.
SORRY.
WUMP
RIGHT. IT'S MEANINGLESS TO READ BOOKS LIKE THIS.
GLARE
IT'D BE QUICKER TO TALK DIRECTLY WITH THEM!
DASH
WHAT?! HEY... MR. YOSHIOA, WHAT ABOUT YOUR FAMILY?!
HE'S SERI-OUS!

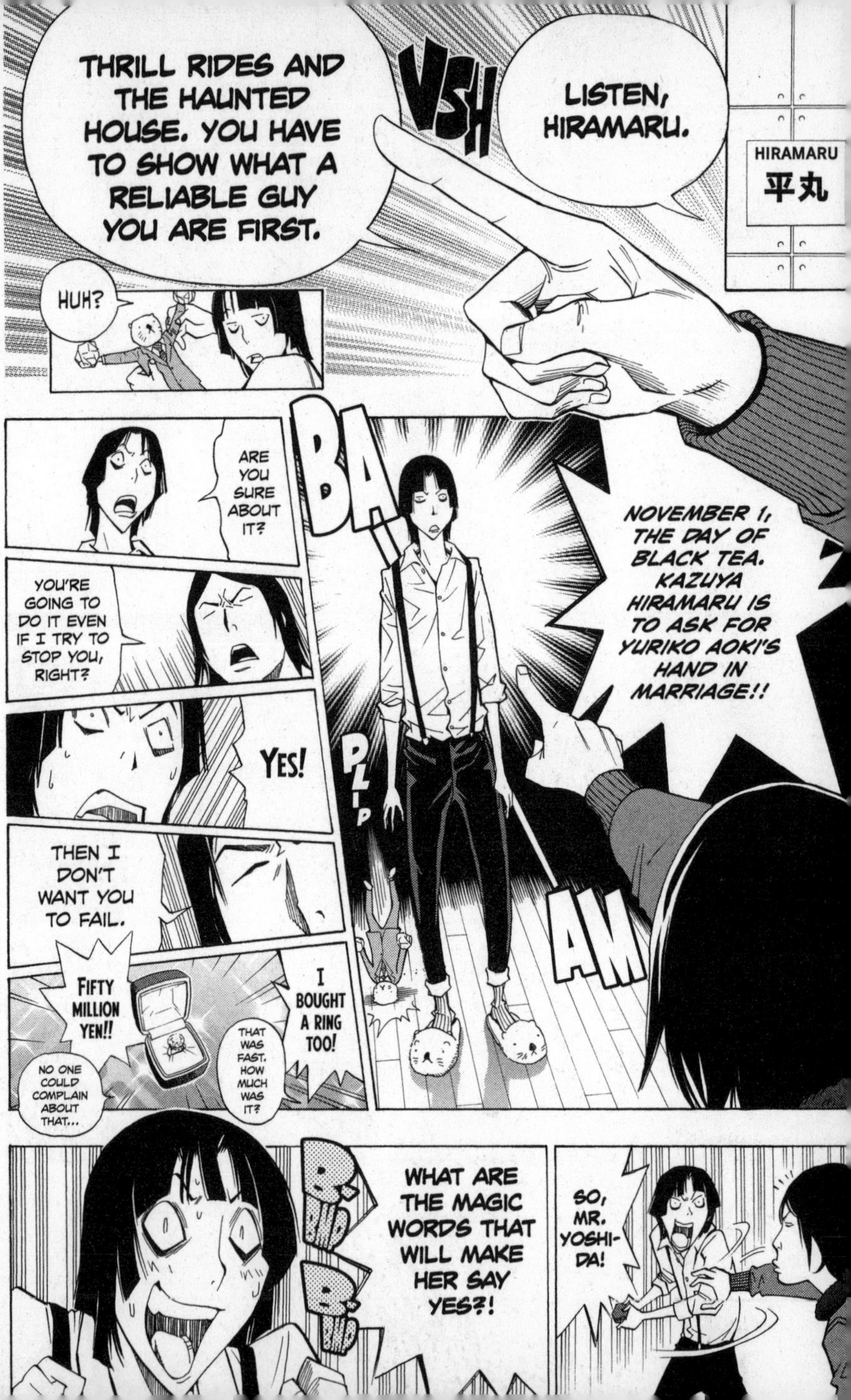
HIRAMARU
平丸
LISTEN, HIRAMARU.
VSH
THRILL RIDES AND THE HAUNTED HOUSE. YOU HAVE TO SHOW WHAT A RELIABLE GUY YOU ARE FIRST.
HUH?
BA
AM
NOVEMBER 1, THE DAY OF BLACK TEA. KAZUYA HIRAMARU IS TO ASK FOR YURIKO AOKI'S HAND IN MARRIAGE!!
DLIP
ARE YOU SURE ABOUT IT?
YOU'RE GOING TO DO IT EVEN IF I TRY TO STOP YOU, RIGHT?
YES!
THEN I DON'T WANT YOU TO FAIL.
I BOUGHT A RING TOO!
THAT WAS FAST. HOW MUCH WAS IT?
FIFTY MILLION YEN!!
NO ONE COULD COMPLAIN ABOUT THAT...
SO, MR. YOSHIDA!
WHAT ARE THE MAGIC WORDS THAT WILL MAKE HER SAY YES?!

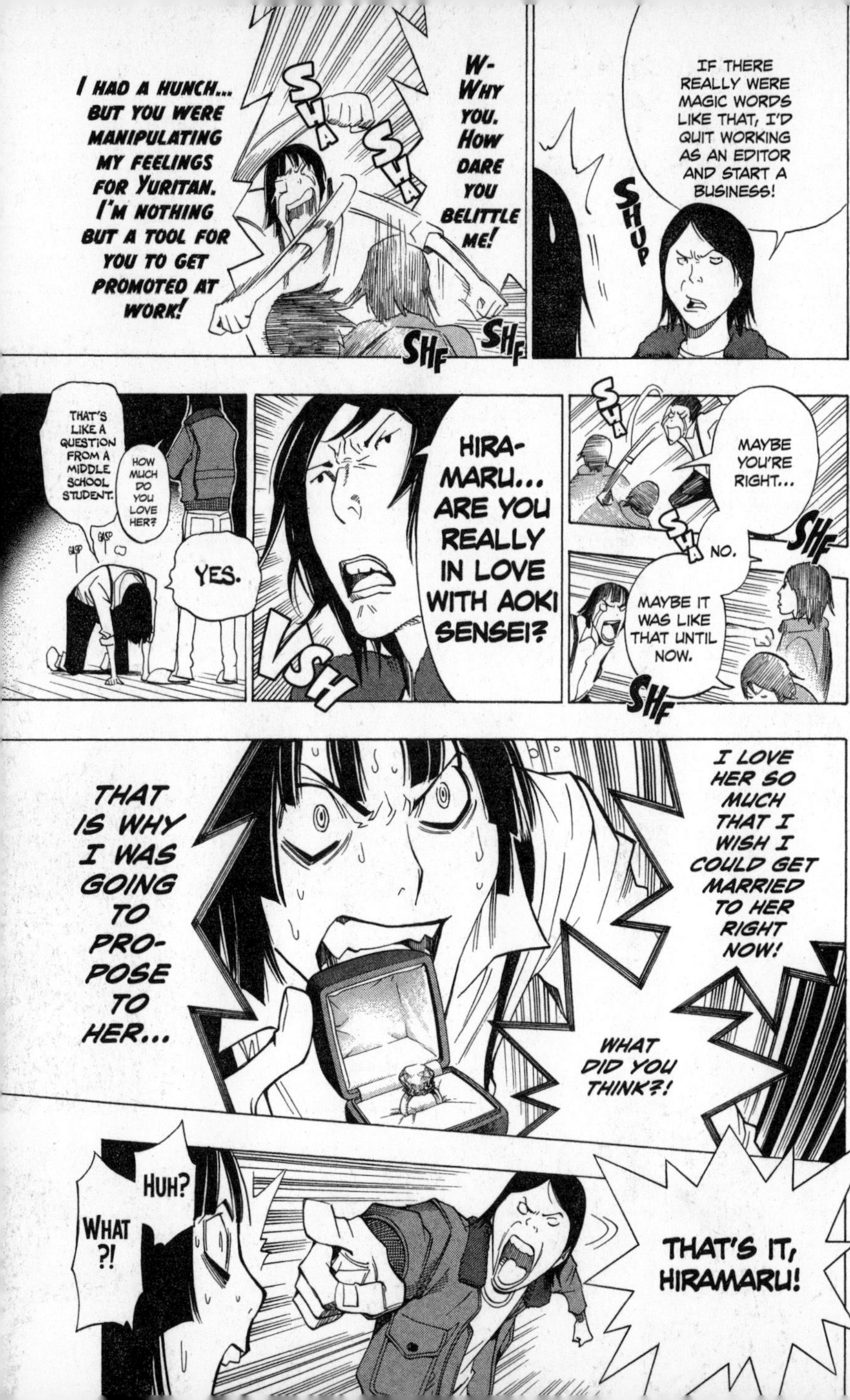
IF THERE REALLY WERE MAGIC WORDS LIKE THAT, I'D QUIT WORKING AS AN EDITOR AND START A BUSINESS!
SHUP
W-WHY YOU. HOW DARE YOU BELITTLE ME!
SHA
SHA
SHA
I HAD A HUNCH... BUT YOU WERE MANIPULATING MY FEELINGS FOR YURITAN. I'M NOTHING BUT A TOOL FOR YOU TO GET PROMOTED AT WORK!
SHF
SHF
SHA
MAYBE YOU'RE RIGHT...
SHF
SHA
NO.
MAYBE IT WAS LIKE THAT UNTIL NOW.
SHF
HIRA-MARU... ARE YOU REALLY IN LOVE WITH AOKI SENSEI?
VSH
HOW MUCH DO YOU LOVE HER?
YES.
THAT'S LIKE A QUESTION FROM A MIDDLE SCHOOL STUDENT.
GASP
GASP
I LOVE HER SO MUCH THAT I WISH I COULD GET MARRIED TO HER RIGHT NOW!
THAT IS WHY I WAS GOING TO PRO-POSE TO HER...
WHAT DID YOU THINK?!
THAT'S IT, HIRAMARU!
HUH?
WHAT?!

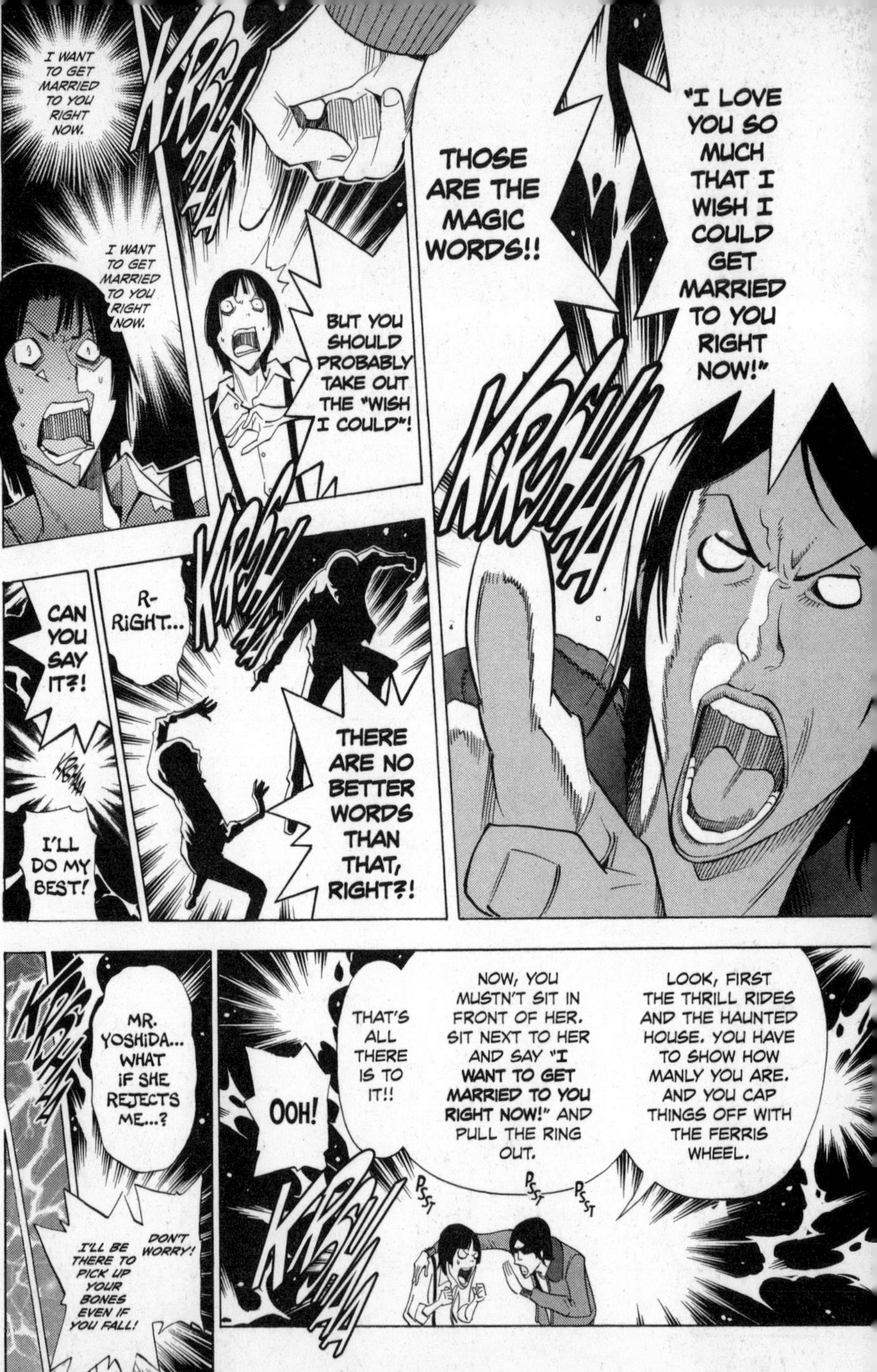
"I LOVE YOU SO MUCH THAT I WISH I COULD GET MARRIED TO YOU RIGHT NOW!"
THOSE ARE THE MAGIC WORDS!!
I WANT TO GET MARRIED TO YOU RIGHT NOW.
BUT YOU SHOULD PROBABLY TAKE OUT THE "WISH I COULD"!
I WANT TO GET MARRIED TO YOU RIGHT NOW.
THERE ARE NO BETTER WORDS THAN THAT, RIGHT?!
R-RIGHT...
CAN YOU SAY IT?!
I'LL DO MY BEST!
LOOK, FIRST THE THRILL RIDES AND THE HAUNTED HOUSE. YOU HAVE TO SHOW HOW MANLY YOU ARE. AND YOU CAP THINGS OFF WITH THE FERRIS WHEEL.
NOW, YOU MUSTN'T SIT IN FRONT OF HER. SIT NEXT TO HER AND SAY "I WANT TO GET MARRIED TO YOU RIGHT NOW!" AND PULL THE RING OUT.
THAT'S ALL THERE IS TO IT!!
OOH!
PSST
PSST
PSST
MR. YOSHIDA... WHAT IF SHE REJECTS ME...?
DON'T WORRY!
I'LL BE THERE TO PICK UP YOUR BONES EVEN IF YOU FALL!

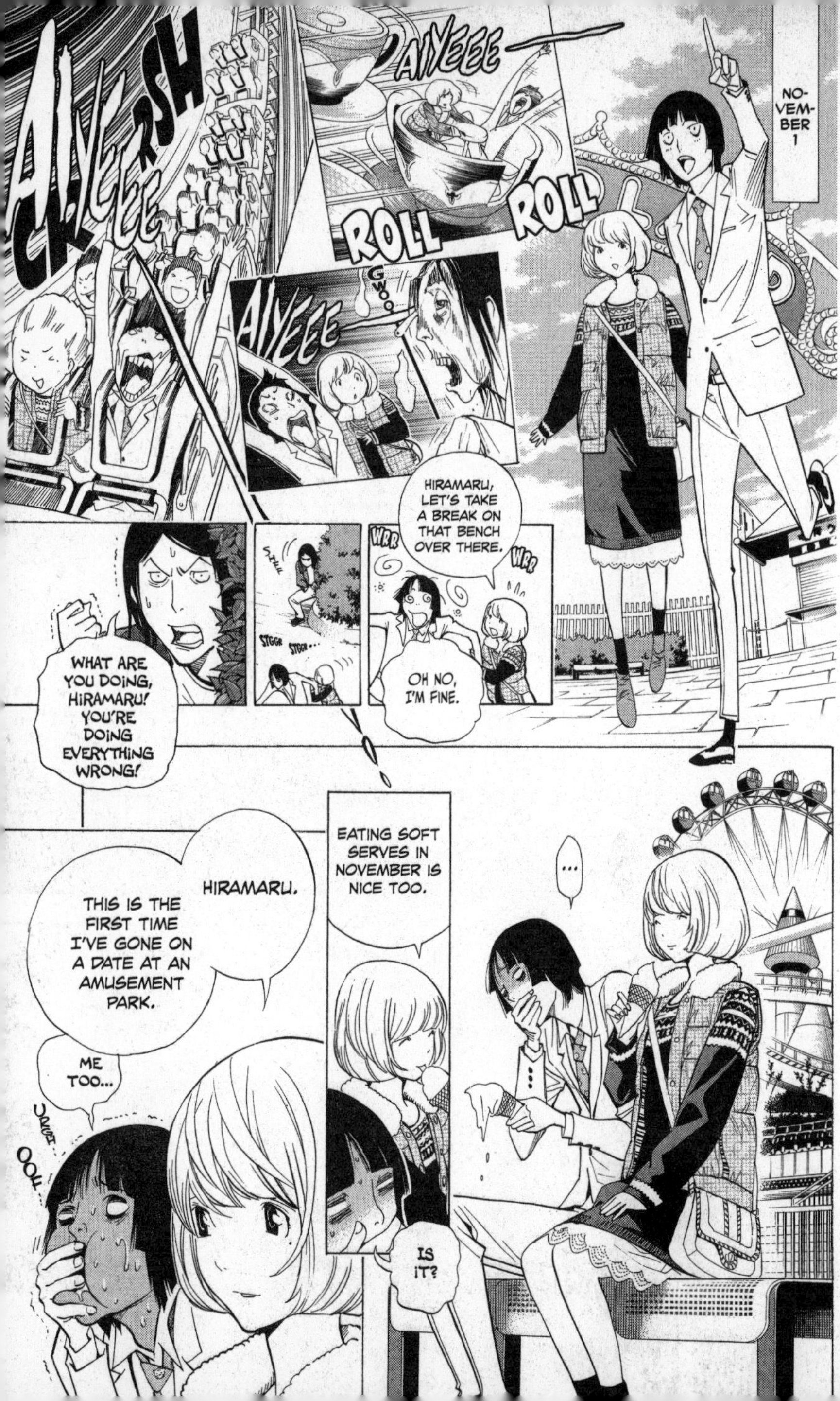
NO-
VEM-
BER
1
AIYEEE
ROLL
ROLL
AIYEEE
AIYEEE
GWOO
WRR
WRR
HIRAMARU, LET'S TAKE A BREAK ON THAT BENCH OVER THERE.
OH NO, I'M FINE.
STGGR STGGR...
WHAT ARE YOU DOING, HIRAMARU! YOU'RE DOING EVERYTHING WRONG!
...
HIRAMARU.
THIS IS THE FIRST TIME I'VE GONE ON A DATE AT AN AMUSEMENT PARK.
EATING SOFT SERVES IN NOVEMBER IS NICE TOO.
IS IT?
ME TOO...
URGH
OOF

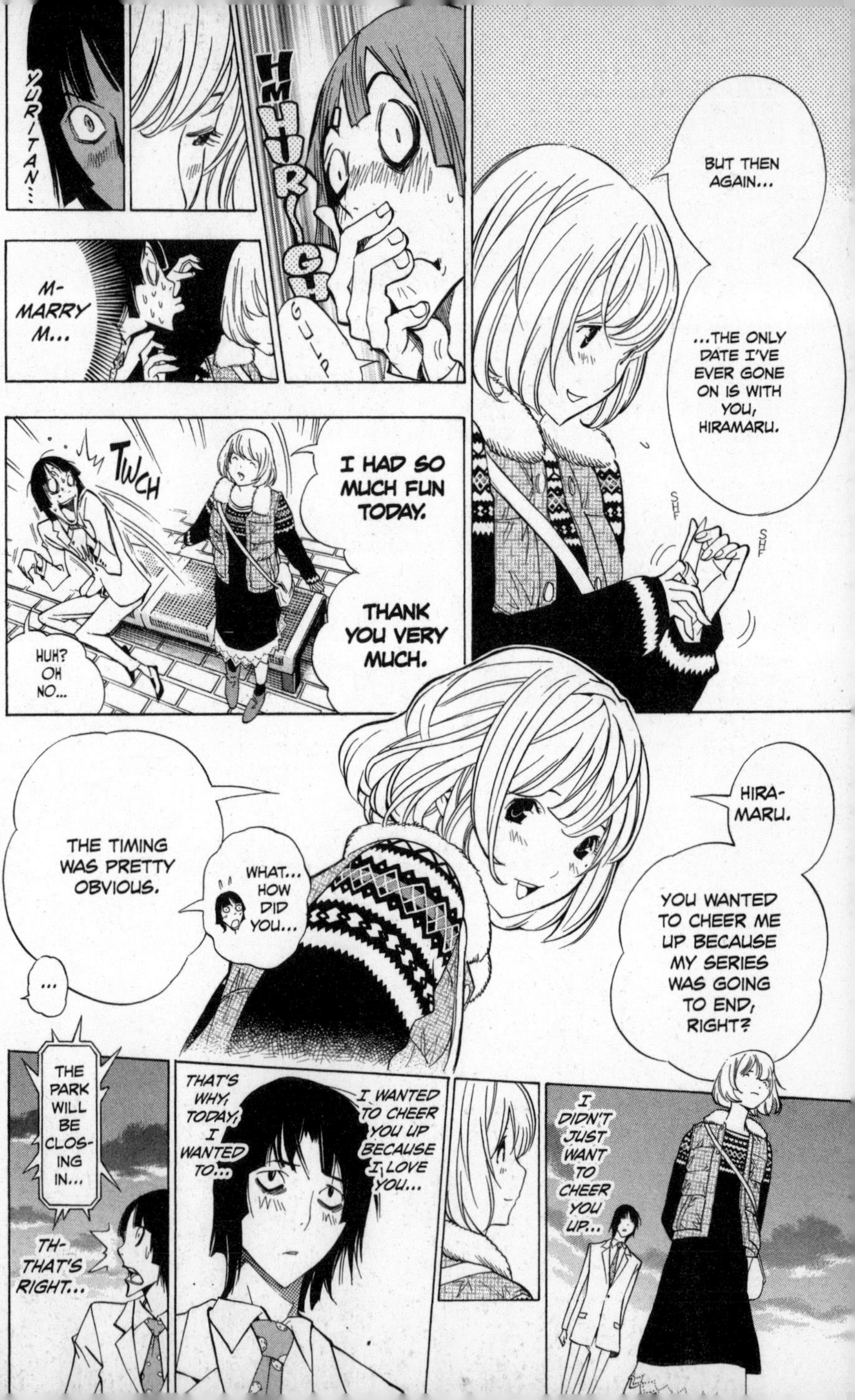
BUT THEN AGAIN...
...THE ONLY DATE I'VE EVER GONE ON IS WITH YOU, HIRAMARU.
SHF
SHF
HMURGH
GULP
YURITAN...
M-MARRY M...
I HAD SO MUCH FUN TODAY.
THANK YOU VERY MUCH.
TWCH
HUH? OH NO...
HIRA-MARU.
YOU WANTED TO CHEER ME UP BECAUSE MY SERIES WAS GOING TO END, RIGHT?
WHAT... HOW DID YOU...
THE TIMING WAS PRETTY OBVIOUS.
...
I DIDN'T JUST WANT TO CHEER YOU UP...
THAT'S WHY, TODAY, I WANTED TO...
I WANTED TO CHEER YOU UP BECAUSE I LOVE YOU...
THE PARK WILL BE CLOSING IN...
TH-THAT'S RIGHT...

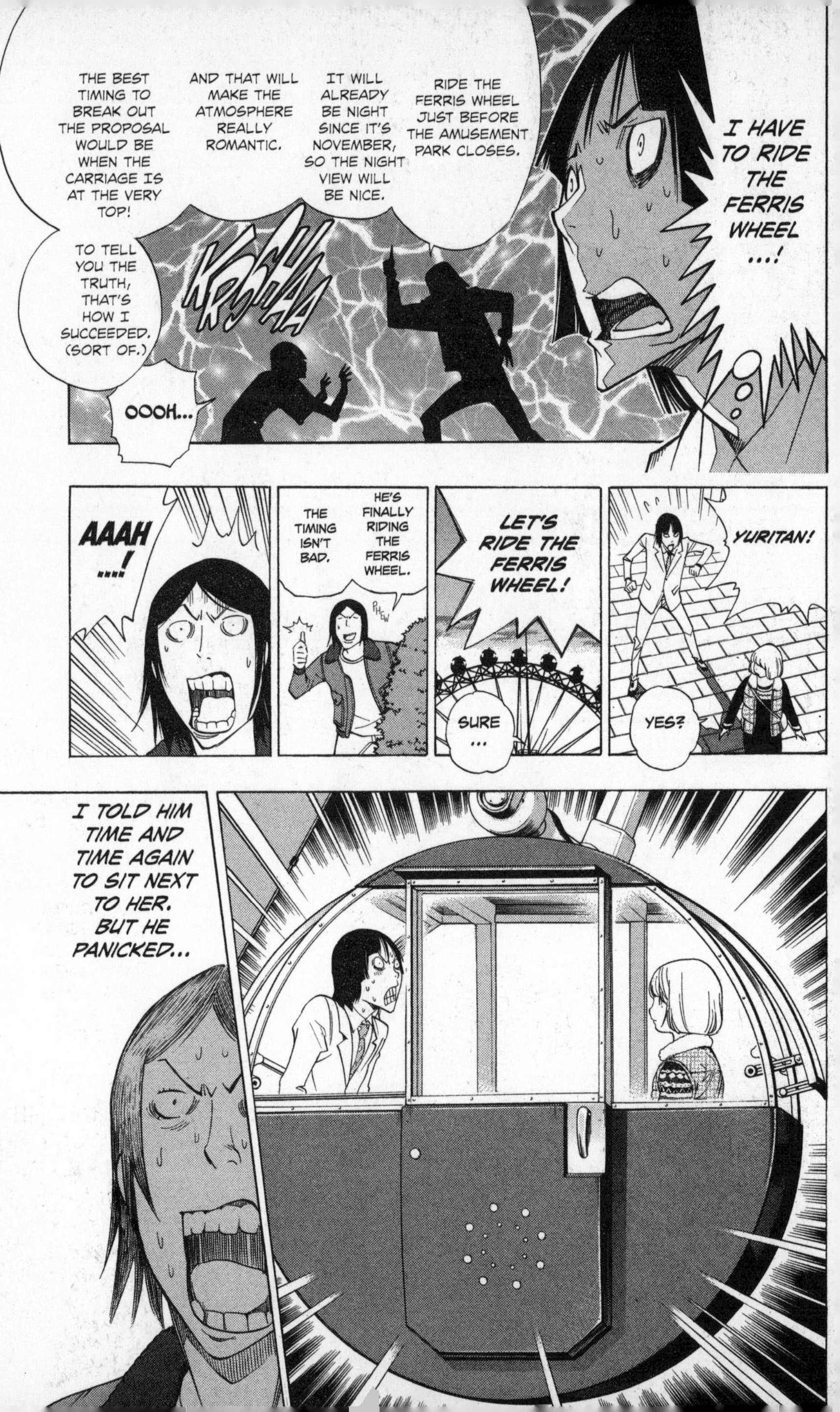
I HAVE TO RIDE THE FERRIS WHEEL ...!
RIDE THE FERRIS WHEEL JUST BEFORE THE AMUSEMENT PARK CLOSES.
IT WILL ALREADY BE NIGHT SINCE IT'S NOVEMBER, SO THE NIGHT VIEW WILL BE NICE.
AND THAT WILL MAKE THE ATMOSPHERE REALLY ROMANTIC.
THE BEST TIMING TO BREAK OUT THE PROPOSAL WOULD BE WHEN THE CARRIAGE IS AT THE VERY TOP!
TO TELL YOU THE TRUTH, THAT'S HOW I SUCCEEDED. (SORT OF.)
OOOH...
YURITAN!
YES?
LET'S RIDE THE FERRIS WHEEL!
SURE ...
HE'S FINALLY RIDING THE FERRIS WHEEL.
THE TIMING ISN'T BAD.
PHEW
AAAH ...!
I TOLD HIM TIME AND TIME AGAIN TO SIT NEXT TO HER. BUT HE PANICKED...

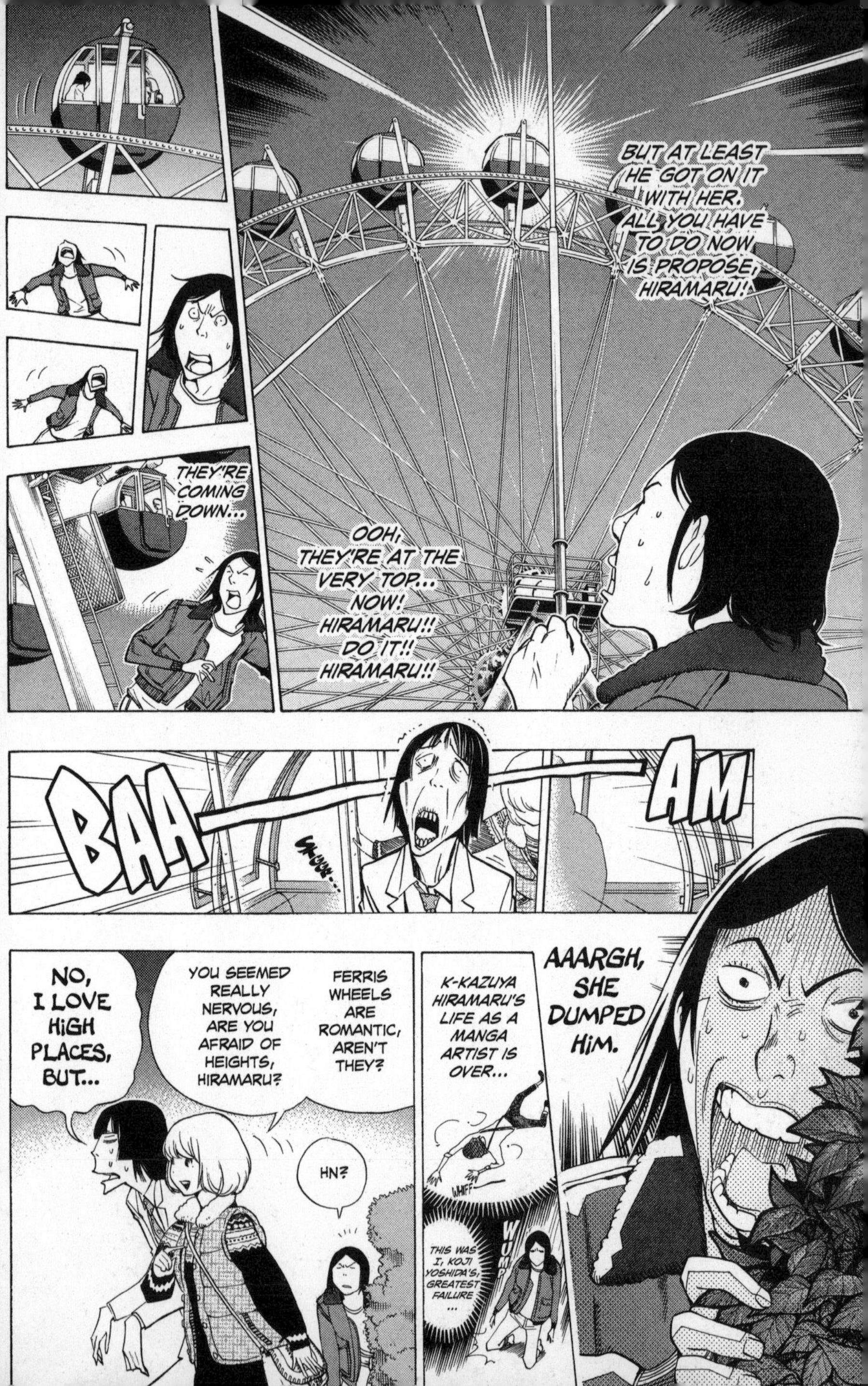
BUT AT LEAST HE GOT ON IT WITH HER. ALL YOU HAVE TO DO NOW IS PROPOSE, HIRAMARU!!
OOH, THEY'RE AT THE VERY TOP... NOW! HIRAMARU!! DO IT!! HIRAMARU!!
THEY'RE COMING DOWN...
BAA
AM
AAARGH, SHE DUMPED HIM.
K-KAZUYA HIRAMARU'S LIFE AS A MANGA ARTIST IS OVER...
WHIFF
WUMP
THIS WAS I, KOJI YOSHIDA'S, GREATEST FAILURE ...
FERRIS WHEELS ARE ROMANTIC, AREN'T THEY?
YOU SEEMED REALLY NERVOUS, ARE YOU AFRAID OF HEIGHTS, HIRAMARU?
NO, I LOVE HIGH PLACES, BUT...
HN?

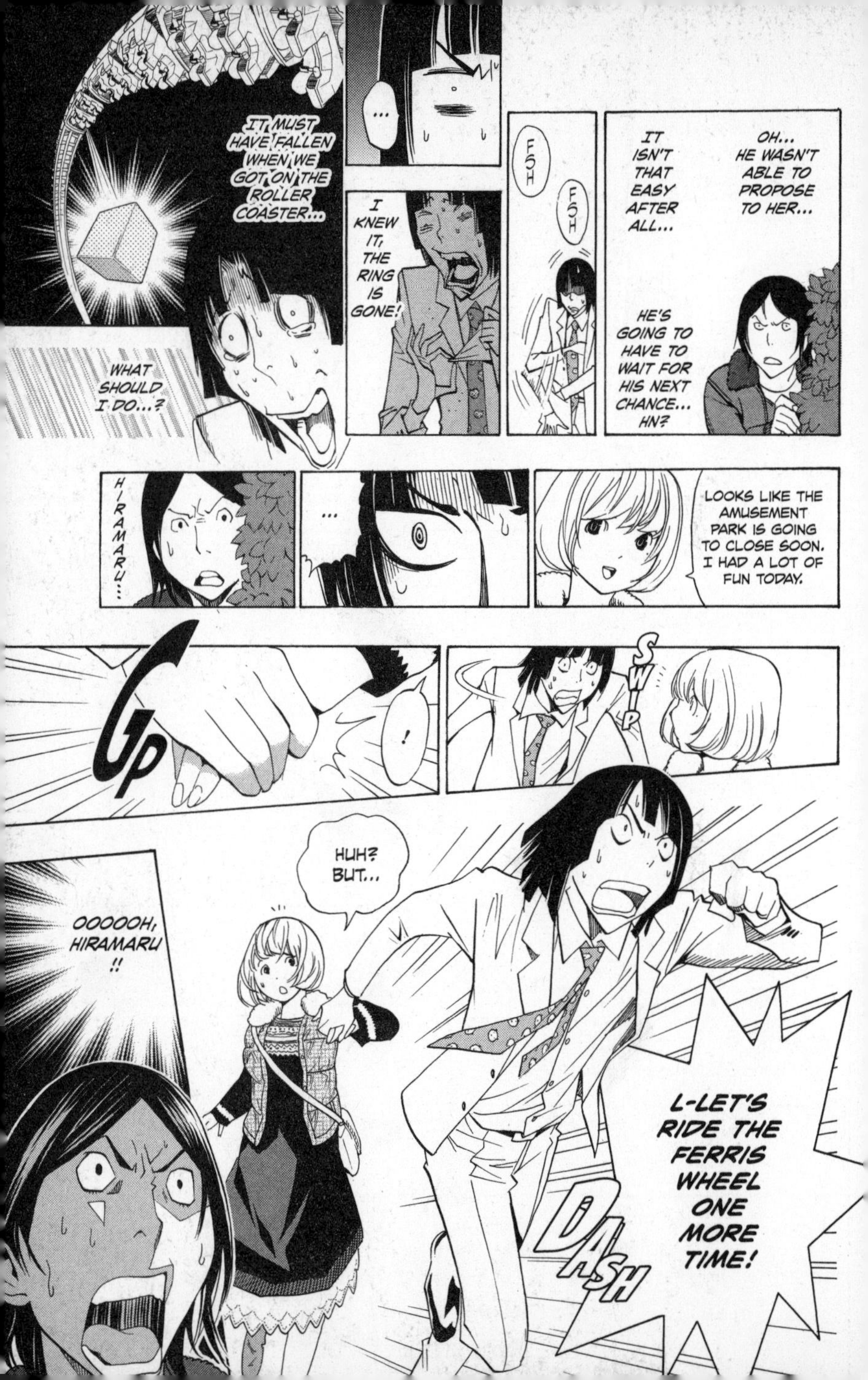
OH... HE WASN'T ABLE TO PROPOSE TO HER...
IT ISN'T THAT EASY AFTER ALL...
HE'S GOING TO HAVE TO WAIT FOR HIS NEXT CHANCE... HN?
FSH
FSH
...
I KNEW IT, THE RING IS GONE!
IT MUST HAVE FALLEN WHEN WE GOT ON THE ROLLER COASTER...
WHAT SHOULD I DO...?
LOOKS LIKE THE AMUSEMENT PARK IS GOING TO CLOSE SOON. I HAD A LOT OF FUN TODAY.
...
HIRAMARU...
SWIP
!
GP
L-LET'S RIDE THE FERRIS WHEEL ONE MORE TIME!
DASH
HUH? BUT...
OOOOOH, HIRAMARU!!

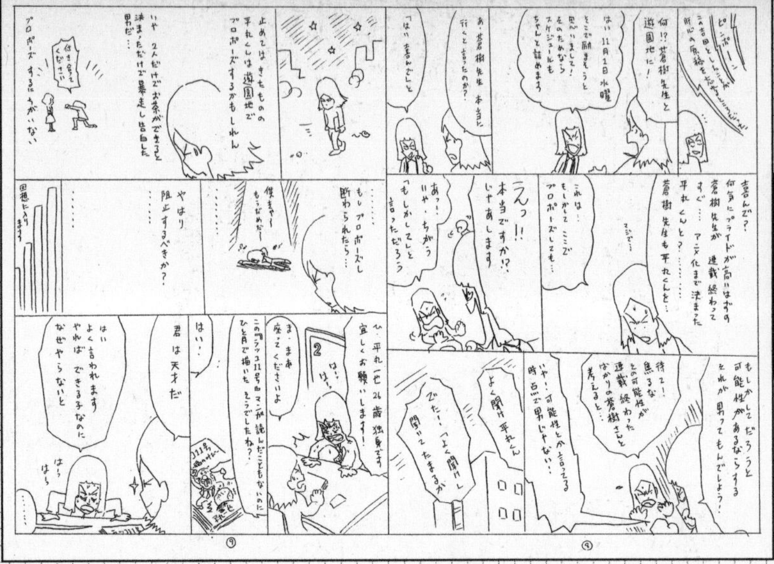
ピンポーン
この吉田としたことが 肝心の原稿を忘れちゃうところじゃった
……
何!? 蒼樹先生と 遊園地に!
はい 11月1日水曜 そこで励まそうと 思いまして! そのためなら スケジュールも ちゃんと詰めます
あ・蒼樹先生 本当に 行くと言ったのか?
「はい 喜んで」と
喜んで? 何事にプライドが高いはずの 蒼樹先生が 連載終わって すぐ… アニメ化まで決まった 平丸くんと? ……
蒼樹先生も平丸くんを…
マジで…
これは… もしかして ここで プロポーズしても…
うんっ!!
本当ですか!? じゃあします
あっ! いや・ちがう 「もしかして」と 言っただろう
もしかしてだろうと 可能性があるならする それが男ってもんでしょう!
待て! 焦るな その可能性が 連載終わった ばかりの蒼樹さんと 考えると…
いや! 可能性とか言ってる 時点で男じゃない…
よく聞け 平丸くん
でた!「よく聞けし」 聞いてたまるか
止めてはきたものの 平丸くんは遊園地で プロポーズするかもしれん
いや 2人だけでお茶ができると 決まっただけで暴走し告白した 男だ…
付き合って ください
プロポーズするに ちがいない
…… もしプロポーズし 断わられたら……
僕もう〜 もうだめだ〜
……
やはり 阻止するべきか?
……
……
回想に入ります
ひ・平丸一也 26歳 独身です 宜しくお願いします!
2
は…っ は…っ
ま・まあ 座ってくださいよ
この『ラッコ11号』 マンガ読んだこともないのに ひと月で描いたそうでしたね?
はい!
君は天才だ
はい よく言われます やれば できる子なのに なぜやらないと
は… は…
……

OHBA'S STORYBOARD

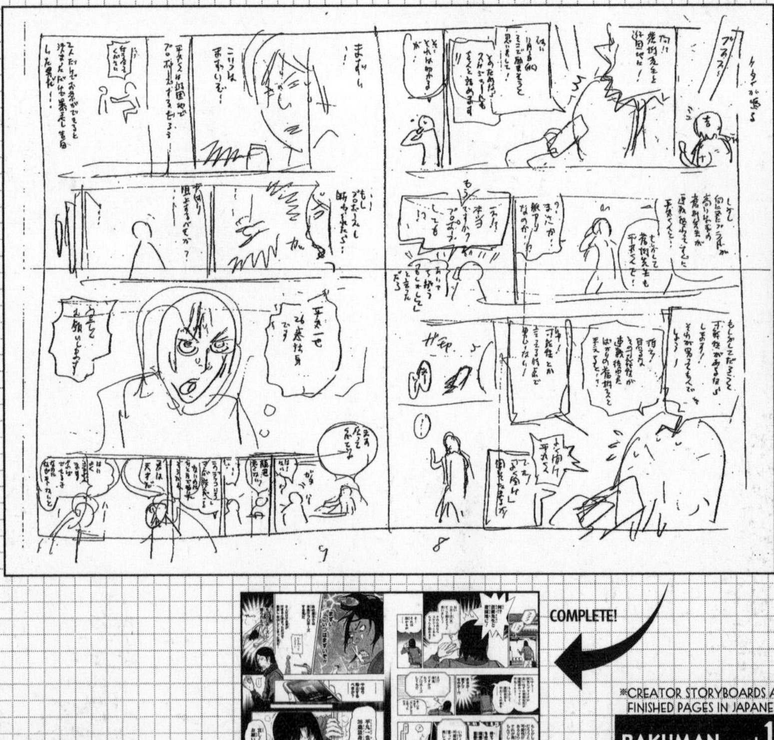

OBATA'S STORYBOARD

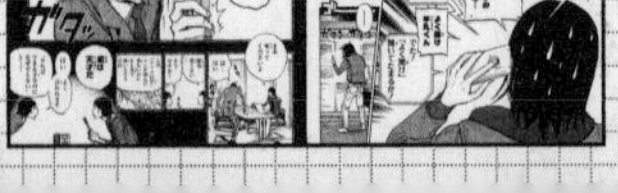

COMPLETE!

※CREATOR STORYBOARDS AND FINISHED PAGES IN JAPANESE

BAKUMAN。 vol.18

"Until the Final Draft Is Complete"

Chapter 169, pp. 158-159

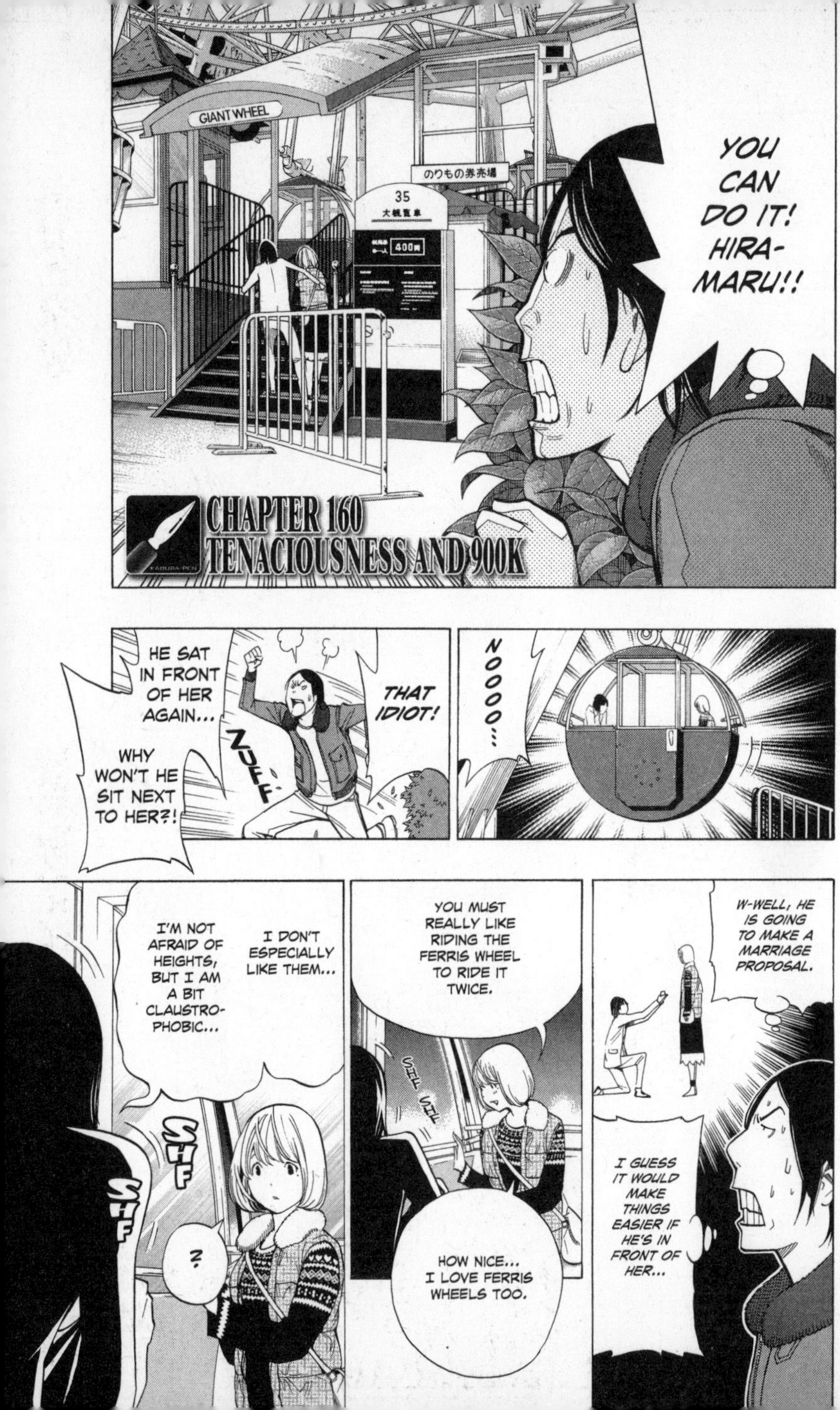
YOU CAN DO IT! HIRA-MARU!!
GIANT WHEEL
のりもの券売場
35
大観覧車
400円
CHAPTER 160
TENACIOUSNESS AND 900K
NOOOO...
THAT IDIOT!
HE SAT IN FRONT OF HER AGAIN...
ZUFF
WHY WON'T HE SIT NEXT TO HER?!
W-WELL, HE IS GOING TO MAKE A MARRIAGE PROPOSAL.
I GUESS IT WOULD MAKE THINGS EASIER IF HE'S IN FRONT OF HER...
YOU MUST REALLY LIKE RIDING THE FERRIS WHEEL TO RIDE IT TWICE.
SHF SHF
HOW NICE... I LOVE FERRIS WHEELS TOO.
I DON'T ESPECIALLY LIKE THEM...
I'M NOT AFRAID OF HEIGHTS, BUT I AM A BIT CLAUSTRO-PHOBIC...
SHF
SHF
?

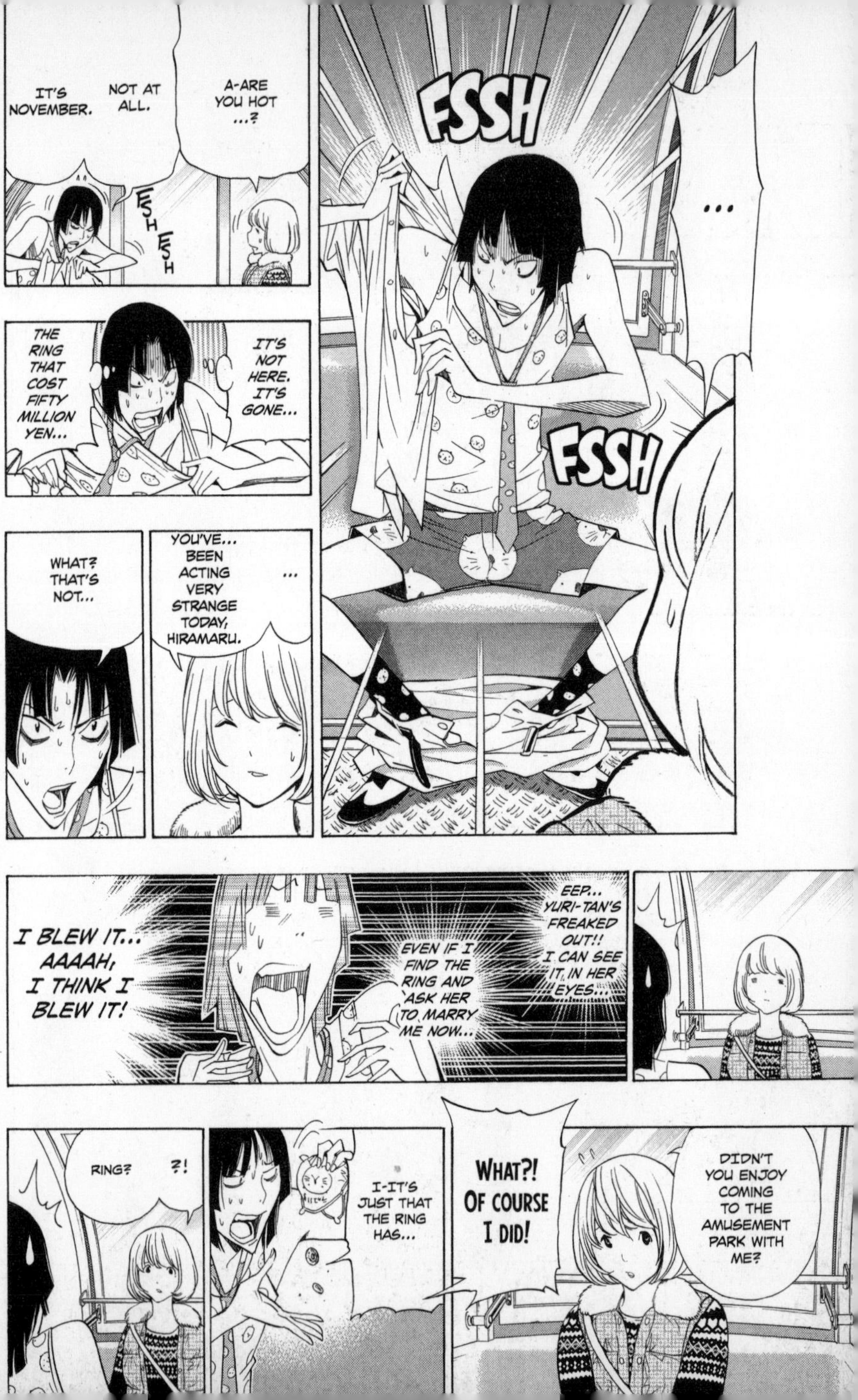
FSSH
...
FSSH
A-ARE YOU HOT ...?
NOT AT ALL.
IT'S NOVEMBER.
FSH FSH
IT'S NOT HERE. IT'S GONE...
THE RING THAT COST FIFTY MILLION YEN...
...
YOU'VE... BEEN ACTING VERY STRANGE TODAY, HIRAMARU.
WHAT? THAT'S NOT...
EEP... YURI-TAN'S FREAKED OUT!! I CAN SEE IT IN HER EYES...
EVEN IF I FIND THE RING AND ASK HER TO MARRY ME NOW...
I BLEW IT... AAAAH, I THINK I BLEW IT!
DIDN'T YOU ENJOY COMING TO THE AMUSEMENT PARK WITH ME?
WHAT?! OF COURSE I DID!
I-IT'S JUST THAT THE RING HAS...
?!
RING?

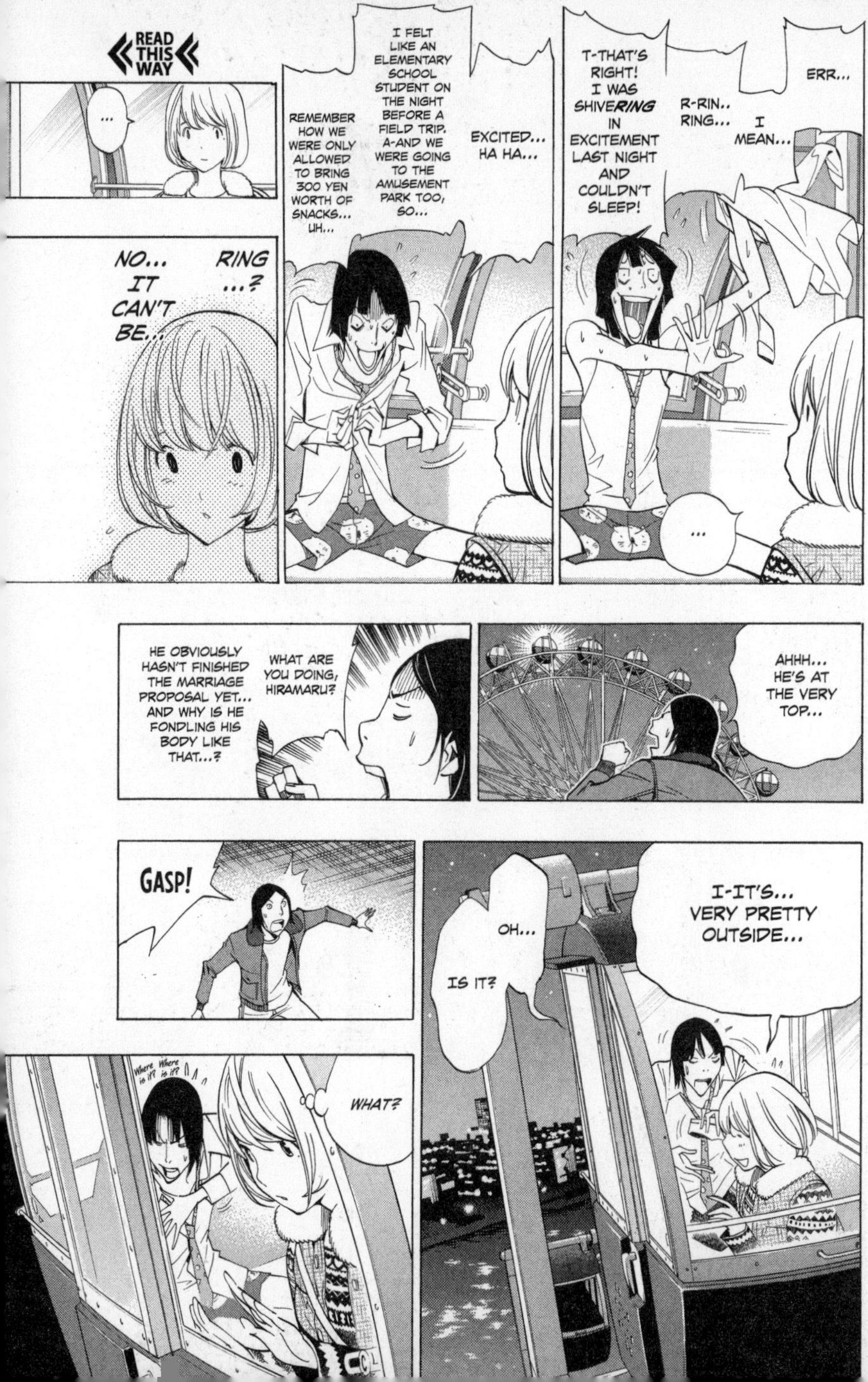
READ THIS WAY
ERR...
R-RIN.. RING... I MEAN...
T-THAT'S RIGHT! I WAS SHIVERING IN EXCITEMENT LAST NIGHT AND COULDN'T SLEEP!
...
I FELT LIKE AN ELEMENTARY SCHOOL STUDENT ON THE NIGHT BEFORE A FIELD TRIP. A-AND WE WERE GOING TO THE AMUSEMENT PARK TOO, SO...
EXCITED... HA HA...
REMEMBER HOW WE WERE ONLY ALLOWED TO BRING 300 YEN WORTH OF SNACKS... UH...
...
RING ...?
NO... IT CAN'T BE...
AHHH... HE'S AT THE VERY TOP...
WHAT ARE YOU DOING, HIRAMARU?
HE OBVIOUSLY HASN'T FINISHED THE MARRIAGE PROPOSAL YET... AND WHY IS HE FONDLING HIS BODY LIKE THAT...?
I-IT'S... VERY PRETTY OUTSIDE...
OH...
IS IT?
GASP!
WHAT?
Where is it? Where is it?

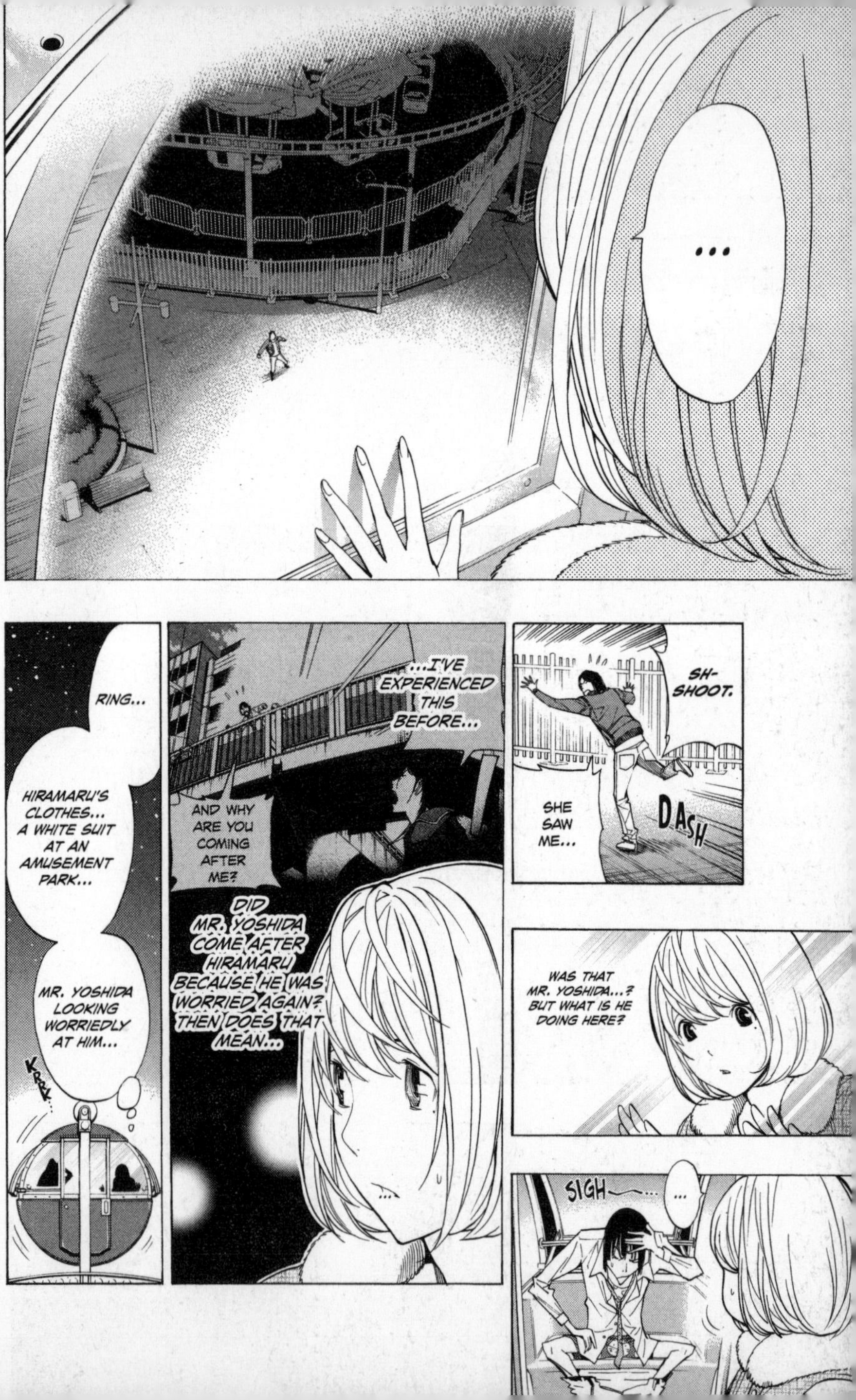
...
SH-SHOOT.
SHE SAW ME...
DASH
WAS THAT MR. YOSHIDA...? BUT WHAT IS HE DOING HERE?
SIGH...
...
...
...I'VE EXPERIENCED THIS BEFORE...
AND WHY ARE YOU COMING AFTER ME?
DID MR. YOSHIDA COME AFTER HIRAMARU BECAUSE HE WAS WORRIED AGAIN? THEN DOES THAT MEAN...
...
RING...
HIRAMARU'S CLOTHES... A WHITE SUIT AT AN AMUSEMENT PARK...
MR. YOSHIDA LOOKING WORRIEDLY AT HIM...
KRRK...

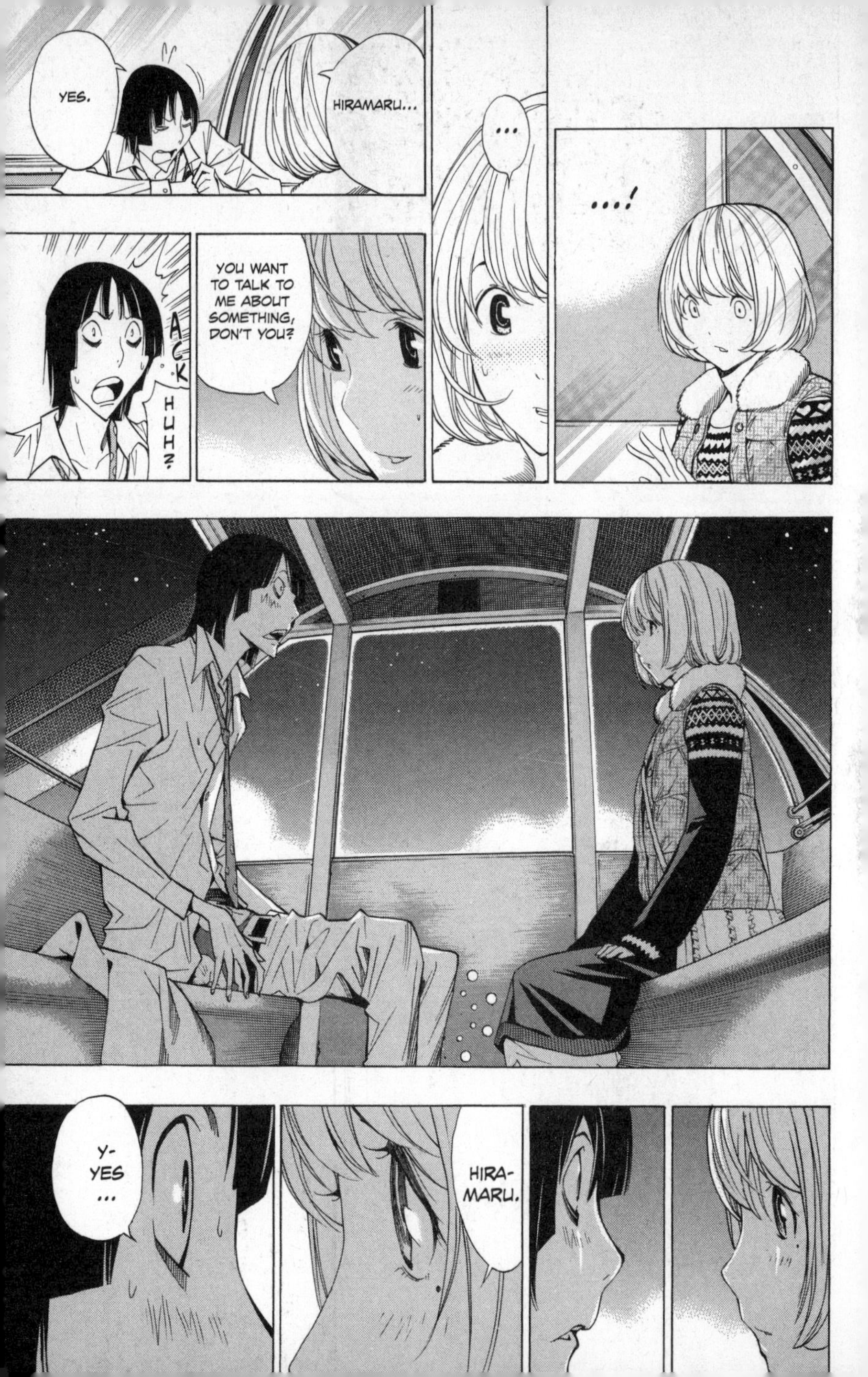
...!
...
HIRAMARU...
YES.
YOU WANT TO TALK TO ME ABOUT SOMETHING, DON'T YOU?
ACK
HUH?
HIRA-MARU.
Y-YES ...

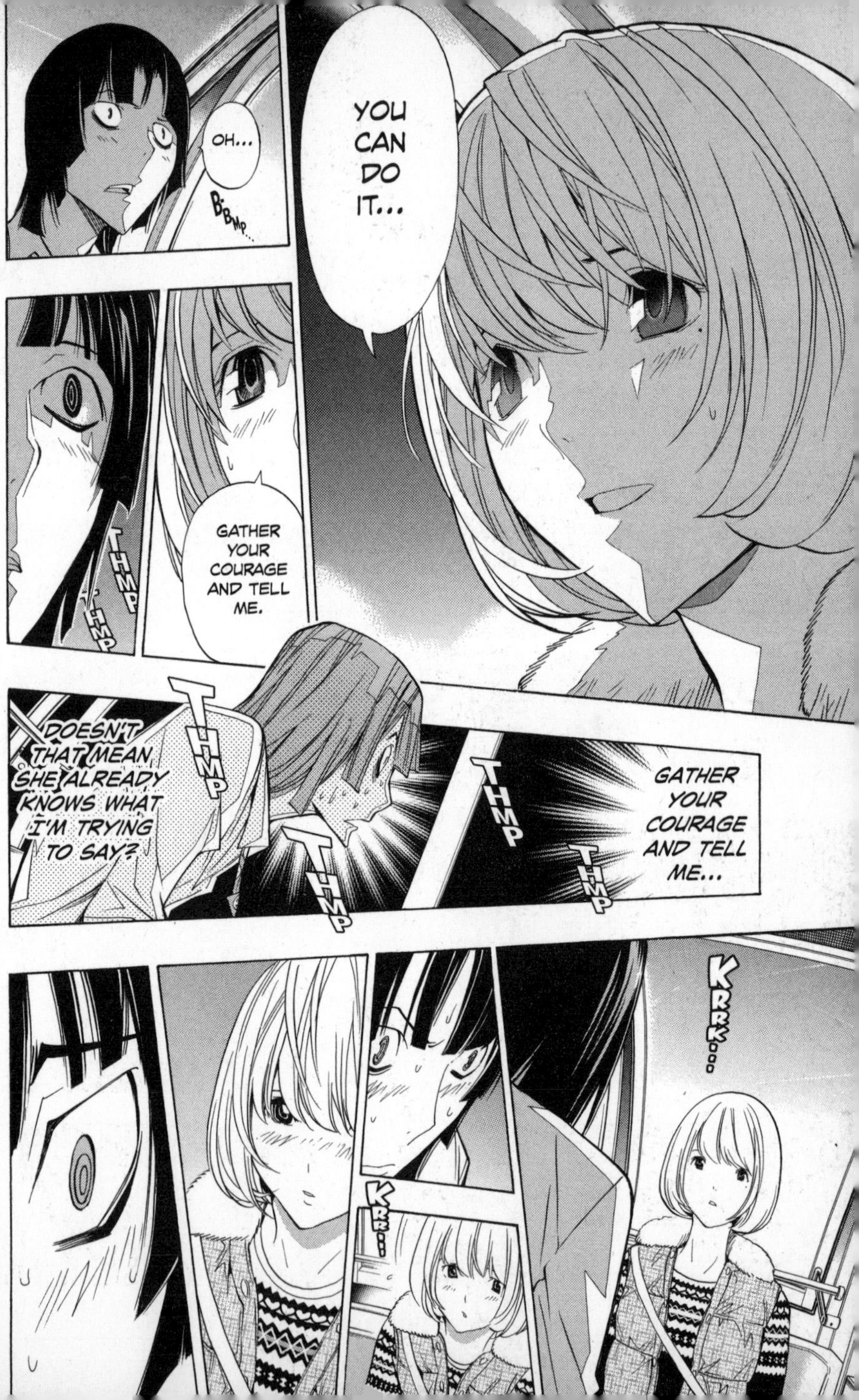
YOU CAN DO IT...
OH...
B-BMP...
GATHER YOUR COURAGE AND TELL ME.
THMP
THMP
GATHER YOUR COURAGE AND TELL ME...
THMP
THMP
THMP
DOESN'T THAT MEAN SHE ALREADY KNOWS WHAT I'M TRYING TO SAY?
THMP
KRRK...
KRR...

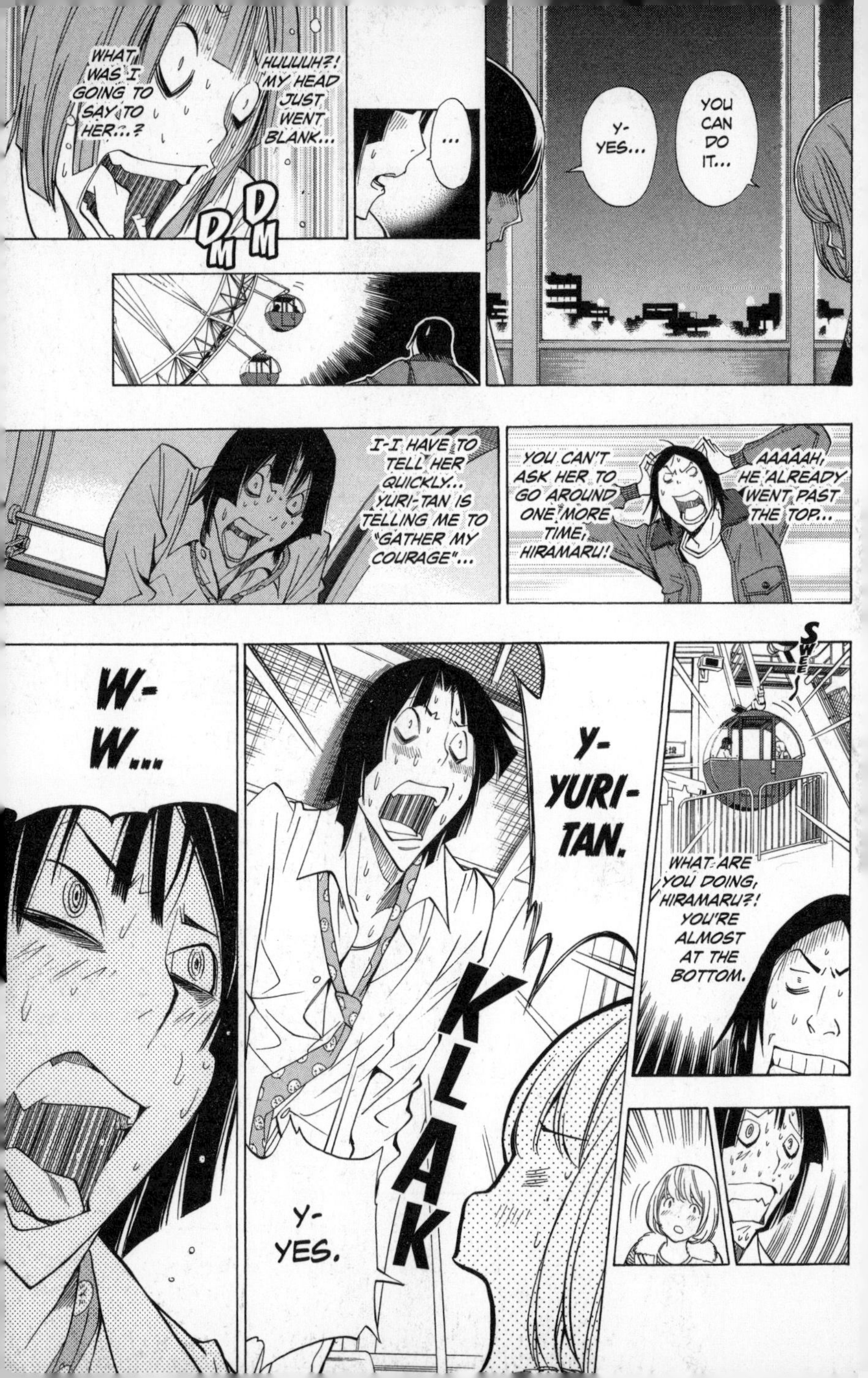
YOU CAN DO IT...
Y- YES...
...
HUUUUH?! MY HEAD JUST WENT BLANK...
WHAT WAS I GOING TO SAY TO HER...?
DM DM
AAAAAH, HE ALREADY WENT PAST THE TOP...
YOU CAN'T ASK HER TO GO AROUND ONE MORE TIME, HIRAMARU!
I-I HAVE TO TELL HER QUICKLY... YURI-TAN IS TELLING ME TO "GATHER MY COURAGE"...
SWEE
WHAT ARE YOU DOING, HIRAMARU?! YOU'RE ALMOST AT THE BOTTOM.
Y- YURI-TAN.
KLAK
Y- YES.
W- W...

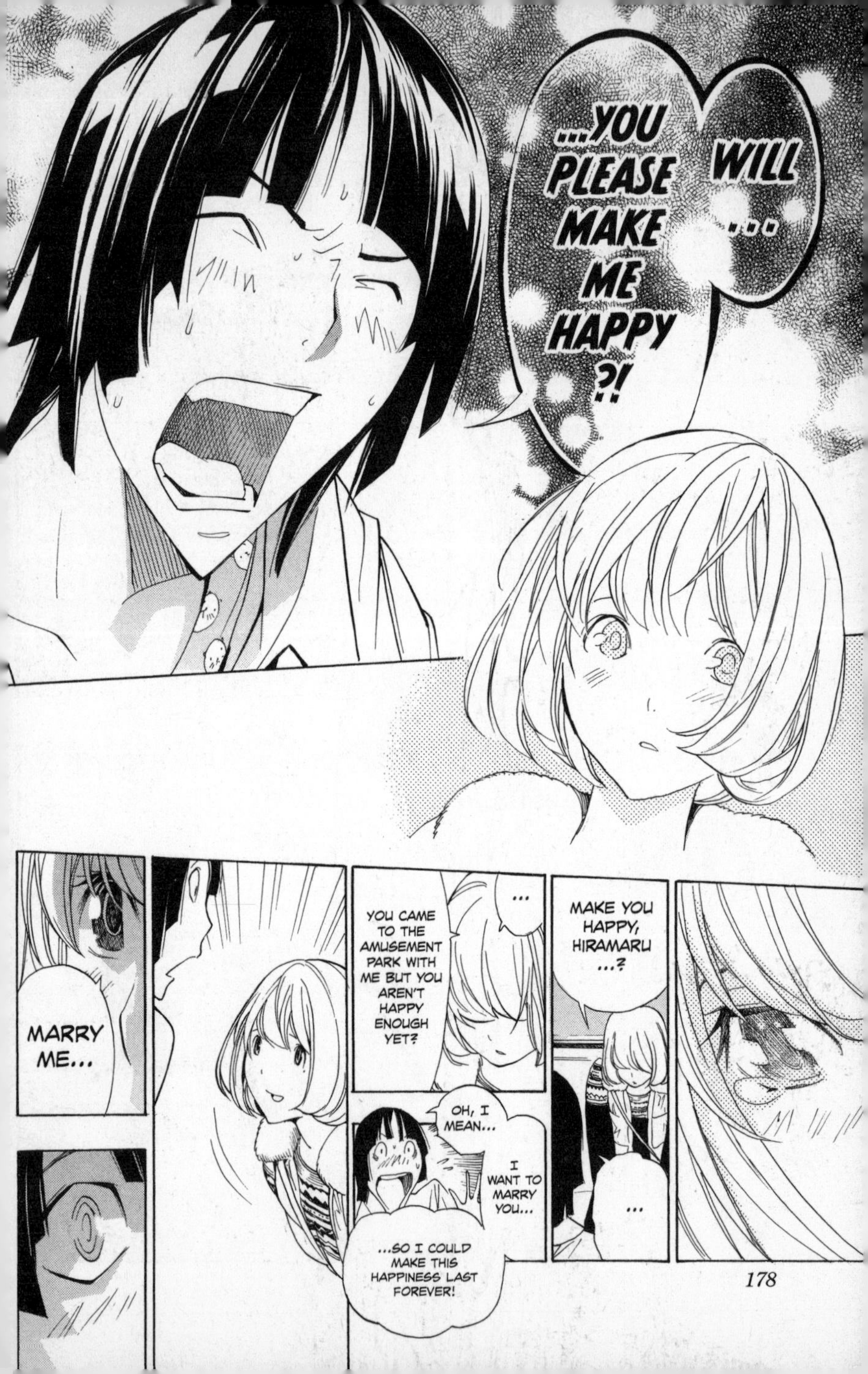
WILL...
...YOU PLEASE MAKE ME HAPPY?!
MAKE YOU HAPPY, HIRAMARU...?
...
...
YOU CAME TO THE AMUSEMENT PARK WITH ME BUT YOU AREN'T HAPPY ENOUGH YET?
OH, I MEAN...
I WANT TO MARRY YOU...
...SO I COULD MAKE THIS HAPPINESS LAST FOREVER!
MARRY ME...

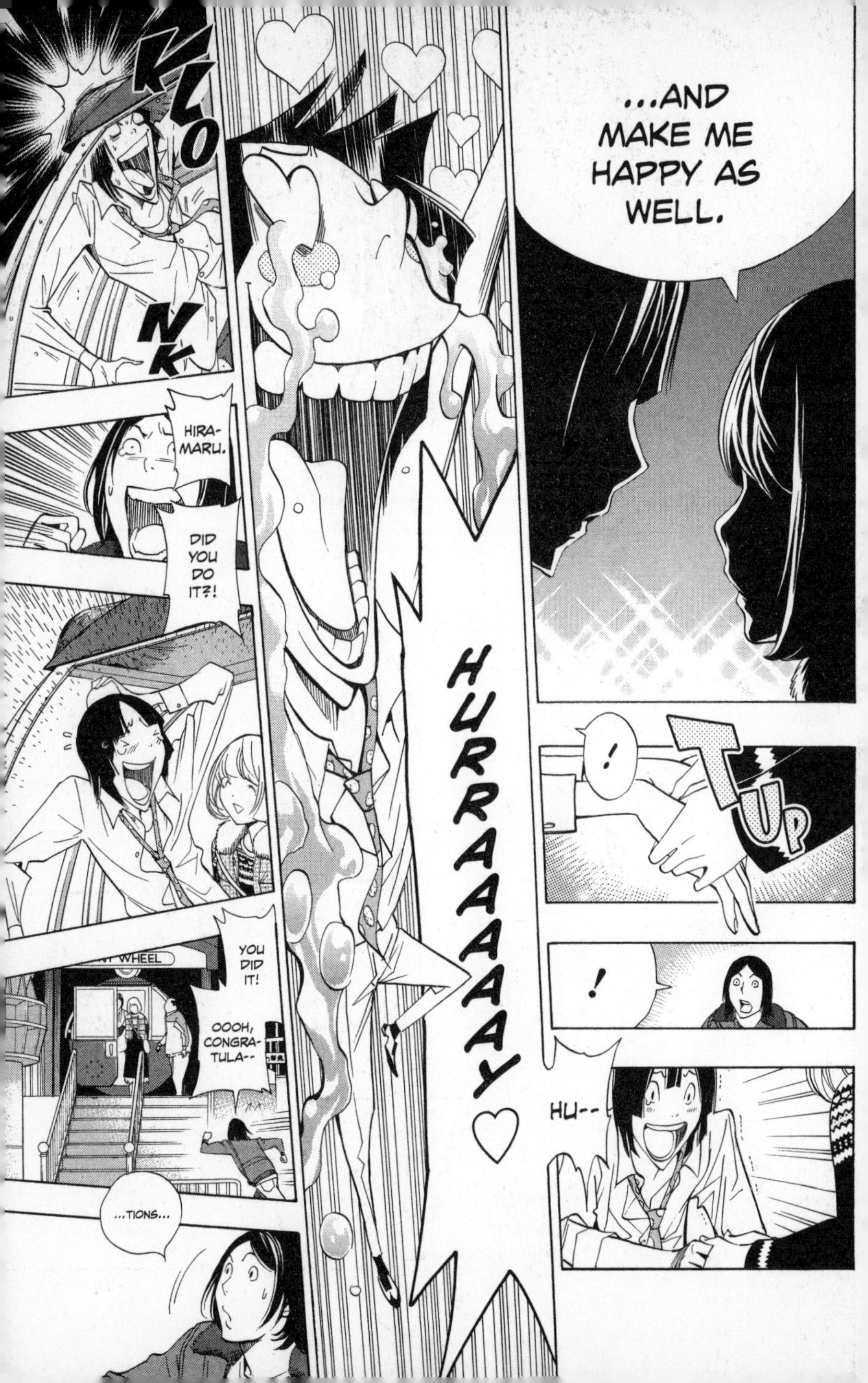
...AND MAKE ME HAPPY AS WELL.
!
TUP
!
HU--
HURRAAAAAAY ♥
KLONK
HIRA-MARU.
DID YOU DO IT?!
YOU DID IT!
OOOH, CONGRATULA--
...TIONS...

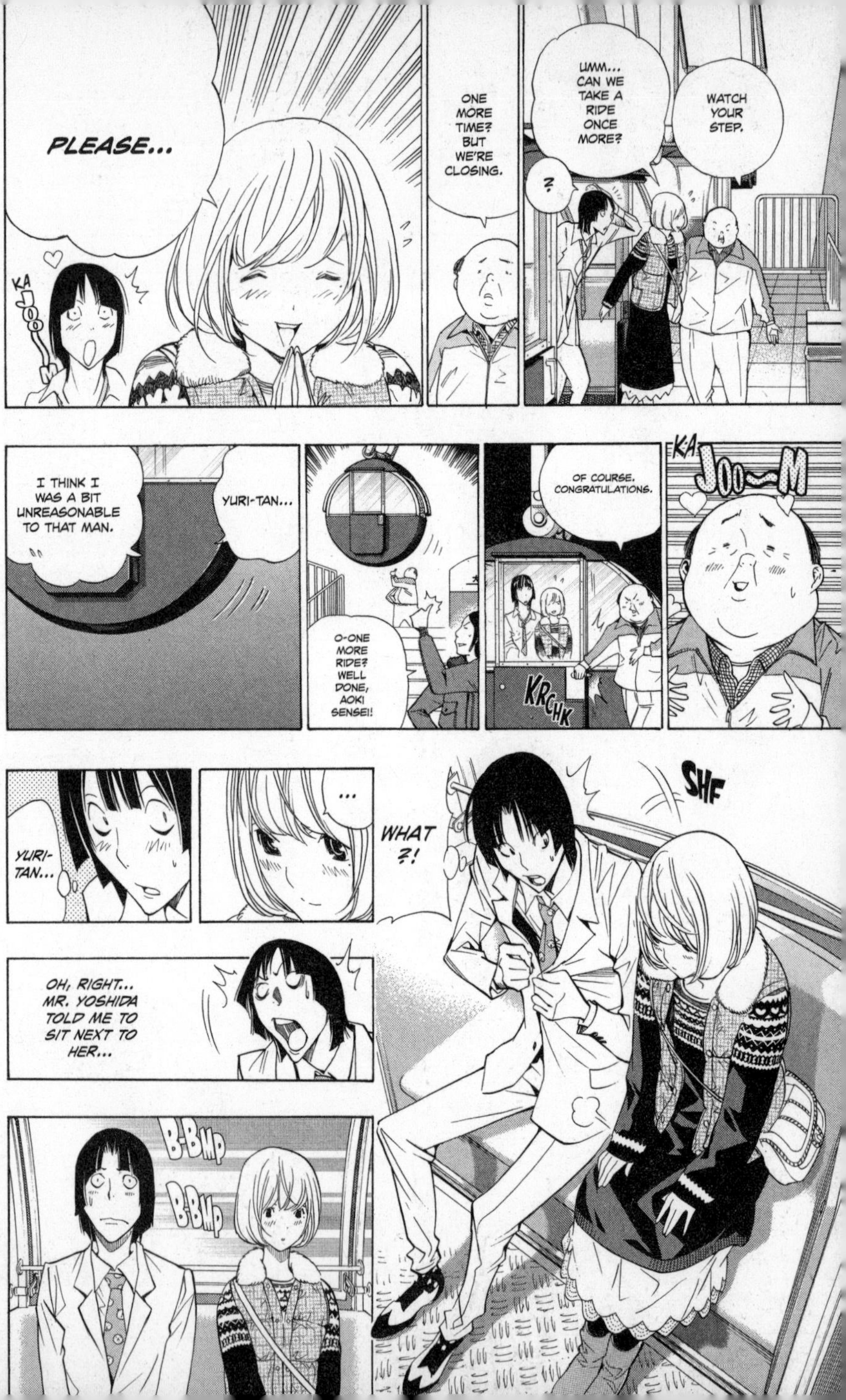
WATCH YOUR STEP.
UMM... CAN WE TAKE A RIDE ONCE MORE?
?
ONE MORE TIME? BUT WE'RE CLOSING.
PLEASE...
KA JOOM
KA-JOO~M
OF COURSE. CONGRATULATIONS.
KRCHK
O-ONE MORE RIDE? WELL DONE, AOKI SENSEI!
YURI-TAN...
I THINK I WAS A BIT UNREASONABLE TO THAT MAN.
SHF
WHAT?!
...
YURI-TAN...
OH, RIGHT... MR. YOSHIDA TOLD ME TO SIT NEXT TO HER...
B-BMP
B-BMP

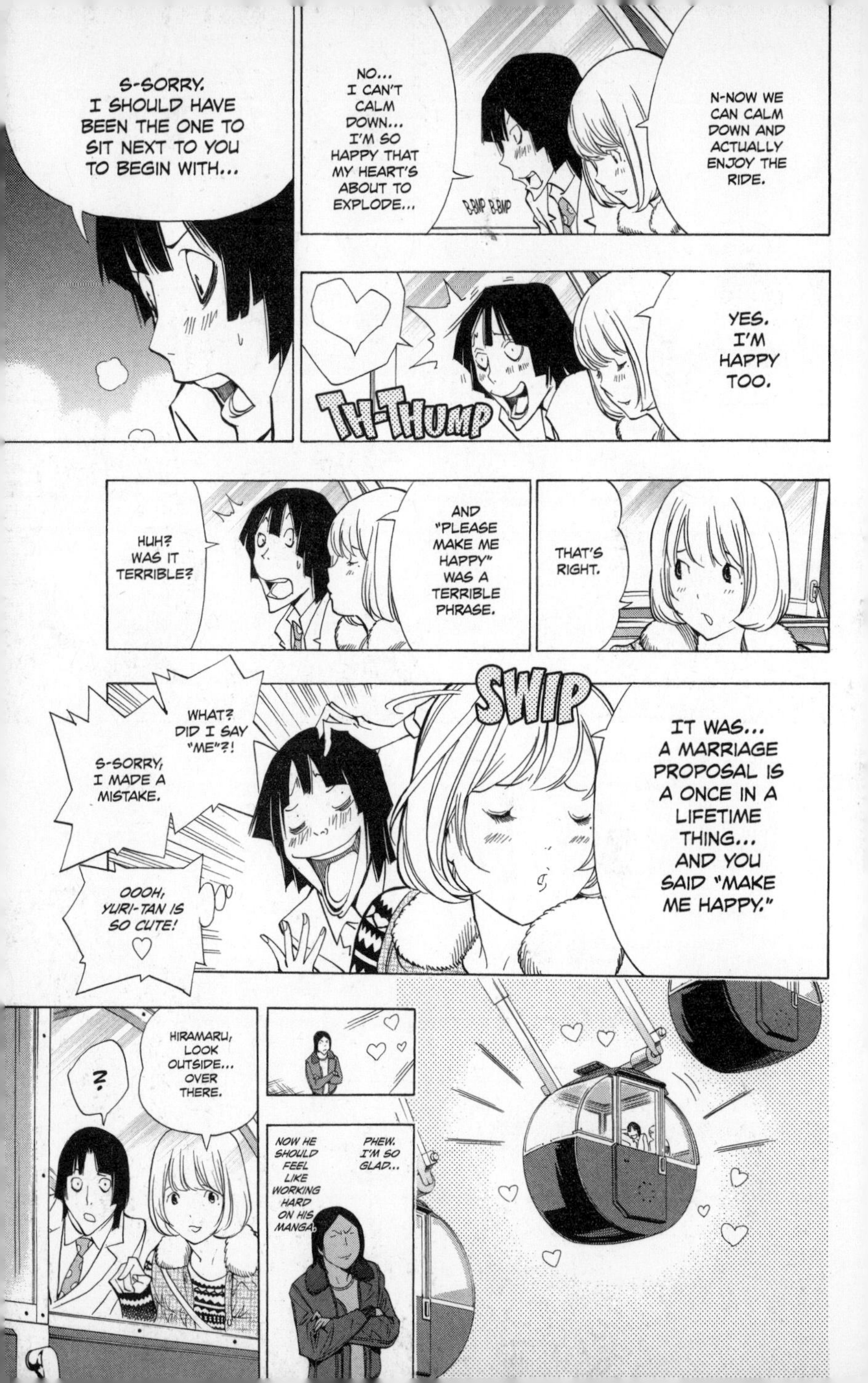
N-NOW WE CAN CALM DOWN AND ACTUALLY ENJOY THE RIDE.
NO... I CAN'T CALM DOWN... I'M SO HAPPY THAT MY HEART'S ABOUT TO EXPLODE...
B-BMP B-BMP
YES. I'M HAPPY TOO.
TH-THUMP
S-SORRY. I SHOULD HAVE BEEN THE ONE TO SIT NEXT TO YOU TO BEGIN WITH...
THAT'S RIGHT.
AND "PLEASE MAKE ME HAPPY" WAS A TERRIBLE PHRASE.
HUH? WAS IT TERRIBLE?
SWIP
IT WAS... A MARRIAGE PROPOSAL IS A ONCE IN A LIFETIME THING... AND YOU SAID "MAKE ME HAPPY."
WHAT? DID I SAY "ME"?!
S-SORRY, I MADE A MISTAKE.
OOOH, YURI-TAN IS SO CUTE! ♡
PHEW. I'M SO GLAD...
NOW HE SHOULD FEEL LIKE WORKING HARD ON HIS MANGA.
HIRAMARU, LOOK OUTSIDE... OVER THERE.
?

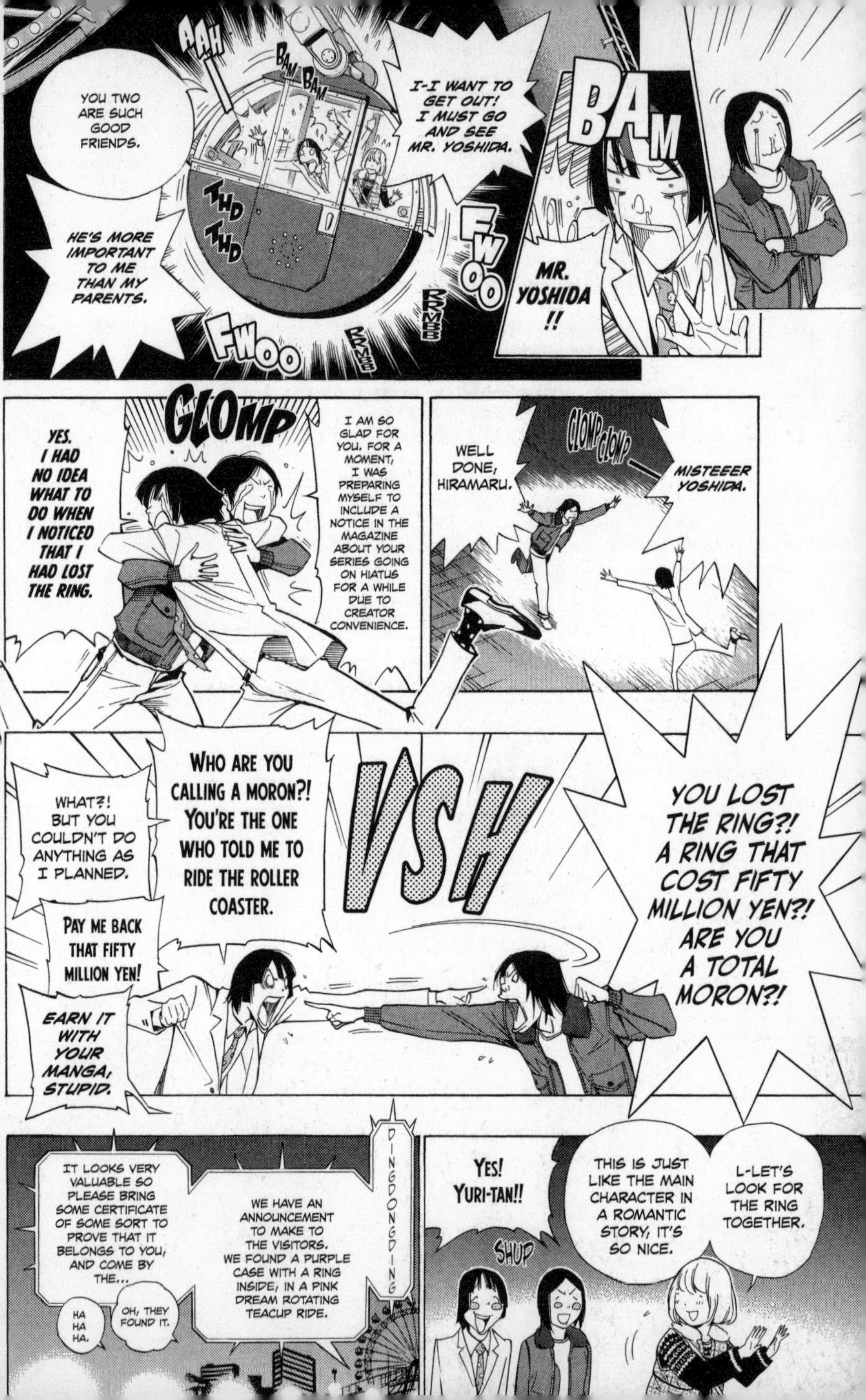
BAM
MR. YOSHIDA!!
I-I WANT TO GET OUT! I MUST GO AND SEE MR. YOSHIDA.
BAM BAM
AAH
YOU TWO ARE SUCH GOOD FRIENDS.
FWOO
RRMBB
THD THD
HE'S MORE IMPORTANT TO ME THAN MY PARENTS.
FWOO
RRMBB
MISTEEER YOSHIDA.
CLOMP CLOMP
WELL DONE, HIRAMARU.
I AM SO GLAD FOR YOU. FOR A MOMENT, I WAS PREPARING MYSELF TO INCLUDE A NOTICE IN THE MAGAZINE ABOUT YOUR SERIES GOING ON HIATUS FOR A WHILE DUE TO CREATOR CONVENIENCE.
GLOMP
YES. I HAD NO IDEA WHAT TO DO WHEN I NOTICED THAT I HAD LOST THE RING.
YOU LOST THE RING?! A RING THAT COST FIFTY MILLION YEN?! ARE YOU A TOTAL MORON?!
VSH
WHO ARE YOU CALLING A MORON?! YOU'RE THE ONE WHO TOLD ME TO RIDE THE ROLLER COASTER.
WHAT?! BUT YOU COULDN'T DO ANYTHING AS I PLANNED.
PAY ME BACK THAT FIFTY MILLION YEN!
EARN IT WITH YOUR MANGA, STUPID.
L-LET'S LOOK FOR THE RING TOGETHER.
THIS IS JUST LIKE THE MAIN CHARACTER IN A ROMANTIC STORY, IT'S SO NICE.
YES! YURI-TAN!!
SHUP
DINGDONGDING
WE HAVE AN ANNOUNCEMENT TO MAKE TO THE VISITORS. WE FOUND A PURPLE CASE WITH A RING INSIDE, IN A PINK DREAM ROTATING TEACUP RIDE.
IT LOOKS VERY VALUABLE SO PLEASE BRING SOME CERTIFICATE OF SOME SORT TO PROVE THAT IT BELONGS TO YOU, AND COME BY THE...
OH, THEY FOUND IT.
HA HA HA.

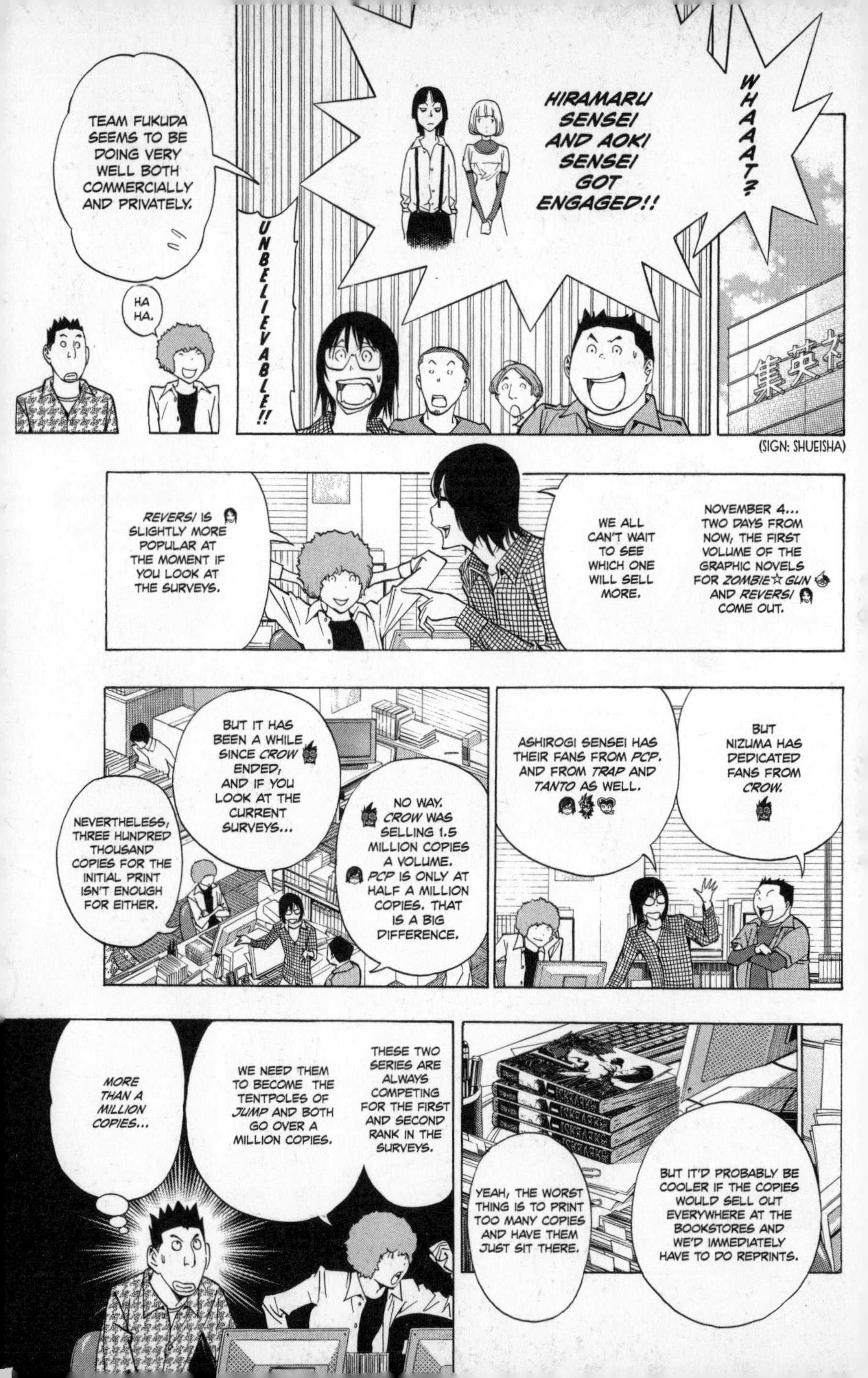
HIRAMARU SENSEI AND AOKI SENSEI GOT ENGAGED!!
WHAAAAT?
UNBELIEVABLE!!
(SIGN: SHUEISHA)
TEAM FUKUDA SEEMS TO BE DOING VERY WELL BOTH COMMERCIALLY AND PRIVATELY.
HA HA.
NOVEMBER 4... TWO DAYS FROM NOW, THE FIRST VOLUME OF THE GRAPHIC NOVELS FOR ZOMBIE☆GUN AND REVERSI COME OUT.
WE ALL CAN'T WAIT TO SEE WHICH ONE WILL SELL MORE.
REVERSI IS SLIGHTLY MORE POPULAR AT THE MOMENT IF YOU LOOK AT THE SURVEYS.
BUT NIZUMA HAS DEDICATED FANS FROM CROW.
ASHIROGI SENSEI HAS THEIR FANS FROM PCP. AND FROM TRAP AND TANTO AS WELL.
NO WAY. CROW WAS SELLING 1.5 MILLION COPIES A VOLUME. PCP IS ONLY AT HALF A MILLION COPIES. THAT IS A BIG DIFFERENCE.
BUT IT HAS BEEN A WHILE SINCE CROW ENDED, AND IF YOU LOOK AT THE CURRENT SURVEYS...
NEVERTHELESS, THREE HUNDRED THOUSAND COPIES FOR THE INITIAL PRINT ISN'T ENOUGH FOR EITHER.
BUT IT'D PROBABLY BE COOLER IF THE COPIES WOULD SELL OUT EVERYWHERE AT THE BOOKSTORES AND WE'D IMMEDIATELY HAVE TO DO REPRINTS.
YEAH, THE WORST THING IS TO PRINT TOO MANY COPIES AND HAVE THEM JUST SIT THERE.
THESE TWO SERIES ARE ALWAYS COMPETING FOR THE FIRST AND SECOND RANK IN THE SURVEYS.
WE NEED THEM TO BECOME THE TENTPOLES OF JUMP AND BOTH GO OVER A MILLION COPIES.
MORE THAN A MILLION COPIES...

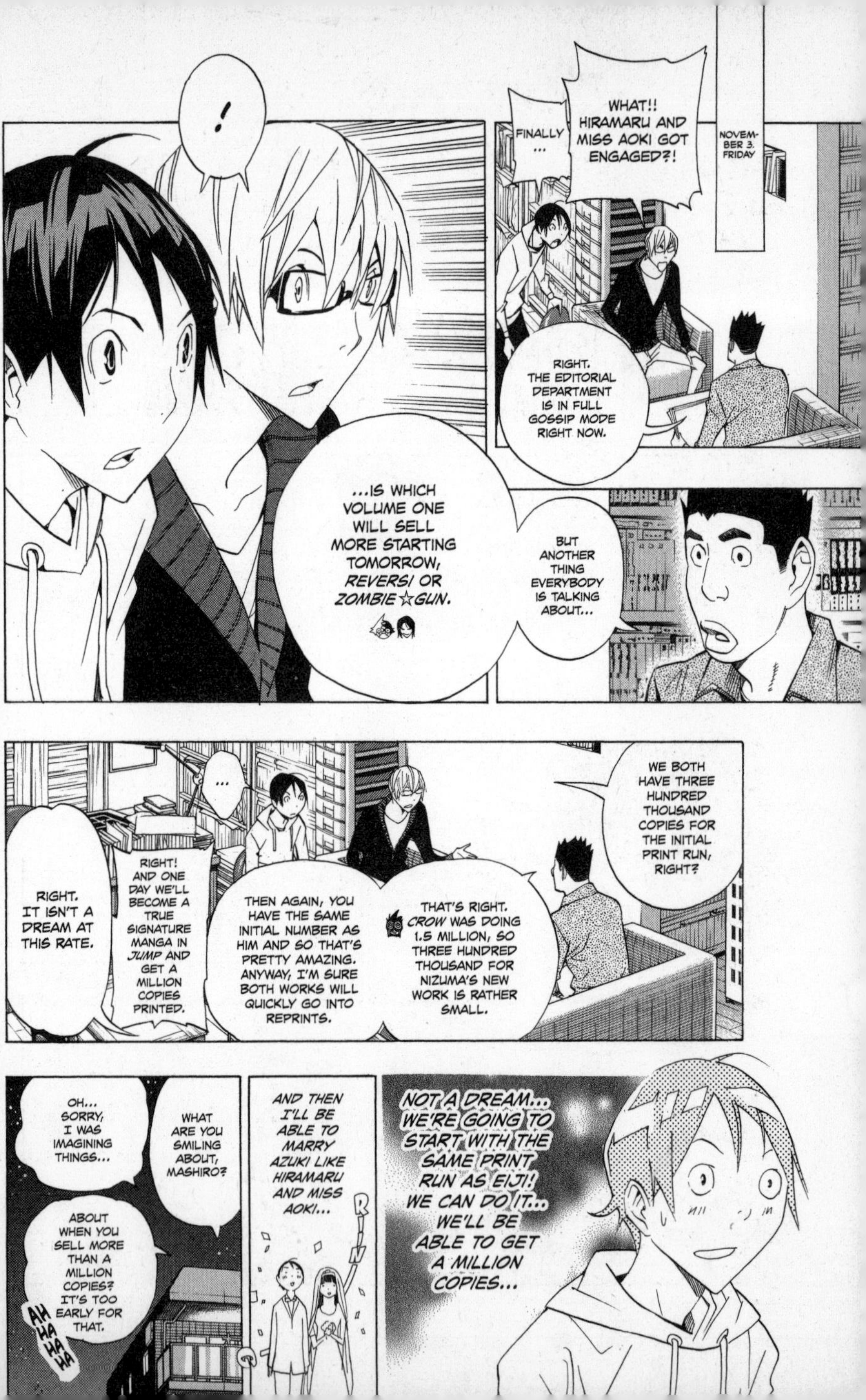
NOVEMBER 3, FRIDAY
WHAT!! HIRAMARU AND MISS AOKI GOT ENGAGED?!
FINALLY...
RIGHT. THE EDITORIAL DEPARTMENT IS IN FULL GOSSIP MODE RIGHT NOW.
BUT ANOTHER THING EVERYBODY IS TALKING ABOUT...
...IS WHICH VOLUME ONE WILL SELL MORE STARTING TOMORROW, *REVERSI* OR *ZOMBIE☆GUN.*
!
WE BOTH HAVE THREE HUNDRED THOUSAND COPIES FOR THE INITIAL PRINT RUN, RIGHT?
THAT'S RIGHT. *CROW* WAS DOING 1.5 MILLION, SO THREE HUNDRED THOUSAND FOR NIZUMA'S NEW WORK IS RATHER SMALL.
THEN AGAIN, YOU HAVE THE SAME INITIAL NUMBER AS HIM AND SO THAT'S PRETTY AMAZING. ANYWAY, I'M SURE BOTH WORKS WILL QUICKLY GO INTO REPRINTS.
...
RIGHT! AND ONE DAY WE'LL BECOME A TRUE SIGNATURE MANGA IN *JUMP* AND GET A MILLION COPIES PRINTED.
RIGHT. IT ISN'T A DREAM AT THIS RATE.
NOT A DREAM... WE'RE GOING TO START WITH THE SAME PRINT RUN AS EIJI! WE CAN DO IT... WE'LL BE ABLE TO GET A MILLION COPIES...
AND THEN I'LL BE ABLE TO MARRY AZUKI LIKE HIRAMARU AND MISS AOKI...
RIIN
WHAT ARE YOU SMILING ABOUT, MASHIRO?
OH... SORRY, I WAS IMAGINING THINGS...
ABOUT WHEN YOU SELL MORE THAN A MILLION COPIES? IT'S TOO EARLY FOR THAT.
AHAHAHAHA

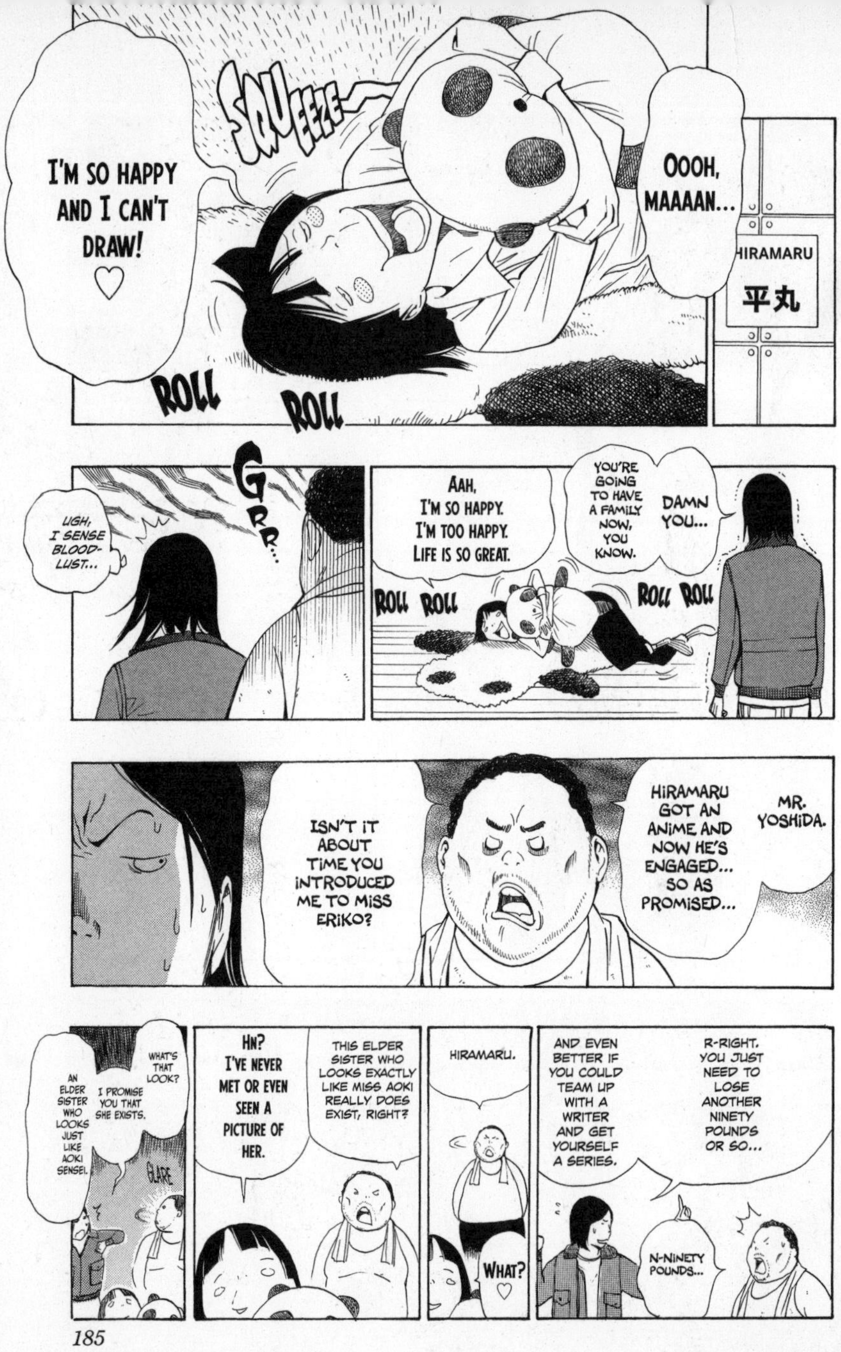
OOOH, MAAAAN...
HIRAMARU
平丸
SQUEEZE
I'M SO HAPPY AND I CAN'T DRAW! ♡
ROLL
ROLL
DAMN YOU...
YOU'RE GOING TO HAVE A FAMILY NOW, YOU KNOW.
AAH, I'M SO HAPPY. I'M TOO HAPPY. LIFE IS SO GREAT.
ROLL ROLL
ROLL ROLL
GRRR...
UGH, I SENSE BLOOD-LUST...
MR. YOSHIDA.
HIRAMARU GOT AN ANIME AND NOW HE'S ENGAGED... SO AS PROMISED...
ISN'T IT ABOUT TIME YOU INTRODUCED ME TO MISS ERIKO?
R-RIGHT. YOU JUST NEED TO LOSE ANOTHER NINETY POUNDS OR SO...
AND EVEN BETTER IF YOU COULD TEAM UP WITH A WRITER AND GET YOURSELF A SERIES.
N-NINETY POUNDS...
HIRAMARU.
WHAT? ♡
THIS ELDER SISTER WHO LOOKS EXACTLY LIKE MISS AOKI REALLY DOES EXIST, RIGHT?
HN? I'VE NEVER MET OR EVEN SEEN A PICTURE OF HER.
WHAT'S THAT LOOK?
I PROMISE YOU THAT SHE EXISTS.
AN ELDER SISTER WHO LOOKS JUST LIKE AOKI SENSEI.
GLARE

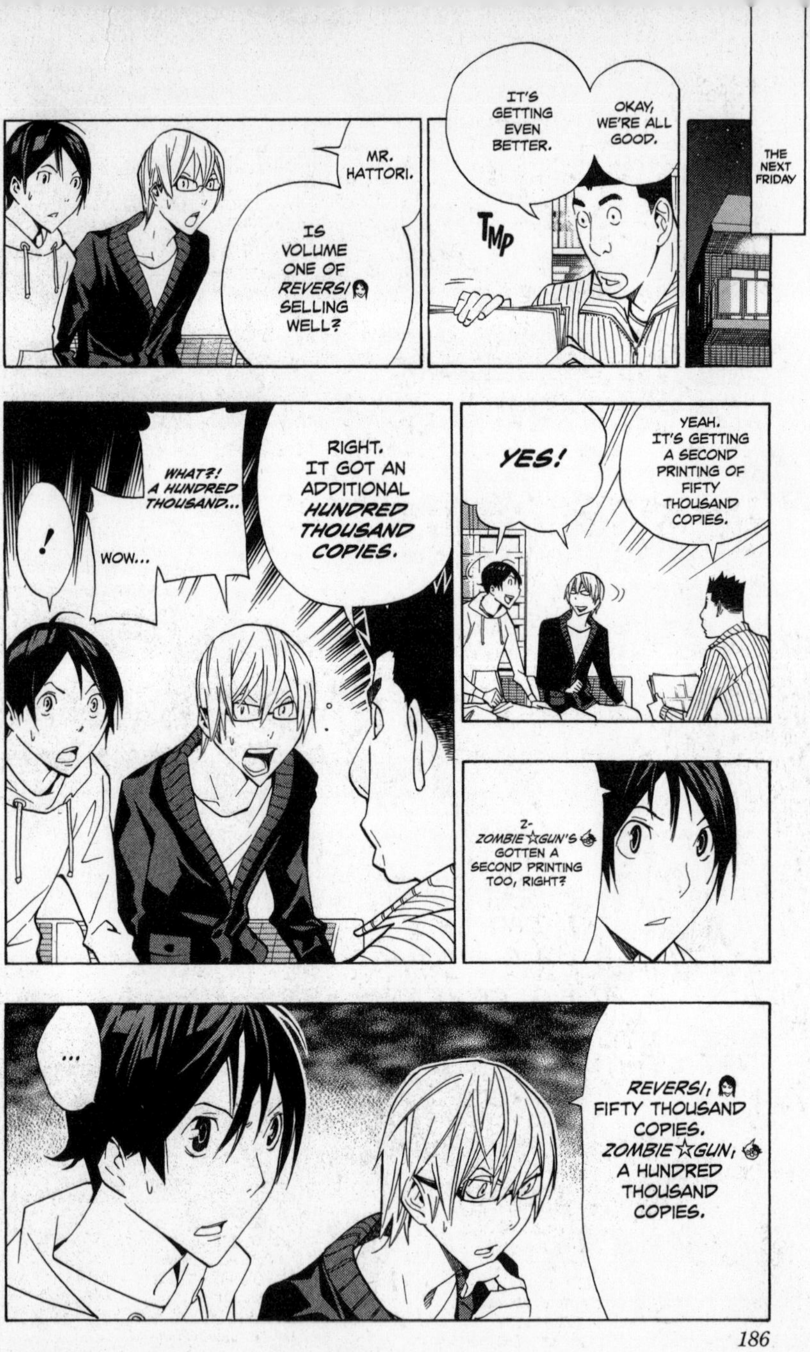
THE NEXT FRIDAY
OKAY, WE'RE ALL GOOD.
IT'S GETTING EVEN BETTER.
TMP
MR. HATTORI.
IS VOLUME ONE OF REVERSI SELLING WELL?
YEAH. IT'S GETTING A SECOND PRINTING OF FIFTY THOUSAND COPIES.
YES!
Z-ZOMBIE☆GUN'S GOTTEN A SECOND PRINTING TOO, RIGHT?
RIGHT. IT GOT AN ADDITIONAL HUNDRED THOUSAND COPIES.
WHAT?! A HUNDRED THOUSAND...
WOW...
!
REVERSI, FIFTY THOUSAND COPIES. ZOMBIE☆GUN, A HUNDRED THOUSAND COPIES.
...

READ THIS WAY

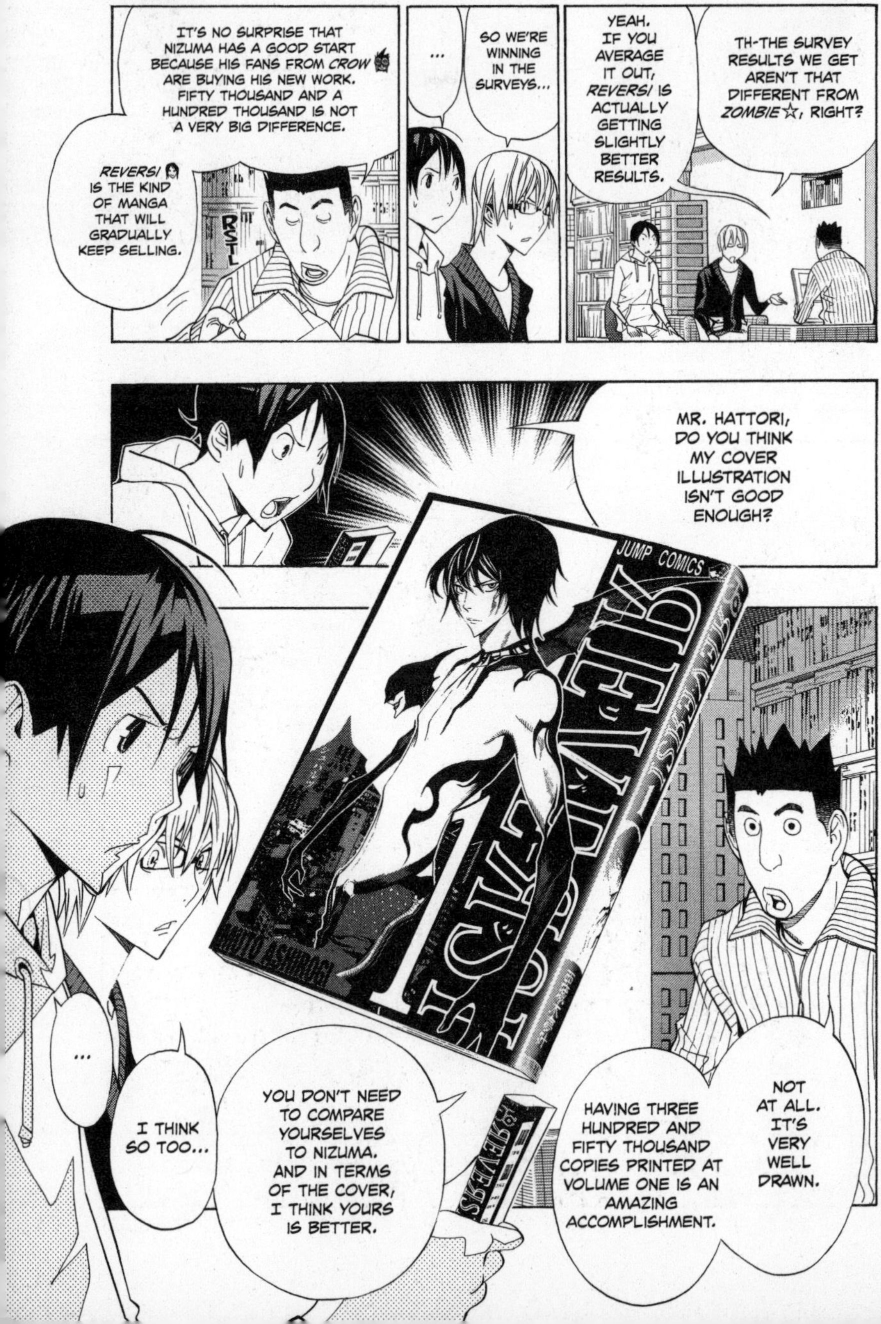
TH-THE SURVEY RESULTS WE GET AREN'T THAT DIFFERENT FROM *ZOMBIE*☆, RIGHT?
YEAH. IF YOU AVERAGE IT OUT, *REVERSI* IS ACTUALLY GETTING SLIGHTLY BETTER RESULTS.
SO WE'RE WINNING IN THE SURVEYS...
...
IT'S NO SURPRISE THAT NIZUMA HAS A GOOD START BECAUSE HIS FANS FROM *CROW* ARE BUYING HIS NEW WORK. FIFTY THOUSAND AND A HUNDRED THOUSAND IS NOT A VERY BIG DIFFERENCE.
REVERSI IS THE KIND OF MANGA THAT WILL GRADUALLY KEEP SELLING.
RSTL
MR. HATTORI, DO YOU THINK MY COVER ILLUSTRATION ISN'T GOOD ENOUGH?
JUMP COMICS
NOT AT ALL. IT'S VERY WELL DRAWN.
HAVING THREE HUNDRED AND FIFTY THOUSAND COPIES PRINTED AT VOLUME ONE IS AN AMAZING ACCOMPLISHMENT.
YOU DON'T NEED TO COMPARE YOURSELVES TO NIZUMA. AND IN TERMS OF THE COVER, I THINK YOURS IS BETTER.
I THINK SO TOO...
...

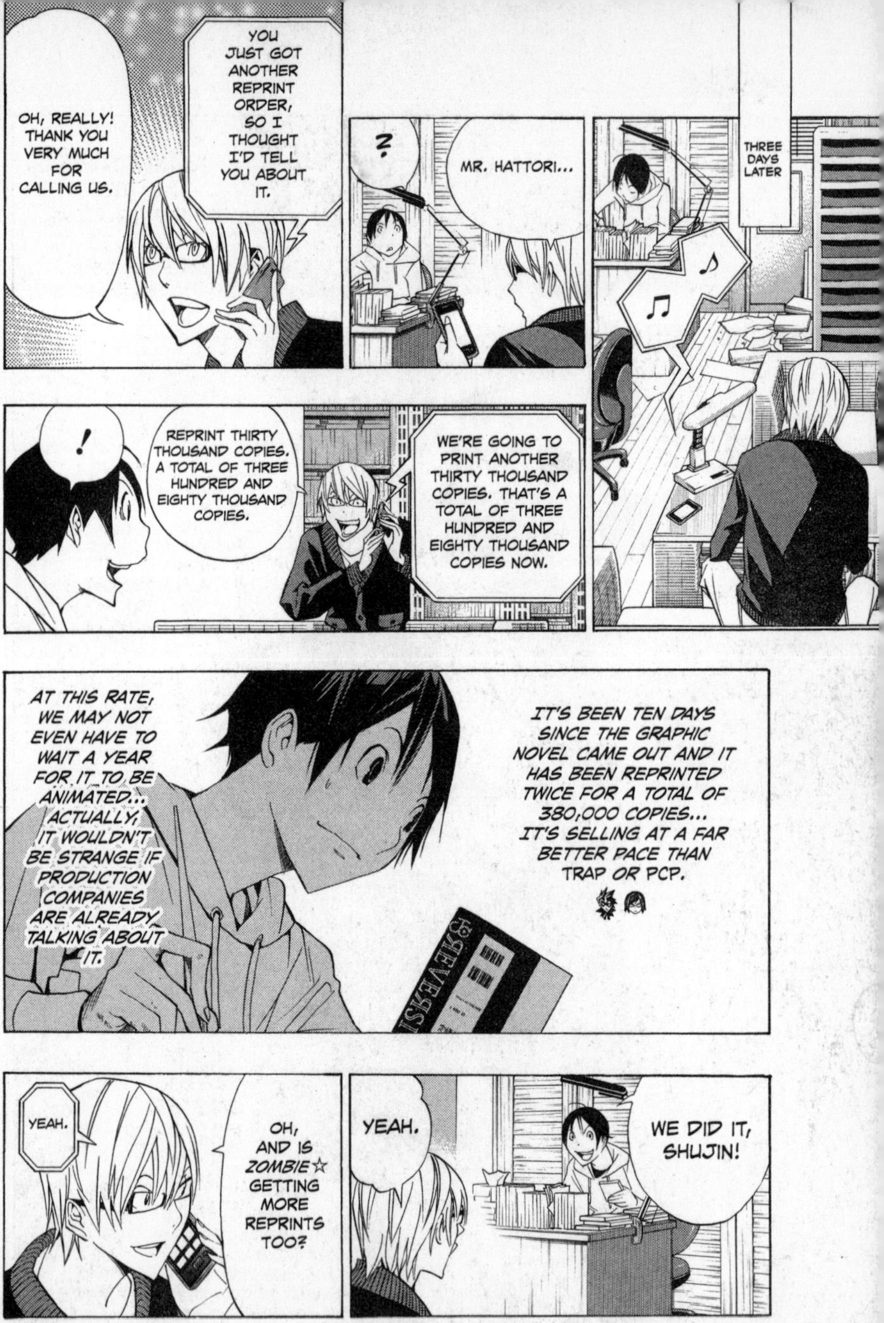
THREE DAYS LATER
♪
♫
?
MR. HATTORI...
YOU JUST GOT ANOTHER REPRINT ORDER, SO I THOUGHT I'D TELL YOU ABOUT IT.
OH, REALLY! THANK YOU VERY MUCH FOR CALLING US.
WE'RE GOING TO PRINT ANOTHER THIRTY THOUSAND COPIES. THAT'S A TOTAL OF THREE HUNDRED AND EIGHTY THOUSAND COPIES NOW.
REPRINT THIRTY THOUSAND COPIES. A TOTAL OF THREE HUNDRED AND EIGHTY THOUSAND COPIES.
!
IT'S BEEN TEN DAYS SINCE THE GRAPHIC NOVEL CAME OUT AND IT HAS BEEN REPRINTED TWICE FOR A TOTAL OF 380,000 COPIES... IT'S SELLING AT A FAR BETTER PACE THAN TRAP OR PCP.
AT THIS RATE, WE MAY NOT EVEN HAVE TO WAIT A YEAR FOR IT TO BE ANIMATED... ACTUALLY, IT WOULDN'T BE STRANGE IF PRODUCTION COMPANIES ARE ALREADY TALKING ABOUT IT.
REVERSI
WE DID IT, SHUJIN!
YEAH.
OH, AND IS *ZOMBIE*☆ GETTING MORE REPRINTS TOO?
YEAH.

READ THIS WAY

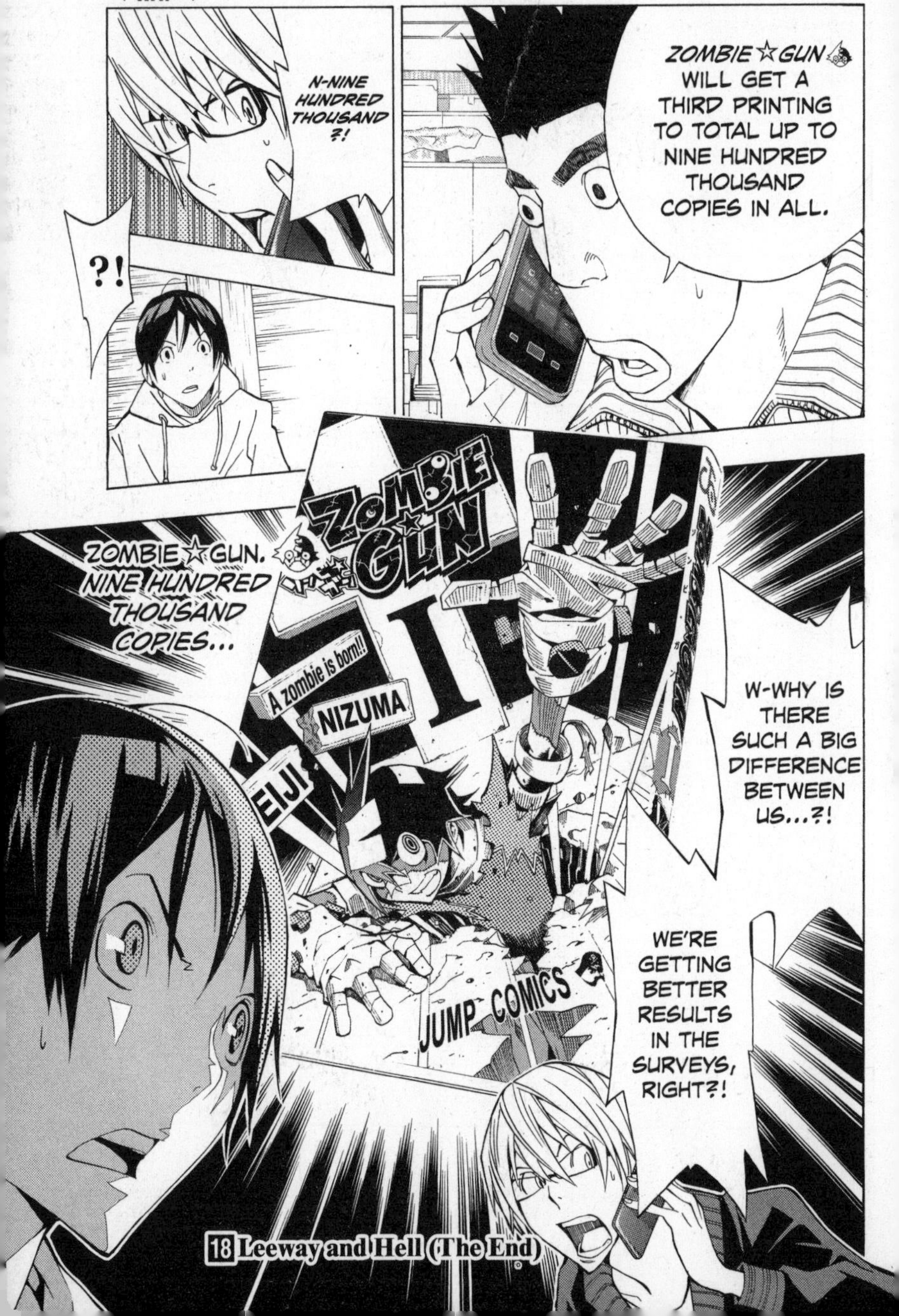
ZOMBIE☆GUN WILL GET A THIRD PRINTING TO TOTAL UP TO NINE HUNDRED THOUSAND COPIES IN ALL.
N-NINE HUNDRED THOUSAND ?!
?!
ZOMBIE GUN
ZOMBIE☆GUN. NINE HUNDRED THOUSAND COPIES...
A zombie is born!!
NIZUMA
EIJI
JUMP COMICS
W-WHY IS THERE SUCH A BIG DIFFERENCE BETWEEN US...?!
WE'RE GETTING BETTER RESULTS IN THE SURVEYS, RIGHT?!

18 Leeway and Hell (The End)

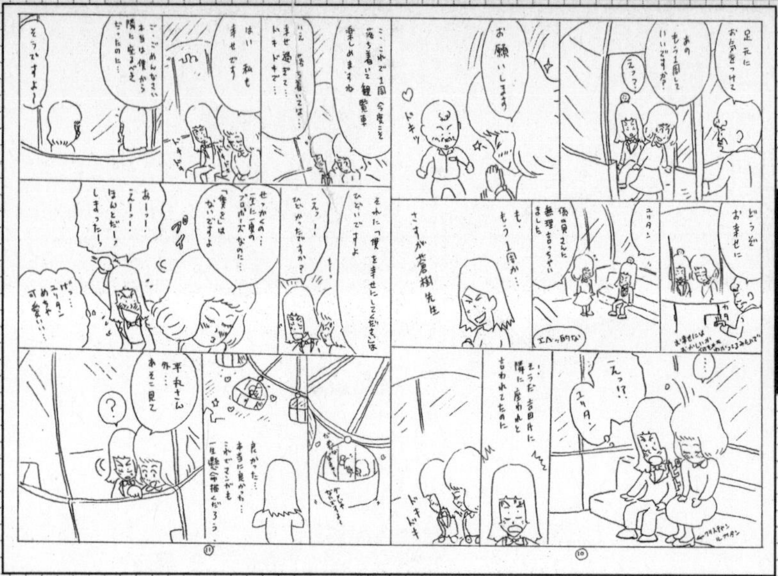

足元にお気をつけて
あのもう1周していいですか?
えっ?
お願いします
ドキッ
どうぞお乗せに
ユリタン
係の人さんに無理言っちゃいました
エヘッ的な
も、もう1周か…
さすが蒼樹先生
ユリタン
えっ!?
まだ吉田氏に隣に座われと言われてたのに
ドキドキ
こ、これでもう1周今度こそ落ち着いて観覧車楽しめますね
いえ落ち着いては… 幸せ過ぎてドキドキで…
はい私も幸せです
ご、ごめんなさい本当は僕から隣に座るべきだったのに…
そうですよ~
それに「僕を幸せにして下さい」はひどいですよ
えっ!ひどかったですか?
せっかくの一生に一度のプロポーズなのに「愛を」はないですよ
プイ
あーっ!えーっ!ほんとだ!しまったー!
げっ…ユリタンめちゃ可愛い…
平丸さん外…あそこ見て
?
良かった…本当に良かった… これで平丸さんも一生懸命描くだろう

OHBA'S STORYBOARD

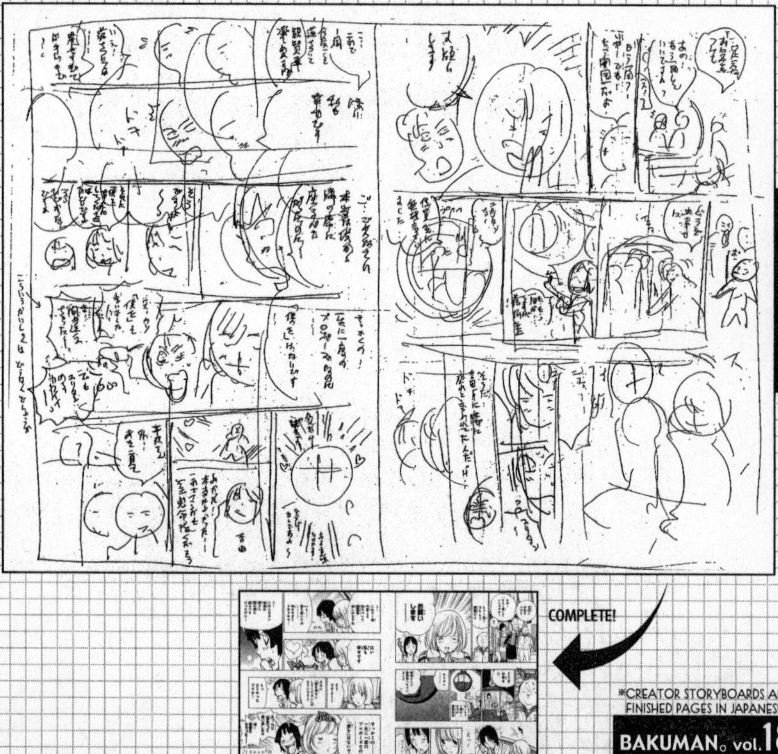

OBATA'S STORYBOARD

COMPLETE!

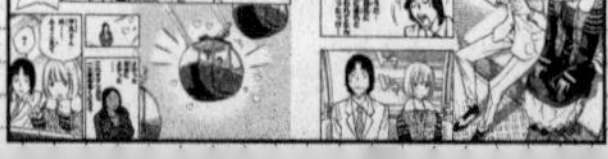

*CREATOR STORYBOARDS AND FINISHED PAGES IN JAPANESE

BAKUMAN。 vol.18

"Until the Final Draft Is Complete"

Chapter 160, pp. 180-181

BAKUMAN。

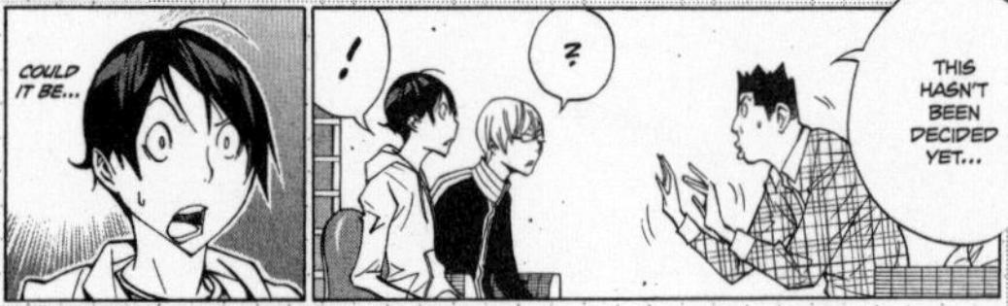
THIS HASN'T BEEN DECIDED YET...
?
!
COULD IT BE...

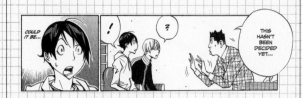

In the NEXT VOLUME

Akito and Moritaka are holding their own against Eiji when it comes to the ranking in *Shonen Jump*, but they're no match for him when it comes to the book sales. But what explains the gap and how can they close it?!

Available May 2014!